PERMANENT COSMETICS:
The Foundation of Fundamental Applications
Second Edition

Marjorie Grimm, CPCP

Published by Society of Permanent Cosmetics Professionals

The techniques describe in this book are intended for reference purposes and not as a substitute for proper/adequate training. The art of tattooing permanent cosmetics can carry a significant risk of liability for the technician. The author, contributors, the SPCP, and publisher do not recommend that anyone use the techniques described unless they have been properly trained through qualified professional instruction and/or guidance, are knowledgeable about the risks involved with tattooing permanent cosmetics, and are willing to personally assume all responsibility associated with those risk.

The Internet addresses listed in the text were accurate at the time of initial publication. The inclusion of a Web site(s) does not indicate an endorsement by the author(s) or the Society of Permanent Cosmetic Professionals, and the Society of Permanent Cosmetic Professionals does not guarantee the accuracy of the information presented at the these sites.

Copyright © 2018. Society of Permanent Cosmetic Professionals All rights reserved.

No part of this publication may be reproduced or distributed in any form or by any means, or stored in a database or retrieval system without the prior written consent of the Society of Permanent Cosmetic Professionals, including, but not limited to in any network or other electronic storage or transmission, or broadcast for distance learning.

Published in the USA by Society of Permanent Cosmetic Professionals
69 North Broadway St, Des Plaines, IL, 60016
www.spcp.org

ISBN 978-1-5323-6852-3

Printed in the United States of America

Second Edition (4th printing) February 2019

TABLE OF CONTENTS

CONTENTS	IV
BIOGRAPHY	IX
PREFACE	XI
SECTION 1 - FACTS ABOUT PERMANENT COSMETICS	**1**
SECTION 2 - PERMANENT COSMETIC DEVICES	**15**
SECTION 3 - TATTOO NEEDLE INFORMATION	**21**
SECTION 4 - SAFE PRACTICES FOR PERMANENT COSMETIC TECHNICIANS	**29**
Medical Asepsis (Clean Technique)	32
Client Skin Preparation	34
Cleaning and Decontamination of Equipment and Tools	34
Surgical Asepsis	35
Sterilization	35
Storage and Handling of Sterile Items	36
Other Considerations	36
Needle Safety and Disposal	36
Personal Protective Equipment	37
Gloves	37
Sterile Water	37
Procedural Protocols	38
Suggested Reading:	41
SECTION 5 - HEPATITIS & METHICILLIN-RESISTANT STAPHYLOCOCCUS AUREUS	**43**
THE HEPATITIS ALPHABET—KNOW YOUR ABCS	45
Hepatitis	45
Hepatitis A	45
Hepatitis B	46
Hepatitis C	46
Hepatitis D	47
Hepatitis E	47
In Summary	48
METHICILLIN-RESISTANT STAPHYLOCOCCUS AUREUS (MRSA)	49
What is MRSA?	49
Who Gets MRSA Infection?	49
Can the Spread of MRSA be Controlled?	50
Symptoms of MRSA	50
How is MRSA Treated?	51
SECTION 6 - SKIN ANATOMY	**53**
The Hypodermis	55
The Dermis	56
The Epidermis	56
SECTION 7 - EYE ANATOMY	**59**
Introduction	61
The Orbit/Eye Socket	62
The Eyelids	62
The Cornea	63

The Sclera 64
The Pupil 64
The Iris... 64
Abnormal Conditions of the Eye..65
Rare but Possible Complications Resulting from Eyeliner Procedures 66
Serious Eye Complication Symptoms 68
When to Seek Medical Attention... 68

SECTION 8 - IMPORTANT MUSCLES OF THE FACE **69**

SECTION 9 - CHOOSING THE RIGHT CLIENT **79**
Is this Prospective Client a Good Candidate?...................... 81
What is the Client's Health Profile?... 81
Is the Client Emotionally a Good Candidate for Permanent Cosmetics? 81
Has the Client Had Permanent Cosmetics Before, and If So, Why Is the Client Not Returning to the Original Technician? 83
Where does the client live?.. 84
Has the Client Discussed the Desire for Permanent Cosmetics with Family and Close Friends? 84
Is the Client a Good Candidate for the Technique Requested? 84
Is the Timing Desired Appropriate Based on Imminent Travel Plans or Social Obligations? 85
DECLINING PERMANENT COSMETIC CLIENTS - GENERAL.............................85
Non-Payment for Services... 85
Time Consumers 85
People Who Ask for Discounts 86
People Who Are Dishonest and Over-Demanding 86
NEGOTIATING THE DISSOLUTION OF YOUR RELATIONSHIP WITH A CLIENT....87

SECTION 10 - PIGMENT (SKIN) TESTING AND PERMANENT COSMETICS **89**

SECTION 11 - CLIENT HISTORY FILES... **95**
CLIENT HISTORY PROFILE: WHAT TO ASK AND WHY 97
INFORMED CONSENT: WHAT TO ADVISE AND WHY................................ 111
PROCEDURE CHART NOTES: WHAT TO DOCUMENT.................................. 113
SAMPLE FORMS.. 113
Client History Profile Form 114
Informed Consent Form 115
Procedure Chart Notes 118

SECTION 12 - DOCUMENTING PERMANENT COSMETIC WORK WITH PHOTOGRAPHY ...**119**
The Client Photograph Consent and Usage Release 122
Selecting Equipment for Photography 123
Common Likeness Photographs 126
Client Positioning and Appearance..127
The Photography Location and Backdrop 127
Presentation Portfolios...128

SECTION 13 - IDENTIFYING SKIN UNDERTONES **133**

Section 14 - Working With Fitzpatrick IV–VI Skin Types 139
Fitzpatrick Skin Evaluation Chart 147
Hyperpigmentation and Hypopigmentation 148

Section 15 - Traditional and Permanent Cosmetic Color Theories 151
The Primary Colors 158
Secondary or Complementary Colors 161
Intermediate and Tertiary Colors 162
Important Elements of Permanent Cosmetic Color Theory 168

Section 16 - Selecting Permanent Cosmetic Procedure Colorants—General Information 173
Eyebrow Color Selection 176
Eyeliner Color Selection 183
Lip Color Selection 184
Permanent Cosmetic Color Correction and Adjustment Guide 187

Section 17 - Basic Facial Morphology and Placement of Procedures 193
Eyebrows 198
Eyes 202
Lips 203
Permanent Cosmetic Designs and the Aging Process 206

Section 18 - All About Procedures 209
Overview of Procedure Techniques and Protocols 211
The Basic Table Setup 212
Client Management Protocols 213
The Eyeliner Procedure 217
The Eyeliner Procedure Sequence 218
Designing Eyeliners Tutorial 223
The Eyebrow Procedure 235
Permanent Cosmetic Eyebrow Tattoo Techniques 236
Lip Color Procedures 251
The Lip Liner and Shaded Lip Liner Tutorial 252
How Will I Look? 263
Can This Procedure Be Saved? 269
What Not to Do 274

Section 19 - Pain and Anesthesia 279
Mind Over Matter 289

Section 20 - The Healing Process 295

Section 21 - Solar Care and Prevention of Premature Permanent Cosmetic Color Fading 303

Section 22 - Herpes Simplex and Permanent Cosmetics 311

Section 23 - Medical Conditions and Permanent Cosmetics 319
Mitral Valve Prolapse (MVP) 321
Latex Allergy 322

VITILIGO 323
ALOPECIA 325
DIABETES 326
HYPERTENSION 327
TRICHOTILLOMANIA (TTM) 329
GLAUCOMA 330
SKIN CANCER 331
OTHER CONDITIONS 333

SECTION 24 - MRI AND PERMANENT COSMETICS 335

SECTION 25 - PSYCHOLOGY AND PERMANENT COSMETICS 341
CONSUMER BEHAVIOR 343
Restoration 344
Considerable Change 344
Convenience 345
Why People Sometimes Resist Change 346
The Familiarity of Design and Color 348
Words that Cause Client Concern 350
Personality Disorders 350
Early Signs of a Potential Challenge 351
WHAT THE BODY IS SAYING 353
Body Language 353
First Contact Analysis 354

SECTION 26 - THE PRINCIPLES OF TATTOO LIGHTENING AND REMOVAL 357
Liability Coverage 359
Considerations 360
How Does Tattoo Lightening Work? 362
The Consultation and Pre-Testing 362
Tattoo Lightening Forms 363
Tattooing Lightening Needle Guidelines 365
Tattoo Lightening Technique Guidelines 365
What to Expect and When to Reschedule 367
Scarring and Procedure Location 375
Challenging colors 376
Procedure-Specific Successes 377
    Eyebrows 377
    Eyeliners 378
    Lips 379
Aftercare: Dry Healing vs. Moist Healing 380
Repigmentation of Lightened Procedure Areas: 382

APPENDIX A - WORKS REFERENCED/WORKS CITED 385

APPENDIX B - LIST OF FIGURES 391

APPENDIX C - ERRORS AND OMISSIONS 403

Biography

Marjorie Grimm, CPCP holds the prestigious position as one of the most credentialed people in the permanent cosmetic industry. As past SPCP board member in 1999 and 2002, she was appointed president of the SPCP and served a two-year term 2003–2005. She has also served as the SPCP's materials and media manager, legislative consultant, the assistant editor for the SPCP Quarterly, and been a major contributor to the SPCP's Train the Trainer Program. Marjorie is a certified trainer and subject matter expert (SME), and an esteemed recipient of the Industry Leader Award.

She began her career in permanent cosmetics in 1993, having been impressed with her hair-stylist's tattooed eyeliner. This led her to seek education in the industry, but there were few who offered training in northern California. Ultimately, she solicited the help of a local tattoo artist, who befriended her. During their one-year time span together, he taught her the basics of tattooing. As happenstance, she met Mary Jane Haake at a beauty show in San Jose, who introduced her to the SPCP. This introduction and association would forever change her career path.

Marjorie began training others in the art of permanent cosmetics in 1999. It was through the development of her training manual and during an update process in 2005 that the concept of writing a textbook for the industry became a reality. In 2005 Marjorie had coauthored a chapter about permanent cosmetics in a medical aesthetics book with Dr. Efran Arrovave, MD Medical Director, Aesthetic Medical Education Resources. This planted the seed to someday publish a book about permanent cosmetics. Kate Ciampi, her friend and mentor, who was assisting with content and editing of the Faces By Design training manual, suggested the content be changed to offer a variety of devices and techniques that all trainers could relate to. Two and a half years later, with the help of other industry leaders who contributed their knowledge to the textbook, *Permanent Cosmetics: The Foundation of Fundamental Applications* became a reality.

Marjorie and the SPCP are very proud to present the new *Permanent Cosmetic: The Foundations of Fundamental Applications*, **Second Edition** textbook which has been over a year and a half in the works. This edition includes up-to-date information on all aspects of our industry and exiting new sections to enhance the reader's learning experience.

Preface

As a permanent cosmetic fundamental trainer for many years, I continually endeavored to compile the best information available for my students. As the industry grew, so did the sources of accurate and up-to-date information. As I embarked upon renewing the contents of my training manual, it became clear that with my experience, and the assistance of other industry leaders, it was an opportune time to produce a textbook and contribute to the industry as a whole - sharing the information with all who desire guidance and seek answers to subjects. This textbook is timeless, uniting science and art, and will serve you throughout your career. My heart and soul are in this book. I was thinking of you when I wrote it.

Many subjects must be explored to provide a sound understanding of permanent cosmetic principles and methodologies. As one applies these practices, there are subjects where science dictates and others where art, and the opinion and technique of an artist, prevail.

> Within the scope of this there are truths, and truth is not subject to belief; it's above opinion. An example of this would be aspects of human anatomy.

Art and the options of artistry, devices used, preferred pigments, needle selection, etc., is different from the truth of science in our industry. Visual art is a personal interpretation of what a person sees, or as an artist, what has been created. An example of interpretation in the permanent cosmetic industry would be the review of an eyebrow design by several trainers. Where one or more trainers may praise the design work as exemplary, one or more trainers may eschew it.

This textbook provides the foundation for fundamental permanent cosmetic applications. If preparing for a fundamental class, the trainer chosen may employ techniques as examples provided, or lead her or his students to alternative methods associated with cosmetic tattooing processes, many times based on unique student characteristics.

If a fundamental class has been completed and this textbook has been selected as a source for supplemental information, the reader will find each section rewarding as an enhancement to class(es) completed.

The information presented in this textbook is not a replacement or substitution for proper and adequate hands-on training from a qualified instructor or for professional medical advice. Be sure to seek qualified hands-on instruction before attempting any of the techniques presented in these materials.

The updated Second Edition is reflective of current industry practices, techniques, and is geographical, gender, product, and device neutral.

Marjorie was instrumental in bringing tattoo lightening to the industry through her work with a major US insurance company and Lloyds of London. She determined that with her vast experience on this subject to include the Principles principal of Tattoo Lightening and Removal in the textbook to support technicians who have either taken a class on this subject and also those in preparation for product-specific training. Also included is the work that she and Greg Shergold, MA, LPC developed, *The Psychology of Permanent Cosmetics.* Technicians will flourish in this industry with knowledge of the different personality types and traits of their clients. The new Permanent Cosmetic Eyebrow Techniques provides a review of the different types of techniques and associated devices currently used for eyebrow procedures.

Several permanent cosmetic industry leaders (many who are also experts in adjunct professions) kindly donated information, pictorial resources, and factual excerpts to this textbook to ensure its accuracy in specialized subject matters. I thank them for their dedication and generosity afforded to the permanent cosmetic industry.

Spyros Aggelopoulos

Konstantinos Angelopoulos

Karen Betts, CPCP

Kate Ciampi Shergold RN, CPCP

Daria Chuprys, CPCP

Sarah Colton, CPCP

Tina Davies

Elizabeth Finch-Howell, CPCP, Bench-Chemist

Mary Jane Haake, CPCP

Jill Hoyer, CPCP

Angie Kwiatkowski, CPCP

Laurna Marika, OSHA Authorized Outreach Instructor, 10-30 hr. General Industry

Erika Mopress

Greg Shergold, MA, LPC

Mytia Story, BS, Biologist and Chemist

Liza Sims, Esthetician

Shelley Turk

David Vidra

Shanan Zickefoose, BSN, RN, CPCP

I appreciate and value all the caring, brilliant people who, over the years, have enriched the industry by freely giving of their time and information; you've inspired many people to be the very best at their trade. To my close friends in this industry, thanks for keeping me focused, making me laugh, and enriching my life.

Although this mention is unauthorized, this textbook would not exist or be what it is without the support of Kate Ciampi Shergold. I've asked that the famous words she spoke to me regarding authoring an industry textbook many years ago be put on my final resting place – "How hard can this be?" Really Kate? Thank you for all you do for the permanent cosmetic industry.

Section 1

Facts About Permanent Cosmetics

Learning Objectives

Introduction

Each notable profession has its fair share of facts from which to draw intellectual information, and fictitious data that may be borne from lack of knowledge.

Early on, the permanent cosmetic industry laid the foundation for fundamentals-truths. Once the concept of tattooing makeup became quite popular, since then, it has not been unusual for incorrect information to infiltrate social media and other technician supported venues; thus, influencing the minds of many who are seeking factual information.

Social media often presents information that may not be completely factual based on chemistry, anatomy, and physiology. Nor are the compete circumstances surrounding a particular permanent cosmetic case study that may be discussed always known or provided.

Objective

Upon completion of this chapter, the technician will firmly anchor popular subject matters into truths and create a foundation of facts to draw on time and time again.

Section 1 - Facts About Permanent Cosmetics

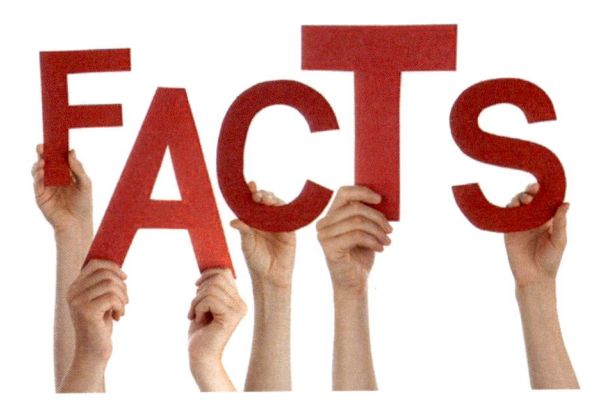

There are facts that support the artistic and technical profession of permanent cosmetics and there is fiction or half-truths, which is misleading to technicians and the public alike. It is important that all technicians separate truths from mistruths on important subject matters. The most effective way to present facts and fiction is to ask questions typically presented for explanation.

How permanent are permanent cosmetics?

If a technician is well-trained, the skin is pricked with a needle and particles of colorants are deposited into the upper dermal layer of the skin. The procedure is considered permanent, but like all color, it is subject to fading over time.

If the technician is *not* well-trained to deposit the colorant(s) into the upper layer of the dermis they may timidly only deposit the color in the outer layer of the skin called the epidermis. Under these circumstances, the deposited color will soon flake off with the natural exfoliation activity of the epidermis during the body's cell renewal activity.

In order to compensate for a lack of experience to place pigment where it rightfully belongs, some technicians have been known to offer procedures indicating they are not meant to be permanent.

The degree and timing of fading does vary from client to client because their bodies and lifestyles are unique. Color can fade due to numerous factors including incidental or excessive exposure to the sun. Other forms of ultraviolet (UV) rays (tanning beds are the most common), unique body chemistry, medical conditions, and facial care maintenance programs also contribute to premature fading.

Fading does not constitute disappearing, and this occurrence furthermore does not support calling permanent cosmetics semi-permanent or any other derivative of this term.

As an industry, we now know that permanent cosmetic formulations and the type of powders used to produce them, along with technician technique and environmental stress, all contribute to the longevity of the appearance of the original healed procedure.

Even if environmental stress were the only factor, expecting clients to remain out of the sun, to never develop health conditions, or to never use facial products that may be contraindicative is not realistic. As a result of the natural aging of color in the skin, environmental stress on color, and client unique health issues, clients must be advised that they will need color refreshers/color boosts from time to time. How quickly or slowly the fading process transgresses is dependent on the client's body chemistry, lifestyle, and formulation properties used for the tattooing procedure.

Are some tattoo devices better than others?

All tattoo devices have the potential of some being considered to be better than others, but usually in relation to the ability of the technician to feel confident operating the equipment properly, and the machine's cross-contamination prevention engineering design.

It is important that the device selected to perform procedures is engineered to prevent cross-contamination during procedures. At one time, for some machine devices (the coil and some rotary machines), reusable tubes that had to be cleaned, disinfected, and sterilized after each use was all that was available. Now single-use pre-sterilized needles and tubes (or single-use machine components and manual devices) are commonplace and conveniently available.

Manual devices are commonly one unit or there are designs that require assembly (the needle assembly is separate and joined with the hand piece by the technician). Either type is disposed of in their entirety after the procedure is completed in a sharps container.

Many different tattoo device types are available. Important factors to consider in regard to devices are the following:

- The device is a safe method to use.
- The device is engineered to prevent cross-contamination of body fluids during a procedure.
- The technician understands the mechanics and maintenance requirements.
- The device is comfortable for the technician to use to during procedures.
- Manual devices are single-use, whether or not they are purchased as one unit or require assembly.

Some technicians are acclimated to a machine, whereas other technicians prefer the manual device. Considering that microblading is very popular, technicians may use both machine and manual devices for different procedure types. Tattoo devices are very technician-specific. A permanent cosmetic procedure is artwork in a living canvas, and as with any form of art, there are many devices available with which to perform the work.

Are permanent cosmetics like tattoos?

Permanent cosmetics/makeup (or any other industry-assigned name) is cosmetic tattooing. There are many titles used to describe the service, but regardless of the name, the service is tattooing. You will find *permanent cosmetics, permanent makeup, cosmetic tattooing, micropigmentation, microblading/microstroking* being a few of the top service descriptions utilized. Microblading has become a top Internet search description for the hair stroke technique with a manual device.

What do technicians who offer cosmetic tattooing call themselves?

Technicians in the industry use a variety of titles. There may be laws in place that dictate professional titles, but in most cases, this is left to the technician. Below are some popular professional titles utilized in the industry.

- Permanent cosmetic technician or artist
- Permanent makeup technician or artist
- Cosmetic tattoo technician or artist
- Micropigmentation technician or artist
- Microblading or microstroking technician or artist

The most popular of these make a statement about the service being offered. It is wise to avoid the use of any descriptive titles that implies medical training associated with cosmetic tattooing. This is misleading to the public and may carry legal consequences. There may be some geographic locations that have laws dictating the title that is to be used which may be different from the common titles listed.

Does the application of permanent cosmetics hurt?

The degree of discomfort during a permanent cosmetic procedure is dependent on several factors:

- The client's unique body properties relating to her or his pain threshold
- The location of the procedure being performed
- The use of anesthetics
- The skill of the technician

Each client will have a client-specific threshold of discomfort. Whereas one client will experience very little discomfort, another may report more discomfort for the same procedure. Discomfort is an unpredictable factor that cannot be foreseen with accuracy.

The majority of experienced technicians agree that characteristically, eyebrow procedures produce the least amount of discomfort. Eyeliner procedures produce more anxiety rather than pain because of the procedure location. (The body is very protective of the wellbeing of the eyes.) Reports indicate that lip procedures seem to result in more discomfort than the eyebrow or eyeliner procedures.

The use of anesthetics is commonplace now, but with varying results. Not all technicians choose to use anesthetics. Also, the legality of using over-the-counter anesthetics is geographically specific.

The client's body chemistry and the breakdown of anesthetics once absorbed by the skin are client-specific factors. If a client reports that she or he is resistant to dental anesthetizing, this is an indication that there may be challenges associated with getting and keeping the procedural area anesthetized during the procedure.

The skill of the technician, her or his stretching techniques, and abilities to coach the client through the process with distractions such as counting and relaxation methodologies all lend to the client's final conclusion that the procedure was or was not more or less uncomfortable.

Regardless of the use of techniques employed and products formulated to reduce discomfort during tattooing, procedures are not performed without some discomfort even if minor or only pressure related. It is considered unethical to imply or promote services as pain-free or any derivative of this concept.

Are permanent cosmetics safe?

This is a question that is often addressed in media articles by people who are not credentialed to speak on the subject. Bad news in the media is headline material.

As we have all seen on a multitude of subject matters, it only takes one high-profile negative incident to discredit an entire industry.

People are routinely exposed to the medical conditions of other people now more than ever before. The public is very aware that there are many serious diseases transmitted through exposure to body fluids and inappropriate use of needles. As a result, the media often presents a negative view of the tattoo profession. They focus on people who offer the service under unsanitary conditions resulting in complications and/or the spread of diseases. Unfortunately, there are those in all public service related industries who have earned a poor reputation for one reason or another, resulting in those who follow the strict letter of the law for public safety to suffer.

> Permanent cosmetics are considered safe when:
> - a trained technician provides services to people who are screened to be good candidates for tattooing which is an invasive procedure;
> - a device that is designed and engineered to prevent cross-contamination is used and the technician follows the Bloodborne Pathogens Standard;
> - professionally manufactured supplies are utilized;

- the technician properly counsels the client how to properly care for the procedure(s) during the healing process.

Trained technicians use client history forms to screen eligibility of clients for the invasive permanent cosmetic procedure, and consent forms to ensure the client is well informed and is agreeable to the terms and conditions. If permanent cosmetic procedures have the potential of causing harm to a potential client, technicians should not proceed with service(s).

Regardless of the safeguards of the device used to perform the procedure in relation to cross-contamination, the technician must follow the Bloodborne Pathogens Standard before, during, and after the procedure. Barrier product must be used to cover common containers and equipment (including machine cords) that will be reused.

The workplace must always be maintained in a clean manner, utilizing disinfectants for cleaning common areas such as the floors and work/equipment surfaces.

Examination gloves are to be worn at all times when touching the client's face, during the procedure (nitrile gloves are recommended), and while disinfecting the area/equipment before and after a procedure.

Products used during the procedure must be deemed safe through any required manufacturer testing, ingredient disclosure, and should not be deemed unsafe by any government agency for over-the-counter limitation standards.

- The Society of Permanent Cosmetic Professionals (SPCP) supplier members provide important product information on their pigments and anesthetics. Because laws are subject to change, it is the responsibility of all SPCP member pigment manufacturers, supplier members, and trainer members to understand and abide by the laws specific to tattoo pigments in the regions where these products are sold and/or used for training purposes.

The client has the responsibility to follow aftercare instructions that are provided or recommended to them by the technician before leaving the studio. For instance, it is not recommended that clients unnecessarily expose just tattooed procedures to germs that are prevalent in high-traffic public areas for several days after the procedure(s). Clients must be discouraged from exposing newly tattooed procedures to UV rays soon after the procedure(s) is performed, and from the use of aftercare products that were not provided or suggested by the technician. The procedural area must be kept clean and the client must comply with aftercare instructions in order for the healing process to commence without incident.

How do people choose their technician?

Technicians are not all equally trained or talented. In some geographic locations, there are few regulations that dictate training or facility practice guidelines. In other locations, there are very strict regulations that specify the training required to offer permanent cosmetic services. Keep in mind, however, that as with any profession, there are technicians who are more sought after than others by virtue of their artistic abilities and the quality of training they have received.

Credentials come in different forms. For instance, the public recognizes training credentials as well as the Society of Permanent Cosmetic Professionals CPCP (Certified Permanent Cosmetic Professional) certification credential.

Certification is a formal recognition of comprehension of a specific body of knowledge demonstrated at the time of the examination. It is a mark of excellence and demonstrates that a certified individual has the knowledge to provide a particular level of quality service. Certification is an investment in a professional's career.

An opponent of permanent cosmetic certificates of completed training may indicate that due to lack of laws requiring supported training programs, certificates of training from independent trainers are insignificant. Training is training and whether or not the program is supported by government agencies, industry leader trainers should not give certificates of training to students who do not demonstrate the abilities necessary to perform the work well.

One of the best forms of credentials is the technician's client photograph portfolio. Also, pleased clients often offer testimonials that can be displayed on websites, provided on review Internet sites, or maintained at the workplace for potential clients to read.

A Bloodborne Pathogens Standard training document evidencing completion of the program (classes are routinely taken periodically) is very important and is a required program by many regulatory agencies.

Longevity in the industry is not necessarily a measurement of talent. There are technicians who initially had inadequate training (if any) and began tattooing substandard work years ago. They may continue to produce substandard work until they pursue additional training. On the other hand, a technician who receives thorough informative fundamental training may have been in the industry for a short period of time but because of their quality of training, they perform high-quality procedures.

The quality of a technician's fundamental class is an important foundation. After their fundamental class, technicians advance to the next level of educational programs (if in a tiered-based training program) or they will pursue continuing education courses independently. Some technicians move into specialized areas of tattooing. The learning process never ends for the technician who strives to remain current in the permanent cosmetic industry.

Often people will rely on word-of-mouth referrals from friends, family members, and co-workers. Also, the media often mentions the SPCP website, www.spcp.org, to read about permanent cosmetic services and to locate a technician or trainer.

Who are the people that benefit most from permanent cosmetics?

Anyone of legal age, who:

- is not pregnant or nursing;
- does not have a health condition that would prevent proper healing;
- does not take medications (blood thinners as an example) that would affect the outcome of the procedure;
- does not have a history of allergies to product ingredients;
- has skin that is healthy and will tolerate the tattooing process without incident.

All others can benefit from receiving permanent cosmetic services. A few of the reasons for considering permanent cosmetics are people:

- who have allergies to topical makeup;
- who have dexterity and eyesight challenges;
- who must look their very best at all times for professional purposes;
- who have lost confidence in their appearance due to the maturing process or other personal reasons;
- who has scarring from congenital cleft lip surgical repair (advanced procedure type);
- who have undergone a mastectomy seeking repigmentation of the nipple/areola complex area(s) after reconstructive breast surgery (advanced procedure type);
- who have medical conditions such as alopecia (resulting in partial or total loss of hair on the body) seeking permanent cosmetic services to restore the appearance of eyebrows or provide definition to their eyes in the absence of eyelashes;
- who have an asymmetric lip shape or who has lost lip definition.

The benefits are endless and very client-specific as to how the benefits apply.

Permanent cosmetic services are thought to be predominantly sought after by women; however, men also pursue services to fill in sparse eyebrows, define their eyes with eyeliner procedures, camouflage scars, and for other appearance enhancing procedures. Regardless of the gender, the motivating factor for seeking our services is quite wide and varied.

There are, however, people who are not good candidates for a particular procedure or at all, in some instances, due to medical conditions. Technicians should not take risks that could result in creating a medical problem for someone. It is also unwise to agree to unreasonable client requested design work that will not serve the potential client long term. People with variegated (two-tone) lips and/or who have deep blue/violet undertones are not normally, if ever, good candidates for lip procedures and they should be advised accordingly. Acting responsibly sometimes means declining work.

Why is color theory so important in the permanent cosmetic industry?

One reason people have unattractive permanent cosmetics is because their technician lacked knowledge of permanent cosmetic color theory (PCCT) and the knowledge of the artistic deposit of color in living tissue. This includes knowledge of skin undertone types.

Reining as a primary reason clients are not pleased with their permanent cosmetic services are those people tattooed with inappropriate colors. To expect the color to perform well long term, the right color formulation must be selected for the appropriate skin type for the procedure being conducted, based on the client's color preferences. If a technician is having consistent problems with the color of recently healed and/or aged procedures, a permanent cosmetic color theory class is the first step to be taken to resolve this problem.

The color that is seen in the container is not the exact color that will be seen in the skin immediately after the procedure, or when the procedure is healed. Inexperienced technicians make the common mistake of assuming that what you see is what you get. They have not been trained that the equation is tattooed color + skin undertone = healed color appearance. Without the benefit of the client's skin healed over the procedure and the effects of light reflecting through the epidermis, the color remains a stand-alone factor. Without knowledge of the formulations of pigments selected for use, and how they perform on certain skin types, technicians have limited insight as to what to expect when the procedure is healed.

The technician's color theory knowledge as it relates to permanent cosmetics and the base color of the formulation used are very important elements associated with the quality of procedures she or he performs. A design may be admirable, the tattooing process performed well, but if the healed color is not as expected, the client may view the entire procedure as less than successful.

There is not a simple ABC guide to color as it relates to tattooing color into a living canvas that has a color of its own. Permanent cosmetic color theory (PCCT) includes subtractive color theory (the science of the behavior of dyes, inks, paints, and pigments). Knowledge of the artistic application of these color theories in a living canvas, and skin undertone identification are all important elements of predicting the final color that will be seen after a procedure heals.

Different eyebrow techniques also affect the temperature of how an eyebrow heals. Microblading is a replication of eyebrow hair stroke patterns. Hair strokes have very little surface area for light reflection compared to other brow technique types. As a result, depending on the formulation (there are some manufacturers who have developed formulations specifically for microblading eyebrows) they may heal to appear cooler and darker than the color used for the procedure appeared in the container or as tested on the surface of the skin.

When did the process of permanent cosmetics emerge?

A permanent cosmetic procedure is cosmetic tattooing. If the skin is pricked with a needle for the purpose of depositing color, the process, regardless of what term is used, is tattooing. The art of tattooing in various forms dates back to historical periods for centuries. There are reports of this person or that person asking for, or performing the *original* permanent cosmetic procedure. Although from a historical or trivia perspective, this may be interesting information to ponder, not only is this not important in the grand scheme of things today, but the process has changed so dramatically in the last twenty-five years that the original procedure performed (on and by whomever) would likely not resemble the service as it is offered today.

How long does a procedure take?

This is very dependent on the procedure being performed and the technician performing the procedure. Typically appointments are scheduled for 1 1/2 to 2 1/2 hours, depending if information regarding client eligibility is scheduled to be discussed at the same appointment before beginning the procedure process. Time for applying design guides and topical anesthetics (if used by the technician) factors into the time allotted.

Considering that over-the-counter pre-procedure type topical anesthetics normally take up to thirty minutes (depending on the manufacturer's directions) to be effective, the actual time spent tattooing the permanent cosmetic procedure consumes only a moderate portion of the time allotted for the entire appointment. The completion and review of forms, the taking of photographs, and discussions regarding aftercare and maintenance requirements are also tasks that require time allotment.

Novice technicians should avoid the feeling that they are on the clock based on the opinion of others as to how long something should take. In the beginning, it is only normal for tasks, including the tattooing process, to take longer than it will once the technician becomes more confident. There are, however, limits to how long a client will be patient with long drawn-out sessions. This is not good advertising. Technicians should strive to move through the elements associated with the permanent cosmetic process efficiently.

As more and more procedures are conducted, the time elements associated with certain tasks will shorten. Most important is that time is adequately allotted for all the steps needed along the way to ensure effective client management, safe practices, and good procedure results.

What usually occurs when performing lip color, eyeliner, and eyebrow procedures?

Procedures will commence and be considered complete in a similar fashion. At the beginning of each procedure type (eyeliner, eyebrows, and lips) in Section 18, a step-by-step guide is provided.

What are examples of what could be considered tattooing for medical reasons?

There are many procedures that are performed as a result of a medical condition, such as alopecia, or the effects of cancer treatments; however, all are not viewed as specific medical procedures.

These are three of the most sought-after procedures that are considered *paramedical* in nature:

- Nipple/areola complex repigmentation, normally in conjunction with breast reconstruction after a mastectomy
- Scar camouflage for scars as a result of traumatic injury or trauma, vs. surgical scars
- Scar camouflage for surgical scars created from cleft lip reconstruction

How successful is permanent makeup at covering things like scars and hyperpigmentation?

Scar camouflage procedures can be very successful. Scar camouflaging is considered advanced procedure work, requiring specialized training and experience to produce successful results.

Scars have many different characteristics and are unique to the skin type in which they reside, the source of the trauma that caused the scarring, and the age and depth of the scar tissue involved.

Hyperpigmentation is a natural darkening of the skin normally caused by sun exposure, hormonal effects, and injury to the skin. Camouflaging over hyperpigmented skin just makes the situation worse by darkening the skin due to trauma from tattooing the area. A well-trained technician never tries to cover hyperpigmentation by attempting to camouflage the area.

Can permanent cosmetics be removed? If so, how? Are camouflage techniques effective for unwanted permanent cosmetics?

Tattooing is permanent. There are many unique elements involved with a successful tattoo lightening and removal procedure. The color that was tattooed into the skin, the size of the tattoo, the location of the tattoo, and the age of the tattoo all have an influence over the possible success of tattoo lightening procedures.

Small areas of tattooed color, at times, may be successfully discouraged from healing into the skin if the problem is addressed *immediately after* the initial procedure (before the client leaves the studio). This normally results in a lightening of the color, but again, success depends on the size, technique employed, color used, etc.

In a non-medical environment (permanent cosmetic studio), the use of products formulated specifically for tattoo lightening by a trained technician is considered a good method for correcting permanent cosmetic work. This is dependent on the specific circumstances of the tattoo (density of color, location, shape of design, client skin undertone etc.) Removing color, especially color that has healed or aged, from the skin is a process. The process is one that may take several visits over an extended period of time; and results will vary.

There is a section in the textbook written specifically on this subject, "The Principles of Tattoo Lightening and Removal" on page 357.

Camouflage cover-up, which is not a removal method, but one used by some uneducated technicians attempting to cover up unwanted design work, is not ever recommended. Attempting to cover up permanent cosmetic procedure mistakes with a flesh tone camouflage tattoo formulation is not considered a professional method of correction and certainly does not result in the appearance of removal or correction. The flesh tone color used mixes with the existing pigment color and creates a third color. Using flesh tone formulations for the purposes of hiding unwanted pigment never works well and ultimately makes things much worse, especially long-term. This should never be done.

In Closing

Networking with well-trained experienced technicians and relying on industry leaders who provide facts, not fiction, provides the opportunity to learn, grow professionally, and conduct business in a truthful manner.

Section 2

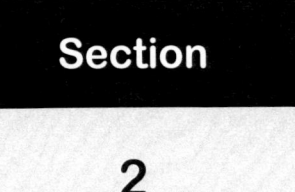

Permanent Cosmetic Devices

Learning Objectives

Introduction

Within the two device type choices, machine and manual, there are countless uniquely engineered designs to choose from. Several are provided as visual references in this section as examples within the same device type grouping.

When searching for the perfect machine or manual device, the primary objective should be to choose one that is engineered to prevent cross-contamination, one that feels right in the hands of the tattoo artist, and one that executes the technician's chosen techniques well. The device chosen should have the potential of producing lovely permanent cosmetics in the hands of a skilled technician.

A device may be acquired in a fundamental training class. This does not mean later on the technician will not choose another type to either add to their inventory or as an additional device for specialized techniques.

There are many technicians who own only one tattoo device type that they are perfectly content with throughout their career, and there are others who own more than one type.

Needle selection for a specific procedure is often unique to the how the technician has been trained. The type and condition of skin being worked on, the technique employed, the procedure being conducted, and the type of device all play an important role in deciding which needle will best deliver the desired results.

By becoming familiar with the primary tattooing concept of permanent cosmetic devices, technicians will ultimately find the one (or more) that meets their needs. Needle configuration availability is specific to each device. Needle selection for procedure types is specific the procedure type, the desired healed appearance, and the technician's preferences.

Objective

Technicians will be better prepared to identify the different devices available in the permanent cosmetic marketplace and develop an understanding of their basic tattooing concept.

Section 2 - Permanent Cosmetic Devices

Permanent Cosmetic Devices

A common myth in the permanent cosmetic industry is that one tattoo device is better than another. In reality, the selection is dependent on technician preferences and training. There are no formal studies that indicate that one device produces more or less trauma or discomfort than another. It is the skill of the technician and the technician's knowledge of the device and needle theory knowledge that causes or reduces trauma elements of a procedure.

If a tattoo device is engineered to meet health and safety standards for preventing cross-contamination, tattoo devices that produce beautiful permanent cosmetics are abundant. There are many manufacturers of manual devices and machines to select from. It was not possible in this textbook to profile each one. The examples below are samples of each type of device that represents a group of industry selection options. The picture examples may lead to a specific manufacturer of the device sample, but there are many manufacturers of manual and machine devices for consideration. Most, if not all, devices used for permanent cosmetic tattooing utilize needles and accessories that are available for purchase in pre-sterilized packaging.

The examples of manual devices used in our industry (see Figure 2-1, Figure 2-2 & Figure 2-3) are modern versions of ancient manual tattoo devices. The needle configuration affixed to the manual device pricks the skin to deposit pigment (colorants/formulations). Technicians who prefer the manual device indicate control, precision, and convenience as positive characteristics.

Figure 2-1: Manual Device
Provided by SofTap

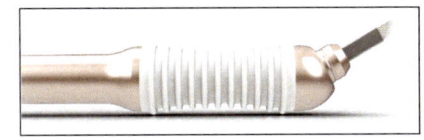

There are many manufacturers of manual devices. There is commonly a large selection of needles configurations for the microblading manual devices for eyebrows. Non-microblading manual devices also offer many needle configuration options in round and in-line needle (some side-by-side rows of needles) designs for a variety of procedure types.

Figure 2-2: Microblading Manual Device
Provided by Harmony

The rotary pen (see Figure 2-4 and Figure 2-4), historically refereed by some as a permanent cosmetic pen, is a rotary machine type device. This device, depending on the specific manufacturer, may offers brand-specific power supply sources and needle configurations. This machine is called a rotary because of the manner in which the electric motor drives the needle up and down via the rotation of the drive shaft. Important in design is the engineering to prevent backflow of pigment (colorants/inks) into the motor assembly. The machine should always be in an off position when not tattooing in the skin.

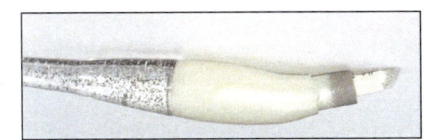

Figure 2-3: Microblading Manual Device
Provided by MeiCha

Needle varieties are unique to the specific manufacturer. Portability and a low level of machine sound (compared to some other machine types) and overall design configuration make this machine popular in the permanent cosmetic industry. Newer generation pen models have various different setting options.

The digital rotary machines (see Figure 2-5 and Figure 2-6) are two examples of the digital rotary machines offered to the permanent cosmetic industry. They have many speed setting functions providing a digital readout of the selected speed. There are many manufacturers of digital permanent cosmetic machines. The needle selections are more often brand-specific, many in cartridge designs. Several models come with a base unit that can accommodate more than one handpiece.

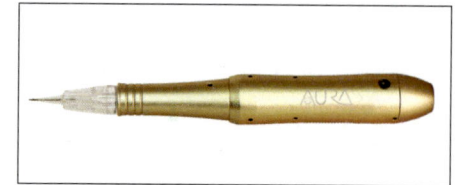

Figure 2-4: Permanent Cosmetic Pen
Photo provide by Daria Chuprys, CPCP

The rotary linear machines (see Figure 2-7) is built for simplicity with low weight, noise, and vibration factors. They accommodate traditional needles, tubes, and supplies, which makes these devices versatile and economical to operate. These machines are available in several model types, some with pre-set or adjustable stroke length options.

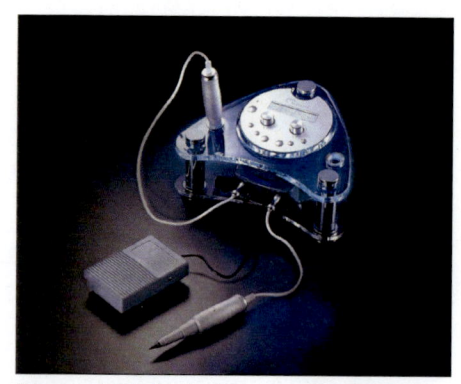

Figure 2-5: Digital Rotary Machine
Photo provide by MeiCha

A new generation of rotary linear device comes in a pen-style design (see Figure 2-8). It provides different operational settings and it can accept a wide variety of different needle-style cartridges.

The coil reciprocating device is a traditional tattoo machine (see Figure 2-9). A coil machine accepts a wide variety of traditional tubes and tattoo needle configurations from a wide variety of different manufacturers.

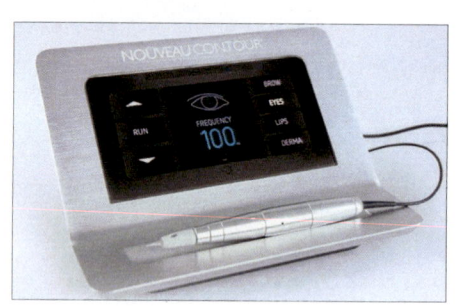

Figure 2-6: Digital Rotary Machine
Photo provided by Nouveau Contour

Needles are held in place inside a tube by being anchored to the machine armature bar post with a nipple/grommet. To create proper tension, one to three rubber bands cross from the needle bar to the frame or designated area. The coils that power the machine have a steel coil and come in a specific number of wraps (wraps equal the number of times the wire wraps around the core). These coils act as electro-magnets. Once current runs through the coil, that coil makes contact with the armature bar by acting as a magnet and attracting the bar. As the armature bar moves down, the needle moves down, eventually breaking the contact and the connection.

Section 2 - Permanent Cosmetic Devices

Technicians normally begin their career having been trained on a particular device during a fundamental training class. It is recommended technician don't look to their tattoo device as the source for problems associated with procedures. Mastering stretching techniques, developing a sense of proper needle selection, and learning about the different speed settings (for machine users) for different skin types and procedures being performed are all part of the learning process.

Figure 2-7: Rotary (Linear) Machine

Figure 2-8: Rotary (Linear) Pen Machine

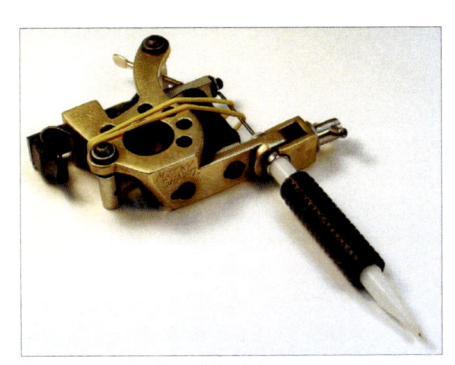

Figure 2-9: Coil Machine

Section 3

Tattoo Needle Information

Learning Objectives

Introduction

It would be very helpful to those who are just entering the permanent cosmetic industry if there was a standard that called out a specific needle for a specific procedure. That will never happen. Technicians and trainers conduct tattoo procedures with a variety tattoo devices and needle preferences. Each tattoo device accommodates a variety of needle configurations, some specific to a particular machine or manual device type.

Training, experience, and ultimately the development of preferences, will dictate which needle configurations are selected within the scope of the device being used and the procedure being conducted.

Objective

Completion of this section will enable the technician to become familiar with the names of the various needle configurations and their properties. This section will provide a quick reference source for review as needed in the future.

Section 3 - Tattoo Needle Informatio

General Needle Information

Needles are the heart and soul of all permanent cosmetic procedures. It is important that technicians study and become familiar with the specific needle(s) they use or may elect to use in the future. Each needle tattoos a pattern in the skin and is the primary influence on how the procedure appears when healed.

Needle Size

Each needle has an associated diameter, regardless of whether it is a traditional tattoo needle, cartridge style, or manual device. All needles have a diameter. This is referred to as the individual needle size. The standard needle sizes are as follows:

- The needle size #12 is .35 mm in diameter
- The needle size #10 is .30 mm in diameter
- The needle size # 8 is .25 mm in diameter
- The needle size # 6 is .20 mm in diameter

Depending on the needle manufacturer, while many call out the needle size as cited above, others may use a numbering system often seen with bug pins.

- The needle size #12 is referred to as 0
- The needle size #10 is referred to as 00
- The needle size #8 is referred to as 000
- The needle size #6 is referred to as 0000

The above-mentioned needle sizes are common to the tattoo industry. There may be others which are considered specialty needles, often associated with one particular brand or tattooing technique device. Manufacturers of specialty needles commonly provide the specific size needles for their products in advertisements, on website information, and when contacted.

In regard to the term *gauge*, often spoken of in relation to needle size, this is not an accurate term for tattoo needles with the exception of the #12, .35 mm size needle, which is considered a standard needle size.

The term *gauge* is a medical needle reference for hollow-bore medical needles. Hollow-bore gauges are based on wire gauges where the smaller the number the larger the diameter of the wire.

23

Permanent Cosmetics: The Foundations of Fundamental Applications — Second Edition

The only exception and commonality of size reference between the medical and tattoo needle industries is only the #12, .35 mm diameter needle.

Needle Taper

Each needle point has a taper. The taper is measurement of the needle point length. Tapers may be one of the following:

- Short
- Medium
- Long
- Extra long

A short taper produces a larger puncture size in the canvas, a medium taper an average puncture size, and long/extra-long tapers create smaller puncture sizes in the skin.

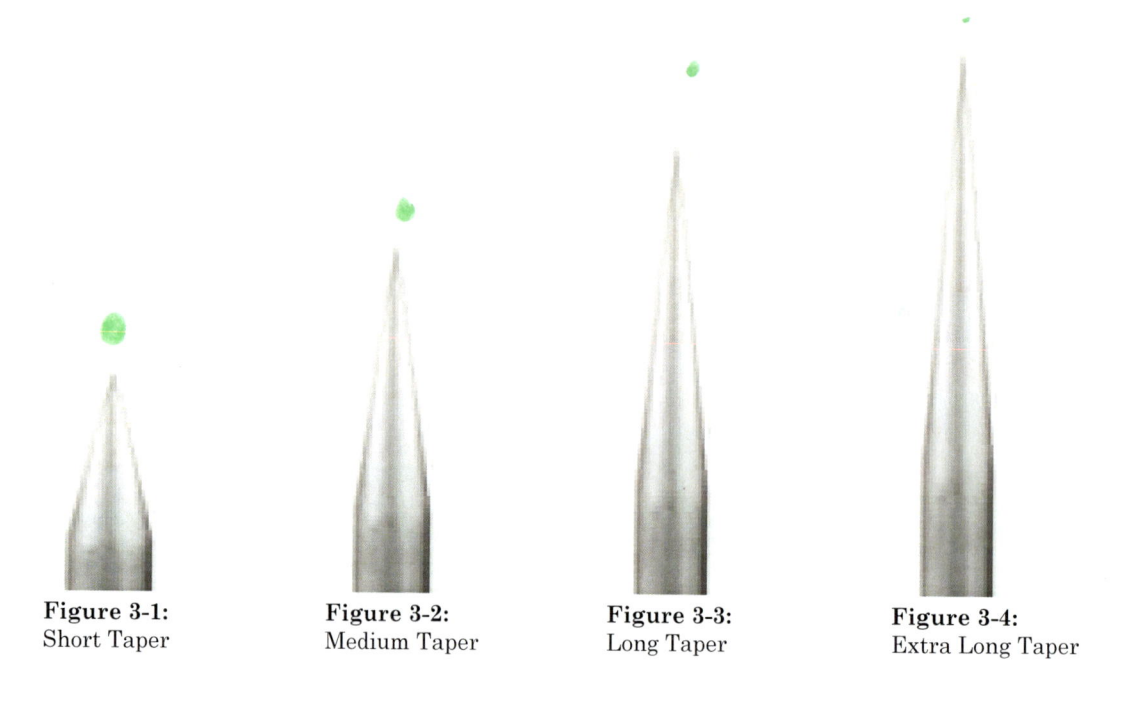

Figure 3-1: Short Taper

Figure 3-2: Medium Taper

Figure 3-3: Long Taper

Figure 3-4: Extra Long Taper

24

Needle Count

Each needle grouping has a count. The following are examples. There are a multitude of needle groupings to choose from.

Figure 3-5: 7-Round Configuration

Figure 3-6: 3-Round Configuration

Figure 3-7: Single Needle Configuration

Configurations (or Groupings)

Configurations/groupings are round, flat/in-line (needles soldered together in a linear alignment) and magnums. A brief description of each is provided:

Rounds

Round liners (Figure 3-8) are a grouping of needles that are soldered together so that the points are close together. The pattern tattooed on the skin is more concentrated.

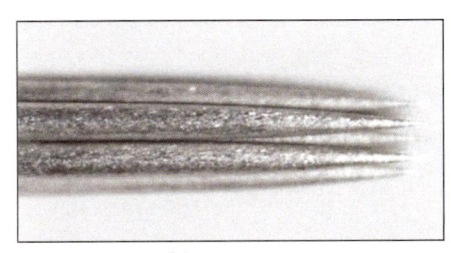

Figure 3-8: 8 Liner

Round shaders (Figure 3-9) are a grouping of needles that are soldered together so that the points are further apart. The pattern tattooed on the skin is more spread out.

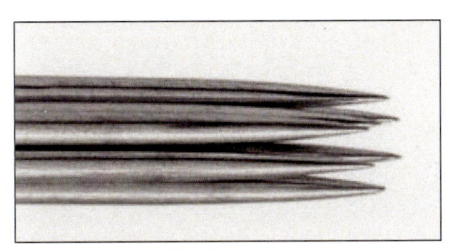

Figure 3-9: 8-Shader

Below is an example of the differences in the liner and shader style needles (Figure 3-10).

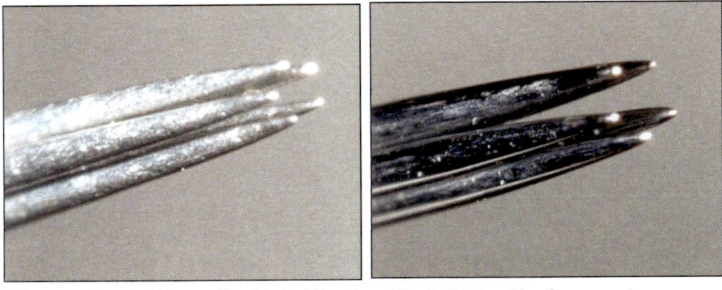

Figure 3-10: Liner (Left) & Shader (Right) Needle Comparison

Flats

Flat configurations (Figure 3-11) are needles in a flat linear pattern and soldered so that there is a certain (manufacturer-specific) space between the needle points.

Magnums

Woven/weaved magnum configurations are one row of needles that woven/weaved in a manner that results in the appearance of two rows needles. They are wider configurations than the stacked magnum.

Woven/weaved magnums are available in either straight (Figure 3-12) or curved/round (Figure 3-13). The two end needles are set back further than the center of the configuration.

Stacked magnum (Figure 3-14) are two rows of side-by-side flat needle configurations with the smaller grouping placed on top of the larger grouping.

Cartridge-Type

Cartridge-type (Figure 3-15 and Figure 3-16) needle style configurations are encased and are inserted into a handpiece of a machine. The needles normally retract back into the encasement when the machine is in the off position.

Manual Device Needle Overview

The in-line needle configurations (Figure 3-17) are arranged in a linear formation some of them multi-row. There are also round configuration styles (Figure 3-18) to choose from. The various in-line and round needles vary in flexibility, rigidity, needle size, method and material by which they are encased, and needle taper.

Microblading needles are configured specifically for eyebrow hair stroke pattern designs and are in-line formation needles. They may be smaller in size (diameter) than the in-line manual non-microblading device needles. They may also be

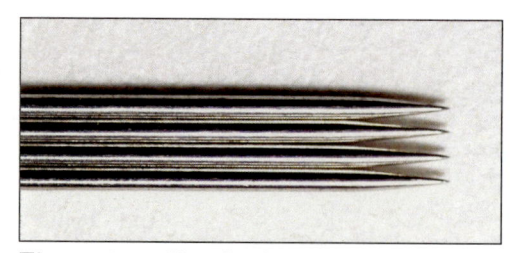

Figure 3-11: Flat Configuration Needle

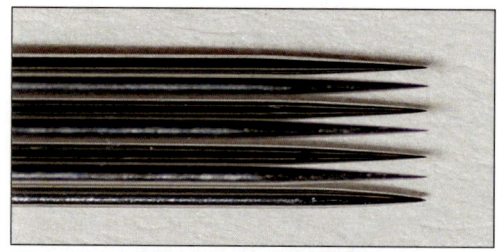

Figure 3-12: 7-Magnum (Straight)

Figure 3-13: 7-Magnum (Curved/Round)

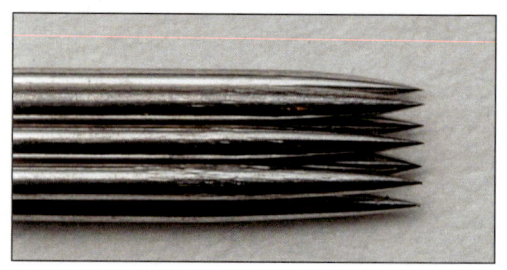

Figure 3-14: 7-Magnum (Stacked)

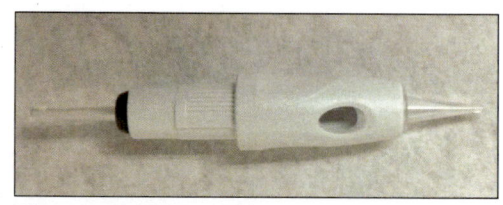

Figure 3-15: Cartridge-Type Needle

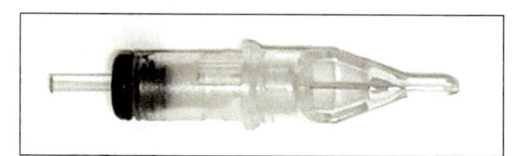

Figure 3-16: Cartridge-Type Needle

Section 3 - Tattoo Needle Information

shorter, more rigid, and depending on the taper, they may be sharper. This information is specific to each microblading needle/device manufacturer.

The microblading needle wrapper or casing may be flexible, or rigid, depending on the material by which it is bound or wrapped. Plastic is more flexible while metal is more rigid. The applications for both depend on the condition of the skin, the experience, training, technician preference, and the desired outcome.

Below are examples of hair stroke in-line formation microblading needles. Note the shorter needle formations (often shorter than the non-microblading needles) and the different materials the needles are wrapped in. The plastic wrap (Figure 3-19) is more flexible while the metal wrap (Figure 3-20) is more rigid.

Figure 3-17: In-Line Formation Double-Row Non-Microblading Manual Device Needle

Needle purchase availability is dependent on the device for which the needles are being purchased. There are machine devices that will only accept their own unique brand needles, while there are other machines that accommodate needles from many manufacturing sources.

Manual devices are often one-unit needle and hand piece (handle) styles, or the needle section is attached to the hand piece (handle) after the sterilized packaging is opened. Regardless of the one-piece needle and handle design, or if the needle comes separate and must be assembled into the handle, at the conclusion of the procedure the entire needle and handle is disposed of in a sharps container.

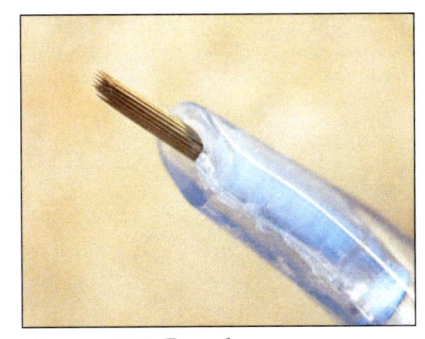

Figure 3-18: Round Configuration Non-Microblading Manual Device Needle.

Depending on the manual or machine device and technique used, technicians choose from the following needle types:

- Traditional tattoo needles that are used for the coil and rotary machines.
- Brand-specific non-cartridge type needles that are not interchangeable between one rotary machine and another. This often relates to the rotary pen machines.
- Cartridge type needles that are brand specific and are not interchangeable between one digital rotary machine and another.
- Cartridge type needles that are not brand specific and can be use with different types of coil and rotary machines.

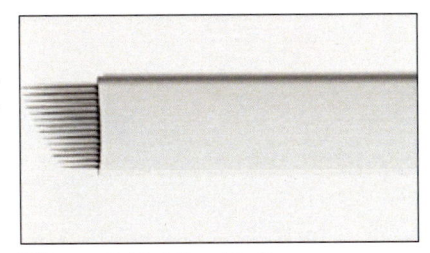

Figure 3-19: Microblading Needle (Plastic Wrapped)

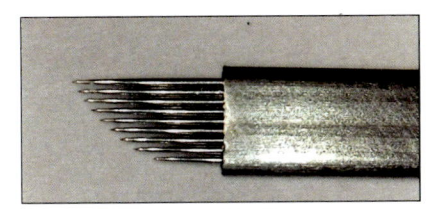

Figure 3-20: Microblading Needle (Metal Wrapped)

- Manual device needles (microblading and non-microblading formations) that also offer a variety of types and sizes with descriptions and recommended uses.

It would not be useful to go into any details about what needle is used for any particular procedure. Trainers and technicians have developed their own preferences for brands and configurations they use for different procedures based on the level of experience, the device they use for tattooing, and how they intend the procedure to appear. The skin condition of the client may also a consideration when choosing needles for a particular procedure.

It is useful to note that during initial fundamental training, students are customarily introduced to a limited number of needle configurations. After training and as technicians become more experienced, they may choose to add different types of needles to their inventory.

Each needle type has manufacturers and distributors that typically maintain websites or provide catalogs that give needle size, configuration, and descriptive information for each needle they offer.

Social media has broadened the exposure to what other technicians are using, and has enabled conversations about the experiences and preferences of others.

References

1. Portions of this section was contributed by Jill Hoyer, CPCP.

Section 4

Safe Practices for Permanent Cosmetic Technicians

Learning Objectives

Introduction

When performing permanent cosmetics, safe practices is a mandated requirement by governing agencies and industry protocols. Safe practices set compliant technicians apart from those who would discredit the tattoo industry and put public they serve at risk.

The public, in general, is aware of health hazards associated with any service or medical treatment that creates bloodborne pathogens. Although they may not be perfectly versed in each step that should be taken to ensure their safety, they are aware of primary principles. Thanks to the Internet and well-distributed articles on the subject in major publications, clients are exposed to a wealth of information on the subject of safety precautions required for invasive procedures.

Technicians are required to serve the needs of their clients in a manner that prevents cross-contamination of their devices, perform proper disposal methods of sharps and other single-use products used during a procedure, maintain the workplace environment in accordance with safe standards, and display impeccable hygienic practices. Clients have a right to feel confident their health has been protected before, during, and after the procedure.

Occupational Safety and Health Administration (OSHA), the Centers for Disease Control and Prevention (CDC), and the Environmental Protection Agency (EPA) are all government agencies in the US. There may be comparable government agencies in other countries.

Objective

The technician will develop a basic understanding of safe practices that are mandated by the industry and governing agencies to ensure technician and client safety during permanent cosmetic procedures.

This is a section you will need to read several times, apply daily, and use as a foundation for classes offered on the same or similar subjects. ✳ ✳ ✳

Section 4 - Safe Practices for Permanent Cosmetic Technicians

In the United States, Occupational Safety and Health Administration (OSHA) Standard 29 CFR 1910.1030 applies to all occupational exposure to blood or other potentially infectious materials (OPIM). Contagious diseases are transmitted (broadcast) by pathogenic organisms through physical contact or by entering the body through mucous membranes, body fluids, airborne inhalation, liquids, food, contaminated objects, or are vector-borne.

OSHA requires all businesses in the United States that employ workers who have the potential of exposure to blood or other OPIM during the performance of their duties to receive Bloodborne Pathogens training annually. Due to the risk of exposure during tattoo procedures, where not mandated by law, it is recommended that technicians attend a live bloodborne pathogens training class presented by an OSHA Outreach Trainer or a web-based class consistent with SPCP guidelines.

Bloodborne pathogens training provides tattoo artists with the knowledge necessary to protect themselves from the risks of occupational exposure to blood and OPIM. Although federally mandated for employers, some states and counties in the US require the class be taken periodically by sole proprietors as well. There may be comparable agencies in other countries with similar standards.

An important component of bloodborne pathogens training is infection control practices. Professionals who conduct invasive procedures, such as tattooing, must do their part to control exposure to infectious organisms and prevent cross-contamination (the process of transferring microorganisms from one surface, object or person to another). To achieve this objective, permanent cosmetic procedures must be conducted utilizing an aseptic technique which involves the use of established practices and procedures to prevent contamination by pathogenic organisms.

The two levels of asepsis are:

- Medical asepsis (clean technique)
- Surgical asepsis (sterile technique)

Medical asepsis practices and procedures are designed to reduce the number of pathogenic organisms present. Examples of medical asepsis utilized within the tattoo studio environment are:

- Correct handwashing technique
- Pre-procedure client skin preparation
- Appropriate cleaning and decontamination of equipment and tools

Surgical asepsis is the set of practices and procedures that are followed to eliminate all microorganisms and spores and prevent their reintroduction into an environment. In the tattoo studio environment, examples are:

- Sterilization of reusable equipment
- Storage and handling of sterile items

Medical Asepsis (Clean Technique)

Hand Hygiene

Hand hygiene is critical in reducing the risk of infection and the transmission of pathogens within the studio environment. Contamination of hands can take place through contact with clients or an unclean surface. Once contamination occurs, microorganisms can survive on practitioners' hands for a period of 2 to 60 minutes.[1] Proper hand hygiene resolves contamination and is the first step in infection control.

In the US, the Centers for Disease Control and Prevention (CDC) recommends the following 11-step process for hand washing to achieve the highest level of hand hygiene:

Duration: 40 – 60 seconds total time

1) Wet hands with water;
2) Apply soap to hands;
3) Rub palm to palm in a rotational manner, creating lather;
4) Interlace fingers palm to back of hand, slide hand back and forth, vice versa;
5) Interlace fingers palm to palm, slide hand back and forth;
6) Scrub back of fingers with palm of opposing hand;
7) Grip thumbs with opposing hand and rub rotationally;
8) Rub fingertips into palm of opposing hand in a rotational manner;
9) Rinse hands with water;
10) Pat hands dry thoroughly with a single-use paper towel, dispose;
11) Use a paper towel to turn off the faucet, dispose.

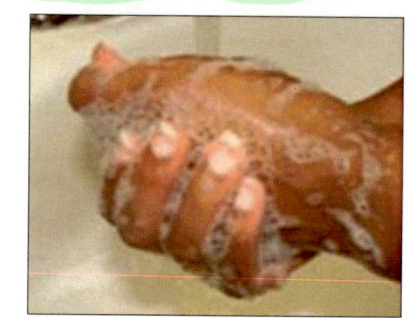

Figure 4-1: Handwashing

The use of antibacterial soap is not required. The purpose of washing with soap is to remove contaminants from the skin. Once contaminants are removed by soap, water, and friction, the surface of the skin is considered clean. Further, the US Food and Drug Administration states there is no conclusive evidence to prove that antibacterial additives to soaps improve the cleaning and antimicrobial qualities of regular soap.

Although handwashing with soap and water is the preferred method for maintaining healthy hand hygiene, hand disinfectants are equally effective for reducing most pathogenic microorganisms when used appropriately. The optimum level of alcohol present in the hand disinfectant/sanitizer should be no less than 60%. If visible dirt or contamination is present, however, then traditional handwashing with soap and water must be performed.

The CDC advises the following method for hand cleaning with alcohol-based hand disinfectants:

Duration: 20 – 30 seconds

1) Apply product to cup of hand (read manufacturer's instruction regarding amount to dispense);
2) Rub palm to palm in a rotational manner;
3) Interlace fingers palm to back of hand, slide hand back and forth, vice versa;
4) Interlace fingers palm to palm, slide hand back and forth;
5) Scrub back of fingers with palm of opposing hand;
6) Grip thumbs with opposing hand and rub rotationally;
7) Rub fingertips into palm of opposing hand in a rotational manner;
8) Continue until hands are dry.

Note: *Many regulators require hot and cold running water and handwashing over alcohol-based hand disinfectants.*

Hand hygiene should be performed:

- before beginning a client procedure;
- before putting on and after removing gloves;
- after contact with blood or other body substances;
- after smoking, eating, using the toilet;
- whenever practitioner leaves the procedure area and then returns to resume the procedure;
- whenever hands are visibly soiled; and
- whenever the risk of contamination of hands could have occurred.

On average, the human hand touches the eyes, nose, and mouth about 15 times per hour.[2] Proper hand hygiene not only prevents cross-contamination of surfaces and clients, but it also prevents the transference of pathogenic organisms to the most vulnerable tissue in the human body, its mucus membrane.

Client Skin Preparation

The client's skin should be cleansed pre-procedure with soap and water or with an appropriate skin preparation product. Use single-use disposable gauze pads and swab the area using a circular motion, starting at the center of the site and moving outward, making sure that pad remains moist throughout the cleansing process. Allow skin to dry before beginning the procedure.

In some situations, individually packaged alcohol swabs (70% ethyl or isopropyl) are instructed to be used for skin preparation. If dispensing from a container, use single-use disposable cups and dispose of leftover fluid after use. Ensure that all products have not exceeded manufacturer's expiration date.

If shaving is required to remove excess hair from the procedure area, a single-use disposable razor must be used and disposed of immediately after use into a designated sharps container.

Cleaning and Decontamination of Equipment and Tools

Prior to disinfection, environmental surfaces and instruments must be cleaned to remove all visible gross debris. Effective cleaning involves friction, detergent, and water.

Disinfection is accomplished by use of a broad-spectrum, chemical disinfectant. In the United States, disinfection is accomplished with Environmental Protection Agency (EPA) registered, hospital level disinfectants that kill viruses, bacteria, fungi, and mycobacterium tuberculosis, in addition to other pathogenic organisms.

Cleaning of tools and equipment should be accomplished according to manufacturers' instructions.

Environmental surfaces should be cleaned and disinfected, working from highest to lowest, cleanest to dirtiest, to prevent cross-contamination. Low-level disinfectants and cleaners may be used in the common areas, with high-level disinfectants reserved for use in procedural and sterilization areas.

Read the manufacturers' instructions when using disinfectants to ensure that wet contact time with surfaces is adequate to kill the microorganisms as intended.

Cleaning schedules must be developed and written for every area within the facility to ensure that cleaning is completed appropriately and on a regular basis. Cleaning schedules should list the areas to be cleaned, the frequency of cleaning, tasks to be performed, products to be used for the cleaning and/or disinfection of the specific area, and the type of personal protective equipment that is to be utilized. Cleaning schedules should be signed or initialed by the individual tasked to clean the specific area to ensure that tasks are performed.

Surgical Asepsis

Sterilization

Autoclaves, also known as steam sterilizers, are the most common piece of equipment used for sterilization in the tattoo studio environment. Autoclaves achieve terminal sterilization (total destruction of all living organisms) by the use of high-pressure saturated steam (121 °C (249 °F)) sustained over a specific period of time, usually 15-20 minutes depending on load size and items.

When not using a fully disposable system, prior to sterilization, reusable tools and equipment such as tubes and tweezers must be thoroughly cleaned and disinfected. Equipment processing is as follows:

1) Isolate & Transport contaminated items
2) Rinse
3) Scrub under water to remove gross debris
4) Rinse & dry
5) Submerge in disinfectant
6) Rinse & dry
7) Place into ultrasonic cleaner with appropriate solution & run
8) Rinse & dry
9) Inspect
10) Package with indicators dated for date of autoclaving (within 24 hrs.)
11) Make sure all packages & indicators are properly marked with the equipment description, date, name or initials of person processing

For technicians who do not use pre-sterilized needles and machine components, a sterilizer on site is necessary. The US Occupational Safety and Health Administration (OSHA) (or other geographical agencies with similar mandates) standards must be met for operational purposes. In the United States, sterilizers must be properly registered with the Food and Drug Administration (FDA) and serviced annually by a licensed authorized sterilizer/autoclave technician as mandated by US OSHA. There may also be health and safety agencies in other countries with associated requirements.

Commercially available pre-sterilized single-use disposable products for the tattoo industry are sterilized using gamma radiation and EO (ethylene oxide) gas. Chemicals (cold sterilization) are not considered an appropriate or safe method for sterilizing needles or reusable machine components (such as metal needle tubes) within the personal services industry.

Storage and Handling of Sterile Items

Sterile supplies should be stored in covered containers and only be accessed with clean gloves to limit potential cross-contamination of packets.

All sterile supplies should be visibly dated and arranged to facilitate stock rotation. Stock should be rotated on a *first in- first out* basis. Packets should not be crushed or grouped with rubber bands as this may compromise the packets.

Storage areas must be maintained to prevent splashing. Do not store sterile items under plumbing valves or traps. Liquids must be stored below dry sterile goods or in a separate area. To facilitate air flow and maintain package integrity, sterile items should be stored 8-10 inches from floor and 18-20 inches from the ceiling.

Other Considerations

Needle Safety and Disposal

Tattoo needles, piercing needles, and razors, referred to as *sharps* (an object that can cut or penetrate the skin), must be discarded immediately after use in a sharps container (Figure 4-2) that meets US OSHA or other comparable agencies' standards.

US OSHA requires that sharps disposal containers be:

- Closable
- Puncture Resistant
- Leak-proof on the sides & bottom
- Color-coded
- Labeled with the universal biohazard symbol affixed to the container

Figure 4-2: Sharps container

Sharps disposal containers should be not be located directly on the working surface. The containers should be placed in a secure upright position. US OSHA recommends the optimal height for wall mounted sharps disposal containers to be at least 52-56 inches above ground level or below eye level.

The use of pre-sterilized single-use disposable needles, tubes and holders is recommended. The removal of needle configurations from *reusable* holders/handles is strongly discouraged as it places the practitioner at greater risk of injury from a needlestick.

In the United States, OSHA federally mandates that when a needle configuration is affixed to a handle or holder, it is regarded as a single unit (Figure 4-3) and therefore must be disposed of accordingly, intact. (29 CFR 1910.1030(d)(2)(vii))

Personal Protective Equipment

Personal protective equipment (PPE) is to be used in every instance where a risk of exposure to bloodborne pathogens (BBP) or other potentially infectious materials exists. PPE must be worn when engaging in client contact, performing a procedure, post-procedure teardown, and disinfection/sterilization procedures. PPE includes: face masks, eye protection, aprons, sleeve protectors, gloves.

Selection of PPE should be based upon:

- the type of exposure;
- the quantity of blood or OPIM that can be reasonably anticipated; and
- appropriateness for the task being performed and degree of exposure anticipated.

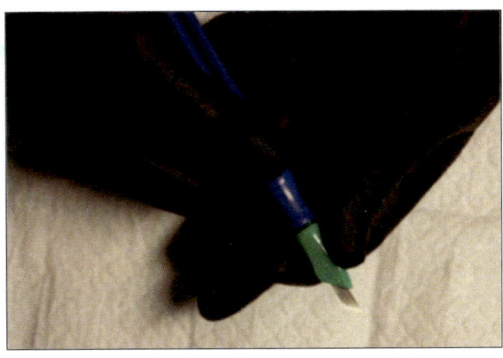

Figure 4-3: Needle affixed to manual device

Face masks and eye protection must be worn where a risk of splash or splatter of blood or other potentially infectious materials is present or can be reasonably anticipated.

Gloves

Although a risk of adverse reaction exists with prolonged skin contact of any glove material, the selection and use of non-latex (nitrile) gloves is strongly advised.

Gloves must be inspected periodically to ensure that glove integrity is intact. If integrity is compromised, such as a hole or tear, gloves must be removed, hands washed and dried thoroughly, and gloves replaced.

Selection of gloves should be based on the following:

- Length of time performing the procedure
- Type of procedure to be performed, i.e. tattoo, piercing, cleaning
- Stresses which gloves may be exposed (chemicals, friction, etc.)
- Practitioner & client sensitivity
- Individual preference

Sterile Water

The Centers for Disease Control and Prevention (CDC) recommends sterile water be used when:

- cleaning client skin in preparation for the procedure;
- diluting pigment, if needed;
- rinsing equipment (e.g., needles) during tattooing.

Bottled distilled or purified water can harbor bacteria. Without a lab test to ensure purity, levels and types of bacteria present are unknown.

In 2012, an outbreak of nontuberculoidal mycobacterium infections in tattoos occurred across several US states. As a result of their investigation, the CDC issued the following recommendations for the tattoo industry:

"Because tattoo pigments are injected intradermally, CDC recommends that pigment manufacturers be held to higher product safety standards, which should include the production of sterile pigments. In addition, tattoo artists should:

- avoid using products not intended for use in tattooing;
- avoid pigment dilution before tattooing, and if dilution is needed, use only sterile water;
- avoid the use of non-sterile water to rinse equipment (e.g., needles) during tattoo placement; and
- follow aseptic techniques during tattooing (e.g., hand hygiene and use of disposable gloves).

To reduce their risk for infection, consumers should:

- use tattoo parlors registered by local jurisdictions;
- request pigments that are manufactured specifically for tattoos;
- ensure that tattoo artists follow appropriate hygienic practices;
- be aware of the potential for infection following tattooing, and seek medical advice if persistent skin problems occur; and
- notify the tattoo artist and in the USA, the FDA's MedWatch program* if they experience an adverse event."[3]

Procedural Protocols

Facility Protocols

- All facilities must have hot and cold running water.
- Floors and walls of the facility must be smooth and nonporous in texture to facilitate ease of cleaning.
- Animals, other than those specifically trained to aid an impaired person and allowed by law in public places, should not be permitted into a tattoo facility.

Technician Protocols

- Prior to washing hands and donning gloves, practitioners must remove all jewelry from hands and wrists. Rings, watches and other jewelry can trap moisture and gross debris, combining with body heat to create an environment that encourages bacterial growth. Jewelry, such as rings,

Section 4 - Safe Practices for Permanent Cosmetic Technicians

   may also tear gloves and comprise glove integrity.
- Artificial nails should be avoided by body art professionals. According to an article published in The American Journal of Infection Control, artificial nails harbor higher levels of bacteria and yeast than natural nails. While handwashing does reduce these levels, it does not remove the contamination completely.[4] Suggested guidelines are:
    - Fingernails should be neatly manicured at a length of no more than 1/8" [3.1 mm] beyond the tips of the fingers.
    - Artificial nail enhancements should not be worn, including but not limited to, artificial nails, tips, wraps, appliques, acrylics, gels, and any additional items applied to the nail surface.
- Nail polish is permissible so long as it is in good repair and not chipped or cracked. Chipped or cracked polish may harbor bacteria in the crevasses or under loose polish.

Procedure Area Preparation

- Barrier film and coverings must be changed between each client procedure. Examples of barrier products:
    - Bottle bags
    - Machine bags
    - Tube sleeves
    - Barrier film
    - Table and chair covers
    - Dental bibs
- During the procedure, cotton wipes or other materials used to wipe a procedure area are used once and then discarded (do not re-dip used wipes back into the water receptacle for reuse).
- All common containers, such as pigments and anesthetics, should be removed from the storage location and taken to the work tray before the procedure; these containers should only be handled with gloved hands. After dispensing into the single-use pigment caps, containers should be immediately recapped and returned to the storage location away from the workstation.
- Machines and clip cords/power cords must be disinfected after each use. Remove and dispose of barrier bags or film and wipe down machines and tools with an appropriate disinfectant.
- Common containers, such as eyewash, that are used before, during, or after the procedure must be properly covered with a barrier film/product. The common containers must be disinfected after barrier film/barrier product is removed, and returned to the storage area.

- Needles should be opened and checked for imperfections (e.g., burs) with gloved hands before use. It is customary to use eye loupes for this practice.

Post Procedure Protocols

- Once the procedure is complete, all barrier products must be removed with clean gloves during the cleanup phase of the procedure.
- All single-use items are to be disposed of immediately after use.
- Lamps and other objects covered with barrier film/product during the procedure must be disinfected after each procedure and new barrier applied before the next procedure.
- Bed/chair covers must be replaced after each client. Surfaces must be disinfected before applying new covers.
- If machine accessories are reusable, such as metal tubes (commonly utilized with the coil machine), they must be placed in a dry leak-proof, puncture resistant container labeled with a biohazard label for transport to the disinfection/sterilization area for cleaning and sterilization, per US OSHA requirements. If needed, a humectant spray, like Prepzyme® or ProEZ®, can be used to keep surfaces wet and prevent adhesion of pigment or other organic material to the surfaces of the soiled tubes and devices while awaiting processing.
- Any items remaining on the work tray post-procedure is considered contaminated and must be disposed of. These include single-use items and products such as poured anesthetics and pigment, unused cotton products, and swabs.
- Dispose of any remaining water used in the procedure by either placing sufficient paper towels in the containers to absorb the water or by use of a superabsorbent powder, such as polysodium acrylate. Once solidified or absorbed, residue may be safely disposed of in the trash, or in accordance with local, municipal and federal guidelines. Check with your local waste disposal provider to ensure that these methods are acceptable. Do not dispose of the used water in a sink or toilet.

The Bloodborne Pathogens Standard in the United States (other countries may have a comparable government agency) in its entirety dictates the proper use of sterilizers, proper housekeeping, hand washing, PPE, proper use of disinfectants, disposal of sharps containers, and a host of other precautionary measures, all which must become routine for the permanent cosmetic technician.

The Society of Permanent Cosmetic Professionals (SPCP) offers Bloodborne Pathogens Standard classes at its events or in the US you may contact your local health department for a referral to a trainer. US OSHA mandates annual Bloodborne Pathogens training. This training should be taken before offering permanent cosmetic services, or as designated by local or state law mandates.

Suggested Reading:

- Occupational Safety and Health Administration, 1910.1030 Bloodborne Pathogens Standard
- Centers for Disease Control and Prevention, *Tattoo-Associated Nontuberculous Mycobacterial Skin Infections — Multiple States*, 2011–2012 Weekly, August 24, 2012 / 61(33);653-656 retrieved from https://www.cdc.gov/mmwr/preview/mmwrhtml/mm6133a3.htm

References

1. World Health Organization (WHO) (2009, July). Guidelines on Hand Hygiene in Health Care: a Summary Retrieved from http://www.who.int/gpsc/5may/tools/who_guidelines-handhygiene_summary.pdf
2. Nicas, M, Best D, J Occup Environ Hyg. 2008 Jun;5(6): A study quantifying the hand-to-face contact rate and its potential application to predicting respiratory tract infection. Retrieved from http://www.tandfonline.com/doi/abs/10.1080/15459620802003896
3. Tattoo-Associated Nontuberculous Mycobacterial Skin Infections — Multiple States, 2011–2012, Weekly, August 24, 2012 / 61(33);653-656
4. Banning Artificial Nails from Healthcare Settings, The American Journal for Infection Control. Retrieved from http://www.ajicjournal.org/article/S0196-6553(02)59151-3/abstract
5. This chapter was contributed by Laurna Marika, OSHA Authorized Outreach Instructor, 10-30 hr. General Industry.

Section 5

Hepatitis & Methicillin-Resistant Staphylococcus Aureus (MRSA)

Learning Objectives

Introduction

Hepatitis is a major health concern throughout the world. Any person who provides a service to the public that can produce bloodborne pathogens is required to know the subject of hepatitis, how the different forms are contracted, and how to prevent transmission. Hepatitis C (HCV), while in some cases is curable, is still a leading cause for the need of liver transplant. This is serious business.

Our lives would be simpler in the permanent cosmetic profession if our clients always knew their health status and passed along that information to their technicians. This is not the case. It is suspected that some people do not divulge a health condition they feel may cause them to be deemed ineligible for a service they desire. Others who have a serious medical condition may not even be aware of it. Many of the early symptoms of some types of hepatitis emulate flu-like symptoms. As a result, all clients must be treated the same, as if they have a medical condition you could contract or pass along to others through cross-contamination if your safe practices are inadequate.

Another health concern for those in the health and beauty services industries is a type of Staphylococcus aureus (staph) that is resistant to treatment with methicillin, thus resulting in methicillin-resistant Staphylococcus aureus-MRSA.

Over the span of a career a permanent cosmetic technician will have thousands of clients, each with the potential of transmitting undesirable and health affecting conditions if proper safety precautions are not adhered to. It is the responsibility of each technician to be knowledgeable about hepatitis and MRSA, and to be proactively dedicated to maintaining impeccable health and safety standards.

Objective

Knowledge of information in this section will provide the technician with an understanding of the different types of hepatitis, how it is transmitted, the associated symptoms, and the available inoculation for hepatitis B. While the alphabet of hepatitis types continues to grow, predominantly discussed types are provided in this section. The reader will also understand MRSA, who is susceptible to this disease, how it is controlled, and how it is treated.

The Hepatitis Alphabet—Know Your ABCs

Hepatitis is an inflammation of the liver caused by certain viruses and other factors, such as bacteria, alcohol abuse, some medications, and trauma. Symptoms include mild fever, headache, muscle ache, fatigue, loss of appetite, abdominal and gastric discomfort and later jaundice, liver enlargement, clay-colored stools, and tea-colored urine.

Depending on the type and cause, hepatitis may be mild and brief with full recovery, or severe with long-lasting symptoms that may develop into a chronic condition. Usually, the liver is able to regenerate its tissue, but severe hepatitis may lead to cirrhosis, chronic liver dysfunction, or cancer.

For the permanent cosmetic professional, strict asepsis utilizing the principles of Standard/Universal Precautions is essential. While the hepatitis B vaccine has been successfully integrated into the childhood vaccination schedule, many currently in our industry may be unprotected. While it may be declined, it is extremely risky to be working without it, but the vaccination should not present a false sense security. Implementation of proper procedures to prevent the transmission of bloodborne pathogens should be routine. It is important to take refresher courses for this annually to always be reminded of what is expected in this industry.

Hepatitis

Hepatitis A

The Hepatitis A virus (HAV) is transmitted by the fecal-oral route and occurs worldwide. It is found in contaminated water and food and may be transferred by direct contact with someone who is infected. In resource-poor countries, it is generally considered that all children have been infected, usually without signs and symptoms of clinical hepatitis. In the United States and other industrialized nations, HAV infections occur sporadically as well as in epidemics. Statistics report 50–75 percent of adults in the United States are positive for antibodies to hepatitis A.

The incubation period of hepatitis A is three to five weeks. While convalescence may be prolonged in some cases, there is no chronic form of the disease. Diagnosis is based on elevated levels of IgM (acute disease) or IgG (prior disease) antibodies to hepatitis A. Pooled ISG (Immune serum globulin) is still recommended for all persons who share a household with a hepatitis A patient.

The disease can be transferred for up to two weeks before any symptoms are displayed, but HAV is not considered communicable after the first week of jaundice. It has previously been called infectious hepatitis. Vaccinations protect up to 25 years in adults and 14-20 years in children. Fortunately, hepatitis A rates of infection in the US have declined by as much as 95% since the vaccine was introduced in 1995.

Hepatitis B

The Hepatitis B virus (HBV) was the first of the hepatitis viruses to be described, and its antigens and antibodies can be used for diagnosis. HBV has been called *serum hepatitis*. It has also been referred to as long incubations hepatitis with an incubation period from six weeks to six months. HBV has been reportedly harbored for up to fifteen years.

HBV occurs worldwide, is endemic in certain parts of the world, and the chronic form of the infection can lead to liver cancer. Historically, hepatitis B has been a serious occupationally acquired infection among healthcare workers and personal service workers who have frequent exposure to blood and body fluids. While direct percutaneous inoculation of HBV by needle from contaminated blood, serum, or plasma is the most efficient mode of transmission, indirect transfer is also possible by means of environmental surfaces.

This means that the permanent cosmetic technician can contract HBV from a contaminated counter or machine clip-cord handled with contaminated gloves. Not only is the technician at risk, but also are their clients.

Many people infected with hepatitis B have no symptoms. About one-third of people infected have a completely silent disease. In addition to symptoms previously mentioned, some patients develop short-term arthritis-like problems as part of a more severe case of HBV. Some people become chronic carriers of the virus, although they may never have had symptoms.

Diagnosis of hepatitis B in acute illness is by identification of hepatitis B surface antigen test (HBsAg) and becomes positive one to seven weeks before clinical disease. Blood containing HBsAg is considered potentially infectious. Hepatitis B antibody (anti-HBs) is an antibody against the surface antigen of hepatitis B and appears weeks to months after clinical illness. The presence of this antibody confers immunity and indicates prior disease or vaccination.

Other studies include hepatitis B core antigen (HGcAg) and E antigen (HGeAg). HGcAg identifies both acute and chronic HBV. Elevation of liver enzymes can also aid in diagnosis. The permanent cosmetic professional needs to seriously understand the need for an HBV vaccination series, which are given at 0, 1-2, and 4-6 months.

Hepatitis C

Hepatitis C virus (HCV) is the etiologic agent of most parenterally transmitted non-A, non-B (NANB) hepatitis worldwide. The transmission of HCV by direct percutaneous exposure to blood has been well documented.

Persons traditionally considered at risk of acquiring HCV infection have included blood and blood product recipients; however, with the advent of tests to screen blood donors since 1990, a very small percentage of persons with HCV currently become infected through blood transfusion.

The highest reported incidence currently has been among the Baby Boomer population and they are at a much greater risk of death from the virus. The majority of people with chronic hepatitis C infection were born during 1945-1965, most of whom are unaware of their infection. That said, HCV is on the rise, particularly among people in their twenties, as a result of the growing opioid epidemic.

Most common identifiable transmission is by injecting drug users, persons with occupational exposure to blood, mother-to-child transmission during birth, and hemodialysis patients. Sexual transmission has also been documented; however, its spread is inefficient and much less likely than that for HBV or the AIDS virus (HIV). Interestingly, in almost 40 percent of HCV cases, transmission cannot be identified.

Hepatitis C is generally a mild condition but it is much more likely than hepatitis B to lead to chronic liver disease in up to 50 percent of infected individuals. The person can remain asymptomatic yet HCV may be slowly destroying the liver. It is the most identifiable reason for liver transplants.

People with acute HBV infection can develop HCV at the same time and may be at particular risk for developing severe, life-threatening symptoms. Hepatocellular carcinoma is also an HCV complication. Previously treatment of HCV was limited to Interferon and Ribavirin, but since 2011, other drugs have become available such as Victrelis (boceprevir) and Incivek (telaprevir), and more recently, Epclusa and Mavyret, among others which are now claiming high cure rates. There is no current vaccine for HCV.

Hepatitis D

Hepatitis D is caused by the delta virus (HDV). It is an incomplete RNA virus that requires helper functions of HBV for its replication and expression. HDV infections only occur in individuals who are hepatitis B surface antigen test (HBsAg) positive and who are either in the acute or chronic phase of HBV infection.

HDV is a potentially severe disease and most cases occur among people who are frequently exposed to blood. Small-scale epidemics have occurred among injection drug users who share contaminated needles. Some believe HDV may be sexually transmitted, but more research is needed to provide more specific evidence.

Diagnosis of delta hepatitis is through a blood test to detect antibodies to the delta antigen. It should be obvious to the permanent cosmetic technician that prevention of HDV will occur through immunization against HBV.

Hepatitis E

The hepatitis E virus (HEV) causes acute infections and is commonly referred to as *enterically transmitted non-A, non-B hepatitis* (ET-NANB). This disease should not be confused with hepatitis C, which is parenterally transmitted non-A non-B (PT-NANB). HEV infection does not lead to chronic hepatitis nor has a carrier state been described. The fecal-oral route transmits HEV by the same modes that have been described for

HAV.

It is a common cause of sporadic and epidemic hepatitis in resource-poor areas of the world where the source of infection is usually contaminated drinking water supplies.

HEV is most often seen in young to middle-aged adults with mild symptoms that usually resolve in two weeks; however, pregnant women appear to be exceptionally susceptible to severe disease, and excessive mortality has been reported, approaching 20 percent.

Diagnosis is based on the characteristics of the outbreak and by exclusion of HAV and HBV by serological tests. Confirmation is through identification of particles in feces of acutely ill patients. Incubation varies from two to nine weeks.

In Summary

To summarize hepatitis therapy, as mentioned, it has improved over recent years with multiple drugs to treat HCV and the childhood vaccination schedule for HBV. Hepatitis is a serious disease, oftentimes chronic and can be life-threatening. It should be clear to all permanent cosmetic professionals that they must accept responsibility regarding hepatitis through available vaccines and by utilizing modes of prevention such as strict infection control measures.

Methicillin-Resistant Staphylococcus Aureus (MRSA)

What is MRSA?

MRSA is the acronym for *methicillin-resistant Staphylococcus aureus*. Staphylococcus aureus are bacteria commonly found on the skin and/or in the noses of healthy people. Although usually harmless at these sites, Staph aureus (staph) may occasionally get into the body and cause infections through breaks in the skin, such as abrasions, cuts, wounds, tattooing, body piercing, or surgical incisions. These infections may be mild, such as pimples or boils, or serious, such as an infection of the bloodstream, bones, or joints.

The treatment of infections due to Staphylococcus aureus was revolutionized in the 1940s by the introduction of the antibiotic penicillin. Unfortunately, most strains of Staph aureus are now resistant to penicillin. This is because Staph aureus has learned to make a substance called B-lactamase (pronounced beta-lactamase) that degrades penicillin, destroying its antibacterial activity.

Some related antibiotics, such as methicillin, are not affected by B-lactamase and can still be used to treat many infections due to B-lactamase-producing stains of Staphylococcus aureus. Unfortunately, however, certain strains of Staph aureus have now also become resistant to treatment with methicillin, thus resulting in methicillin-resistant Staphylococcus aureus—MRSA.

MRSA skin infections can present in a number of forms:
- **Cellulitis**—Inflammation of the skin
- **Impetigo**—Blistered lesions or abraded skin with honey-colored crust
- **Folliculitis**—Infection of the hair follicle (like a pimple)
- **Furunculosis**—Deeper infection below the hairline
- **Carbuncle**—Multiple adjacent hair follicles and substructures are affected
- **Abscess**—Pus-filled mass below skin structures
- **Infected laceration**—Preexisting cut that has become infected

Who Gets MRSA Infection?

Skin infections with MRSA are transmitted by close skin-to-skin contact with an infected person or by contact with objects or surfaces contaminated with MRSA. A large majority of MRSA infections occur in hospital/infirmed patients; however, reports of MRSA infections acquired outside a hospital setting (community-acquired) are now commonplace. As with ordinary strains of Staph aureus, some people harbor MRSA on their skin or in their nose without harm, whereas other people may develop infections.

People with an increased risk of developing infection include those with breaks in their skin due to abrasions, cuts, wounds, tattooing, body piercing, or surgical incisions; those with certain types of immune system disorders, such as low number of white cells in their blood; athletes participating in contact sports; IV drug users; and those living in crowded, unsanitary conditions.

When MRSA spread from a site where they are harmless to a site where they cause infection, this results in an infection described as *endogenous*. In addition to causing endogenous infections, MRSA can spread between people, usually by direct or indirect physical contact. For example, a tattoo artist performing a procedure on an infected client may become contaminated with MRSA. The technician may then spread the bacteria to other clients with whom she or he subsequently has contact. These clients may then become infected. The spread of MRSA (as well as other bacteria) from client to client is called cross-infection.

MRSA can also survive on inanimate objects or surfaces such as tables, sinks, floors, and even mops.

Can the Spread of MRSA be Controlled?

There are several steps that can be taken to minimize the spread of MRSA.

- Body modification practitioners should wash their hands scrupulously, using soap and water, and disposable towels.
- Single-use exam gloves should be worn for every instance of client contact.
- The skin of the area where the tattoo procedure will be performed should be properly cleansed.
- Carefully dispose of materials that come in contact with blood or other potentially infectious material (OPIM).
- Personal protective equipment (PPE) should be worn whenever handling contaminated items.
- All work surfaces and other potentially contaminated surfaces and objects should be thoroughly cleaned and disinfected as soon as possible using an EPA (an agency of the United States federal government) registered, hospital level disinfectant. There may be comparable government agencies in other countries.

Symptoms of MRSA

MRSA is a type of staph, so the symptoms of a MRSA infection and the symptoms of an infection due to other staph are initially similar. Pimples, rashes, pus-filled boils, especially when warm, painful, red or swollen, can indicate a staph skin infection and a doctor should be seen. See figures 5-1 and 5-2 for examples of MRSA infections.

Because MRSA can't be identified without special lab tests, it is not always identified and treated correctly when antibiotic treatment is needed. This potential delay in recognizing and treating MRSA infections effectively can result in more serious infections such as severe skin infection, surgical wound infections, prolonged illness, and rare life-threatening illnesses in the blood, heart, and bones.

The symptoms could include fever, chills, muscle aches, malaise-symptoms of flu; chest pain, shortness of breath, leading to heart infections (endocarditis), toxic shock syndrome, and septicemia (blood poisoning). Essentially, people can become very ill and die from MRSA infection.

How is MRSA Treated?

Individuals COLONIZED with MRSA

Individuals colonized with MRSA may be treated with an antibiotic such as Bactroban (mupirocin), applied onto their skin or inside of their nose. This helps eliminate MRSA and reduces the risk of the bacteria spreading to other sites on the body where they may cause infections, or to other people. However, some strains of MRSA are resistant to these drugs. Individuals colonized with MRSA may also be directed to wash their skin and hair with suitable antiseptics, such as chlorhexidine.

Individuals INFECTED with MRSA

Medication options for MRSA skin and soft tissue infections may also include:

- clindamycin
- tetracycline drugs - doxycycline and minocycline
- trimethoprim and sulfamethoxazole
- rifampin
- linezolid

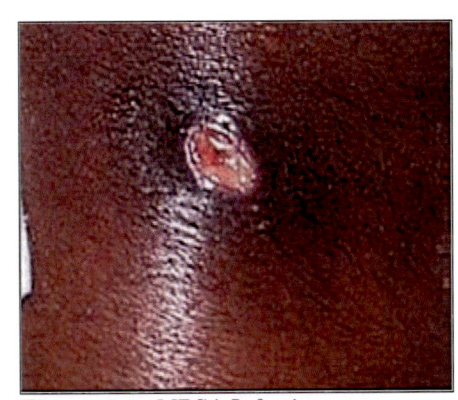

Figure 5-1: MRSA Infection

When resistant to other drugs, MRSA most times remains susceptible to glycopeptide antibiotics, such as vancomycin. Vancomycin must be administered by infusion or injection, and for this reason, it is used for treatment only in hospitalized patients. In addition, injection of vancomycin into muscle is painful and thus not used, while rapid administration into a vein may produce an allergic-type reaction. To overcome these problems, vancomycin must be given by slow infusion into a vein.

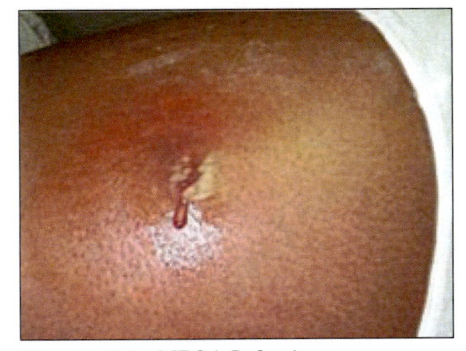

Figure 5-2: MRSA Infection

Vancomycin Resistance

MRSA has developed resistance to drug therapy in some cases: For general knowledge, they are called Vancomycin Intermediate Staphylococcus aureus, (VISA) and Vancomycin Resistant Staphylococcus aureus, (VRSA). There are additional treatments for them.

References

The section *The Hepatitis Alphabet—Know Your ABCs* was prepared with the assistance of Kate Ciampi Shergold, RN, CPCP.

1. CDC Foundation (2018). Viral Hepatitis Action Coalition | CDC Foundation. Retrieved from https://www.cdcfoundation.org/vhac#
2. Health Union, LLC (2018). Hepatitis C Statistics - HepatitisC.net. Retrieved from https://hepatitisc.net/what-is/statistics/
3. American Association for the Study of Liver Diseases and the Infectious Diseases Society of America (2018). Initial Treatment of HCV Infection | HCV Guidance. Retrieved from https://www.hcvguidelines.org/treatment-naive
4. US Department of Human Services Centers For Disease Control and Prevention (2018). Hepatitis C Information | Division of Viral Hepatitis | CDC. Retrieved from https://www.cdc.gov/hepatitis/hcv/index.htm

The section *Methicillin-Resistant Staphylococcus Aureus (MRSA)* was prepared with contributions by David Vidra, LPN.

Section 6

Skin Anatomy

Learning Objectives

Introduction

Permanent cosmetic technicians who have a working knowledge of the different layers of the skin are, simply put, better technicians than are those who would skim over this important element of tattooing. This is not to say one must have the vast knowledge of an esthetician to tattoo properly, but it is fact -- the more you know, the better you become. Yes, there is much to learn, but that is exactly why you purchased or were provided this book.

The skin has many layers that all provide a particular function. Not to present information that is forthcoming, but to tease with a thumbnail of information -- it is not uncommon for improperly trained technicians to complain about pigment not holding in the skin through the healing process (which will be discussed in a later section of the book). They jump to the conclusion that it was the pigment brand they used. They may listen to those who would gain from this type of incorrect conclusion and pour hundreds of more dollars into what they foresee as a good remedy for the problem.

There are also others who would blame the device they use. Again, out to the marketplace to find the best-advertised device only to find this did not resolve the problem. Some even may go so far as to accept failure as the norm and convince their clients that touch-ups are required every few months. What was likely their problem? As novice technicians, they grazed only the epidermal layer of the skin and during the cellular renewal process, the pigment naturally exfoliated with the dead skin cells the epidermal layer of the skin is composed of.

So, right up front, a treasure chest of information is provided that over time, might save thousands of dollars in new products, new devices, and the cost of classes to learn about both.

Objective

Completing this section will provide the reader with an understanding of the different layers of the skin -- the living canvas, used to produce permanent cosmetic procedures. It will be important to thoroughly understand the names, the placement of, and the properties of each of the layers of the skin and related cells..

Section 6 - Skin Anatomy

Pigment is tattooed in the upper dermal layer of the skin. This is easy to say, but easy to do? For those that are just beginning their study of cosmetic tattooing, it is important to understand the different layers of the skin.

The skin, the major component of the integument or integumentary system, is made up of multiple layers of cells and is the largest organ of the body that acts as a barrier to protect the internal body against a number of external environmental and potentially harmful factors. The skin is the major player in the tattooing game. In many instances, it will dictate needle configurations, machine speed, pigment color selection, and influences how soon you see your client for a follow-up appointment.

The skin is the ultimate vessel for the human body; it receives and transports, accepts and expels, according to the body's needs. It is a container, defender, regulator, breather, feeler, and adaptor. But success in these roles is not accomplished automatically. As sturdy as it is, the skin requires attention and maintenance to function properly. Without such care, the complex organization of the skin breaks down, making it and the body it protects susceptible to injury and disease. Thus, the body's coverall organ is as fragile as it is seemingly unyielding.

The skin is perhaps the organ that brings us closest to an understanding of organ function because its anatomy and function can be partially observed by the naked eye. In addition to its ability to communicate internal physiological information, such as the presence of fever, the skin also reacts to external stimuli, such as sun exposure, toxins, topical product applications, and even psychological stimuli.

The skin accounts for roughly fifteen percent of total body weight. The average square inch of skin contains six-hundred-and-fifty sweat glands, twenty blood vessels, sixty-thousand melanocytes, and more than a thousand nerve endings. As an organ that interacts directly with its external surroundings, the skin's primary function is to protect our bodies against the invasion of pathogens. The skin has many other important functions including temperature regulation and sensation.

Because skin is the canvas upon and within which we perform our work, understanding its functions and structure are important not only for a pleasing permanent cosmetic result but for the safety and proficient wound management for our clients. The skin's strata (parallel layers of material arranged one on top of the other) are divided into three main categories:

The Hypodermis

The hypodermis (subcutaneous) is the deepest layer of skin and acts to affix the skin to adjoining organs. The hypodermis stores adipose tissue (fat) to act as a shock absorber, protecting the internal organs from injury. The hypodermis is not present in areas of very thin skin such as eyelids, genitals, nipples, and shins. It also acts as an insulation layer to conserve body heat.

The Dermis

The dermis is the middle layer of skin and contains many specialized cells and structures. Hair follicles and their attached erector pili muscles (tiny muscles attached to hair follicles causing hair to raise) are located in this layer. The dermis also contains sebaceous (oil) glands, sudoriferous (sweat) glands, blood vessels, and nerves. The nerves transmit sensations of pain, itch, heat, and cold. The dermis varies in thickness depending on its location on the body. It may range from .3 mm thick on the eyelids to 3.0 mm thick on the back. The dermis is composed of three types of tissue: collagen, elastic tissue, and reticular fibers. These three types of tissue are found throughout the dermal layer, not in separate layers.

The two layers of the dermis are the papillary and reticular layers. The papillary layer is the outermost layer and contains a thin arrangement of collagen fibers. The lower, reticular layer is thicker than the papillary layer and made of thick collagen fibers that are arranged parallel to the surface of the skin. When tattooing, the papillary/upper reticular level of the dermis is the target level for the pigment/ink. If deposited below this target, the pigment will look hazy, spotty, and can blue out in appearance. If deposited above the dermis, the pigment will desquamate, or slough off with the naturally occurring shedding of skin cells.

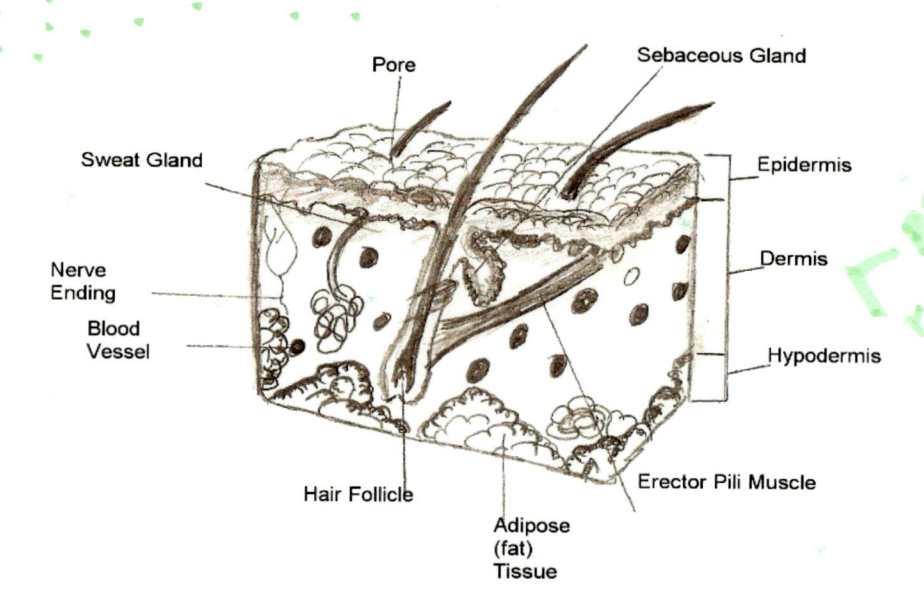

Figure 6-1: The Skin
Drawing by Liza Sims.

The Epidermis

The epidermis is the outermost layer that is visible to us when we look at our skin. The epidermis varies in thickness throughout the body. Forces of friction primarily determine its thickness, such as represented by the thick nature of the palms of the hands and the soles of the feet. The epidermis comprises the following layers:

- **Stratum Germinativum** or stratum basale is the layer of keratinocytes (a protein producing epidermal cell) that lies at the base of the epidermis, just above the dermis. This layer consists of a single layer of columnar epithelial cells lying on a basement membrane (the dermal-epidermal junction). These cells experience rapid mitosis (birth, by means of cell division), replenishing the regular loss of skin (desquamation).

- **Stratum Spinosum** is a multilayered arrangement of cuboidal cells, joined by desmosomes (cell adhesion and linking proteins) giving the cells a spiny appearance. This is the layer where epidermal cell death begins. The cell's nutrients and oxygen (found in interstitial fluid) have become exhausted by this level and therefore unable to nourish the skin cells.

- **Stratum Granulosum** contains three to five layers of flattened cells whose cytoplasm (nutritional fluid between the cell membrane and the nucleus) contains small granules. These granules are proteins in the process of transforming into the waterproofing protein keratin. The skin is preparing its barrier defense at this level.

- **Stratum Lucidum** cannot normally be identified in areas of thin skin. In areas of thick skin, such as the soles of the feet and the palms of the hands, the stratum lucidum consists of a thin clear layer of flattened dead cells forming a transition layer from the stratum granulosum and the stratum corneum. The cells of the stratum lucidum do not have distinct boundaries and are filled with an intermediate form of keratin. Because permanent cosmetics are normally only applied to areas of thin skin (face), this layer of skin is not often encountered.

- **Stratum Corneum** or horny layer is the outermost layer of the skin's epidermis and may be 6 to 40 layers thick, depending on age and photo-damage. The cells are embedded within a dense matrix of proteins. The cells are difficult to see individually because they are very flat and the spaces between the cells are filled with lipids, which cement the cells together in a visually continuous membrane. As the cells move closer to the surface they appear looser and scale-like and are constantly being shed in a process known as desquamation. Thickness variations of the epidermis are primarily due to stratum corneum thickness differences, but other layers may also vary in thickness. This layer of skin is recognized for its ability to repel moisture, thereby guarding the underlying layers against bacterial assault.

The following are epithelium cells that play important roles in the application of permanent cosmetics:

Keratinocytes are protein cells responsible for the actual formation of the epithelium.

Langerhans cells play a role in the organic immune system. They are dendritic in shape (having dendrites; tentacles) and are located in the stratum spinosum. They function as antigen-presenting cells that bind antigens entering through the skin and transport them to the lymph nodes.

Melanocytes are located in the stratum basale and are responsible for producing melanin (darkened skin color). People have the same number of melanocyte cells, but the darker the natural skin tone (ethnicity) of a person, the more melanin the melanocytes are capable of producing. Melanin production is a natural response to ultraviolet (sun) ray exposure as a means of protecting the dividing mother cells from UV damage. The melanocyte is of concern to those performing permanent cosmetics because UV assault is not the only trigger of overproduction of melanin. Any wound or damage to the surface of the skin, including thermal damage, lesions, and punctures may trigger the rapid production of melanin in a protective response. Caution should be observed when working on dark skin.

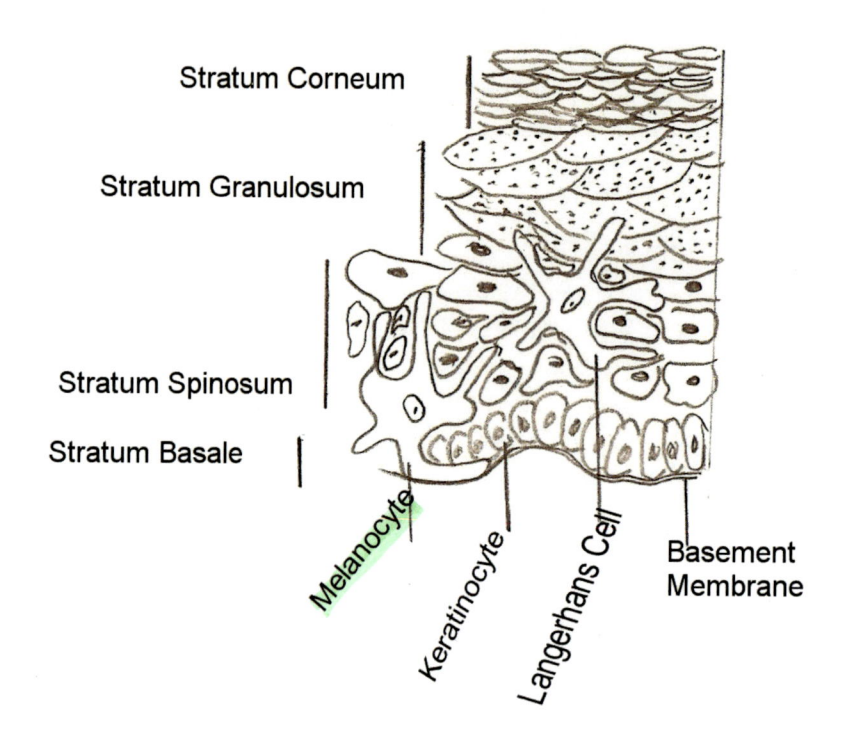

Figure 6-2: The Epidermis
Drawing by Liza Sims.

References

1. This section was contributed by Liza Sims.

Section 7

Eye Anatomy

Learning Objectives

Introduction

There are few things people value more than their sight. The body is very protective of the eyes and many people psychologically have difficulty trusting others with any service that includes working in the eye area. So why do people pursue permanent eyeliner? Because it represents freedom, convenience, and no longer spending time and effort applying a beauty enhancement that merely sweats or washes off only to need reapplication. Allergies to topical makeup also make the top ten for why people ask for tattooed eyeliner.

Notwithstanding all the pros they may feel about the service, there still may be reluctance, either before or during the procedure, to yield control of this organ to another. It is not uncommon to hear a client say, "I feel (operative word "feel" due to the body's guardian system that protects the eyes) you are too close to my eyeball." It is also not uncommon for clients to report that the procedure was not painful but rather stressful. This is a normal reaction. People are concerned about the safety of their eyesight. It is the technician's responsibility to understand the important functions of the eye, to incorporate client safety measures during eyeliner procedures, and to effectively communicate information to the client to ensure she or he feels safe during the procedure.

Objective

Completion of this section will enable the technician to become knowledgeable about the anatomical structure of the eye, the functions of eyelids, abnormal conditions of the eye, and become proficient regarding the risks that are associated with permanent cosmetic eyeliner procedures. The information provided is basic to a well-trained permanent cosmetic technician. If the subject matter appears complex, it is because it is.

The majority of permanent cosmetic technicians are not medical doctors. Because of our close proximity to the eye when performing eyeliner procedures it is, however, very important to understand the basics of the anatomy of the eye and how it functions; how to recognize obvious abnormalities of the eye, the need to inquire about less obvious conditions, and how to complete permanent cosmetic eyeliner while keeping the eyes safe.

The eye serves a very important function, the sense of sight. Sight is an intricate activity with a range of physical and perceptual confines, yet it is the primary source of information about the world around us. Most people would agree that vision is the most used of our five senses (sight, hearing, taste, touch, and smell) and the sense most people would state as the most valued. It is for these reasons clients are naturally very protective of their eyes. Permanent cosmetic technicians must have the training and confidence to perform eyeliner procedures in a manner that controls and protects the client's eyes at all times.

Introduction

"Human vision is a highly complex activity with a range of physical and perceptual limitations, yet it is the primary source of information about the outside world. Visual perception can be divided into two stages: the physical reception of the stimulus from the outside world, and the processing and interpretation of that stimulus."[1]

"The eye is basically a mechanism for receiving light and transforming it into electrical energy. The receptors in the eye transform it into electrical signals, which are passed on to the brain. The eye has a lot of components. The cornea and lens at the front of the eye focus the light into a sharp image on the back of the eye, the retina. The retina is made up of rods and cones."[1]

"Rods are highly sensitive to light and allow us to see under low levels of illumination. However, they are unable to resolve fine detail and are subject to saturation. This is the reason for the temporary blindness that is caused when we move from a dark room into the sunlight. There are approximately 120 million rods per eye which are mainly situated towards the edges of the retina."[1]

"Cones are less sensitive to light than rods and can tolerate more light. There are three types of cones, each of which is sensitive to a different wavelength of light. These cones which number about 6 million are mainly concentrated on the fovea, a small area of the retina on which images are formed."[1]

Permanent cosmetic technicians should also be aware that people with lighter-colored eyes, cataracts, and those who suffer from migraine headaches are more likely to notice sensitivity to light and glare. The positioning of a lamp during eyeliner procedures may need adjusting to accommodate for this sensitivity.

The Orbit/Eye Socket

The orbit is the eye socket. The cheekbone, the forehead, the temple, and the side of the nose form the eye socket.

"The eye is cushioned within the orbit by pads of fat. The orbit is surrounded by layers of soft, fatty tissue, which protects the eye and enables it to turn easily. Three pairs of extraocular muscles regulate the motion of each eye: the medial and lateral rectus muscles, the superior and inferior rectus muscles, and the superior and inferior oblique muscles."[3]

It is important to watch or direct the movements of the eye during eyeliner procedures. Specific instructions should be given to the client to keep the eyeball in a stationary position. Random eye movements can affect the position of the needle.

The Eyelids

The eyelids are two folds of skin that protect the eyeball from the environment, damage, and light. The eyelids maintain a smooth corneal surface by distributing tears evenly over the eye. The eyelids are made up of an exterior layer of skin, a middle layer of muscle, tissue that gives them form, and an inner layer of moist conjunctival tissue. The conjunctiva is a thin, clear layer of skin covering the front of the eye, including the sclera and the inside of the eyelids. The conjunctiva keeps germs and foreign material from getting behind the eye and causing damage.

Several muscles work in concert to control the actions of the eyelids. The orbicularis oculi muscle closes the lids. It is a circular muscle located in the middle layer of the eyelid. The levator muscle is attached inside the upper lid and upon contraction, elevates it. The orbicularis oculi and levator muscles must be controlled with an effective stretching technique during the eyeliner tattooing process to avoid protective involuntary movements of the eyelids, which can be spontaneous or forceful, such as closing or squinting.

The Mueller's muscle, smoother in texture, gives the lids tone and helps preserve elasticity. Tiny oil-producing Meibomian glands line the Tarsal Plate (a medical term for the strong fibrous connective tissue supporting the lids). These glands produce oil that lubricates the eye. Some technicians feel tattooing the inner edge of the lids (commonly known among cosmetic tattoo artists as mucosal or wet line eyeliner tattooing), is not potentially harmful, while the majority considers this practice risky. The closer the tattooing process is in proximity to the eyeball, the higher the risk of corneal abrasions and/or damage to the eyeball. A mucosal eyeliner technique also has the potential of creating dry eye syndrome, resulting from damage to the Meibomian glands from the tattooing process.

The corners of the eyes represent the inner and outer canthus areas. Tattooing too far into these areas can result in pigment migration, as the skin is very delicate and thin.

Rows of lashes on the top and bottom lids protect the eyes from the elements and debris. The eyelash lines represent the template for eyelash enhancement and small to medium eyeliner procedures. Wider top eyeliners depart from this template and should be attempted only by technicians trained in techniques that will ensure the wider top eyeliner designs are consistent on both eyes.

The Cornea

"One-sixth of the outer layer of the eye bulges forward as the cornea, the transparent dome that serves as the outer window of the eye. The cornea is the primary structure focusing light entering the eye, along with the secondary focusing structure, the crystalline lens. It is composed, for the most part, of connective tissue with a thin layer of epithelium (the type of tissue that covers all free body surfaces) on the surface."[3]

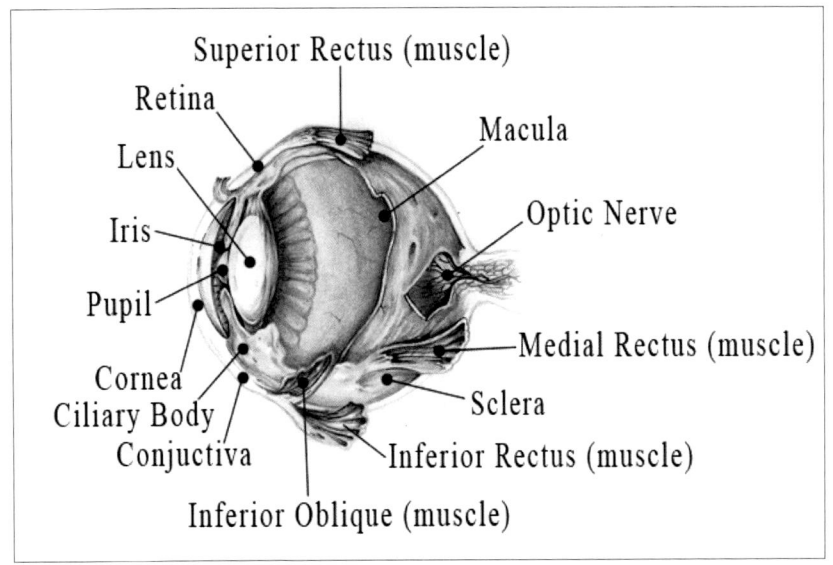

Figure 7-1: Reference diagram of major components of the eye

The cornea is clear and although it seems to lack substance, in reality, it is a highly organized group of cells and protein. A fluid called the aqueous humor and tears that fill the chamber behind it provides needed nourishment. The cornea's construction does not include blood vessels, like other tissues of the body, to guard against infection. It is important that it remains transparent to refract light properly. The presence of even the smallest possible capillaries would obstruct this process.

The cornea provides a physical barrier to the inside of the eye and protects against environmental elements and other harmful substances. It shares this protective task with the sclera, also called the white of the eye. During eyeliner procedures, the cornea is protected with the proper placement of anesthetics (avoiding direct contact with the eyeball), the application of moisturizing eye drops, rinsing the eye frequently with eyewash, and allowing the client appropriately timed blinks.

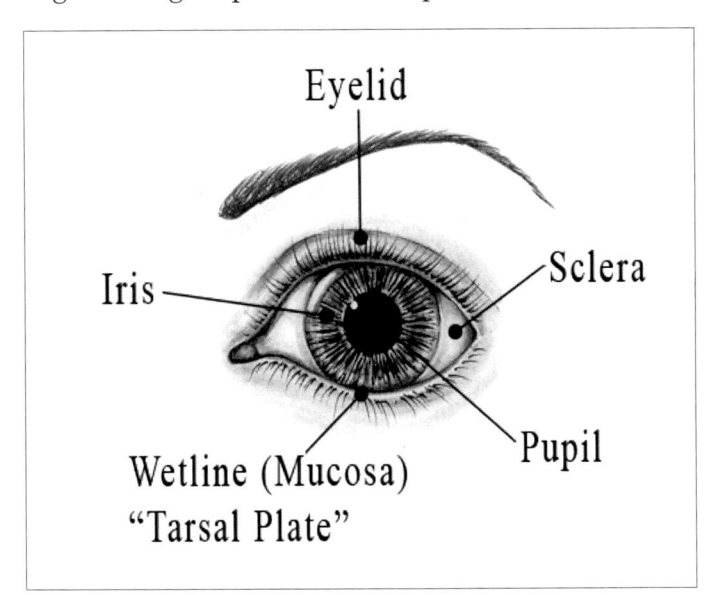

Figure 7-2: Frontal view of the eye

63

The Sclera

The sclera is commonly known as the white of the eye. This tough, opaque tissue serves as the eye's protective outer coat and makes up the back five-sixths of the eye's outer layer. Muscles connect to it around the eye and manage the eye's movements. The optic nerve is attached to the sclera at the very back of the eye.

The Lacrimal System

The eye's tear production and drainage are found in the lacrimal system. *Lacrimal* originates from the Latin word *lacrima*, which means tear. The lacrimal gland, which is part of the orbit and located underneath the exterior portion of the upper eyelid, produces tears that help lubricate and moisten the eye, as well as wash out any foreign matter that may enter the eye. The tears drain away from the eye through the nasolacrimal ducts, which are located at the inner corner of the eyelids. Safe eyeliner designs intentionally do not include tattooing in close proximity to the nasolacrimal ducts.

A safe eyeliner procedure also recognizes the need for the client to blink (or the technician structured movement of a controlled blink by using one of the eyelid stretching fingers to lower the top eyelid downward to replenish the tear film across the eyeball). People normally blink the eyelids about every six seconds.

The Pupil

"The central black portion of the eye, the pupil, regulates light by expanding and contracting. When you are in a room with low lighting, the pupil expands to allow more light to enter the eye. If you are in bright sunlight, the pupil shrinks to reduce the amount of light entering the eye."[4]

If anesthetic is allowed to get into the eye, the pupil may appear dilated. This is most often evident when an anesthetic with epinephrine is used, which is a vasoconstrictor. Every effort should be made to prevent this.

The Iris

"The colored portion of the eye, the iris, also helps regulate the amount of light entering the eye. You'll find most of the muscle structure that controls the opening and closing of the pupil within the iris."[4]

Abnormal Conditions of the Eye

It is the responsibility of permanent cosmetic technicians to be on alert for any obvious abnormal conditions of the eyes before commencing with eyeliner procedures. In most instances, permanent cosmetic technicians are typically not physicians. Our job is to ask important questions about and to inspect for conditions that are contraindicative to the eyeliner tattooing process, not to diagnose. If in doubt, request that the client consult with her or his medical care provider. The following are obvious eye conditions that warrant resolution before proceeding with eyeliner.

- **Eye Allergies**—Similar to processes that occur with other types of allergic responses, the eye may overreact to a substance perceived as harmful even though it may not be. For example, dust that is harmless to most people can cause excessive production of tears and mucus in eyes of overtly sensitive, allergic individuals. Eye allergies are often hereditary.[5]
- **Blepharitis**—Blepharitis refers to inflammation of the eyelids, particularly at the lid margins. It's a common disorder and may be associated with a low-grade bacterial infection or a generalized skin condition.[5]
- **Acquired (Adult-Onset) Nasolacrimal Duct Obstruction**—Tear duct obstruction that results in excess tearing (tears may run down the face) and mucus discharge.
- **Stye**—A stye (also spelled sty) develops when a gland at the edge of the eyelid becomes infected. Resembling a pimple on the eyelid, a stye can grow on the inside or outside of the lid. Styes are not harmful to vision, and they can occur at any age.[5]
- **Conjunctivitis (Pink Eye)**—Pink eye is the most obvious symptom of conjunctivitis, which involves inflammation of the clear membrane covering the white of the eye and interior lining of the eyelids. Pink eye can refer to all types of conjunctivitis, or just to its contagious forms.
  - *Viral conjunctivitis*—usually affects only one eye and causes excessive eye watering and a light discharge.
  - *Bacterial conjunctivitis*—affects both eyes and causes a heavy discharge, sometimes greenish.
  - *Allergic conjunctivitis*—affects both eyes and causes itching and redness in the eyes and the nose accompanied by excessive tearing.
  - *Giant papillary conjunctivitis*—usually affects both eyes and results in intolerance to contact lenses, itching, heavy discharge, excessive tearing, and visible red bumps on the underside of the eyelids.[5]
- Any obvious abnormality associated with the tissue on or surrounding the eyeliner canvas.

The following eye conditions may not prevent a person from having successful eyeliner procedures but are very important to be aware of and in most instances, will require the client's medical care provider's advice. These conditions may not be evident upon inspection of the eyeliner canvas and would become known by providing the client with a history form to fill out, requiring all conditions to be documented. If in doubt, every technician has the option/responsibility of advising a client she or he requires a medical clearance before proceeding.

- **Dry Eye Syndrome**—Dry eye syndrome is a chronic lack of sufficient lubrication and moisture in the eye. Its consequences range from subtle but constant irritation to ocular inflammation of the anterior (front) tissues of the eye.[5]

- **Ocular Herpes**—Herpes of the eye is a reoccurring viral infection that affects thousands of people with herpes. Although ocular herpes can result from the sexually transmitted herpes simplex II virus, it is usually caused by herpes simplex virus I (HSV I), which is the virus responsible for cold sores.

- **Glaucoma**—Glaucoma refers to a category of eye disorders often associated with a dangerous buildup of internal eye pressure (intraocular pressure or IOP), which can damage the eye's optic nerve that transmits visual information to the brain.[5]

- **Floaters**—Floaters are minute spots or specks that float across the field of vision. Most people notice them in a well-lighted indoor environment or outdoors on a bright day. Floaters often are normal, but sometimes they represent a warning of serious eye problems such as impending retinal detachment, especially if they happen with flashes of light.

- **Macular Degeneration**, often called AMD or ARMD (age-related macular degeneration)— is the leading cause of vision loss and blindness in Americans aged 65 and older. Because older people represent an increasingly larger percentage of the general population, vision loss associated with AMD is a growing problem. AMD occurs with degeneration of the macula, which is the part of the retina responsible for the sharp, central vision needed to read or drive. Because the macula primarily is affected in AMD, central vision loss may occur.[5]

Rare but Possible Complications Resulting from Eyeliner Procedures

- **Corneal Burn**—A corneal burn may occur as a result of an irritant, or a burn resulting from contact with an alkali or acidic product. The acidity or alkalinity of a product, such as the anesthetics used for permanent cosmetics, is referred to as the pH of a substance. The pH of a substance is measured on a scale from 1 to 14 with 7 indicating a neutral substance.

    Permanent cosmetic technicians should strive to use safe products that are or are near the 7-pH factor. These products are more agreeable to the eye and less likely to cause a corneal burn or other eye irritation if a small amount of the product should drift into the eye from applications to the eyelids. The risk of a corneal burn is one of the primary reasons why eye drops for lubrication are used, and why the eyes should be rinsed with eyewash frequently during the eyeliner procedure.

Corneal Abrasion—A corneal abrasion is a scrape or scratch of the surface of the cornea. This represents a very painful condition to the person it has happened to.

In the permanent cosmetic industry, corneal abrasions are thought to occur when pigment (also called color, colorant, and formulation) is not properly rinsed from the eye, often lodging under the upper eyelid and scraping across the eye during closure of the eye. The use of a dry cotton swab used to remove pigment particles from the eye is prohibited and can cause a corneal abrasion if contact is made with the eyeball. Cotton swabs should be moistened with eyewash before being used on or around the eye, and pigment particles should be rinsed toward the nasolacrimal ducts and rolled out at the inner canthus position of the eye. The less direct contact with the eyeball, the less risk of abrasion.

Another source of corneal abrasion is at the hands of the client inspecting their new eyeliner, improper application of a healing ointment, or rubbing their eyes soon after the procedure. Providing directions to the client as to how to care for a new eyeliner procedure is a part of the procedure process. Clients can unknowingly cause harm to their eye if not advised properly.

- **Eye Irritation**—It doesn't take much to upset an eye, which can result in visible irritation. Reading for long periods, time spent looking at a computer screen, taking a walk on a windy day or on the beach all can contribute to eye irritation. The stretching techniques, tattooing process, and products used during the procedure can all, or independently, lend to an irritated appearing eye. It is advisable to allow the client to rest and apply cool compresses to the eyeliner area after the procedure is completed. Then conduct a final eye inspection (a final rinse with eyewash is common) before allowing the client to leave your establishment. Eyes that are merely temporarily stressed from the procedure process will likely calm soon after the procedure.

More serious conditions such as a corneal burn or abrasion, on the other hand, will not resolve and will require immediate medical attention. This may not be apparent until the client has left for home. Because of the possible delay of the symptoms of a serious condition, many technicians provide access to their cell phone numbers for emergency calls after hours.

Serious Eye Complication Symptoms

- Painful eye movements
- Eye discharge
- Abnormal swelling
- Loss of vision
- Severe headache
- Excessive tearing

When to Seek Medical Attention

Permanent cosmetic technicians can never be too careful when observing or being available to be advised about an unusual eye condition after eyeliner procedures. If a client reports any of the serious eye complication symptoms listed above, or others of concern, directions should be provided to seek treatment with their medical care provider, or one you have developed a relationship with in the absence of a client having one of her or his own. If the event occurs after standard medical office hours, do not hesitate to direct a client to an emergency room for care, requesting that you be kept advised of the diagnosis.

Eye injuries associated with permanent cosmetic eyeliner procedures are rare, but possible if the technician does not adhere to safety precautions needed to keep the eye safe. Clients also are responsible for following aftercare instructions that would prevent injury or infection.

It is wise that all technicians develop a relationship with an ophthalmologist.

References

1. http://www.cc.gatech.edu/classes/cs6751_97_winter/Topics/human-cap/senses.html 03/26/2017 http://www.zainbooks.com/books/computer-sciences/human-computer-interaction_7_human-input-output-channels-1.html
2. Ted M. Montgomery, O.D., Anatomy, Physiology and Pathology of the Human Eye, 03/26/2017, http://www.tedmont-gomery.com/the_eye/. Used with permission.
3. Ted M. Montgomery, O.D., Anatomy, Physiology and Pathology of the Human Eye, 03/26/2017, http://www.tedmont-gomery.com/the_eye/cornea.html#keratoconus.
4. Central Valley Eye Association, 01/14/08, http://www.centralvalleyeyeassociation.org/centralvalleyeyeassociation_002.htm. Used with permission.
5. http://www.rivervalleyvision.ca/your-eye-health/eye-conditions/eye-allergies/3/26/2017

Section 8

Important Muscles of the Face

Learning Objectives

Introduction

Muscles of the face dictate facial symmetry and asymmetry. The nervous system's interaction with muscles prompts spontaneous expression, which if not controlled with effective stretching techniques and client control can result in misplacement of the needle positioning during tattooing.

Knowing about these important muscles, where they are located, and how they function is essential to recognizing client discomfort and working safely.

Objective

Upon completion of this section, the technician will have a working knowledge of the important muscles of the face that can affect safety aspects of the procedure, alert her or him to client discomfort, and how to predict and control involuntary muscle movements affecting the procedure area.

Section 8 - Important Muscles of the Face

A thorough understanding of important muscles of the face is important to accurate design work, predicting facial movements—sometimes involuntary—during a permanent cosmetic procedure, and to developing adequate stretching techniques for procedures conducted.

Much of the information in this section is medical in terminology, and for those who are nonmedical technicians, possibly confusing, but once studied and learned, we become better technicians with a better understanding of our canvas and the muscles that dictate movement, an element associated with completed quality work.

Anatomy is a descriptive science, and as a result, a good amount of the effort associated with learning it requires memorizing terms. However, as more knowledge is acquired in this specialty through association, structures (in this case muscles) and their functions are easily recalled. In other words, at the outset, description of the important muscles (important in relation to permanent cosmetic procedures) is generally remembered through a process of memorization. Keep in mind that relating the function of a muscle to its morphology as well as to other muscles, as appropriate, is the basis for an in-depth retention of knowledge of muscles of the face.

The uses of muscles of the face present interesting and important observations and challenges for the permanent cosmetic technician. As an example, a woman who arrives for a lip procedure who has used her triangularis muscles (creates a down turned appearance at the corners of the mouth) may prove to be a challenge when applying a design guideline for lip liner. The corners of the mouth naturally droop and this is not a desirable shape to compound upon.

Another example is an eyebrow client's natural tendency to raise one eyebrow or the other. She or he has developed a habit of using the outer frontalis muscle (forming wrinkles in the lateral part of the forehead and an arched shape to both or either of the eyebrows), which is very likely to be very obvious when a mirror is used or when photographs are taken. Observations such as these must be made, and the client asked to relax her or his face so that photographs and/or design work does not reflect spontaneous habits. There are many examples that you as the reader can apply to each of the muscles listed below. The more you associate them with a vision and an example of how the use of the muscle affects (positively or negatively) you as a technician, the more prepared you will be to work with each client's facial morphology uniqueness.

Muscles of the face have two different designs: circular muscles that surround the eyes and mouth openings, and long muscles whose muscle bundles interweave at the edges of the circular ones and pull the circular ones when they contract. There are also muscles that attach to the skin and move it, causing puckering.

Figure 8-1 (next page) shows an anatomical diagram of important muscles of the face (as they relate to permanent cosmetic procedures) listed and their location. A brief description is provided.

Frontalis—"The Frontalis muscle runs vertically on the forehead, originating in tissues of the scalp (galea aponeurotica) above the hairline and inserting into the skin in the forehead and near the eyebrows. (It is considered the front part of the Epicranius muscle or Occipito-frontalis which covers the scalp from the forehead to the back of the head.) Contraction of the entire frontalis draws the eyebrows and skin of the forehead upwards and forms horizontal wrinkles running across the forehead. It is composed of inner (medial) and outer (lateral) parts, which can function relatively independently."[1]

"Frontalis is innervated by temporal branches of the facial nerve (VII) and is supplied with blood by the superficial temporal artery. The inner frontalis is the medial part of the frontalis muscle. Its contraction raises the medial part of the brow and eyebrows, forming slanted wrinkles in the forehead and creating a slant up towards the center in the eyebrows. The outer frontalis is the lateral part of the frontalis muscle. Its contraction raises the lateral (outer) part of the brow and eyebrows, forming wrinkles in the lateral part of the forehead and an arched shape to the eyebrows."[1]

Permanent cosmetic technicians often must remind clients they are exercising the inner or outer frontalis muscle(s), causing eyebrow asymmetry either when they are looking in a mirror to approve design work or when their photograph is taken.

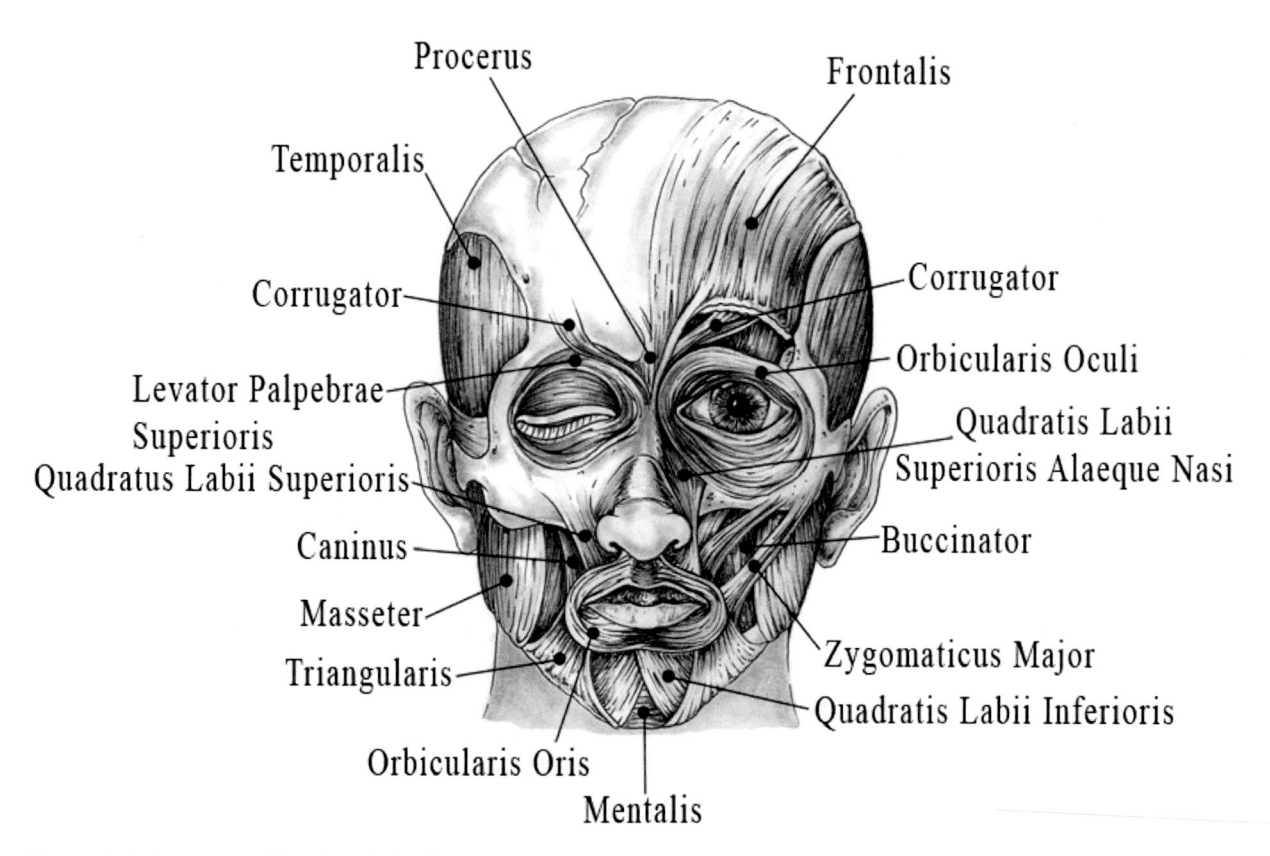

Figure 8-1: Important Muscles of the Face

Corrugator—"The Corrugator muscle originates at the inner orbit of the eye near the root of the nose and inserts into the skin of the forehead above the center of each eyebrow. It pulls the eyebrows and skin from the center of each eyebrow to its inner corner medially and down, forming vertical wrinkles in the glabella area and horizontal wrinkles at the bridge of the nose. It most often acts simultaneously with two nearby smaller muscles, the depressor supercillii and the procerus. It is one of the most important of expressive muscles. Some suggest this is the muscle of grief and suffering (research suggests much more diverse roles). It produces a frown in the eyebrows and forehead. Corrugator is innervated by zygomatic and temporal branches of the facial nerve (VII) and is supplied with blood by the superficial temporal artery."[2]

When designing eyebrows deep glabellar lines can affect the positioning of one or the other or both eyebrows in the bulb area. When performing an eyebrow procedure it is important to maintain a good focused stretch when working in the eyebrow bulb area to control the client's strong corrugator muscle movements. This area of the eyebrow lies on thicker skin as well. Additional attention to the eyebrow bulb area is, at times, necessary to ensure good pigment implantation.

Temporalis—"The Temporalis muscle originates in the scalp above the temporal region and inserts into the upper part of the jaw. It acts to elevate the jaw and clench the teeth."[3]

During an eyebrow or eyeliner procedure, the technician's hand may rest on this area for support. When a client is under stress or is experiencing discomfort, often the technician can feel the temporalis muscle tighten. Reminding the client to relax or considering a momentary break in the tattooing process is advisable. This is a primary reason why we never allow our clients to chew gum during a procedure.

Orbicularis oculi—"Orbicularis oculi is a sphincter muscle around the eye and acts, in general, to narrow the eye opening and close the orbit of the eye. This muscle has important functions in protecting and moistening the eye as well as in expressive displays. These muscles constrict skin around the eye, reduce the eye opening, and close the eye. It has three parts, an outer or orbital part, an inner or palpebral part in the eyelids, and a small lacrimal part near the tear duct. The outer part originates in the medial part of the orbit and runs around the eye via the upper eye cover fold and lid and returns in the lower eyelid to the palpebral ligament; the palpebral part originates in the palpebral ligament and runs above and below the eye to the lateral angle of the eye. These two muscles form concentric circles around the eye. Action of the palpebral part is often involuntary, as in the blink reflex."[4]

During an eyeliner procedure, the technician must control this muscle to ensure the eyelid does not close at an inopportune time. Controlled blinks, allowing the orbicularis oculi to function, ensure the eye remains moist.

Levator palpebrae superioris—The levator palpebrae superioris muscle is the muscle in the orbit that lifts the upper *eyelid*, pulling it back into the eye socket revealing the top of the iris and sclera around it. This action serves to open the eyes in a wide-open position.

During an eyeliner procedure, the technician must control this muscle to ensure the eyelid remains in a position that does not interfere with the implantation process. Controlled blinks, allowing the levator palpebrae superioris to function, ensure the eye remains moist.

Procerus—"The Procerus (also known as the depressor glabellae or pyramidalis nasi) muscle originates in the fascia of the nasal bone and upper nasal cartilage, runs through the area of the root of the nose, and fans upward to insert in the skin in the center of the forehead between the eyebrows. It acts to pull the skin of the center of the forehead down, forming transverse wrinkles in the glabella region and bridge of the nose. This horizontal wrinkle at the root of the nose is sometimes referred to as the 'champion pucker' because this muscle often contracts in effortful activities. It usually acts together with corrugator and/or orbicularis oculi and/or the nasal part of levator labii superioris. It is very difficult to contract deliberately without involving these other muscles."[5]

Movement of the procerus muscle during an eyebrow or eyeliner procedure can cause skin movement and pigment displacement. It is important to remind the client to relax as eyebrow and eyeliner procedures are being conducted. Movement of this muscle can be seen often in response to discomfort.

Quadratus labii superioris—The quadratus labii superioris muscle (also known as the levator labii superioris) is the elevator of the upper lip, moving it at the same time slightly forward. Its angular head serves as a dilator of the nostrils. The infraorbital and zygomatic heads assist in structuring the nasolabial furrow, which passes from the side of the nose to the upper lip and gives an expression of sadness or disappointment to the face. The quadratus labii superioris lifts the angle of the mouth and aids the Caninus in generating the nasolabial furrow.

Involuntary movements of the quadratus labii superioris muscle during a permanent cosmetic lip liner procedure can result in an irregular implanted line.

Caninus—"The Caninus muscle (also known as levator anguli oris) originates in the upper jaw bone area near the canine and inserts near the corner of the mouth in tissues of the other muscles there (e.g., o. oris). It pulls the corner of the lip up in an almost vertical direction, sharply angling the lip corners up in a kind of 'smile.'"[6]

Involuntary caninus muscle movements during a permanent cosmetic lip liner procedure can result in an irregular implanted line.

Zygomaticus major—The zygomaticus major is a muscle that extends from each zygomatic arch (cheekbone) to the corners of the mouth. It raises the corners of the mouth when a person smiles.

During lip procedures, the technician's hand may rest on this area of the cheekbone. The technician must be acutely aware of any movement of the zygomaticus major muscle, as this can result in unintentional movement of the tattooing device.

Masseter—"Masseter is one of the most powerful muscles for its size in the body. It originates in the lateral part of the cheekbone (zygomatic arch) and inserts in the angle of the mandible. It acts to raise the jaw and clench the teeth. This muscle functions to chew food and derives its name from the Greek for chewing, and is associated with angry and aggressive states. When this muscle is chronically too tense, the abnormal condition called 'Temporal-Mandibular Disorder,' also known as TMJ, can occur."[7]

When clients feel stressful during a procedure, it is not unusual for them to clench their teeth. Technicians can typically feel the masseter muscle contract when a client clenches their teeth because the tattooing hand can rest on the cheek when performing eyebrow, eyeliner, and lip color procedures. When this occurs, many technicians take this as an opportune time for a rest before proceeding.

Buccinator—"Buccinator originates in the maxilla and mandible in the area of the molar teeth and inserts into various muscles at the corner of the mouth. It acts to compress the cheeks tight to the teeth, and tighten and pull the lip corners inwards and somewhat laterally, often dimpling the cheeks. It forms a large part of the lateral wall of the mouth. Its functions include keeping food in the mouth where it can be masticated by the teeth. Because of its importance in expelling air through pursed lips, blowpipes, or wind instruments, it has been called the 'trumpet muscle.'"[8]

There are clients who will breathe in and out through their mouth to control short periods of discomfort exercising the buccinator muscle. Although this is discouraged and controlled with stretching techniques during a lip procedure, it is probable to see it more often with an eyeliner procedure. Technicians must be aware that if their tattooing hand is resting on the upper jaw area, this can cause movement in the tattooing positioning.

Triangularis—"Triangularis, a name based on its shape, (also known as Depressor anguli oris) originates in the mandible and platysma and inserts in the skin and orbicular muscle at the corner of the mouth. It is a muscle whose evolutionary connection to the platysma is evident, being continuous with it and extending to the mouth. This muscle causes the corners of the mouth to turn down and form the lips into an inverted U, an action stereotyped as indicating grief. It produces a frown in the mouth."[9]

When a client is uncomfortable, it is not unusual to see the lips respond in a frown. Control over the lip muscles with effective stretching techniques and brief periods of rest are important when conducting a lip procedure. Extreme caution to discourage an involuntary movement of the triangularis muscle must be exercised, particularly when tattooing in the corners of the mouth.

Quadratus (levator) labii superioris alaeque nasi muscle—The quadratus (levator) labii superioris alaeque nasi has the longest name of any muscle. This muscle lifts the upper lip and is also referred to as the 'wing' of the nose. The muscle attaches to the upper frontal process of the maxilla and inserts into the skin of the side part of the nostril and upper lip. The action of this muscle raises the lip into a snarl. Envisioning Elvis Presley's famous snarled lip expression when singing is a good example.

Technicians must be aware of the possibility of some involuntary lifting of the upper lip during a lip liner procedure. Short span stretching techniques encompassing small areas of the lip during tattooing will help discourage involuntary movement.

Quadratus labii inferioris—"Depressor labii inferioris (also known as quadratus labii inferioris) originates in the chin part of the mandible and inserts into the skin of the lower lip and muscles of the lower lip (o. oris). Its action pulls the red parts of the lower lip relatively straight down and the skin of the lower lip somewhat laterally and down, baring the lower teeth. It has been suggested by some to express irony."[10]

The bottom lip is typically larger and more buoyant than the upper lip. Technicians must maintain short span stretching techniques when conducting lip procedures to control and discourage quadratus labii inferioris muscle movements.

Mentalis—"Mentalis is so named because it is associated with thinking or concentration, although the justification for this view is lacking. It also has been said to express doubt. It originates in the part of the mandible below the front teeth and inserts into the skin of the chin, and acts to push the chin boss upwards, wrinkling it and curving the lips upward in an inverted U."[11]

Movement of the mentalis muscle can result in movement of the technician's tattooing positioning and misplacement of the pigment during a lip procedure. Technicians must maintain short span stretching techniques when conducting lip procedures to control and discourage movement of the mentalis muscle.

Orbicularis oris—"Orbicularis oris is the sphincter muscle around the mouth, forming much of the tissue of the lips. It has extensive connections to muscles that converge on the mouth. This muscle acts to shape and control the size of the mouth opening and is important for creating the lip positions and movements during speech. Several different strands can be distinguished that allow it to form the lips into versatile shapes. As an expressive muscle, four relatively distinct movements can be produced by orbicularis oris, a pressing together, a tightening and thinning, a rolling inwards between the teeth, and a thrusting outwards."[12]

Effective firm stretching techniques, encompassing smaller sections at a time during lip procedures, are recommended to keep the mouth from naturally compressing due to the orbicularis oris muscle movement when discomfort is experienced.

References

1. Joseph C. Hager, PhD, DataFace, Psychology, Appearance, and Behavior of the Human Face, 01/15/08, http://www.face-and-emotion.com/dataface/expression/frontalis.html.
2. Joseph C. Hager, PhD, DataFace, Psychology, Appearance, and Behavior of the Human Face, 01/15/08, http://face-and-emotion.com/dataface/expression/corrugator.html.
3. Joseph C. Hager, PhD, DataFace, Psychology, Appearance, and Behavior of the Human Face, 01/15/08, http://face-and-emotion.com/dataface/expression/other.html.
4. Joseph C. Hager, PhD, DataFace, Psychology, Appearance, and Behavior of the Human Face, 01/15/08, http://face-and-emotion.com/dataface/expression/o_oculi.html.
5. Joseph C. Hager, PhD, DataFace, Psychology, Appearance, and Behavior of the Human Face, 01/15/08, http://face-and-emotion.com/dataface/expression/procerus.html.
6. Joseph C. Hager, PhD, DataFace, Psychology, Appearance, and Behavior of the Human Face, 01/15/08, http://face-and-emotion.com/dataface/expression/caninus.html.
7. Joseph C. Hager, PhD, DataFace, Psychology, Appearance, and Behavior of the Human Face, 01/15/08, http://face-and-emotion.com/dataface/expression/masseter.html.
8. Joseph C. Hager, PhD, DataFace, Psychology, Appearance, and Behavior of the Human Face, 01/15/08, http://face-and-emotion.com/dataface/expression/buccinator.html.
9. Joseph C. Hager, PhD, DataFace, Psychology, Appearance, and Behavior of the Human Face, 01/15/08, http://www.face-and-emotion.com/dataface/expression/triangularis.html.
10. Joseph C. Hager, PhD, DataFace, Psychology, Appearance, and Behavior of the Human Face, 01/15/08, http://face-and-emotion.com/dataface/expression/depressor_labii.html.
11. Joseph C. Hager, PhD, DataFace, Psychology, Appearance, and Behavior of the Human Face, 01/15/08, http://face-and-emotion.com/dataface/expression/mentalis.html.
12. Joseph C. Hager, PhD, DataFace, Psychology, Appearance, and Behavior of the Human Face, 01/15/08, http://face-and-emotion.com/dataface/expression/orbicularis_oris.html.

Section 9

Choosing the Right Client

Learning Objectives

Introduction

Frequently, the history of a liability lawsuit indicates that problems could have been avoided if the technician had been tuned in to red flags that many unsuitable potential clients presented during the consultation. Problems should be identified before proceeding with the requested procedure. Of primary importance is the client's health and emotional profile suitability for the specific permanent cosmetic service.

Another consideration is the client's location. Is this a person who is not hampered by travel limitations, or is in a locale that would allow an unscheduled appointment in the event there are reasons you need to view and discuss? Notwithstanding the possibility of complications, many times a client needs reassurance and will request a few minutes of our time. Clients out of one's locality prove to be a challenge in these respects and can result in undue stress or concern.

Timing is everything. Well-timed procedures result in appropriate down time (as appropriate) for a client before she returns to normal activities. Down time is often associated with unique personal information provided by the client, i.e., one's hobbies, work-related responsibilities, age, and any health considerations.

Objective

At the completion of this section, the reader will discover what key questions one should ask and behaviors to watch for during consultations to ensure the timing is right for a procedure and that the client is a good candidate, both medically and emotionally. For those who are not a good fit for being a client, information on how to negotiate the dissolution of a relationship with a client is provided.

Section 9 - Choosing the Right Client

The title of this section has many implications.
- What is the client's health profile?
- Is the client emotionally a good candidate for permanent cosmetics?
- Has the client had permanent cosmetics before, and if so, why is the client not returning to the original technician?
- Where does the client live? Can you easily ask the client to return to observe any concerns the client may have during the healing process?
- Has the client discussed the desire for permanent cosmetics with family and close friends? Some people are dependent on the opinions of others; it doesn't hurt to ask this question.
- Is the timing desired appropriate, based on imminent travel plans or social obligations?

Is this Prospective Client a Good Candidate?

What is the Client's Health Profile?

Permanent cosmetic technicians must obtain an overview of a client's health profile and other information that assists with determining if the person is a good candidate for permanent cosmetics. Regarding physical health conditions, the primary issues include *will the client heal normally?* and *will I cause any health issues by conducting permanent cosmetic services?*

Is the Client Emotionally a Good Candidate for Permanent Cosmetics?

There are many emotional issues that people in today's society are confronted with. It is interesting that some medical professionals might advise us not to provide services to anyone who is takes an antidepressant. Unfortunately, it is not uncommon for people of all appropriate ages to take an antidepressant for a number of reasons, some of which may have little to do with depression. For example, it is common for people who are trying to quit smoking to be prescribed certain antidepressants because they are reported to help dull the desire for nicotine. Some clients report they were prescribed antidepressants to help overcome the changes experienced during menopause. Just because someone is on an antidepressant, that alone may not necessarily rule them out as a good candidate for tattooing. It is the reason *why* a person is on an antidepressant that is important. If a person has been truly diagnosed as depressed, proceeding with a permanent cosmetic procedure is worth serious consideration. You are always in charge of whom you do or do not accept as a client as long as your reasoning is ethically and legally sound.

Most of the emotional issues we are presented with are focused on whether potential clients can handle change. They must be prepared to accept the fact that when they leave your establishment after their initial procedure, the procedure area(s) will look darker and bolder than they will appear after a few days of healing. There may be slight to noticeable swelling. The eyebrow procedure produces little or no noticeable swelling, eyelash enhancement and narrow eyeliner procedures normally produce a puffy appearance (as if the client has been crying), wider eyeliner can result in more noticeable swelling and slight skin discoloration depending on the skin type/age of the client, and the lips produce the most noticeable swelling. The procedure area will eventually fade somewhat and appear softer because approximately 15 to 20 percent of the pigment is trapped in the epidermal layer of the skin and will ultimately exfoliate along with dead skin cells. There is a healing process that each good candidate for permanent cosmetics must accept and agree to deal with emotionally, and care for according to written aftercare instructions.

Another emotional issue that frequently arises is whether the client accepts that the procedure is tattooing, and that tattooing is not a pain-free process. Those who need constant reassurance that it will not hurt much, or those who continue to remind you they have a low tolerance to pain, or are subject to fainting, etc., most likely will not be easy clients to deal with, and technicians will work far more with these types of clients than they will with clients who just accept that the *no pain, no gain* slogan applies to all invasive beauty services. This is not to imply that a client who asks questions about pain is not a good candidate for tattooing. Those who make the subject of discomfort they may experience during the procedure a major issue will, in all likelihood, be more challenging and require more attention and time. For those technicians who work in a medical environment who can legally do so, and choose to offer anesthetics that are injected by a licensed medical professional, this may sound attractive to the client that has a legitimate pain issue and may calm her or his fears. It is the opinion of many industry leaders that topical anesthetics made specifically for our industry work better than, or as well as, anesthetics that are injected. Technicians who have worked in a medical environment where injected anesthetics were used have reported that the injections can cause bruising and more discomfort than the tattooing process with topical anesthetics and can also interfere with design work. Noteworthy is that bruising associated with injected anesthetics frequently outlasts any swelling or other typical telltale signs of a recently performed procedure. Technicians have to choose whether they want to deal with a client that constantly reminds them of how much she or he fears pain.

Compulsive disorders are headliners in our business—big red flags. Many people with compulsive disorders are often not happy with themselves on a variety of subjects, including how they look. During the consultation, clients who stare at themselves for long periods of time in a mirror, trying to get a point across about design work, or who bring a variety of topical makeup products as examples of preferred colors for reference (not being able to decide between one or the other) either may not trust their technician, or go through this inspection and color-selection process every day in the privacy of their home, never being satisfied even with their own choices. Those who are compulsive also may not be trustworthy to follow aftercare instructions. Leaving the procedure alone except for cleaning and aftercare maintenance as directed and refraining from applying topical makeup on the area for a few days, waxing or tweezing eyebrow hairs, etc., may just be too much for this type of person.

The client's dependency on another person's opinion for final approval of design or color selection is something technicians occasionally must deal with. Having a potential client who has discussed her or his desire for permanent cosmetics with those they are close to is not necessarily a sign of dependency; it just simply may be a matter of being considerate or having open discussions with friends and family. Beware, however, of the client who has to bring another person or people to be involved with the process because she or he cannot make decisions without the input of others. There will also be those clients who might prefer for their partner to be there because they do everything together, not necessarily because decisions cannot be made under any other circumstances. For instance, there are some people who would just not make any major decision without the approval of their partner or a relative.

Allowing a partner, relative, or friend to accompany a client to the appointment is each technician's decision. Some people have physical challenges that prevent them from driving. There is also the client who may have consulted with a physician and obtained a prescription for a relaxant or pain medication. It would seem unreasonable to ask a designated driver to sit in their car for an unspecified period of time. So if there is a waiting area available, this is the appropriate location for that person or any other person accompanying the client to the appointment during the procedure process. Be on guard, however, for the client who cannot make up their own mind and needs the reassurance of others outside the scope of what might be considered normal. Under those circumstances, technicians will never have just one client to please; they will also be answering to the person the client needs to help her or him make procedure-related decisions. There is a difference between a person being dependent on others, and being considerate of others or needing a little reassurance; learn to recognize it.

Clients who have the need to be in constant control are normally very difficult people. A demanding, bossy, or sarcastic attitude is one that requires time to determine if a working relationship can be established to the satisfaction of both parties.

Clients who have recently gone through major life changes may or may not be ready to make good, sound decisions. A good consultation typically gives the technician the information needed to help determine this one way or the other.

Has the Client Had Permanent Cosmetics Before, and If So, Why Is the Client Not Returning to the Original Technician?

This is an important subject to discuss with the client who is seeking services for correction or touch-up procedures. First of all, regardless of what the client conveys, technicians have no idea what actually transpired. Be cautious. There are legitimate reasons why people change technicians. Technicians and clients move out of reach of one another. Clients sometimes feel another technician is more qualified for additional procedure work. What you need to listen for is if the person badmouths the prior technician and mentions any threats relating to lawsuits. The client who recognizes that she or he made a mistake when choosing the original technician is voicing responsibility for not having done the proper research necessary before choosing a technician. This happens, and when clients admit they are partially responsible for whatever it is about the procedure that is unacceptable, it is a good indication that the client is emotionally sound and merely looking for help or to establish a relationship with a new technician because the original technician is no longer available.

Where does the client live?

Many technicians do not see any problem with offering services to clients that live out of their vicinity for touch-ups or an office visit if anything transpires that would warrant coming in for observation. Other technicians feel it is important to have easy access to clients.

Has the Client Discussed the Desire for Permanent Cosmetics with Family and Close Friends?

Even though we all prefer to believe our clients are not really concerned about what other people think or say about something so personal as how they look, face it, we all seek approval from others about our appearance in some respect or another. Whether or not the client has discussed this with family and close friends isn't necessarily a good or bad indication. Dependency on others versus being considerate of others was discussed earlier. Some people are very independent (a characteristic technicians normally admire about a client) and private and would consider the fact that they are going to have a permanent cosmetic procedure none of another person's business. It is always pleasing to a technician when the client says that she has discussed getting the procedure with others and they don't care, they think it is a great idea, or they are waiting to see how the procedure goes, etc. That is usually somewhat of a relief to the technician inasmuch as the technician won't plan on getting a call advising that the client's partner, friend, or relative thinks the client made a mistake, or the color is too dark, wrong, or a multitude of other situations that can arise. Technicians get all sorts of responses when asking clients questions about what other people say about them pursuing permanent cosmetics. The responses may or may not cause a potential client to be considered a good candidate, but all responses provide valuable information.

Is the Client a Good Candidate for the Technique Requested?

Several experts in the microblading segment of our industry have made it clear that not all skin types (oily, large pores, sensitive skin, etc.) are good candidates for the eyebrow microblading technique. The same concept of eligibility applies to eyeliner. Some clients have eyelids that literally droop over the eyeliner area which can affect the healing process or distort the design work, they request tips on the eyeliner that are not appropriate for the skin that would support proper placement. There are also qualifications for lip procedures to ensure the color heals evenly as expected and hyperpigmentation does not affect the final color.

Is the Timing Desired Appropriate Based on Imminent Travel Plans or Social Obligations?

Potential clients often call for an appointment very close to a planned vacation date, many times to a sun-drenched part of the world or an important event. Brides are so busy planning their weddings, many times they will think of the convenience of permanent cosmetics at the last minute. Procedures should be scheduled to allow ample time for healing and a follow-up appointment (and healing time for touch-up work) before planned vacations and high-profile social events.

There is much to learn about client management, recognizing problems, solving problems, etc. The most detailed book on this subject is *The Client Management Book* offered by the Society of Permanent Cosmetic Professionals, www.spcp.org.

Declining Permanent Cosmetic Clients - General

There are several reasons or occurrences that may lead a technician to decline new work or to sever the relationship with a client they have provided services to. There are far too many to list to discuss all the possibilities, but the following are some frequently discussed situations.

Non-Payment for Services

Although I believe most technicians are paid at the time services are rendered, clients have the option with most credit card companies to file a dispute for recorded charges or to stop payment on a check written. This can occur when a client leaves perfectly happy but meets with critical reviews from family or friends. There are other reasons that may apply but ultimately, regardless of the reason, this creates an administrative problem that must be resolved.

This is an uncomfortable occurrence which requires time, energy, and subsequent conversations with the client, the bank or credit card company as to the reason why payment should not be stopped. This tarnishes the relationship and if further work is provided to finish the original service, often technicians find it reasonable to advise the client it would be best to locate another technician for future work.

Time Consumers

Technicians book clients based on a reasonable amount of time to provide the service requested at a professional pace. There have been instances where technicians have accepted a client for permanent cosmetics who do not recognize or respect that their time with the technician is scheduled according to the service; in other words, this is not a social event. Some clients can be easily and gently reminded of the allotted time for their permanent cosmetics, while others don't seem to be easily persuaded to adhere to time restraints. Often this personality type can be recognized during a consultation; another valuable reason why consultations are important.

If the prospective client insists on more time than scheduled, is a no-show, or is chronically late, and the technician feels uncomfortable with this type of relationship, the technician may want to impose a consideration for the time consumed. People do seem to expect the technician to call or write to them a few days ahead of time as a reminder of the date and time allocated for the service or consultation

Some technicians make their policy clear in their Informed Consent form. Late or no-show fees are outlined for the client to review and agree to which gives the technician the perfect opening to remind the client of their written agreement.

One professional in the medical industry has a similar statement shown below on their consent form:

> *If you miss an appointment or are chronically late for appointments, we will assume you prefer to do business with another professional, and we will decline any requests for further appointments with our office.*

People Who Ask for Discounts

Although this is more likely to occur during the consultation or on a phone request for information about pricing, a long-term client may develop a sense of relationship that their loyalty deserves rewarding with a lesser fee for continued services. Or, another frequently heard message is that the client just needs a few minutes of your time to do something that in reality will take much longer. A gentle reminder that your fees apply to everyone, regardless of their circumstances or long-term relationship with your office often discourages any further requests for discounts.

People Who Are Dishonest and Over-Demanding

People who are not honest and people who want to be in charge are usually not people technicians develop a good relationship with. A person who arrives at their consultation with residual permanent cosmetics and swears she or he has never had a previous service is likely not going to be honest during the time the new technician spends with them. This could branch out into whether or not the client will follow aftercare instructions and be honest about it if they do not. Over-demanding people often take up a good amount of time telling a professional how to do their job and have a need to feel in charge of the time spent together.

No one looks forward to turning down work, or to ask an existing client to look for another technician for their future work. As an industry built on helping others often it is an extremely awkward conversation to have with a prospective or existing client. And there's always the fear of someone who feels offended by being called out on their behavior venting on social media. Our businesses depend on happy clients who refer their friends and family to us for their procedure work and good social media reviews.

The alternative to turning down people who you are not compatible with (for whatever reason a technician should decide to work with a questionable client) is to be openly acceptable to the whims of clients you may not want to do business with. Every industry has this challenge; how to plan your professional time with people who are dependable and pleasant to work with.

Negotiating the Dissolution of Your Relationship with a Client

Most permanent cosmetic professionals are eager to attract clients. This client-technician relationship is based on a mutual-value premise—providing a valuable service in exchange for compensation. But unless you follow strict guidelines, some client relationships are doomed to fail.

Turning away a client is the last thing anyone envisions when they launch a permanent-cosmetics business. However, there are times when the words or actions of a client lead to a significant loss on the part of the technician, and continuation of a business relationship cannot be justified or could even result in a legal challenge. This is when it makes good sense to set these clients free.

One of the hardest challenges we face as professionals is learning how to gracefully say *"No, thank you"* to a problem client. Recognizing when you can't meet a client's expectations makes the difference between a successful business and a failure. One unhappy client can destroy your life emotionally and financially in a short period of time.

We should never discriminate again a prospective client solely based on race, color, sex, sexual orientation, gender identification, religion, national origin, age, or disability. However, there is no reason you can't deny services due to: personality conflicts, medical contraindication, requested work being out of the scope of your training/expertise, etc.

It is very important to develop a protocol for distinguishing between good clients and identifying those that aren't right for you *before you work on them*. If you find yourself with a client you do not want to do business with, there are professional and ethical ways to accomplish this.

Some clients are quite insistent (another bad sign) and refuse to allow you to say no. Other problem situation may arise when a potential client seems to be emotionally distraught. This could be due to a major negative life event they are experiencing. Find a good solid reason to turn people away who seem to be in a life-changing situation until at such time in the future they are more emotionally stable.

People tell you who they are right up front. Put your ego aside and listen to what they are saying. If during the consultation you get the feeling this person is not right for you, don't proceed. Learn to distinguish between someone who is just having a bad day and someone who is having a bad life. Be willing to say to yourself, *"No matter what, I'm not taking this business."*

Sit down and analyze exactly what type of client you want and what type of individual you are not comfortable working with. *Then integrate as much of that information into your contract or consent forms.* Clearly spell out in writing and during the consultation what you expect from your clients. This is an interview between two people. You are not applying for a job as much as the client is soliciting your expertise. Disengaging from current clients should also be done in a formal manner with notes written in their files and a formal letter.

When you are sure all your contractual obligations have been met, you can prepare and send dissolution correspondence*. Keep it professional and courteous.

*Note: the SPCP recommends that all dissolution type correspondence and/or agreements to refund money should be reviewed by and coordinated with your insurance carrier.

Just as there is no universal *Dear John* letter, there is not a single best way to turn down a client or break away from them. In fact, the discussion does not have to be face-to-face with new clients, if you have already booked the appointment but are having second thoughts. Write them an email or private message them dissolving the relationship.

If, during the consultation you feel the person is not right for you, whether in writing or in person, it is best to never blame the client even when she or he richly deserves it. Turn the situation back on yourself and your capabilities. For example, suggest that what they are wanting is beyond my skill level. It takes a very determined person to still demand work after they hear something like that.

This is the reason to have a consultation for any type of permanent cosmetic procedure. Make it clear in the consultation that you are going to get to know each other to determine if you are a good fit. If not, you might want to say, *"I don't think I am the person to produce the look you desire"* or *"I don't specialize in the type of look you desire."*

At a minimum, you want your client to walk away thinking they were treated respectfully. Nobody likes to be told no, even if there is a good reason for it.

Dissolving relationships with individuals may be acting in their best interest. Give them the gift of allowing them to find the proper person to fulfill their needs.

References

1. Portions of *Negotiating the Dissolution of Your Relationship with a Client* were contributed by Mary Jane Haake CPCP.

Section 10

Pigment (Skin) Testing and Permanent Cosmetics

Learning Objectives

Introduction

Pigment (skin) testing (or may be referred to in other terminology depending on the locality) is a pre-procedure practice accepted by some technicians and pigment manufacturers, consisting of implanting a small amount of pigment (also called color, colorants or formulation) in the client's skin with the purpose of attempting to determine if a client is allergic to the pigment selected for a procedure.

This practice is called out differently by technicians and pigment manufacturers (there is not an industry set standard) in the permanent cosmetic industry. It is variously referred to as pigment testing, skin testing, patch testing (discouraged as this relates to a medical test conducted only by physicians, i.e., patch testing for food allergies), scratch testing, and so forth.

While the concept of pre-procedure testing, in theory, seems prudent, there are factors that affect the testing process and test results. What do the manufacturers of your pigment line state on this subject on their product labels? Is this test practice recommended? Required? Are they silent on the subject? What do your insurance policy or your regulatory provisions state?

Objective

The technician will have a full understanding of the pros and cons associated with pigment (skin) testing, and how these procedures are performed, upon completion of this section.

Section 10 - Pigment (Skin) Testing and Permanent Cosmetics

Pigment (skin) testing as it relates to the permanent cosmetic industry is a process conducted by some technicians intended to determine if the client is allergic to the pigment that will be used to perform a procedure. Caution to nonmedical technicians: a patch test in the United States (and possibly other countries) for example, is a term associated with medical coding for a medical test. It is advisable not to cross the professional line and refer to any test conducted as one identical to one a physician may perform and code on a medical document. While this section of the textbook does not suggest or provide any processes associated with pigment (skin) testing, it is an important subject to discuss.

Normally a pigment (skin) test consists of a small amount of pigment tattooed in the skin of the client. Unless the manufacturer of the pigment gives directions as to how long to wait to see if the test yields a positive or negative result, technicians report they allow a waiting period of anywhere from seven to thirty days if no reaction has occurred before performing a procedure. Without direction, technicians are on their own to determine if they feel comfortable going forward with a procedure after a pigment (skin) test has been conducted. Some manufacturers that require or suggest a pigment (skin) test give specific instructions as to how and where on the body to conduct the test and how long to wait before proceeding with a procedure, assuming there has been no evident reaction. Reading a pigment (skin) test of any kind can be construed by some as diagnosing, which can only be performed by a physician. For this reason, some technicians who use pigments that do not require this type of test may not offer one, or if they do, they advise the client to see their physician for a medical opinion of the result.

If pigment (skin) testing were a science, and all tests yielded conclusive information, this type of testing prior to a procedure would indeed be a method by which we could always determine if the client and the pigment are systemically compatible. Unfortunately, pigment (skin) testing is not an exact science and the process does not consistently allow technicians to accurately foresee whether a client will ultimately have a reaction to the pigment. An allergic reaction could happen months or even years after testing and/or a procedure is conducted.

In order for a test to be considered reasonably practical, the color that the technician and client have selected for the procedure should be used. Hypothetically, to be an effective measurement of allergic reaction, the pigment would be placed in the area on the face where the procedure is ultimately to be performed, at the same depth in the skin, and in significant amounts so that the body will have a sufficient substance with which to react.

This is not normally the manner in which the test is known to be performed. More often than not, the client does not want a mark of pigment in the eyebrow, eye, or lip area unless the entire procedure is being performed, and the technician is typically not keen on placing a mark in an area that may prove to be an eyesore if for any reason the procedure is not conducted at a later date. As a result, it has become commonplace to locate the test on other parts of the body (referred to as a surrogate area) such as behind the ear, on the shoulder, or as directed by the pigment manufacturer, etc., so that it is hidden away from sight during the testing period.

The amount of pigment utilized for the test is also an issue. A minimal amount is usually used and only applied to a small area. As a result, it is questioned if the body has adequate amounts to which it can react. Use the example that a person who is allergic to strawberries eats one strawberry and has no adverse reaction. However, the same person eats a pint of strawberries and the allergy becomes obvious. Some technicians use a lancet to perform the test, which can produce more blood on the surface of the test area than pigment being placed into the skin. As a result, the pigment bleeds out of the procedure site and the patch test is negligible. It is recommended that the pigment used for a pigment (skin) test be tattooed into the location selected.

Timing is yet another unpredictable element of a possible allergy. What a person is not allergic to today, they may be allergic to tomorrow, or next year, or in several years. On the other hand, they may never develop an allergy to the pigment. Moderate to extreme exposure to UV rays also has made the list of unpredictable elements that are thought to contribute to the onset of some reported pigment allergic reactions.

There are indeed many volatile elements that may affect the pigment (skin) test concept and the manner in which it is agreeably conducted with the client's consent.

Although pigment (skin) testing for every client may not be deemed practical by a technician, or even considered logically necessary in the technician's opinion, there may be particular clients technicians may prefer to test based on answers to a client history profile.

Clients who technicians may consider good candidates for a pigment (skin) test if for no other reason but to set their minds at ease, include clients who:

- indicate that they are allergic to topical makeup products or metals such as gold or silver jewelry;
- are allergic to hair dyes;
- have a history of skin sensitivities;
- indicate they have chronic allergy problems.

These are the communities of people that might seem as being an obviously high risk to pigment allergies. Some inorganic and organic pigment colorants are also ingredients in topical cosmetic products such as eyebrow pencils, eyeliners, and lipsticks. Not that the test results could be considered entirely decisive long term; a negative response could, as a minimum, reveal that your client at the time of and during the waiting period of the pigment (skin) test, was not allergic to the pigment to be used in a procedure. This is assuming enough pigment was placed in the skin to allow for a reaction if there was indeed going to be one at all.

Pigment manufacturers may require a pigment (skin) test to be conducted. As a result, if a technician chooses to use pigments with this labeling requirement, in order to comply with the product directions, the technician must conduct and document a test as directed for every client with every pigment used on that client for procedures. If the pigment manufacturer requires or suggests a pigment (skin) test, ensure that directions are provided to as to where the test is to be conducted, whether it should be conducted topically or intradermally, and what the manufacturer considers to be an adequate waiting period before the commencing with a procedure. Technicians also need to read their permanent cosmetic liability insurance policy as well to determine if their insurance carrier requires pre-procedure pigment (skin) testing (this process may be addressed by various names in the text of an insurance policy).

Whitney Tope, M.D., a past Director and Medical Advisor for the Society of Permanent Cosmetic Professionals (SPCP), wrote in his article *Patch Testing: Is It Worth It?* "As in the performance of all medical or paramedical procedures, the best course is to educate and inform the client to the best of your ability and allow them to make a rational decision about patch testing for themselves."

Dr. Tope has provided good guidelines. As a result, you will find on the consent form that is provided with your manual, a designated place for your client to indicate whether she or he chooses to have a test conducted. As the technician you always have the option of performing a pigment (skin) test on clients who you feel may be high risk. Notwithstanding the minority of high-risk clients who a technician may insist are tested, the majority of clients must make that decision (unless regulatory requirements dictate otherwise), and document their decision on the client's consent form by circling or initialing that they do or do not request a pigment (skin) test. For those localities where pigment (skin) testing is a regulatory requirement, information should be documented on designated forms as appropriate. Remember, it is not the inconvenience of a pigment (skin) test that is the primary concern; it is the inconclusive data supporting this type of testing that is the ultimate issue for technicians and clients.

If you wish to read more about pigment (skin) testing, Dr. Tope's *Patch Testing: Is It Worth It?* This article can be obtained through the Society of Permanent Cosmetic Professionals (SPCP) in the Medical Issues book at www.spcp.org.

Section 11

Client History Files

Learning Objectives

Introduction

All professionals who offer personal services maintain client history files. A service as familiar as hair coloring, for instance, is supported by files indicating the colors used and other important information that would be impossible for the cosmetologists to recall for all the clients they serve.

Computers have enabled many industries to keep very detailed purchase/activity related historical information and develop instant recall for the attendant to retrieve in order to make the caller feel welcome, remembered, and important.

In the permanent cosmetic industry, client history files provide several purposes, all of which are important and useful, and in some instances essential for efficient operational practices. Insurance providers and some regulatory agencies require technicians to prescreen clients to ensure the person requesting procedures is a good candidate. And just imagine trying to recall the pigment color used for an eyebrow, eyeliner, or lip liner client several years after the date of the original procedure.

Objective

Completion of this section will enable the technician to become familiar with frequently used questions asked of a potential client during a consultation, and what a yes response to a presented question may mean to the interviewing technician.

Section 11 - Client History Files

At the end of this section, there are examples of a Client History Profile Form, Informed Consent Form, and a Client Chart Notes Form.1 These forms are provided as examples only and all technicians are advised to seek legal counsel for the version of forms ultimately accepted as their official business forms. Trainers may also offer forms for consideration and the Society of Permanent Cosmetic Professionals (SPCP at www.spcp.org) also offers examples of forms in the Members Only section. However, in order to provide guidance to technicians regarding client health profile information, and the value of informed consent and charting, the forms provided at the end of this section will be used as references.

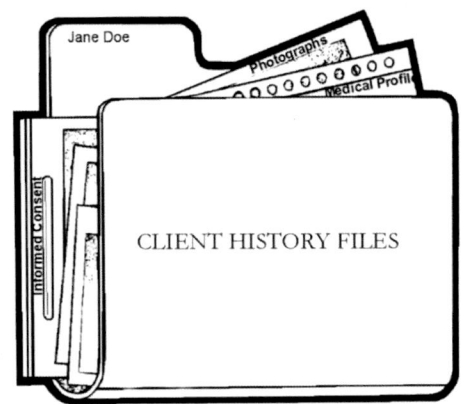

Every person for whom you provide permanent cosmetics should complete client history profile and informed consent forms. These client-completed, technician-signed documents represent evidence of a client's history profile at the time of the procedure and written confirmation that the client understood all elements of the procedure before consenting to the procedure(s) being performed.

Client History Profile: What to ask and why

Depending on your locality, it may be a requirement to comply with state, local, or country governing agency mandates for client screening that are not included in this section. Always comply with governing agency mandates. Review by your liability insurance provider is also recommended.

As providers of services that require breaking the skin, technicians will want to be confident that a person seeking the services does not have medical conditions or contraindications that would prevent a healthy healing process.

So that technicians are better prepared during prospective client consultations, a form is completed that allows for documenting health conditions. This section will explore many common conditions that prospective clients may indicate they have. Compare it to the information that follows, which provides a reasonable explanation as to why the questions are on the form and what the implications are if the prospective client indicates a yes to any of the questions. Answers are provided from a technician perspective only and based on industry experiences. Guidance provided is not intended to substitute for that which might be given by licensed medical professionals. Also, this textbook is provided to students from many regions in the United States and internationally. All technicians have an obligation to follow the laws of their state, county, and country. If any such law(s) prohibits a procedure or a procedure provided to persons with a particular health condition, or under any stated conditions, the laws of the state, county, or country where the procedure is to be performed prevail and the technician must refrain from offering that service. If for *any reason* technicians feel it necessary, or are required by the laws in their state, county, or country, to refer clients with certain medical conditions, or those on prescription medications, or any other circumstances causing concern for the well-being of the prospective client, to their physician for clearance before the procedure, they should do so before accepting the person as a client and commencing with the procedure.

Each question on the provided client history form is addressed below and its significance to the technician is explained if your client answers yes to any of the questions. These are general guidelines.

1) Are you pregnant or nursing?

   It is recommended technicians refrain from providing procedures to prospective clients who are pregnant or nursing. A person who is in their second or third trimester of pregnancy may be unable to lie on their back comfortably; in fact, it has the potential of negatively affecting the fetus in some cases. If at any time this person or their baby develops distress or disease of any kind, or the baby is born prematurely, the technician of a permanent cosmetic procedure might be held responsible. Offer services once the child is born, and baby is no longer breast feeding.

2) Have you had any alcohol within the last 24 hours?

   People that have had alcohol, especially wine it seems, tend to bleed more during the procedure. Bleeding is normally minimal and a controllable issue for an eyebrow or eyeliner procedure; however, this is unpredictable and if being conservative or if the prospective client is having a lip procedure, rescheduling is recommended.

3) Have you ever had cold sores/herpes/fever blisters?

   If consulting with a prospective client about a lip procedure and the person has a history of cold sores / herpes / fever blisters, it is very important that technicians advise the prospective client that she or he should see a physician for advice. Often, the physician will prescribe an antiviral medication to be taken as prescribed *prior* to the procedure and for a physician- designated period of time after the procedure. Proper use of an antiviral medication will assist in the prevention of the development of herpes viral eruptions on the lip tissue. Advise the prospective client that permanent cosmetic lip procedures will require more than one session and that it would be appropriate to discuss adequate quantities of antiviral medication with their physician for three procedures: the initial and two touch-ups.

4) Do you have any allergies to latex?

   Latex protein is found in latex gloves and can cause immediate hives (urticaria) or a more delayed contact dermatitis, or a more serious health condition. Nitrile gloves are the standard in the permanent cosmetic industry. There are powder-free alternative glove types if circumstances warrant.

5) Have you had a laser or chemical peel within six months?

Chemical and laser exfoliation treatments (peels) can (depending on the chemical or laser used) result in a thinning of the layers of the skin. As a minimum, people who have had these beauty or medical treatments may also have very sensitive skin if the treatment was recent. If the treatment was within the past six months, ask them to consult with their provider to determine if their skin is in good condition for permanent cosmetics. The laser and peel treatments do not normally directly affect the actual tissue you will be working on; providers typically do not use the chemicals or lasers in the eyebrows, lash line, around the eyes, or on the lips. However, to perform permanentcosmetic procedures, technicians must stretch the skin surrounding these areas and do not want to cause any skin irritation by doing so.

6) Have you ever had any permanent cosmetics or tattoos?

A *yes* answer to this question is an open door to inquire and observe as to how the prospective client healed, if the procedure(s) resulted in any scar tissue, and how the pigment in the tattoo or permanent cosmetic procedure appears now.

7) Do you bruise easily?

Technicians will find that the majority of their clients will not have any bruising from the procedure; however, there are some clients who bruise very easily. If the prospective client answers yes to this question, advise that she or he may see a slight discoloring in or around the procedure area. Because bruising is not common, the question is asked to single out those that have very fragile skin types and advise them what to expect so they are not alarmed. If fragile skin surrounding the procedure area is torn or in any way compromised during the procedure process, and then pigment is wiped into that area during the procedure, the skin is open and will accept minuscule levels of pigment that may heal to a shadowy appearance. Be aware and be careful. If the surrounding skin is slightly compromised during the procedure—if this is going to be a problem at all, this is usually a rare issue around the sensitive frail tissue of the outer corners of the eyes—cover the area with an ointment and cotton square as the procedure continues in order to prevent wiping any pigment into the open area.

8) Do you routinely use Retin-A®, glycolic, or other exfoliating products?

Request that the prospective client indefinitely refrain from using these products on the procedural area. The exception may be a lip treatment product that contains a small amount of alpha hydroxy or other light exfoliation product. The lip color looks more vibrant when the lips are not chapped and the alpha hydroxy (or other similar agents) helps exfoliate the dry chapped lip conditions that can veil good color.

9) Do you wear contact lenses?

If the procedure to be performed is eyeliner, advise the prospective client to remove the contact lenses prior to conducting the procedure. In general, contact lenses should not be worn until there is no sign of swelling and the tissue around the eyes has returned to normal. If advice is requested in regard to how long before contacts can be worn after the eyeliner procedure, refer the person to their eye doctor for advice. The eyeliner procedure produces slight swelling. If the eyelid is swollen, each time they blink the swollen eyelid has the potential of rubbing against the contact lens, causing irritation. Also, in the event *any* anesthetic or pigment has found its way into the eye and is not completely rinsed away during the final eye cleansing process, placing a contact lens in the eye is much like placing a lid on top of these substances. This can result in a chemical burn or scratch to the eyeball. The primary concern is based on the fact that even just blinking may cause harm to the eye with lenses in place when the eyelid tissue is at all swollen.

10) Are you allergic or sensitive to any metals, for instance, metals used for jewelry?

Many pigments contain iron oxide or other metallic salts/oxide materials. If a prospective client answers yes to this question, technicians have the option of conducting a pigment (skin) test in accordance with the manufacturer's direction with the pigment selected for the procedure prior to proceeding. *Note*: Many people are allergic to nickel. This is not unusual. Tattoo needles contain a small amount of nickel. If a person can wear jewelry made of gold, silver, etc., but reports itching from inexpensive earrings or other jewelry, a yes answer under these circumstances normally indicates a minor reaction to the metal nickel. An option is to advise clients of the nickel content in the needles and tell them if they experience slight itching, it will in all likelihood be as a result of skin contact with the needles used during the procedure, and that it will subside. Or if there is further concern, have the client consult with their physician.

11) Do you have any problems healing from small wounds?

This is an extremely important question. In order to perform a healthy procedure, the prospective client's health profile must support proper healing. If the prospective client answers yes to this question, determine what the source of the problem is that causes slow healing. If the reason is an autoimmune condition or any other medical condition, ask the prospective client to consult with their physician before going forward with the procedure. There are many health conditions that result in the inability to heal or have a slower healing process. A client that cannot heal well is not a good candidate for permanent cosmetics.

12) Do you use any other eyelash growth product?

The manufacturers of Latisse® as well as other eyelash growth products have not provided scientific-based information to our industry regarding the effects of these products on the eyeliner tattooing procedure. However, permanent cosmetic artists have reported different experiences that in some cases have resulted in a less than optimal procedure outcome. It is recommended that an extended before and after eyeliner wait period be implemented.

13) Do you use tobacco?

Depending on the amount of tobacco used, it can cause the prospective client to heal slower than someone who does not use tobacco. Schedule the follow-up/touch-up/top-up (there are a variety of terms used for the appointment after the original work has healed) visit one to two weeks further out than normally would be scheduled for a healthy nonsmoking client the same age. The reasoning is to ensure the skin is well healed before any touch-up procedures are performed.

14) Do you have a heart condition?

Depending on the condition, it is always wise to be aware of any conditions that could put a prospective client in harm's way. If a client is aware of the heart condition, in most cases, they are also under a physician's care and take appropriate medications. Clients with Mitral Valve Prolapse Syndrome (MVP) were frequently required to be pre-medicated with antibiotics prior to an invasive procedure. By today's standards, this is more uncommon, but as a non-medical technician, it is appropriate to inquire. *Do not* advise a client to alter prescription medication dosages or frequencies, or refrain from taking any medications prescribed by a physician. Clients should contact the prescribing physician for appropriate medication directives in relation to the condition and the cosmetic tattoo procedure. Some states may require a doctor's clearance before technicians provide procedures for clients with medical conditions.

Many clients report that they are on blood thinners such as Coumadin®. This is normally a controllable issue for eyebrows and eyeliners, but may prove challenging, at least for the first pass during a full lip procedure. The blood under these conditions is thinner and the client may bleed more than others who are not on these blood-thinning products. It has proven to be helpful to schedule a client's procedure right after their regularly scheduled bleeding time check with their doctor. In this way, you will be able to avoid a time where the bleeding time is too prolonged. Some technicians feel clients on Coumadin or other similar prescription blood thinners are not good candidates for permanent cosmetics, especially lip procedures.

15) Are you diabetic?

There are varying degrees of controlled or uncontrolled diabetes our clients may have. Some types are controlled by diet, some by oral medications, and some require insulin injections. In any event, it is always a good practice for prospective clients to consult with their physician before going forward with the permanent cosmetic procedure. In some instances, diabetics may not heal well. This is a condition that warrants their physician's clearance to proceed safely. A technician must be aware of signs of low blood sugar in the event they get clearance from the physician to work on the diabetic client. Stress can ultimately drop the blood sugar level. If the prospective client is known to have this problem, it is advisable to ensure she or he eats before the start of the procedure and that she or he informs you of any difficulties during the work.

16) Do you have any autoimmune disorders?

    People with autoimmune disorders do not have a healthy or dependable immune system. This can affect the healing process. In some instances, such as alopecia clients, technicians will find that clients with this autoimmune disorder may scab up soon after the procedure (scabbing is discouraged by the aftercare maintenance process) and thus may lose more pigment during the exfoliation process. Other conditions such as diabetes and lupus affect the body's ability to heal. Technicians may want to consider requesting that a prospective client with these medical conditions consult with their medical provider before going forward with the permanent cosmetic procedure.

17) Are you sensitive or allergic to hand creams or body lotions?

    There are preservatives in many hand and body lotions that are also used in pigments as a preservative, namely *propylene glycol*. If the prospective client answers yes to this question, try to determine if she or he is sensitive or allergic to *all* hand and body lotions, or just a specific brand. If the prospective client is specific about the ingredient that causes the sensitivity, contact the manufacturer of the pigment that will be used and ask if the pigment contains that ingredient.

18) Do you have your lips injected with filler materials?

    Lip filler materials are used frequently by physicians to enlarge the appearance of the client's lips. There are several factors to consider. It is discussed within our industry (no scientific proof) that repetitive injections in the lips result in unseen scar tissue. This could affect the way pigment sits in the tissue on a lip procedure. Restylane and other hyaluronic acid (HA) products may cause a bluing effect when injected too close to the surface, or in the very thin skin of the lip. Lip implants are more challenging to deal with because the implants may actually move slightly during the procedure. If in doubt about the filler substance or the implant materials, request that the prospective client consult with their attending physician before going forward with the procedure.

19) Do you menstruate?

    It is a well-accepted fact that women who are on or near their menstrual period are less tolerant and more sensitive. If possible try to schedule around a woman's period.

20) Do you hyperpigment?

    Hyperpigmentation factors are usually associated with Fitzpatrick skin types IV–VI, but hyperpigmentation is not limited to these skin types. Clients that tend to darken where the skin has been broken may cause the pigment selected to appear the same as seen immediately after the procedure or one to two shades darker after healing. It is a factor that must be taken into consideration when selecting eyebrow and top and bottom eyeliner colors. Hyperpigmentation does not normally affect a top eyelash enhancement procedure because this procedure is conducted on the ridge of the lash line and not on eyelid skin.

The hyperpigmentation factor does *not* work in your favor in any manner during a lip procedure. That is why many clients with Fitzpatrick skin types III–VI may not be good candidates for lip procedures. Considering the fact that their lips are often variegated in color (darker on the top or bottom than the other lip), when an additional pigmentation factor is added, the possibility of success is poor. Ask to look at the prospective client's elbows, knees, or any surgical area to determine how the skin reacts to friction, or how previously wounded areas appear after healed. Analyze the natural lip color as well to determine just how strong the hyperpigmentation issue is for the prospective lip client.

21) Do you tend to develop keloid or hypertrophic scars?

Ask to see an example of the scar tissue. Cosmetic tattooing is not a surgical procedure; however, there are people that scar very easily. Technicians have to be the judge on a client-by-client basis to determine if there are any risks associated with the procedure. Keloid and hypertrophic scars are two different types of scar tissue. People can develop keloid scarring after a surgical procedure or serious injury. Some industry concerns have been expressed regarding keloid scarring and people of color. Keloid scarring resulting from permanent cosmetic procedures is not common in our industry, but not impossible. Do not initiate a permanent cosmetic procedure if there are concerns that the procedure may result in scarring.

22) Do you scar easily from minor skin injuries?

A prospective client does not have to develop keloid or hypertrophic scars to scar easily from an injury. Ask to see an example of the scars on which the prospective client has based her or his yes answer. Technicians have to be the judge on a client-by-client basis to determine if there are any risks associated with the procedure. Do not proceed if there are concerns about the procedure resulting in scarring.

23) Do you have any seizure-related conditions?

If the prospective client has seizure related conditions such as epilepsy, the first request is that the prospective client consults with their physician to determine if a procedure can be safely conducted without incident. If physician clearance is obtained, then ask that someone who is familiar with the client's condition and can react properly to a seizure incident, drive her or him to and from the procedure, and remain there during the procedure.

24) Do you have a tendency to faint or become dizzy?

Fainting can be a normal reaction by some to the sight or discussion of blood. Make it a point that the prospective client does not see the cotton wipes or swabs that are used during the procedure and don't say the B (blood) word during the appointment. If the prospective client has a medical condition that results in fainting spells, technicians will want her or him to consult with their physician to determine if they are a good candidate for permanent cosmetics. If so, require that the client have someone accompany them to the appointment, remain in the facility during the appointment, and drive them home after the procedure is finished. Many times fainting is caused by low blood pressure. If the prospective client has low blood pressure, it would be best to sit them up at regular intervals and never have them stand up fully from a lying down position without sitting up for a bit first.

25) Do you bleed excessively from minor cuts?

This is a very important question. Technicians should not provide services to a client that is a hemophiliac (a mostly inherited genetic condition that impairs the body's ability to make blood clots) due to the body's impaired ability to clot blood. There are other blood conditions that can cause abnormal platelet levels. One would not expect a person with an abnormal blood condition to be pursuing an invasive procedure; however, many people may be undiagnosed and only report that they bleed excessively.

People who routinely take aspirin to thin their blood for related or unrelated heart conditions may bleed more easily than those who do not take aspirin on a regular basis, but they will not bleed as excessively as someone with a platelet disorder. It has become very commonplace for a person to take aspirin on a daily basis. Many of the anesthetics used for broken skin during the tattooing process contain a small amount of epinephrine, which is a vascular constrictor and usually successfully controls a normal amount of bleeding associated with permanent cosmetic procedures. If in doubt, request that the prospective client consult with their physician before initiating a permanent cosmetic procedure, and do not offer services to anyone who indicates that they have a bleeding disorder.

26) Do you have prosthetic implants?

This group includes an array of people with artificial implants in their body. It is important to determine if the prospective client is required to pre-medicate with antibiotics before invasive procedures. If so, ask that the prospective client consult with their physician in order to obtain clearance and/or proper medication directives (some regulations may require physician clearance) before going forward with the permanent cosmetic procedure. By today's standards, this is more uncommon, but as a non-medical technician, it is appropriate to inquire.

27) Do you consume aspirin on a daily basis?

See the answer to question 25.

28) Are you under treatment for depression?

If a prospective client is under treatment for depression, an attempt must be made to determine the severity in relation to their judgment and decision-making abilities. Some depressed individuals may make hasty decisions that they later regret. They may also have more challenges dealing with the healing maintenance requirements and the changes inherent to the permanent cosmetic process. On the other hand, many people take different dosages of antidepressants for common stress-related conditions and some as a stop smoking aid, or other reasoning based on a physician's determination. If in doubt, require that the prospective client consult with their physician before initiating the permanent cosmetic procedure. Keep in mind that not all clinically depressed people take medication or manage their condition with the help of a physician. These are the people who will be more difficult to identify during the consultation.

Any life-changing event, such as a logistic move, a divorce, loss of a loved one, or job change can affect the state of mind, temporary or otherwise. These life-altering events can cause some people to act emotionally, and until their lives are back in order, technicians do not want to contribute to their problems by prematurely conducting a permanent cosmetic procedure. Be mindful of the client that is obsessive or compulsive in regard to their appearance. People who constantly find fault with themselves or with the work of other service providers will rarely be satisfied with anyone's work, including a permanent cosmetic technician's.

29) Do you have a history of cold sores/fever blisters?

This question is specifically important for those clients who wish to have lip procedures. Cold sores/fever blisters (HSV-1) is a viral condition that warrants a physician's determination in regard to an appropriate antiviral medication before and after a lip procedure as directed by their physician.

30) Are you sensitive to petroleum-based products?

If a prospective client is sensitive to petroleum, technicians will want to suggest a non-petroleum-based product for aftercare use. If the prospective client is sensitive to lanolin, check the labels of aftercare single-use packages (if it is policy to provide an aftercare ointment to clients) to ensure the prospective client will be receiving a product that will not cause skin allergy or irritation. Because healing ointments are just a part of life, ask the prospective client what they normally use for minor injuries, and advise accordingly before the procedure is conducted so that the proper aftercare ointment may be provided or suggested. There are petroleum and lanolin-free products available.

31) Do you have Botox® injections?

Botox injections can temporarily alter the eyebrow positioning. It has been recommended to conduct the procedure when the effects of Botox have subsided and the site has returned to normal. If this timing is not realistic, a substantial number of prospective clients will have some eyebrow hair as a guideline for design placement purposes. Use this guideline and don't be tempted to make adjustments to compensate for the effects of wrinkle-reducing injections.

If there are questions regarding proper timing, ask the prospective client to consult with the medical provider who conducted the Botox service as to appropriate timing.

32) If you have permanent cosmetics or tattoos did you have any problems with healing?

Other healed permanent cosmetics or tattoos are a good indication of a prospective client's healing properties, unless they were tattooed many years ago and their health profile has since changed. The body's ability to heal changes over time and current health conditions may deem a yes answer to this question impractical to use as a guide for determining if a prospective client heals well now from tattooing.

33) Are you undergoing radiation or chemotherapy treatment?

This indicates that the prospective client has been diagnosed with a serious health condition and is undergoing aggressive medical treatment. Postpone procedures until a clearance to proceed with permanent cosmetic services has been received from the prospective client's physician.

34) Are you now, or have you ever been on the acne treatment Accutane®?

People who are or have been on Accutane are often advised to wait one year after treatment before they pursue permanent cosmetic procedures. Accutane affects the condition and structure of the skin. Physician advice before scheduling a permanent cosmetic procedure is recommended.

35) Do you have an implanted cardiac device (ICD)?

Technicians always want to be aware of any heart-related conditions a prospective client may have and any medical equipment associated with keeping the heart stable. Find out if the prospective client has any restrictions associated with the medical condition. Technicians may ask a prospective client to consult with their physician prior to initiating a permanent cosmetic procedure. Things have changed a lot over the years, but at one time there were concerns expressed regarding the pacemaker and the magnetic properties of a traditional coil machine. It is recommended to consult with the client's physician if they have an ICD.

36) Do you take prescription drugs?

Only a small percentage of permanent cosmetic technicians are also physicians. As a result, the majority of technicians do not have the knowledge required, or the legal right as a nonmedical professional to make determinations about medications. Technicians can never go wrong by referring prospective clients who are on prescription medications to a physician for a consultation regarding the safety associated with medications they take for associated health conditions and the permanent cosmetic process. However, with that said, there are some common medications that historically have not caused contraindications during the permanent cosmetic procedure. Environmental allergy medications, birth control pills, hormone replacement therapy medications, and other such common prescription strength medications have not been reported as being contraindicative.

37) Are you anemic?

Anemia is a condition that can be associated with a number of serious diseases. Those at risk include people with chronic kidney disease, diabetes, heart disease, and cancer; chronic inflammatory conditions like rheumatoid arthritis or inflammatory bowel disease; and persistent infections such as human immunodeficiency virus (HIV).

The most common reason for a woman to be anemic is a heavy menstrual period, but to work conservatively, be aware of other conditions that anemia may represent. Technicians must use good judgment.

38) Do you have a history of skin sensitivities?

The procedural area must be free and clear of any signs of skin conditions such as rashes, pimples, unusual pigmentation properties, and any other obvious abnormalities. The area should not be subject to topical medications in order to maintain normalcy. If the prospective client's skin is not healthy, do not perform the procedure until the skin condition has been properly and professionally treated and all indications of the condition have subsided. If there are no obvious signs of a medical condition, but the prospective client indicates their skin is sensitive, during the consultation try to determine the source of the sensitivity. The sensitivity may be related to topical cosmetics that contain a host of ingredients like perfumes and talc, which permanent cosmetics do not.

Because clients with sensitive skin react to touch and topical applications of products more easily than others, advise the prospective client that during the tattooing procedure it is necessary to stretch the skin; this can cause blotchiness and that anesthetics used (if the technician chooses to use anesthetics) may also cause slight irritation to the surrounding area, resulting in a pink or red-violet appearance.

39) Do you have any medical condition that has resulted in a medical professional requiring you to pre-medicate with an antibiotic prior to a dental or other invasive procedure?

There are several medical conditions, some quite serious, that require a person to pre-medicate before dentistry. Request that prospective clients consult with their physician to determine if they are good candidates for permanent cosmetics and if so, their physician will advise them of any premedication requirements. Regulations in some states may require a person who is required to pre-medicate before a dental procedure to have a doctor's clearance before proceeding with a permanent cosmetic procedure. By today's standards, this is more uncommon, but as a non- medical technician, it is appropriate to inquire.

40) Do you have allergies to topical makeup?

> Allergies to topical makeup are a primary reason for pursuing permanent cosmetic services. The area of concern is that base of topical makeup is often ingredients found in organic and inorganic permanent cosmetic pigments. The difference is that topical makeup, in addition to also may contain other ingredients as well that are not found in our pigment formulations. Additional ingredients may include, but are not limited to perfumes, talc, and different species of alcohols and wax among others. The ingredients label for some topical makeup reads like a science project, and it is little wonder more people do not develop an allergy to at least one of the components. However, because of the probability of some common organic and inorganic ingredients in topical makeup and permanent cosmetic pigments, anyone who indicates they are allergic to topical makeup poses a concern, even though permanent cosmetics is often a solution to makeup sensitivity.
>
> Ask the prospective client if they are unable to wear *all* topical makeup or if there are particular brands that cause the eaction. Ask if it has been determined what the primary ingredient is in the topical makeup that causes the reaction. Many people have gone through the identification process with their physician to determine what ingredient should be avoided.
>
> More often than not, you will find through inquiries that through trial and error a prospective client has found some products that do not cause allergic reactions.
>
> These clients may remind technicians that it does not hurt (although the test may not prove to be conclusive) to conduct a pigment (skin) test with the pigment to be used for the procedure. Please read Section 10 about pigment (skin) testing.

41) Do you have dry eyes?

> Prospective clients with dry eyes will require more moisture applied to the eyes before, during, and after eyeliner procedures than clients who don't suffer from a dry-eye condition. Insufficient applications of lubricant moisture and not allowing natural blinking during momentary breaks can result in the requirement for medical attention. Keep in mind that some clients with a severe dry-eye condition may have had a surgical occlusion of the punctum, whereby tiny plugs were inserted to block the tear ducts from draining much-needed fluid or they are surgically closed altogether. Take care in performing stretching techniques so as not to dislodge the plugs. For clients who report a serious dry-eye syndrome, consider asking the prospective client to obtain a medical clearance, as a dry-eye sufferer's worsening condition might be attributed to the eyeliner procedure. For the most part, however, eyeliner is a very welcome procedure for people who suffer from a dry-eye condition. A dry-eye condition does not affect an eyebrow or lip procedure process, although a related dry-eye condition like Sjögren's Syndrome can also cause dry mouth.

42) Do you intentionally tan—direct sun or tanning bed?

Clients who intentionally tan will find their pigments will fade much sooner than that of a person who avoids UV rays. Please read the section regarding solar exposure and care of permanent cosmetic procedures for more information.

43) Do you personally have a history of cancer?

Technicians will want to inquire as to the cancer type, location, treatments that resulted, and current medications associated with the condition. If the cancer history is recent or occurred in the area that will now be tattooed, request the prospective client to consult with their physician to determine if they are a good candidate for permanent cosmetics.

44) Do you have a history of stroke or heart attack?

Technicians must use good judgment based on when this history occurred. If there are medications involved, and the prospective client remains under a physician's care for the condition, request that she or he consult with their physician to determine if they are a good candidate for permanent cosmetics.

45) Do you have problems being anesthetized for a dental procedure?

A *yes* answer to this question is a good indication that there may also be problems getting the prospective client anesthetized and continue to keep them comfortable with our anesthetics. Clients who are resistant to anesthetics have enzymes more efficient at breaking down anesthetic agents. They are known as fast acetylators. Please read Section 19, which addresses effective use of anesthetics, for detailed information. Some prospective clients may say they cannot have normal anesthetics during dental procedures because they get heart pounding or similar reports. This may be due to the epinephrine in some anesthetics. The topical use of epinephrine which is an ingredient in some post–broken skin anesthetics made for the permanent cosmetic industry is not usually considered a problem but if in doubt, use an anesthetic that does not contain epinephrine.

46) Do you hypopigment when the skin is compromised?

Hyperpigmentation (darkening of the skin) is far more common, especially for Fitzpatrick skin types IV–VI, than is hypopigmentation (lightening of the skin color or absence of color in the skin). True hypopigmentation occurs when the skin cells lose pigment and skin tissue becomes whiter. However, there are various types of *whitening* of skin including *paleness* (not actually related to pigment but related to a reduced blood supply). Hypopigmentation, whitening, or other *skin color changes* need prompt professional medical investigation for correct diagnosis. It is suggested technicians do not work on any area that is obviously hypopigmented until the prospective client has received a diagnosis and clearance to proceed with the procedure from a physician.

47) Are you allergic to colorants?

It is common thinking that people who are allergic to colorants generally are not also sensitive or allergic to ingredients in permanent cosmetic pigments. Many still feel if a prospective client answers *yes* to this question, technicians may want to suggest a pigment (skin) test before initiating a permanent cosmetics procedure. Pigment (skin) testing is a complex subject and rarely considered conclusive, but there is no harm in conducting the test especially for a person with extreme allergy issues as long as not prohibited by regulations in your geographical area. With that said, however, nonmedical technicians cannot read or diagnose the results of the test. The prospective client should be directed to see their physician for a medical determination regarding the results of a pigment (skin) test area.

48) Do you have glaucoma or other medical eye condition?

It is recommended by many in the industry that technicians do not provide eyeliner services to a client who has glaucoma, as a minimum without clearance from a doctor. Many glaucoma patients are well controlled by medication and/or surgical intervention, but this is a medical condition affecting pressure on the optic nerve, and during eyeliner procedures stretching techniques are employed. Consider the liability if a client with glaucoma reports their condition has worsened after an eyeliner procedure. If other eye diseases are present, request a prospective client to obtain clearance from their physician before proceeding with an eyeliner procedure, or just consider the fact that this person is not a good candidate for permanent cosmetic eyeliner.

49) Do you have arthritis?

People with arthritis may require assistance onto and off the procedure bed or chair. In order to remain comfortable during the procedure, depending on where the arthritis is active, technicians may want to take short breaks and allow the client to sit or stand up. Sometimes a properly covered pillow behind the knees, etc., provides great relief. Communicate frequently with the client during the procedure.

50) Do you have high or low blood pressure?

People with high blood pressure may be on prescription or over-the-counter (OTC) medications. Inquire and determine if this affects the ability to safely or effectively perform the procedure. If in doubt, ask the prospective client to consult with a physician regarding the safety of the procedure.

51) Do you have sinus problems?

Procedural activity at the eyebrow bridge and bulb areas and at locations near the inner canthus of the eye can cause clients to sneeze and need to blow their nose. Always provide clients with a tissue and be prepared to stop the procedure to allow them to sneeze and blow their nose.

52) Have you been diagnosed with any type of hepatitis?

> Hepatitis is a disease of the liver and can be life-threatening. A prospective client with hepatitis B or C may be in very poor health and those in poor health do not heal well. Request a prospective client who has ever been diagnosed with hepatitis B or C to consult with their physician before scheduling a permanent cosmetics procedure. Please read Section 5, which addresses hepatitis, for more details.

Informed Consent: What to Advise and Why

An informed consent document is the prospective client's verification and acknowledgment that the risks and permanency of the tattooing process/procedure are effectively stated and understood.

The form, provided as an example, at the end of this section is used as an example and consists of acknowledgments, understanding, and/or agreements to the following:
Note: Depending on your locality, it may be a requirement to comply with state, local, or country governing agency mandates for informed consent information that is not cited in this section. Always comply with governing agency mandates. Review by your liability insurance provider is also recommended.

- That the nature and method of the proposed permanent makeup (cosmetic tattoo) procedure has been explained, including the usual risks inherent in the procedure process, and the possibility of complications during or following its performance.
- That there may be a certain amount of discomfort or pain associated with the procedure and that other adverse side effects may include minor and temporary bleeding, bruising, redness, or other discoloration and swelling.
- That fever blisters (herpes simplex virus type 1) may occur on the lips following lip procedures.
- That fading or loss of pigment may occur.
- That secondary infection in the area of the procedure may occur; however, if properly cared for, it is rare.
- That you cannot fully determine if a procedure would result in an allergic reaction.
- That the pigment (skin) test has been explained and the client has had the opportunity to request or decline the test. If a pigment (skin) test has been requested, that it is the client's responsibility to seek the advice of a medical professional (a physician) to determine the outcome of the test.
- That you have been informed of any existing health conditions and the prescription or nonprescription medications (if any) taken for those conditions.
- That the client acknowledges that complications are always possible and that following the pre-and post-procedure instructions are mandatory.
- That hyperpigmentation or hypopigmentation is a possibility.

- That the client has received written aftercare instructions.
- That the procedure is permanent and no representations have been made as to the ability to later change or remove the results of the procedure.
- That future laser or other skin-altering procedures such as plastic surgery may alter and degrade the permanent cosmetics.
- That permanent cosmetics is not an exact science and no guarantees are made.
- That the client agrees to pre- and post-procedure photographs and that you have the client's permission to use these photographs at your discretion. *Note*: A client may not give permission to use the photographs taken at your discretion. If there are limits to the use of the photographs, these limitations should be so noted on the consent form. However, as a minimum, the client must agree to pre- and post-procedure photographs for their official client file. It is recommended to decline to provide services to anyone who refuses to do so.
- That the choice to have permanent cosmetic procedures performed is the client's choice alone and that the client agrees to any actions or conduct reasonably necessary to perform the procedure.
- That the client is aware that the herpes simplex virus type 1 (HVS-1) may manifest as a result of a lip procedure. This statement is made twice to emphasize the importance of the client's understanding.
- That the client understands that tattoos may cause MRI (Magnetic Resonance Imaging) artifacts and that there may be a warming and/or tingling sensation in the permanent cosmetic procedural area during the MRI due to the properties of some pigments. That the client understands she or he should advise a physician she or he has had permanent cosmetics (a tattoo) in the event an MRI procedure is prescribed.
- That the fee for permanent cosmetic services has been discussed and agreed upon.
- That due to the fact that client approval is obtained prior to final selection of color and design applications, a no refund policy is employed.
- That the permanent cosmetic procedure may be a multisession process.
- That the appearance of the procedure as it appears (darkness specifically) and the lightening process has been explained.
- That all color fades and the client is aware that color refreshers will be needed in the future.
- That the client has read and understands the contents of each provision above and has received no warranties or guarantees with respect to the benefits to be realized from or consequences of the permanent cosmetic procedure.
- That the Informed Consent Form remains in effect throughout the entire period of time they are your permanent cosmetic client.
- That the client has had every opportunity to ask questions before signing the form.

Procedure Chart Notes: What to document

Client chart notes provide instant recall for discussions post-procedure. An example of a procedure chart notes form is provided at the end of this section. When the client returns for a follow-up visit, chart notes will reflect what procedure was performed, what device was used, the needle configuration utilized, and which anesthetics were used. Most importantly for liability purposes, consider providing space for the client to initial evidencing that sterilized needles were opened in the client's presence (reference the provided procedure chart notes example) and that if eyeliner was performed, she or he is being released in good condition.

There should be a separate section for procedure notes. Technicians will use this section for each procedure performed, by date, to enter professional observations and information about the client and the procedure.

The chart notes are also the appropriate place to note a number of important elements of the procedure. As examples, if the client was more comfortable with the anesthetics used at the onset of the procedure or if anesthetic brands were changed during the process; if the client preferred to design their own eyebrows prior to the procedure; if the client sought a physician's clearance before proceeding with the procedure; or a host of other comments technicians find imperative as a matter of record. Any important data may be documented for the sake of future conversations with the client, or as a matter of record for liability defense purposes should be recorded in this section of the chart notes.

All files with the exception of photographs that clients may have released for the technician's use are considered confidential to clients and must be securely protected for the privacy of their health data. All client files should be kept in a storage area that is not accessible to others.

Sample Forms

On the following pages are sample for you to review. Included are the three forms discussed in this section (client history profile, informed consent, and procedure chart notes). These samples can be used as a starting point when designing your forms. No one form can be considered all-inclusive for all regulatory jurisdictions, so be sure to contact your local regulatory authorities to ensure you are collecting the required data. Also, it is advisable to have your forms reviewed by your insurance provider and legal representative to ensure the wording is appropriate and acceptable.

Client History Profile Form

Name		Date	Gender - F☐ M☐	Age
Address		City	State	Zip
Employer/Occupation		Ph-H	Ph-W	Ph-Cell
How did you select me for your permanent cosmetic services?		E-Mail	Physician's Name	Physician's Ph. No.

#			Question	#			Question
1	YES	NO	Are you pregnant or nursing?	27	YES	NO	Do you consume aspirin daily?
2	YES	NO	Have you had any alcohol in the last 24 hours?	28	YES	NO	Are you under treatment for depression?
3	YES	NO	Have you ever had cold sores/herpes/fever blisters?	29	YES	NO	Do you have a history of cold sores/fever blisters?
4	YES	NO	Do you have any allergies to latex?	30	YES	NO	Are you sensitive to petroleum-based products?
5	YES	NO	Have you had a laser or chemical peel within 6 months?	31	YES	NO	Do you have Botox injections?
6	YES	NO	Have you ever had any permanent cosmetics or tattoos applied?	32	YES	NO	If you have permanent cosmetics or tattoos did you have any problems with healing after they were applied?
7	YES	NO	Do you bruise easily?	33	YES	NO	Are you undergoing radiation or chemotherapy treatment?
8	YES	NO	Do you routinely use Retin-A, glycolic, or other exfoliating products?	34	YES	NO	Are you now, or have you ever been on the acne treatment Accutane?
9	YES	NO	Do you wear contact lenses?	35	YES	NO	Do you have an implanted cardiac device (ICD)
10	YES	NO	Are you allergic or sensitive to any metals, for instance, metals used for jewelry?	36	YES	NO	Do you take prescription drugs?
11	YES	NO	Do you have any problems healing from small wounds?	37	YES	NO	Are you anemic?
12	YES	NO	Do you use Latisse® or any other eyelash growth product?	38	YES	NO	Do you have a history of skin sensitivities?
13	YES	NO	Do you use tobacco? If you use tobacco you may heal slower and this affects the timing on scheduling a touch-up appointment, if applicable.	39	YES	NO	Do you have any medical condition that has resulted in a medical professional requiring you to pre-medicate with an antibiotic prior to a dental or other invasive procedure?
14	YES	NO	Do you have a heart conditions?	40	YES	NO	Do you have allergies to topical makeup?
15	YES	NO	Are you diabetic? If so, Type 1 or Type 2?	41	YES	NO	Do you have dry eyes?
16	YES	NO	Do you have any autoimmune disorders?	42	YES	NO	Do you intentionally tan—direct sun or tanning bed?
17	YES	NO	Are you sensitive or allergic to hand creams or body lotions?	43	YES	NO	Do you *personally* have any history of cancer?
18	YES	NO	Do you have your lips injected with filler materials?	44	YES	NO	Do you have a history of stroke or heart attack?
19	YES	NO	Do you menstruate? If yes: Next cycle date	45	YES	NO	Do you have problems being anesthetized for a dental procedure?
20	YES	NO	Do you hyperpigment? (Tendency to develop dark spots in the skin from wounds or sun)	46	YES	NO	Do you hypopigment (lack of pigment in the skin)?
21	YES	NO	Do you tend to develop keloid or hypertrophy scars?	47	YES	NO	Are you allergic to colorants?
22	YES	NO	Do you scar easily from minor skin injuries?	48	YES	NO	Do you have glaucoma or any other medical eye condition?
23	YES	NO	Do you have any seizure related conditions?	49	YES	NO	Do you have arthritis?
24	YES	NO	Do you have a tendency to faint or become dizzy?	50	YES	NO	Do you have high or low blood pressure?
25	YES	NO	Do you bleed excessively from minor cuts?	51	YES	NO	Do you have sinus problems?
26	YES	NO	Do you have prosthetic implants?	52	YES	NO	Have you ever been diagnosed with hepatitis?

If you answered Yes to any questions above, use the space below and the reverse side of this form to provide an explanation. Correlate your explanations to a specific question number. A yes answer does not indicate you are not an acceptable candidate for permanent cosmetics. It may simply be information that is valuable to me as your technician as each person's body is unique, or it may indicate that based on any health conditions that affect healing, it would be advisable or required for you to consult with your physician before proceeding. If this form has not addressed a medical condition you have, please list it below.

Client Signature: _____ Date: _____

Informed Consent Form

Client Name: _____

The nature and method of the proposed permanent cosmetic (cosmetic tattoo) procedure has been explained to me by my technician and/or by her or his associate(s) including the usual risks inherent in the tattooing process, and the possibility of complications during or following its performance. I understand there may be a certain amount of discomfort or pain associated with the procedure and that other adverse side effects may include minor and temporary bleeding, bruising, redness, or other discoloration and swelling. Fever blisters may occur on the lips following lip procedures. Fading or loss of pigment may occur. Secondary infection in the area of the procedure may occur; however, if properly cared for, is rare. _____ *(Init)*

- I understand a pigment (skin) test of the pigment to be used for my procedure is offered upon request and the test result is not assessed by a medical professional unless I make arrangements to have this done myself. A nonreactive skin test does not prevent an allergic reaction occurring at a future point in time. I accept all associated risks of requesting or declining pigment (skin) test.

    I decline the skin test _____ (Init) OR **I request a skin test** _____ (Init)

    Please initial one of these options.

    Client Signature _____ Date _____

- I have informed my permanent cosmetic technician and/or her or his associates of any existing health problems. _____ *(Init)*

- I acknowledge that complications are always possible as a result of the permanent cosmetic procedure, particularly in the event my post-procedural instructions are not followed. _____ *(Init)*

- I acknowledge that hyperpigmentation (darkening of the skin) or hypopigmentation (the absence of color in the skin), or scarring is a possibility as result of my body's reaction to the skin being broken during the procedure. I realize that my body is unique and that my permanent makeup technician and/or her associate(s) cannot predict how my skin may react as a result of this procedure. _____ *(Init)*

- I acknowledge the receipt of written instructions advising me of the proper care of my procedures and I recognize the absolute necessity for following these instructions. _____ *(Init)*

- I acknowledge that the procedure will result in a permanent change to my appearance and that no representations have been made to me as to the ability to later change or remove the results. _____ *(Init)*

- I understand that future laser treatments or other skin altering procedures, such as plastic surgery, implants, and injections may alter and degrade my permanent makeup. I further understand that such changes are not the responsibility of my permanent makeup technician. I further understand that such changes in my appearance may not be correctable through further permanent makeup procedures. _____ *(Init)*

- I am aware that cosmetic tattooing is not an exact science, and I acknowledge that no guarantees have been made to me as to the results of the procedure. _____ *(Init)*

- I authorize my permanent cosmetic technician and/or her or his associate(s) to obtain pre- procedural and post-procedural photographs, and give her or him permission to use such photographs for publication and/or for teaching purposes, as she or he chooses. _____ *(Init)*

- I am aware that the herpes simplex virus type 1 (HSV-1) (fever blisters or cold sores) may occur as a result of a lip procedure due to trauma to the lip tissue. The anticipation of an outbreak may be pretreated with antiviral medication, available by prescription from your physician. _____ *(Init)*

- I understand that tattoos may cause MRI (Magnetic Resonance Imaging) artifacts and that there may be a warming and/or tingling sensation in the permanent cosmetic procedural area during the MRI due to the iron oxide (metallic salts) properties of some pigments. It is understood that I should advise my physician that I do have permanent cosmetics (a tattoo) in the event an MRI procedure is prescribed. _____ *(Init)*

- The fee for permanent makeup services has been explained to me and has been agreed upon. I understand the total fee for services rendered is due upon completion of the initial procedure(s) and that there will be separate fees for any future modification of the design(s) or major color change(s). _____ *(Init)*

- Due to the fact that my approval is obtained prior to final selection of color to be implanted and design application(s) to be applied, my technician employs a no refund policy. _____ *(Init)*

- For some skin types and procedures, permanent cosmetics may be a multisession process. In addition to your initial application, you are entitled to a post-evaluation appointment. At the post-evaluation appointment, it will determined if a touch-up to the initial application is required. You must schedule your post-evaluation appointment within 45 days after the initial procedure. _____ *(Init)*

- It has been explained to me that immediately after the procedure(s) is completed, the color will appear darker than when the procedure heals. It has also been explained that within a short period of time, during the healing process, the color will soften. _____ *(Init)*

- All color fades—this is a fact that also applies to pigments (also called colors, colorants, and formulations) used for cosmetic tattooing. After your procedure(s) has been performed and any subsequent work performed at the post-procedure appointment, the pristine appearance of your permanent cosmetics is very dependent on daily maintenance of avoiding direct sunlight (intentional tanning), avoiding strong chemicals applied to the procedural area, and applying a sun block product daily (frequently if in a situation where activities take you in the sun). Color refreshers will be needed at some point in the future. The time frame for that need cannot be predicted, as this aspect of permanent cosmetics is very

client specific. If the procedural area is dense enough (can be easily seen) that one application of pigment will bring the color back to its original appearance, a color refresher fee will be charged that represents a lower charge than the fee charged for new work. If the procedural area is extremely light and only represents a weak version of the original procedure, or if it is not visible, a procedure fee for new work in effect at the appointment when the color is reinstated will be charged.
_____ *(Init)*

- I have read and understand the contents of each paragraph above. I have received no unrealistic warranties or guarantees with respect to the benefits to be realized from, or consequences of, the aforementioned procedure(s). _____ *(Init)*

- Your signature below represents consent for permanent cosmetic services and shall remain in effect during the entire period you remain a client of XXXXX.
  _____ *(Init)*

I acknowledge by signing this consent form, I have been given the full opportunity to ask any and all questions about the permanent makeup procedure(s) and process(es) from my permanent makeup technician and/or her associate(s).

Client: _____ Date: _____

I personally reviewed the above information with my client, or the client's representative.

_____ Date: _____
Permanent Cosmetic Technician

Procedure Chart Notes

Client Name (First, Last)_____

Consultation Date: _____ **Procedure Date:** _____

Procedure Type and Pigment Used: _____

Machine and needle(s) used: _____

Anesthetic Used: Unbroken: _____ **Broken:** _____

Before Photo Taken: _____ **After Photo Taken:** _____

Design of procedure was agreed to, pigment color selection was agreed to, sterilized needles and tubes were shown in manufacturers packaging before opening, and clear aftercare instructions were given and fully understood. **Client initials:** _____

If eyeliner was performed, client verifies (s)he was released in good condition.

Client initials _____
PROCEDURE NOTES: _____
_____
_____

Consultation Date: _____ **Procedure Date:** _____

Procedure Type and Pigment Used: _____

Machine and needle(s) used: _____

Anesthetic Used: Unbroken: _____ **Broken:** _____

Before Photo Taken: _____ **After Photo Taken:** _____

Design of procedure was agreed to, pigment color selection was agreed to, sterilized needles and tubes were shown in manufacturers packaging before opening, and clear aftercare instructions were given and fully understood. **Client initials:** _____

If eyeliner was performed, client verifies (s)he was released in good condition.

Client initials _____
PROCEDURE NOTES: _____
_____
_____

References

1. Kate Ciampi RN, CPCP assisted with the compilation of information contained in this portion of the textbook.

Section 12

Documenting Permanent Cosmetic Work with Photography

Learning Objectives

Introduction

Most people enjoy taking casual pictures with friends and family, they are precious keepsakes for gathering and represent fond memories. Selfies for Internet postings are popular.

Well-taken photographs of permanent cosmetic work represent a business interest and the opportunity to build an impressive portfolio for marketing purposes and to offer prospective clients the opportunity to see the various aspects of permanent cosmetics. Business camera selections and photographs taken require planning.

In the business arena, all photographs taken of a client before, during, and after a procedure has been conducted represent a record that may be called upon to support a contested issue. Pictures also provide historical images that technicians may want to study and/or review with clients at some point in the process.

Technicians should purchase equipment that is easily operated (or from a source that offers classes/professional direction) and that allows consistently clear close-up photographs to be taken.

Objective

The following section provides insight into the world of permanent cosmetic photography. The technician will become acquainted with the many purposes client photographs serve in a permanent cosmetic business. Completing this section will also ensure the reader recognizes the importance of being an accomplished operator of the camera selected to support this element of required business documentation.

Section 12 - Documenting Permanent Cosmetic Work with Photography

Photography is a tool that is utilized as a powerful means to demonstrate, communicate, and document through the presentation of images. The concept that one picture says a thousand words remains as true today as the day the words were first uttered.

Makeup artists, medical professionals, estheticians, and numerous other professionals rely on images to support client files and to showcase the benefits and results of services rendered.

Before and after photographs are essential elements of the permanent cosmetic business and all technicians should begin to develop a professional portfolio immediately upon offering services. Photographs serve many purposes in the permanent cosmetic workplace:

- A showcase of procedures conducted documenting how clients appear before, immediate after, and healed;
- Documents to support any inquiries made on behalf of an insurance provider or legal representative;
  (**Note:** Before and after photographs may be a requirement for insurance coverage;)
- A visual file to refer to for follow-up (top-up, perfection appointments) and touch-up (color boosts) appointments;
- A visual document to study for educational purposes.

Client photographs are an integral part of our services. It is important that permanent cosmetic technicians acquire quality photography equipment that allows them to develop the skills to operate the selected equipment well and easily take clear close-up photographs. Remember, there is only one opportunity to take a before picture of a client. Once the permanent cosmetic service(s) has been performed, the image of how the client appeared before the procedure is lost forever.

During the consultation, many prospective clients will voice their concern about how they will look immediately after the procedure is performed. Will they look swollen or bruised? Will the color of their procedures appear darker than when healed? Will the timing of the procedure interfere with scheduled events? The unknown is sometimes far worse when imagined. When prospective clients are shown photographs of different clients immediately after a procedure is performed, this brings reality into the conversation. These photographs will put many fears at ease and help a prospective client determine appropriate scheduling for the procedure.

The healed version of permanent cosmetic photographs provides equally important information. By comparing the immediately after and healed versions of the service performed, a prospective client learns more about how the procedural area changes in appearance as it heals. She or he also witnesses the immediately after versus the softer appearance that evolves after inflammation has subsided and new skin has healed over the procedure area. The color is then seen through the filter of the skin.

The eyebrow procedure is typically bolder in color than it will once healing is underway due to inflammation and color that is trapped in the epidermis before exfoliation commences. Clients are often relieved to see how the appearance of boldness diminishes in a short period of time.

Lip procedures may sometimes require a lengthy explanation about how it is normal for there to be a certain percentage of color loss on the vermilion border and vermilion, and how the exfoliation process may cause the lips to appear very chapped during healing. Lip procedures typically appear swollen and the color much more vibrant than after the healing period; especially full lip procedures. This could be of concern to the client who has requested a natural appearing color. This prolonged explanation can be better clarified with the support of a few before, immediately after, and healed photographs of lip procedures. Some very obliging clients may agree to come in a few days after the initial procedure and allow photos to be taken of how the lips appear at different intervals during the healing process.

Eyeliner procedures often require an explanation as to why the immediately after appearance may differ substantially in appearance from the healed version. The eyelids can swell from the trauma of tattooing causing the eyeliner to appear wider than it will after the swelling has subsided. Also, the color of the eyeliner is more vibrant than it will appear after exfoliation and new skin has healed over the tattooed color.

Overall, photographs are a substantial benefit when consulting with a client to prepare them for the service(s) requested, and to schedule at a time when they can clear their calendar for appropriate aftercare attention.

Being a good communicator helps; however, all attempts to explain different phases of the permanent cosmetic procedure are usually not as quite as effective as a collection of photographs.

Regardless of the choice of equipment, practice makes perfect and before depending on acquired skills to capture the perfect set of photographs for historical client files portfolio presentation and marketing purposes, practice is recommended. If necessary, acquire the needed skills through a photography class at a community college or an adult education class.

The Client Photograph Consent and Usage Release

An informed consent form (an example is provided in Section 11), should always include a request for a client release of photographs. In the event a client refuses to provide a photograph release, technicians should advise the client that as a minimum, photographs are required for their confidential client file. If a client refuses to have photographs taken entirely, even under the circumstances that they will be kept private in their client file, it is recommended to advise the client that photographs are a contingency of providing the requested service(s).

Photographs are evidence to show how a client appeared before, immediately after the procedure(s), and when healed. People are unpredictable and it is very important to have documents (photographs) that reflect exactly how a client appeared during each segment of the process. This applies to all work performed during the professional relationship with each client.

Selecting Equipment for Photography

There is a wide variety of cameras available that work well for taking photographs of permanent cosmetic procedures, including camera features on mobile devices and tablets; each has its own strengths and weaknesses for consideration.

For documenting permanent cosmetics, one of the primary considerations is the ability to take good indoor photographs without the need for additional professional lighting equipment. The clarity of detail is also important to capture. Preferences and needs will vary from between technicians and their studios where the photographs will be taken.

All cameras by design are generally meant to take clear photographs. While manufacturer marketing and reviews will often state *their* camera does a better job than all others, fundamentally, it comes down to knowing how to operate the camera properly. An expensive camera does not equate to good photos if the owner doesn't know how to use it as intended. A good photographer can usually get nice pictures on a variety of camera types; even if the camera is less expensive.

Although there may be some who prefer the film or instant type cameras (e.g. Polaroid), for the purposes of this section, digital options will be addressed. The primary downside of cameras that require film development is that the results of pictures taken are not instantly known. Although not thought to be as commonly used, instant type cameras and self-developing file are still available. Both the film and instant cameras produce hard copy pictures, that when added to client files may result in the need for increased physical file space.

A digital camera is a common selection that is available in an array of different styles, sizes, and costs. The good news is these cameras are relatively easy to operate with manufacturer directions and operational information. Many are advertised as a *point and shoot* camera with auto function settings.

For the more advanced camera setups, taking a beginning photography class at a community college or joining a photography club are options to become more comfortable with the operation of the camera. If a person is more self-study oriented, there are countless books on how to take better pictures at your local library or that can be purchased. There are also many instructional articles, videos, and message forums on the Internet. Don't forget the operational manual that came with the camera, tablet or mobile phone – it will also be a great resource.

Digital cameras have become commonly used in the permanent cosmetic industry because the technician can immediately view the photos taken. Cameras on mobile devices also provide good photography options. There are also optional lens attachments specifically for mobile devices that can help extend the capabilities of the device.

For digital cameras, memory card storage capacity is important to understand, but first one needs to understand the size of files that are produced by the camera. This is expressed as the number of mega-pixels (MP) a camera can capture. In recent years, the number of mega-pixels (MP) reported in the specifications of cameras, has become less important. The mega-pixel war has subsided – any camera rated at 5 mega-pixels or higher will be sufficient for documentation purposes. A larger number of mega-pixels does not necessarily equal better once an 8-10MP or higher has been reached. A larger number of mega-pixels is desirable for large prints (16"x20" or larger) or other specialized applications (e.g. wallpaper, banners, or billboards). Today, a person would be hard-pressed to find a digital camera with a capability of less than 8MP – even for a low-end camera, mobile phone, or tablet.

With regards to the size of a camera's memory card, the greater number of mega-pixels, the larger the digital picture (files) will be. This will be a driving force on determining the size of memory card that will be needed. Also remember, a camera with a larger MP rating will create larger files, and that will take up more space on a computer and backup/cloud storage than a camera with a lower MP rating.

The Date and Time Stamp Feature

Many cameras provide the ability to imprint a date to each photograph taken, and in some instances, the time as well. These are important features that authenticate client records as to when the procedure was performed and the correlating photographs that were taken before, immediately after the procedure, and when the procedure has healed. There may also be a feature to create albums. This is very important information if client photographs taken during the permanent cosmetic tattooing process are ever called upon to support an insurance or legal question. Also, clients sometimes forget how they once appeared and photographs provide historical documents to remind clients of certain physical characteristics they may need to be reminded of.

The Red-Eye Reduction Feature

Nothing could be more distracting than a photograph of a client with perfectly tattooed permanent cosmetics who appears to have blazing red eyes. Red-eye is caused by the reflection from the subject's eye (retina) caused by an on-camera flash. When a picture is taken with an on-camera flash, the brightness/light from the flash is reflected directly back into the camera lens which creates red-eye. With red-eye reduction features, a pre-flash (or series of quick flashes) occurs just before the picture is taken. This causes the subject's pupils to constrict which reduces the amount of light that can enter the eye. In this brief pupil constricted state, the picture is taken with the flash. The constricted state of the pupil decreases the amount of light able to enter the eye, and as a result, less light is reflected back from the eye, thereby reducing the amount of red-eye captured.

The Flash Feature

The need for a flash is solely dependent on the environment in which pictures are taken and the available natural or professional lighting. Ideally, when possible, using available light, rather than an on-camera flash can be preferable. In a very way similar that red-eye is created from the flash, reflections/hotspots can appear on the procedure areas when using an on-camera flash. Using available light without a flash will help avoid this, or reducing the flash output power (if the camera device has that option, check your camera instructions/manual) can help reduce these hot-spots. More recently, digital cameras have become better at internally processing these hot-spot areas so they are less evident in photos.

Often camera equipment has an auto-flash function. This leaves the decision to use the flash up to the camera's internal algorithms to determine if the flash needs to be used or not.

Macro (Close-up) Feature

Close-up pictures are very important, but moderation for publication is advised. People can find fault with any work if they look close enough, especially newer work that is not completely healed. Nothing is perfect and the closer a person looks, the more minor imperfections they may find. Extreme close-up pictures are fine to use for analytical purposes, but unless the photograph details an important element that could not otherwise be presented, it is not recommended to include them in portfolios. Extremely close-up photographs can show skin imperfections that a person would otherwise not notice. Clients who review a technician's before and after portfolio book are looking to see how normal and natural clients appear, and extreme close-ups don't always represent that concept well.

Some of the best advice offered to a novice photographer is to seek professional advice from those who offer a large selection of photography equipment before making a purchase. Write down the environmental properties of the workplace where the pictures will be taken. Record the quality needed, source of light, the color of a backdrop, and the average distance from which pictures will be taken. Knowledge of these environmental conditions will help people who specialize in photography equipment recommend an appropriate selection.

Post-Processing Software

There are many different options for editing and organizing photographs. Common commercial products such as Adobe Photoshop and Adobe Photoshop Lightroom are available for both Apple and Windows PC. There are platform specific programs such as Apple Photos and iPhoto, and other cross-platform and open-source photo editing software (GNU Image Manipulation Program or GIMP). All provide ways to adjust and enhance photos.

While it can be beneficial to use software to enhance client photos, it is important to remember the purpose of *documentation photos* is to provide verification of the quality of work that has been provided in a sequential form. This at a minimum should include before, immediately after, healed, and any follow-up (top-up) and touch-up (color boosts) visits. Since these are for documentation purposes, the amount of manipulation should be kept to a minimum and original unaltered photo should be kept. Software such as Adobe Lightroom is considered non-destructive to the original photos. The originals are kept in the unmodified states, and any changes made to the photo are tracked in a catalog and are not applied to the original photo; those changes are applied when a photograph is exported or printed. This allows any changes/modifications recorded in the catalog to be undone at any point in time, even weeks, months, or even years later.

There has been a recent backlash against overly manipulated photos in the beauty industry. While a person can become extremely proficient correcting and fixing model or client photos, one needs to remember the importance of ensuring the photos are realistic. Over *photoshopping* can create misleading results and expectations. Cropping, exposure, color temperature, and contrast adjustments would be within the acceptable limits. Using post-production software to completely reshape brows or redesign a lip procedure would create false expectations, misleading results, and should be avoided.

There are also many apps for mobile devices and tablets that can be used to create collages, captions, watermarks, etc. on photos that can easily be shared and posted to social media. A quick search on a device's app store or an internet search on a preferred search engine will provide many different options.

Common Likeness Photographs

At times we see photographs of clients appearing unhappy or sad in the before picture and conversely to appearing as if they just won the lottery in the after pictures. The general public is wary of before and after photographs and they routinely look for how another person may be trying to mislead them. Don't give a prospective client the opportunity to develop mistrust and take the chance they will not look at photographs as an honest representation of permanent cosmetic work performed.

In order to keep the before, immediately after, and healed photographs consistent, take the photos from the same distance in all shots. It is wise to make a mark on the floor to stand on each time a photograph is taken. Once becoming familiar with a selected camera's zoom properties, it will become easier to automatically and consistently zoom in for close-ups of the procedural area.

Client Positioning and Appearance

After lying down for an hour or so during the procedure, it is not uncommon for a client to want to freshen-up. Freshening-up is a good thing unless during the freshening-up they client may apply makeup that they did not have on in the before picture. Discourage the application of any makeup the client did not have on in the before photo. The hair should also be tidied up for the after picture. When rearranging tousled hair back to the before picture look, take special care that hair is not obscuring the procedure area(s).

In preparation for photographs of a client, tell the client to sit up straight and give a slight smile, but without showing teeth. Not everyone has nice teeth and then there are some clients who can just dazzle others with their veneers and whitening results. Either way, a good or bad set of teeth can take attention away from the work a technician is attempting to display, so keep the smile to a pleasing minimum. Poor posture causes people to appear unconfident or sad, whereas someone who is sitting up straight appears proud and alert.

If the photograph is full-face and the client is sitting up, ask the client to look directly into the camera and not be tempted to look up or down as the picture is snapped unless being directed to do so (some close-up pictures of eyebrow and eyeliner procedures are best taken with the client's head angled slightly upward and taken from the side of the client). It is also important to watch closely for clients who tend to raise one eyebrow when posing for eyebrow pictures. For some this is a natural inclination but can cause the appearance of inappropriately placed eyebrow procedures. To discourage this if the client has an inclination to do so, ask the client to close their eyes as if they are resting. Then have the client slowly open their eyes and look at the camera. Snap the picture before the client automatically raises one of their eyebrows.

The point of consistently creating a similar environment and pose, for the before, immediately after, and healed pictures is an attempt to visually convince the viewer that the only physical difference (the client may be wearing different clothes in the healed photo) between these pictures is that of the permanent cosmetic work that has been performed.

The Photography Location and Backdrop

By experimenting with photography equipment, determine the best location to set up an area for taking photos. Although it is common to take close-ups of a client's procedure service while lying down on the procedure bed, for their client records at least one full-face photograph should be taken. A close-up of an eyebrow, eyeliner, or lip area doesn't identify who the client is, and that is important for insurance purposes and the client's historical files. Once the best location has been determined based on lighting availability, consider the color of the backdrop that will serve as the background for each photo taken; some colors are better than others for good photography depending on the lighting in the studio.

The color of the backdrop is important. Backdrop colors that are white, gray, or black are often recommended. There is an assortment of information and options on the best colors for a photography backdrop available on the Internet. If a consistent backdrop for photography is chosen, select one that is agreeable to good photography while keeping the aesthetics of the studio décor in mind. Backdrops can be purchased from a variety of sources. Search *Photography Backdrops* on the Internet. There is a large selection of colors and sizes to choose from.

A common backdrop in each portfolio photograph gives professional presentation flair to photography work. If portfolios appear confusing, the viewer may become distracted by the variety of backdrops (a variety of locations where photographs are taken) behind the same client. With consistency, potential clients will not be distracted when looking at a photo portfolio and will make assessments of the tattooed work more easily; consistency is important.

Presentation Portfolios

Presentation, presentation, presentation. Once good photographs have been taken, how they are received is often very dependent on how they are presented. The value of photographs decreases if they are not readily available and grouped together by client or service type so that comparisons can be easily viewed.

When technicians are just beginning to offer permanent cosmetic services it takes time to acquire a large number of photographs of permanent cosmetic work. It is a challenge each new technician is faced with. On the other hand, the beginning of your new career is just the right time to acquire good photograph equipment, decide how photos will be grouped for potential client viewing, and remain consistent so that you are not later faced with a large project of going back in time and searching for or rearranging a large number of photographs.

People who have a mobile device or tablet that they use for photographs may allow for album collections, or use an app which can be used to group photos by each client. Websites are perfect for displaying work performed in an organized manner that tells a story of your work.

Presentation Placement

Many potential clients will not be able to remember from one photo to another the prior photograph looked like. Showcase photos side-by-side when possible, or if displaying the before, immediately after, and healed photos grouped on one image (made possible with photo software on a computer by arranging digital images), be consistent with size from one set of images to the next. Don't confuse the viewer with inconsistent placement and size of the before, immediately after, and healed versions of permanent cosmetic work. See Figure 12-1 and Figure 12-2 on the next page.

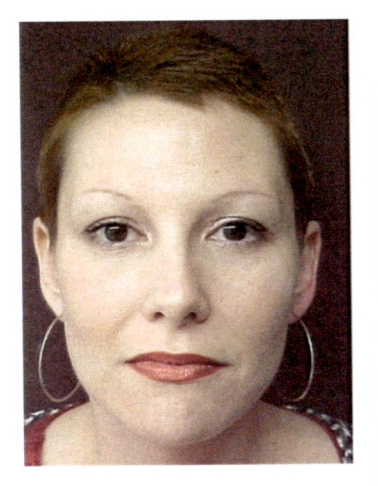

Section 12 - Documenting Permanent Cosmetic Work with Photography

Before Eyebrow Procedure

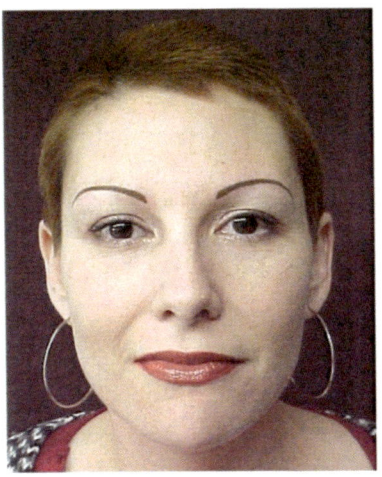

Immediately After Eyebrow Procedure

Eyebrows Healed 30 Days Post Procedure

Figure 12-1: Inconsistent Placement and Size

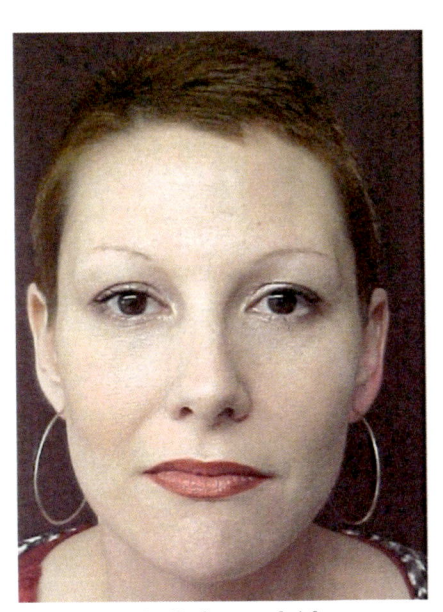

Figure 12-2: Before and After

Summary

- Select a camera, mobile device, or tablet that allows you to take sharp and consistently clear photographs by getting to know and use the equipment properly.

- Practice taking pictures before using the equipment for business photography purposes.

- Designate a location in the workplace that serves as the client photography area. This will help with taking constant appearing photos without having to adjust the camera for different lighting conditions, subject distances, etc.

- Construct or purchase a backdrop using a color that is pleasing to the eye of the camera.

- After the procedure, allow the client to freshen-up but **without** applying makeup that was not present in the before photograph.

- Advise the client to sit up straight, tell them where you want them to look, and ask them to avoid raising either or both eyebrows when posing. A slight smile without the client showing her or his teeth is recommended.

- Stand a consistent distance from the client when taking pictures or be prepared to crop the photos to a consistent size.

- Take photos of a client from a conversational distance as well as close-ups of the procedural area. Close-up photographs allow the technician with the ability to analyze work.

- Arrange the before and after pictures side-by-side or in a manner that reflects the before, immediately after, and healed photographs in proper sequence.

- Investigate photo apps for digital devices and tablets that allow for editing and grouping photos together.

- Keep original/unaltered photos for documentation purposes.

- If using computer-based software that provides the capability of text identification of the photographs, identify what procedure was performed and the status of the photo, i.e., before, immediately after, or healed procedure.

- Watermarking photographs is recommended but do so in a manner that does not distract from the subject being presented (procedure type). Pictures are sometimes seen with watermarks placed directly across the face, obscuring eyebrows, eyeliner, or lip procedures. While it is recognized that watermarks identify ownership, on the other hand, clients, when viewing your portfolio, need a clear view of the examples of the work that they are being shown.

- For instant recall and study purposes maintain client pictures in specific client-based folders or by procedure type as preferred.

Resources

- Specialty camera stores will have a wide variety of camera types to select from and experienced personnel to work with to select a camera appropriate for the intended use and environment.
- Community colleges and adult education programs offer evening photography courses, which is an economical way to learn basic camera operation and photography skills.
- Camera magazines offer overview articles and ratings about different cameras available on the market.
- Mobile devices and tablets provide for photography, some of which have options for date identification and the creation of client or procedure-specific albums.

The Internet is a convenient source of information for research on camera, mobile device, tablet cost, and the local distributors in any given area. Reviews from people who have previously purchased a particular type and model of equipment are commonplace on the Internet.

Section 13

Identifying Skin Undertones

Learning Objectives

Introduction

The subject of skin undertones is an important topic frequently discussed in the permanent cosmetic industry. Are the client's skin undertones cool or warm? Technicians often struggle with the task of identifying the base (underlying) color of the client's skin in the procedural area where they will be depositing colorants/pigments. For educational purposes, all tattoo powders from which formulations are developed are colorants/pigments (both terms are interchangeable).

The analysis is complicated by the skins' overtone appearance which has been subject to UV rays (incidental sun exposure/ tanning practices) and topical makeup. From conclusions drawn, and with the client's preferences for color considered, tattoo formulations with the appropriate base colors are selected.

Objective

Upon completion of this section, the reader will better understand diverse skin undertones and be prepared to more easily identify them for color selection purposes.

Section 13 - Identifying Skin Undertones

Skin undertone is one of the two factors to be considered in the equation of *skin undertone + tattooed color = healed true color*. They help guide technicians during the color selection evaluation process to one that will appear as anticipated when healed.

Many factors influence how the eyes perceive skin undertones. For instance, people with darker (Fitzpatrick IV–VI) skin overtones may tan and appear a golden bronze (warm appearing) color. This represents the person's skin *overtones*. In reality the person with a golden bronze, warm appearing overtone actually has a green, violet, or blue (cool) skin undertone.

Even incidental sun exposure may also cause lighter skin types to appear warm (overtone appearance) when in reality their skin has blue, red-violet, or violet (cool) skin undertones. These are examples, as true skin undertone types will vary as they are masked by overtones (the effects of sun exposure, tanning, or cosmetic products).

The technician's workplace lighting is also a factor. If several different lighting sources (lamps) are lined up side by side and a bare arm moved under each one, the skin on the arm will likely appear a slightly different color under each different lamp. Under one lighting source to another, the arm would appear cooler, warmer, and some more neutral than under the more cool or warm lighting sources.

Although not an exact science, identifying ancestral backgrounds sometimes will reveal generalized skin undertone information which can be helpful during the skin analysis and color selection phase of the procedure.

Below are skin samples and a description of each skin undertone type. Once a technician has identified the client's skin undertone, and the client has voiced their color preferences (from lighter to darker and warmer to cooler) the formulation to be used for the procedure to be conducted becomes clearer.

NOTE: *The skin samples are provided to give an idea of the different color/tones of the described skin - but due variations during digital capturing of the skin types and the associated difficulties with color matching in the printing process, the printed version may not be a completely accurate representation, despite the authors and publishers best attempts.*

Also, complete faces were purposely not included to prevent creating any biases when skin undertone types are being assessed. The color samples shown were taken from the cheek area of a person representing the described skin undertone and magnified with digital imaging. Under normal circumstances (not magnified and digitized) the technician would not see this obvious of skin undertone and other factors discussed would be important during the analysis.

Undertones in the specific procedural area should be identified. The eyelids and lips may reflect more extremes of coolness because of the thinner skin in these areas; the vascular system has more influence and it is more easily seen. As an example, a more mature client may indeed have cooler undertones on the lips or eyelids than they do on their forehead eyebrow area. *Identify skin undertones based on the procedural area, not an overall assessment of the faces in its entirety.*

Figure 13-1 and Figure 13-2 are two examples of how color in the eyelids and lips appear (due to the thinner skin and noticeable vascular activity in those areas) vs. the surrounding skin.

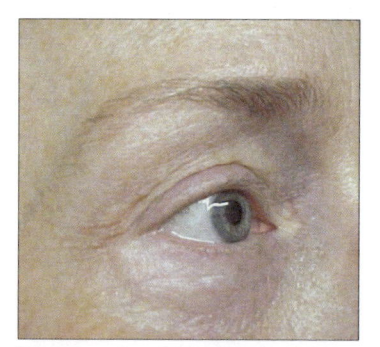

Figure 13-1: Thinner eyelid canvas

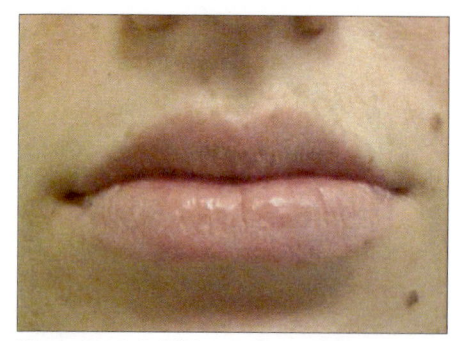

Figure 13-2: Thinner lip canvas

The skin samples below and assigned skin undertone type is based on taking a photographic sample from an area of the cheek (magnified). Other areas of this skin type such as the eyelids or lips may appear different.

Transparent skin (cool)—skin types will appear cool porcelain sometimes with a violet influence that can be seen around the eyes. This is most obvious when the person has lighter skin. As younger adults, the scalp hair of transparent types may appear darker shades of ash brown or more mature clients a soft ash gray. Because many younger clients with this skin type and true scalp hair coloring feel washed-out, they may tend to alter their hair color adding more red or golden highlights.

Ruddy (cool)—skin types have a red-violet, rose-beige, soft pink, or rosy cast to the skin. People who burn and either tan minimally or not at all have significantly less visible melanin, which results in a pink, reddish violet (ruddy) skin undertone. In addition, look for telltale signs: people with ruddy skin tend to flush easily, the ears and décolleté may appear pink or reddish, and usually have distended or broken capillaries near the surface of the skin.

The designator of cool associated with ruddy skin may come as a surprise. Ruddy skin undertones may appear red to the naked eye, and according to traditional color theory, the primary color red is designated as a warm temperature color. However, the excessive vascular factor that contributes to a ruddy undertone is a *red-violet* which is cool.

Many ruddy types may develop *rosacea* (classic symptoms are patchy flushing (redness) and inflammation, particularly on the cheeks, nose, forehead, and around the mouth as they mature). The eye color may vary significantly and the natural scalp hair ranging from a golden blonde, red, reddish brown, or a rich copper color in younger clients. When scalp hair ages and changes color, it often appears to have a graphite or dull grey tone. If more salt than pepper, the white is not a brilliant white, but has more a dull/yellow appearance. Their lips often have a purple or lavender hue to them.

Translucent skin (cool)—skin types will appear cool ivory-porcelain sometimes with a blue influence around the eyes. The lips may appear a pink or lavender color.

This skin type will be most obvious if the person has lighter skin. Younger people with translucent skin undertones may have very dark hair contrasting with their pale skin while more mature people tend to gray early in life. Snow white natural scalp or eyebrow hair is a worthwhile indicator of some mature translucent skin types.

Olive (cool)—skin types appear a golden bronze, or olive. Many people of Mediterranean, American Indian, and some Hispanic descent have olive skin. The natural hair color of olive skin types is often medium or dark brown (brunette).

Sallow (more neutral)—skin types are pale yellow, ivory, or sallow (more neutral than other skin types) undertones without the olive appearance of the Mediterranean skin type. If there is a greenish cast, it will normally appear a yellow-green. This skin type typically has no blue or red cast. This is a common (but not limited to) Korean, Japanese, Taiwanese, and Chinese skin types. The eyes are typically dark and the natural color of hair ranges from medium and dark brown, or black. More mature people may have a warmer gray coloring to their scalp hair.

Peaches and Cream (warm)—skin types are younger (usually under 30 years of age). Their skin appears a pale honey undertone. This is considered a more rare (uncommon) skin undertone type in the permanent cosmetic industry. The peaches and cream types blush easily. Their scalp hair tends to range from a lighter to a deeper golden or strawberry blonde (not auburn or red-brown) to golden gray. The eye coloring is often light but brown eyes are not uncommon.

Rosy (cool)—The rosy skin *overtone* (not undertone) is associated with the traditional cosmetic industry. They type it as warm based on how they would treat it with topical cosmetic colors, not how the skin interacts with a colorant/pigment when tattooed. For the purposes of permanent cosmetic skin undertone evaluation, any skin type with pink or red-bias undertones is cool.

If evaluating a person with a red-violet, rose-beige, or rosy/ruddy cast to the skin, it is ruddy. For the purposes of providing some educational direction, if you see a rosy skin overtone, consider this person a *milder version of ruddy skin undertone.*

Brown Skin (cool)—People with brown skin are cool; but their overtone many appear very bronze and warm. Don't be misled. All brown skin has some degree of cool blue, green, or violet undertones. This group includes but is not limited to people of African-American, some Hispanic, Indian, or West Indian descents. The natural scalp hair coloring is normally dark brown or black and the eyes are typically dark brown.

Extreme black (includes very dark brown) or white (very/extremely cool)—These skin types are often easier to identify than some of the other skin types because of the extreme nature of the skin coloring. This skin type often applies to African Americans or those with Scottish and Welsh ancestry respectively. These type skins appear black (or very dark brown) or appear white (pale) to the extreme. Extremes are typically extremely cool with blue undertones.

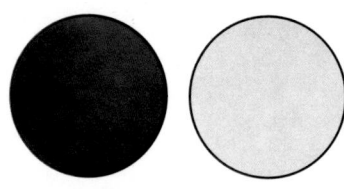

People with a specific ancestral background may be more readily identified as being one of the skin undertone types listed above. However, we live in a multicultural world with innumerable variations of ancestral heritage, so it is important to remember that skin undertones should not be solely be identified by ancestral heritage alone. Some people also tend not to be as dedicated to wearing sunscreen, and as a result what the technician may be viewing is skin that has been subjected to sun exposure that will change seasonally.

Formulation selections are based on what is analyzed and seen on the day of the procedure, however, what isn't often discussed in the permanent cosmetic industry, are the effects of the skin's aging process on healed permanent cosmetic colors.

As people mature, their skin goes through different stages. Among the many changes, the epidermis thins, which results in a cooler appearing skin undertone sometimes obviously rosy or ruddy on people with lighter skin.

As the skin ages, this affects how a colorant/pigment color is seen through the filter of the skin. As a result, depending on how many color refreshers a client may have during their different life stages, color adjustments may need to be considered to accommodate the aged cooler skin undertone. Skin undertones don't get warmer as people age, they get cooler.

Section 14

Working With Fitzpatrick IV–VI Skin Types

Learning Objectives

Introduction

Fitzpatrick IV–VI skin types present professional challenges that can be overcome with proper education. Technicians who take the approach that all skin types will react the same to tattooing fail to make considerations for the probable response of darker skin to a permanent cosmetic procedure. Technicians need to be aware of the biological differences that Fitzpatrick Skin Types IV-VI represent.

Many technicians live in localities where clients with Fitzpatrick IV–VI skin types represent a large percentage of potential clients and for that reason, this subject is included at the fundamental level of education.

For educational purposes, all tattoo powders from which formulations are developed are colorants/pigments (both terms are interchangeable).

Objective

At the completion of this section, the technician will become familiar with many of the unique skin characteristics of clients with Fitzpatrick IV–VI skin types. The technician will be better prepared to know which permanent cosmetic formulations and services are appropriate for clients in this Fitzpatrick skin type range.

Section 14 - Working With Fitzpatrick IV–VI Skin Types

Training that has included information about working with Fitzpatrick skin types IV–VI, which have a propensity to develop post-inflammatory hyperpigmentation (PIH) or scar, is a benefit that prepares novice technicians to professionally evaluate when the odds are for or against completing a successful procedure.

Some trainers may advise their fundamental class students to refrain from offering services to these skin types until they have been further educated on this subject, as there are variables to consider for a novice technician. In many respects, the concerns are justified. There is not an abundant amount of information from skin experts published in our industry on the subject of invasive procedures and Fitzpatrick skin types IV–VI, commonly associated with (but not limited to) Latino, Asian, Indian, Italian, and African American ethnicities. However, considering that a large percentage of the world's population is comprised of people of color, some basic training at the fundamental level is necessary to accommodate the increasing requests for permanent cosmetics. It is important to know when going forward with the procedure may or may not be appropriate.

Fitzpatrick IV–VI skin types generally seem to be, based on the opinions of experienced technicians, more tolerant to the tattooing process of the permanent cosmetic eyebrow and eyeliner procedure. This assumes the client has healthy skin that is unaffected by medical conditions, prescription medications, or extreme sun exposure. The skin of Fitzpatrick IV–VI skin types usually appears and feels thicker to the touch (by degrees depending on the specific skin type involved) and not as thin or fragile as some Fitzpatrick I-IV skin types. This is also a variable depending on the age and health profile of the client and the general overall condition of the skin. Generally speaking, the darker the skin, the more a technician may notice the skin to have a thicker, more compact texture.

Figure 14-1: Ashy Cool Healed Eyebrow

A note of precaution is that it has been published that people of color may tend to develop keloid scarring from injuries to the skin. Based on this concern, always ask about and look for this factor during the consultation. Below is an excerpt that was taken from an article on this topic:

"Black skin is 60 to 70 percent higher in lipid content than white skin and has larger sebaceous glands. A layer of cells in black skin, although thinner, has a higher concentration of cells than white skin. Because the stratum corneum is, therefore, denser in black skin, and the oil glands are larger, black skin is much more prone to lesion formation through follicular impaction."[1]

Scarring any skin type can result from overworking the skin, plain and simple; however, the concern for scarring skin that is a darker color prevails as a common subject discussed among technicians. Photographs have been seen during technician networking sessions of eyebrow procedures conducted on darker skin that resulted in a shiny or slightly raised appearance (indicating scarring). Eyebrows that healed too cool (*ashy*) (see Figure 14-1) and multi-tone and/or hyperpigmented lip liners have also been shown as examples of procedures performed for people of color by technicians who were not well informed.

Proper procedure color selection to achieve the client's expectations and the possibility of the client developing PIH during the healing process are legitimate concerns. For instance, although a medium brown color for an eyebrow procedure may be selected, there are some skin types that will hyperpigment the color to the degree of seeing a darker brown, black-brown, or black color during the healing process. It takes time for skin that develops PIH to return to its normal appearance. This information is offered as a reference to the concept that darker skin may have a tendency to react differently to the permanent cosmetic process than lighter skin.

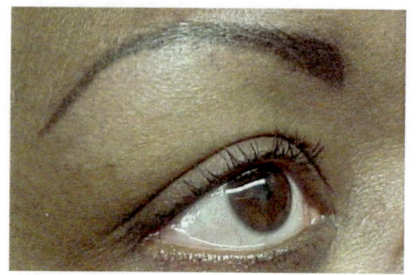

Figure 14-2: Immediately After the Eyebrow Procedure

The right shows examples of a normal healing process (Figure 14-2 through Figure 14-5). During healing, as with all tattoo procedures, the epidermis that heals over the tattooed procedure appears opaque. It takes time for this to resolve and the epidermis become more translucent and show the true color, which can also involve some degree of PIH for several weeks or longer. As a result, schedule the follow-up appointment accordingly. These photos were taken in different lighting.

Figure 14-3: Day 4 of the Healing Process

There are considerations when selecting colorants/pigments for people of color. Fitzpatrick skin types IV–VI may produce some degree of hyperpigmentation when the skin is compromised (broken). A reference point is to look at the knees, hands, and elbows of the potential client. When the skin on people of color has been compromised or comes in contact with friction, the skin may naturally darken due to additional melanin production during the healing process. There may also be evidence of hyperpigmentation around the eyes where people frequently rub their eyes when tired or their eyes water.

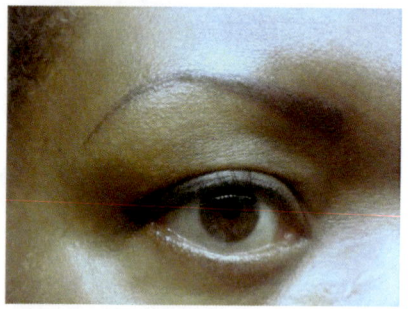

Figure 14-4: Day 5 of the Healing Process

This is not a science, but it often gives some insight to the technician as to what degree of hyperpigmentation the client has produced under other circumstances. Technicians can also ask how the skin reacts to insect bites; look at the prospective client's complexion. Is there evidence of darker spots resulting from acne? If the face has been shaved, is there any sign of hyperpigmentation where the skin may have been nicked with a razor? Analyze how the skin has

Figure 14-5: Day 11 of the Healing Process

reacted to past minor injuries. The answer to these inquiries and observations may have an influence on the color selected for the procedure and some insight as to what to expect.

In regard to technique, a lighter hand during tattooing and a conservative number of passes are recommended. This is actually a good, sound practice for *all* skin types, but the reasoning for emphasizing this point specifically in this section is to caution the novice technician that the skin of people of color may have a propensity to scar more easily than that of lighter skin. There are no set-in-stone tattoo industry guidelines because each client is unique, however, the consensus is *less is better*.

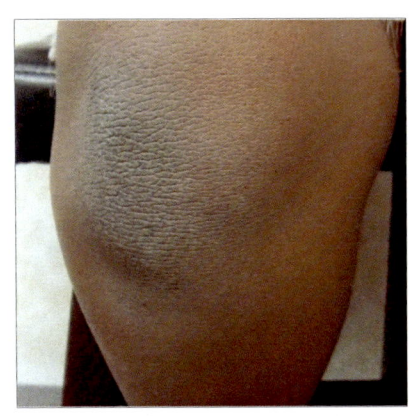

Figure 14-6: Hyperpigmentation on Knees

Another consideration is the ability to make small adjustments to design work. Because of the possibility for Fitzpatrick skin types IV–VI to hyperpigment to different degrees, lightening or removal of color in small areas that could make a big difference in the overall appearance of the procedure is difficult. Although lightening or removal of tattoo colorants/pigments may be successfully accomplished with products made specifically for this procedure, it may be more difficult or improbable to accomplish for people of color. It is likely the area where color has been lightened (or removed) may hyperpigment and ultimately heal to appear darker in the area where there once was tattoo color.

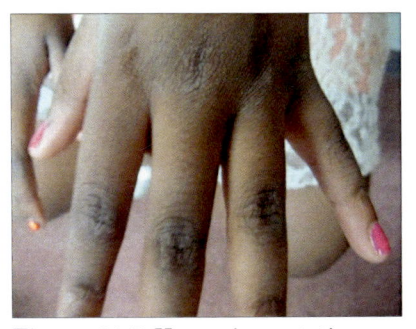

Figure 14-7: Hyperpigmentation on Hands

Always ensure that if there is any modification to the design work needed on the follow-up visit, it will be to make the design larger or the color darker. Again, this is a good way to proceed on all skin types but emphasized for people of color in this section. In this respect, many technicians will initially make eyebrows and eyeliners slightly thinner until the client has had the opportunity to become accustomed to the permanent cosmetics. Choose design work and colors carefully; reversals on darker skin are far more challenging.

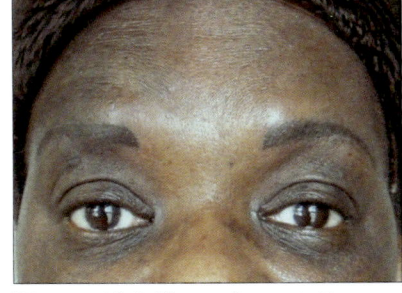

Figure 14-8: Hyperpigmentation around the eyes

Generally, when tattooing Fitzpatrick skin types IV–VI technicians can count on healed eyebrow procedures appearing to be similar to, or one and occasionally two shades darker, than the color used for the procedure. This is assuming a medium range brown colorant/pigment was used. Again, this is specific to each client. Technicians who use brown-black, black-brown, or black because any other color would not have provided the needed contrast on the client's darker skin (usually Fitzpatrick V and VI) may see only a slight change. This is because darker colorants/pigments will usually only result in a dark healed procedure on people with darker skin, although they may see a *too cool* eyebrow result if the technician did not take precautions by adding some degree of warmth to a cool colorant/pigment (the darker the colorant/pigment generally the cooler the colorant/pigment) on a cool skin undertone.

If a technician decides to offer eyebrow or eyeliner services to Fitzpatrick IV–VI, proceed conservatively, inquire about, or observe, hyperpigmentation/hypopigmentation, or scarring from minor injuries, and know when to recognize if additional training is needed.

Figure 14-9 shows an eyebrow procedure conducted with a lighter warm brown formulation for a woman who asked for a softer appearance. It was a foregone conclusion that because of her skin type, the lighter brown would darken somewhat during healing.

The majority of permanent cosmetic clients ask for standard eyeliner colors (dark brown, black-brown, brown-black, black, or charcoal). If hyperpigmentation on a Fitzpatrick IV-VI skin type occurs, this can work to the technician's advantage. Unless the prospective client shows a propensity to scar from minor wounds, eyeliner procedures for people of color should be safe ground, as long as a conservative design is applied. The question is - *Will the eyeliner color provide an adequate contrast to the skin to meet the client's expectations?*

Figure 14-9: Lighter warm brown formulation on Fitzpatrick 5 Skin Type

Figure 14-10 is a top and lower eyeliner tattooed with a black formulation on a Fitzpatrick V skin type. The client was advised early-on that there may not be an adequate contrast to her skin once the procedure healed to meet her expectations. The client was satisfied with the healed results, but once the eyeliner begins to fade, the contrast will not be as obvious.

On the other hand, Figure 14-11 (next page) is a lower eyeliner tattooed with a black formulation on a Fitzpatrick VI skin type. The immediately after the procedure photo looked as the client expected the healed procedure to appear. Unfortunately, there was only a barely detectable contrast with her skin once the procedure healed (see Figure 14-12).

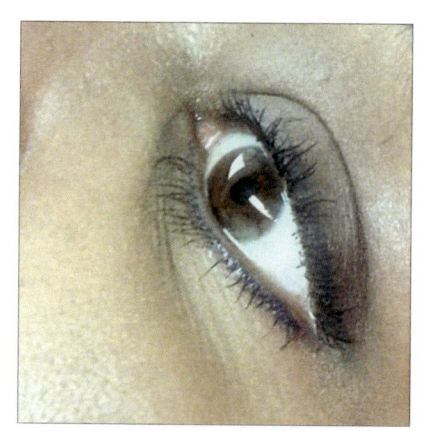

Figure 14-10: Black eyeliner tattooed on a Fitzpatrick V skin type

Tattooing lip color on darker skin type clients is a predominant concern regarding working on tissue that tends to hyperpigment, scar, has strong bluish or violet undertones, or has variegated (multicolored) lip color.

Making sound decisions about whether a client is a good candidate for lip procedures requires technicians to recognize contraindications that affect the healed outcome. It is common knowledge, and voiced by experienced technicians in the industry, that there are rarely (if ever) instances when Fitzpatrick skin types V–VI are good candidates for lip color. It is not necessarily rare for a Fitzpatrick skin type IV to also be considered a non-candidate. Below are conditions to observe when considering a lip procedure:

- Are both the top and bottom lips the same natural color? If it is noted that the top and bottom lips are not the same or similar colors, this client is not a good candidate for lip procedures. This appearance is referred to as variegated (multi-toned) lips. Our industry has realized that a dark natural lip color cannot be tattooed to appear lighter Also, any expectations of making the lighter lip of a client with variegated lip color appear identical to the darker lip by tattooing a closely related color is not a task for a novice technician.

- Are the lips a dark blue or violet color? This characteristic is normally impossible to overcome to the client's satisfaction. Remember this is a person who has skin that may tend to hyperpigment and the dark areas of the lip may heal even darker because the skin has been compromised.

- Do the sides of the lips (outer corners) or vermilion border appear darker? A client of color may appear to have the same upper and lower lip tones until a more thorough inspection is conducted. The sides (inner corners) of the lips are well-known for being more bluish, violet, or darker appearing on people of color and after tattooing, hyperpigmenting to an even darker or cooler color when healed.

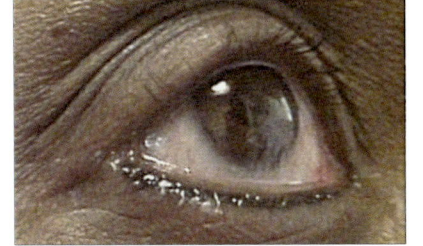

Figure 14-11: Black lower eyeliner tattooed on Fitzpatrick VI skin type – immediately after

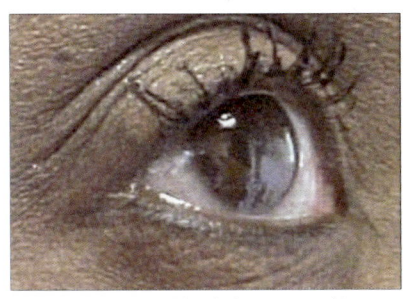

Figure 14-12: Black lower eyeliner healed on Fitzpatrick VI skin type

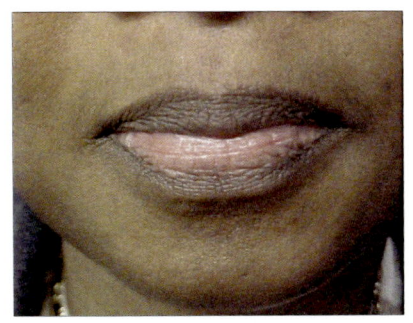

Figure 14-13: Variegated lips with cool undertones

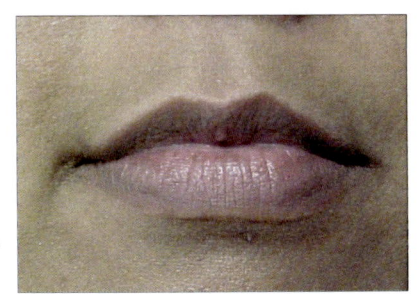

Figure 14-14: Variegated lips with cool undertones

If the potential client has differences in the colors of the upper and lower lip color (variegated lip color) or strong bluish or violet (sometimes uneven in placement) lip coloring to overcome, considering the probable hyperpigmentation factor from tattooing, and possible scarring tendencies, it is common to suggest they take advantage of the long-lasting lipsticks on the market.

Figure 14-13 and Figure 14-14 are two examples of variegated lips and hyperpigmentation that would rule out the possibility of a successful permanent cosmetic lip liner or shaded/blended lip procedure.

Working on different skin types can be a joy when the characteristics of the skin work for the technician and the client, but beware and be conservative when considering working on skin that has obvious properties that are contraindicative to the tattooing process and the procedure that has been requested.

On the following page, there is a Fitzpatrick chart that provides for client Fitzpatrick skin evaluation.

Fitzpatrick Skin Evaluation Chart

The Fitzpatrick Scale:

Type 1 (scores 0–7) White/Subject to sunburn

Type 2 (scores 8–16) Tan/Capable of tanning

Type 3 (scores 17–25) Dark/Capable of tanning – Prone to hyperpigmentation

Type 4 (scores 25–30) Dark – Prone to hyperpigmentation

Type 5–6 (scores over 30) Very dark – Prone to hyperpigmentation

Fitzpatrick Skin Evaluation

Score	0	1	2	3	4	Score
What is the color of your eyes?	Light blue, Gray, Light Green	Blue, Gray or Green	Dark Blue or Hazel	Dark Brown	Brownish Black	
What is the natural color of your hair?	Sandy or Red	Blonde	Chestnut/ Dark Blonde	Dark Brown	Black	
What is the color of your non-exposed skin?	Reddish	Very Pale	Pale with Beige Tint	Light Brown	Dark Brown	
Do you have freckles on unexposed areas?	Many	Several	Few	Incidental	None	

Total Genetic Disposition Score: _____

Score	0	1	2	3	4	Score
What happens when you stay in the sun too long?	Painful redness, blistering, peeling	Blistering followed by peeling	Burns sometimes followed by peeling	Rarely burn	Never had burns	
To what degree do you turn brown?	Hardly or not at all	Light color tan	Reasonable tan	Tans easily	Turns dark brown quickly	
Do you turn brown within several hours after sun exposure?	Never	Seldom	Sometimes	Often	Always	
How does your face react to the sun?	Very sensitive	Sensitive	Normal	Very resistant	Never had a problem	

Score	0	1	2	3	4	Score
When was the last time you exposed your body to the sun, tanning bed or self-tanning cream?	More than 3 months ago	2–3 months ago	1–2 months ago	Less than a month ago	Less than 2 weeks ago	
How frequently do you expose the area to be treated to the sun?	Never	Hardly ever	Sometimes	Often	Always	

Total Combined Score: _____

Hyperpigmentation and Hypopigmentation

Hyperpigmentation is a common, usually harmless condition showing as patches of skin darker in color than the normal surrounding skin. This darkening occurs when an excess of *melanin*, the brown pigment that produces normal skin color, forms deposits in the skin. These deposits include light brown to darker brown or black color. While skin pigmentation abnormalities can occur at any age and on any part of the body, they become accelerated during the aging process due to a breakdown of melanin production and can affect the skin color of people of any ethnicity.

Melanin production is stimulated by a pituitary hormone called *melanocyte stimulating hormone* (MSH) which causes melanocytes to product melanin. Age spots, freckles, and *melasma* (a tan discoloration of the face that is associated with pregnancy or with the use of oral contraceptives or with some medical conditions) are examples of hyperpigmentation.

The amount of pigment in the skin is determined by the amount of melanin being produced by the body. Loss of pigment (*hypopigmentation*) can be caused by an absence of melanocytes, malfunctioning cells, exposure to cold or chemicals, or some types of medical conditions (see Figure 14-15).

An increase in pigment (hyperpigmentation) may be caused by skin irritation and friction (see Figure 14-6 thru, Figure 14-8, page 148), hormonal changes, aging, a metabolic disorder, or another underlying problem. Exposure to UV rays can cause the skin color to become darker. Sun exposure is the primary source of exposure to UV rays, but tanning beds and lamps are also a source.

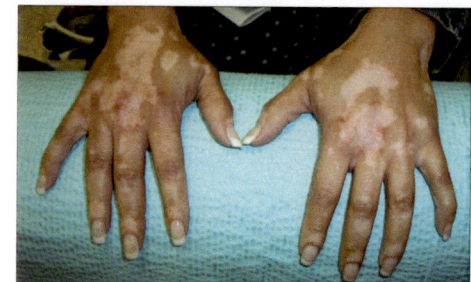

Figure 14-15: Loss of pigment (hypopigmentation)

At birth, the skin color seen is the genetically determined skin color that has not been exposed to the sun. All people also have a genetically determined response to sun exposure.

The Fitzpatrick Skin Type Chart provides a correlation between genetically determined skin (prior to sun exposure) and tanning response categorized as skin phototypes.

Skin Type   **Tanning Response**

I   Always burns, never tans
II   Sun-sensitive, burns easily, tans minimally
III   Sun-sensitive, burns minimally, slowly tans to a light brown
IV   Minimally sun sensitive, tans to a moderate brown
V   Sun-insensitive, rarely burns, tans to a dark brown
VI   Sun insensitive, never burns, tans to a black

This information is important because people of color, who typically represent Fitzpatrick IV–VI skin types, almost always respond to injuries to the skin, including tattooing with some degree of hyperpigmentation (increased melanin production in the epidermis).

Post-inflammatory Hyperpigmentation (PIH)

There are studies that theorize that some persons have an inherited tendency for weak melanocytes that respond to inflammation by decreasing melanin production, or for strong melanocytes that respond by increasing melanin production. While the effect is more evident when lighter-skinned persons respond with hyperpigmentation or darker-skinned persons respond with hypopigmentation, persons of all ethnicities can respond to inflammation with hyperpigmentation or hypopigmentation. With time and resolution of the inflammation, the pigmentation changes can normalize.

How does all this information about hyper- and hypopigmentation affect us as cosmetic tattoo artists? The primary relationship is that the end result of our procedures is tattooed color + skin tone = the healed result. If the skin we are working with has a propensity to become darker when injured, the healed result of our procedure, or parts of the procedure, may be darker than expected for an undetermined period of time. Areas of procedure location are important:

Hyperpigmentation is normally not a concern at all in the instance of eyeliner. A good majority of people ask for dark top eyeliner, often the darker the better. There are exceptions to this when a client requests a fashion eyeliner color, but a majority of the time clients request standard eyeliner colors (dark brown, black-brown, brown-black, black, or charcoal eyeliner). The lower eyeliner is typically such a small fine line that the color must be dark and contrasting to the skin to some degree to be seen after the healing process. Again, there are exceptions when clients request fashion eyeliner colors or a lighter lower liner.

Hyperpigmentation can influence the selection of eyebrow pigment but rarely ever rule a client out as a good candidate for eyebrows. While some technicians would anticipate PIH (if this condition should occur) to subside over time and the skin to return to its pre-hyperpigmentation color, some clients will simply not be satisfied if their eyebrows heal darker than expected and would be hard-pressed to wait for the hyperpigmented skin to return to its normal color. As a result, to act conservatively for the initial eyebrow procedure, some technicians will offer a color that will provide contrast for their eyebrow clients, but would not be considered too dark if hyperpigmentation were to occur. The healed eyebrow color is evaluated at the follow-up visit and adjusted to a darker color if necessary.

This is a good practice to apply to all eyebrow procedures, regardless of skin type, but emphasized in this section because of the propensity of people of color to hyperpigment. There will be those instances, however, when the skin is dark to the degree that only a very dark colorant/pigment would show in the skin (provide contrast) and the offering of a lighter color is not an option.

Hyperpigmentation is one of the major factors dictating who is and who is not a good candidate for lip procedures. This is also where the Fitzpatrick Skin Type Chart is influential. The darker the skin, i.e., skin types IV–VI, typically darker and/or more variegated lip tones will be observed. The top lip is often a different color than the bottom lip and both top and bottom lips may range from a soft pink, brown, or a darker brown or violet. The thin outer edges of the lips or vermilion are well-known for hyperpigmenting (see Figure 14-13 and Figure 14-14, page 145).

Also, an anticipated degree of hyperpigmentation factor of any client can be evaluated. For instance, a person who is a Fitzpatrick I or II skin type (light skin) may have some slight lighter brown tones in their lips, but this may not be a deciding factor to deny a lip procedure. Another person, however, with brown tones in the natural lip that is a skin type Fitzpatrick type V or VI gives more merit to the probability that tattooing the lip will result in considerable hyperpigmentation. Evaluate each client and make determinations accordingly.

Much of this section of your textbook has been dedicated to the subject of *hyper*pigmentation. *Hypo*pigmentation is, as explained earlier, the absence of skin pigmentation, leaving the skin lighter in spots than the surrounding normal skin color. All subjects relating to hypopigmented skin (camouflage techniques, scar tissue, etc.) are advanced subjects not appropriate for in-depth fundamental training discussion.

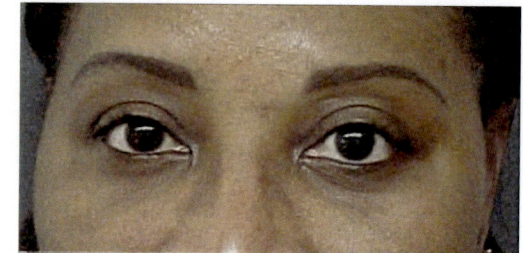

Figure 14-16: Healed Eyebrow Procedure

There are considerations for certain procedure types when working with Fitzpatrick IV-VI skin types, but unless there are medical implications that would dictate otherwise, as long as there is potential for appropriate contrast with the skin when healed, eyebrows are a very popular and successful procedure.

References

1.   Heathman, C. (2003). *Acne and Skin of Color*. Dermascope, May 2003.

Section 15

Traditional and Permanent Cosmetic Color Theories

Learning Objectives

Introduction

Standing along with device knowledge and accomplished design work, knowledge of permanent cosmetic color theory (PCCT) and how to apply our color theory is unquestionably one of the heart and soul elements of successful permanent cosmetic procedures.

Permanent cosmetic color theory (PCCT) differs from traditional color theory (TCT) and the associated artist's color wheel. It is, however, commonly used as a color theory reference guide to the extent where there are agreements with PCCT. Where there are agreements between these two theories and where there are deviations are important elements of our industry. This section approaches color from both theory avenues, each with its own destination.

Objective

Upon completion of this section, the technician will have a good understanding permanent cosmetic color theory (PCCT).

Section 15 - Traditional and Permanent Cosmetic Color Theories

The title of this section may appear out of step (indicating more than one color theory) with the basic color theory taught in other educational venues (cosmetology or traditional art, as examples). In reality, there are many color concepts and associated materials to support each theory. The foundations of pre-21st century color theory were built around *ideal or pure colors* (without a bias toward other primary colors), characterized by sensory experiences rather than attributes of the physical world. This has led to a number of inaccuracies in traditional color theory principles that are not always remedied in modern presentations.

> *An important challenge has been the confusion between the behavior of light mixtures, called additive color mixing, and the behavior of dyes, inks, paints, and pigments mixtures, called subtractive color mixing. This challenge arises because the absorption of light by material substances follows different rules from the perception of light by the eye.*[1]

In additive color theory, the primary colors of light (red, **green**, and blue) are added to create white light. In subtractive color theory, the primary colors of dyes, inks, paints, and pigments (red, ***yellow***, and blue) *absorb* or *subtract* white light when mixed together.

An example would be to compare viewing a brown car in two different mediums. One brown car is viewed on a computer or TV monitor. This is a brown image created by the projection of colored light-additive color theory; the behavior of light mixtures applies. Conversely, a brown car is painted on a canvas. In this example, subtractive color theory, the behavior of dyes, inks, paints, and pigments applies. The primary colors are different for both additive and subtractive theories.

After research, it is apparent that in regard to tattooing color into living tissue (a canvas that has its own color), the permanent cosmetic industry required a color theory presentation that relates more specifically to our medium (the skin) accompanied by the behavior of the formulations we use for tattooing (subtractive color theory).

Permanent cosmetic formulations may be one or the compilation of two or more colors, with a dominant color being referred to as the *base*. As technicians who work with these formulations, we employ subtractive color theory in a rather unorthodox manner. During the tattooing process, we are depositing a color (our formulation), with another color (the skin undertone). The client's skin undertone has an influence on the color selected for the procedure and how the procedure appears when healed.

Lighting is a considerable factor in our studios when selecting a color and often an issue when a client views the procedure in various lighting environments; the color can appear different.

Traditional Color Theory History Reference

A tradition of color theory begins in the 18th century, initially within a partisan controversy around Isaac Newton's theory of color (Opticks, 1704) and the nature of the so-called primary colors. From there it developed as an independent artistic tradition with only sporadic or superficial reference to colorimetry and vision science.[2]

As a reference point for traditional color theory (TCT), the artist's color wheel is used as a baseline with red, yellow, and blue (RYB) being identified as the three primary colors. This is, however, somewhat inadequate in practicality for our industry at times as you will read in this section. It is little wonder novice technicians find color theory confusing as it applies specifically to permanent cosmetics artistry. We use the subtractive theory behavior of dyes, inks, paint, and pigments as a baseline, and then adapt it to available formulations that will be tattooed into a living tissue medium that has its own color.

This is quite the undertaking and it does take time. Nonetheless, it is TCT and the associated traditional color wheel calling out pure red, pure yellow, and pure blue (RYB) as the primary colors that traditional artists who paint on non-living canvases depend on to a great degree. Notice I did not say *exclusively*. The use of the word *ideal* or *pure* in regard to traditional color theory relates to the fact that the human eye cannot see pure colors (colors without a bias toward another color). The traditional artist's color wheel primary colors red, yellow, and blue do not show any bias (one primary color leans toward one of the two other primary colors).

The traditional color wheel does provide source materials from which to draw and deviate from for the purpose of establishing guidelines for creating permanent cosmetic formulations. With that said, customizing TCT must be considered to formulate permanent cosmetic colors for tattooing and to predict the behavior of these formulations in living tissue (the skin). So much of the complexities become learned information after seeing healed procedures using the same formulations in different mixtures in different skin undertones.

A much-discussed challenge in our industry is that people see color differently. There is the technician who, in the controlled lighting environment of their studio, is the expert at selecting an appropriate procedure color for the skin undertone medium. The technician applies her or his knowledge of permanent cosmetic color theory, anticipating how the color will appear when tattooed into the client's skin undertone and how the procedure will appear when healed.

Then there is the aspect of how the client sees the color. The memory of the color she or he is accustomed to seeing in their own lighting environment(s) applied with cosmetics may greatly influence how the permanent cosmetic color is perceived. Comments such as, *"Oh, this is too dark (or light)"* may simply be her or his emotional response to not being able to accept something different from what they are accustomed to seeing. Friends/family/co-workers who are ever so generous to voice their opinion, discuss the appearance of the immediately-after and ultimately healed color with your client. While much of this dialogue is going on without the technician present, on-lookers are not taking into consideration that the color they are looking at is also greatly influenced by the environmental light source, which affects how the color appears at any given time. Why would they not take this into consideration? They are merely casual judges in the grand scheme of things offering opinions. Critics are not color or lighting experts.

In office settings where the quality of lighting is a variable, color may appear differently than it does when in natural light or in a makeup mirror with its own lighting sources. Also, there are people who are color vision deficient and may not even be aware of it. Our color task as technicians is providing the right color for the procedure being conducted on the right skin undertone that will also be seen as a good color by the client when viewed in a variety of lighting environments. This is challenging and requires a good permanent cosmetic color theory education.

How Lighting Affects the Perception of Color

Lighting in the workplace greatly affects how color is seen. All lighting sources influence color perception to some degree. A well-equipped studio should have full-spectrum natural lighting in order to see colors more accurately.

Imagine on a more personal basis how lighting affects how we see color. People who do not have good lighting at home occasionally will find themselves wearing one black sock and one navy blue sock. In poor or low lighting these two colors can appear the same. Think how often colors of clothing or cosmetics are selected under artificial lighting of a department store only to inspect the item outdoors and find the color looks completely different in natural lighting.

Proper lighting is important for an accurate reading of the colors we offer clients. Technicians who have windows in their studios that allow for natural light and those who have invested in lamps and lighting that provide the effects of natural lighting definitely have an advantage. All technicians' disadvantage is that clients take their permanent cosmetic procedures into a variety of lighting environments where the colors can appear somewhat different than they did in the technician's studio. Even in natural lighting, there are variances to the amount of sun depending on the weather and the time of the day.

Geographically throughout the world, the natural environment is different. As an example, one location may be consistently sunny with very little filtered sunlight for a good portion of the year; while in other locations the norm may be more consistently overcast with filtered sunlight. The same color could look somewhat different in both locations. The color seen in an overcast environment will often appear cooler, and possibly darker than it will in a sunny geographical location.

Tattooing technique also affects how light reflects color and its presentation in the skin. Microblading (manual device) and machine hair stroke techniques tend to produce cooler eyebrow procedures when healed. The small independent replications of hair do not reflect light as well as larger surface areas of filled eyebrows (such as shaded techniques).

Color Terminology

- *Hue* identifies the color by name and distinguishes it from other colors. It is the answer to "*what color is this?*"
- The *value* of color describes the lightness or darkness of a hue created by adding black or white.
- The *saturation* of color is the relative intensity of color from vivid to dull.
- *Chromaticity* is the amount of identifiable color in a hue. Highly chromatic colors contain maximum hue (a specific color) with little or no impurities such as white, black, or gray. The less chroma in a color, the more dull and gray it will appear. An achromatic color is unsaturated or near neutral.
- *Relative temperature* of color describes the amount of warmth or coolness of a specific hue.
- *Neutralizing* color relates to the loss of vibrancy in an existing color by introducing the appropriate complementary color. As an example, orange is the complementary color to blue. By introducing orange into an existing blue color, blue loses its vibrancy and appears more neutral (some shade of brown or tan). This is subtractive color theory at its best.

To further our education on permanent cosmetic color theory, the definitions of inorganic and organic colorants are as follow:

- The definition of an *organic colorant* is: A colorant that contains carbon atoms. Organic colorants are typically synthesized (made from a chemical formula). This differs from the agricultural definition of an organic food.
- Organic colors used for cosmetic tattooing are not natural as the word organic might imply (from nature). The natural organic colorants such as Natural Yellow #26, Carotene (carrots); or Natural Yellow #6, Saffron (a plant); or Natural Red #4, Cochineal (crushed beetles); and others like them are typically not known to be used for producing permanent cosmetic color formulations. The organic colorants used for permanent cosmetic formulations are typically thought to be synthetically produced. For those who wish further information on this topic, the *Wiley-Interscience Pigment Handbook, a Wiley-Interscience Publication* is an excellent resource.

Organic colorants can be divided into two types:

- Type 1 - Soluble organic dyes combined with a material to make the color insoluble. This type of organic colorant is termed as a *lake pigment*. It is normally formed using insoluble but universally accepted as biologically safe metals such as aluminum and calcium.

Section 15 - Traditional and Permanent Cosmetic Color Theories

- ♦ Type 2 – Insoluble colorants, which tend to have a higher lightfastness and brightness. Contrary to popular belief, most organic colorants contain atoms of metals.[4]
- The definition of an ***inorganic colorant*** is: Naturally mined or synthetic colorants such as metallic oxide, sulfide, and other salts. They do not contain the carbon atom. Inorganic colorants are:
  - ♦ Iron Oxide
  - ♦ Ultramarine Blue, Violet, and Pink
  - ♦ Chromium Oxide Green
  - ♦ Hydrated Chromium Oxide Green
  - ♦ Titanium Dioxide
  - ♦ Manganese Violet

Color Perception

- The perception of color is an aspect of our visual capabilities and a psychophysical response consisting of the physical reaction of the eye and automatic interpretive response of the brain to wavelength characteristics of light above a certain brightness level.
- Eyes contain sensors that respond to various wavelengths of light.
- Eyes efficiently break down the visible spectrum into the three primary regions of additive color theory *red*, *green*, and *blue*.

Figure 15-1: Visible color spectrum of the human eye

As traditional color theory principles are explored, the deviations from these principles to accommodate for color formulations either mixed together (permanent cosmetic mixing techniques) or ready-made color formulations will be annotated.

Permanent cosmetic color theory is presented in this manner because we have all been taught and exposed to traditional color theory and the traditional color wheel. By first presenting what we are more familiar with (traditional color theory- TCT), and then introducing the deviations from that theory for permanent cosmetic color theory (PCCT) this approach seemed a logical step-by-step approach.

Based on the traditional artist's color wheel, the primary colors are red, yellow, and blue (RYB).

The primary colors red, yellow, and blue are not mixed from other colors; rather, they generate all other colors.

The traditional color wheel consists of a 12-step color wheel. At this juncture, the 12-

157

step color wheel will be built, beginning with the traditional primary colors, red, yellow, and blue. The secondary colors orange, violet, and green will be added, and then the intermediate colors yellow-orange, red-orange, red-violet, blue-violet, blue-green, and yellow-green.

For educational purposes, all tattoo powders from which formulations are developed are colorants/pigments (both terms are interchangeable). The term ink is an informal industry word assigned for colorants/pigments, and although used in the industry by many, is generally not recognized as being different from colorants/pigments in the permanent cosmetic manufacturing industry. Whether or not the term pigment/color/colorant/ink is used as a description, it is the ingredients that matters, not what it is called.

The proper flow sequence is as follows
- Colorant/Pigment
  - Inorganic
  - Organic

Because the industry uses different references for their tattoo color products (some formal and some informal) which may be inorganic, organic, or a mix of both, the following traditional and permanent cosmetic color theory comparisons will primarily use the words *colorant(s)*, *color(s)* and *formulation(s)* more than other terms. The definition of a colorant is a dye, pigment, or other substance that colors something. A formulation is a material or mixture prepared according to a particular formula, in other words, the finished product. The word *pigment* in this section is only used occasionally.

The Primary Colors

The 12-step traditional artist's color wheel starts with the three primary colors, red, yellow, and blue placed in an equilateral triangle (see Figure 15-2).

Traditional Color Theory (TCT)—Red is medium in brightness and density of the three traditional primary colors and is considered a warm color relative to yellow and blue.

Permanent Cosmetic Color Theory (PCCT)—Permanent cosmetic red colorants usually have a bias toward a warmer orange version, or a cooler violet version, although there are reds that have less of a bias than others. PCCT is in agreement with the medium brightness and density factors of TCT.

In practice, reds with a bias toward warm or cool as designated above are commonly, although not exclusively, used in the formulation of lip colorants. Even the brightest iron oxide reds are less vibrant and dull, appearing rust or brick colors. The brighter, more vibrant reds are organic, some of which may have more or less transparent properties.

Lip formulations may contain iron oxide (less vibrant more dull appearing), other inorganic colorants (such as manganese violet, ultramarine violet, ultramarine pink, or titanium dioxide as examples) and/or organic (bright and vibrant) colorants.

TCT –Yellow— Yellow is the lightest and brightest of the three traditional primary colors with little density, but extreme intensity. Yellow may have a warm (yellow-orange) or a cool (yellow-green) bias. There are yellows which have less of a bias to green or orange that will appear more neutral when compared to a cooler or warmer version of yellow.

PCCT–Yellow— In theory, permanent cosmetic theory is in agreement with traditional color theory. Yellow is a TCT primary color that may be either warm or cool. Permanent cosmetic yellows are either warm, having a bias toward orange, or cooler having a bias toward green. As stated earlier, there may be yellows when compared to one another that will have less of a bias toward orange or green. In order to provide more neutral bases for eyebrow formulations, a cool, warm, or a yellow with less of a bias may be the principal color agent. PCCT is in agreement with the lightness and brightness factors of TCT. It is used as a complementary (neutralizing) color for violet.

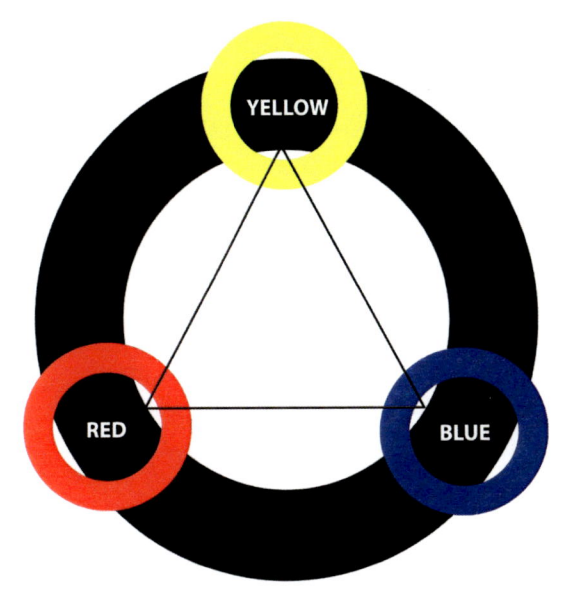

Figure 15-2: Primary Color Wheel

Manufacturers purchase yellow colorants such as iron oxide (dull in appearance) or organic (bright, more vibrant colorants) for permanent cosmetic color formulations. In practice, yellow is said to be one of, if not *the* most, important colors in the permanent cosmetic industry.

TCT–Blue— Blue has the most depth and density of the traditional three primary colors, and is considered a cool color.

PCCT–Blue— Blue is designated as a cool color in the permanent cosmetic industry. In practice, blue is a color that is not thought to be often, if ever, used for permanent cosmetic formulations unless it is being used as a fashion color for an eyeliner.

Blue could be a component of technician color mixing, as in mixing the secondary colors red and yellow to make orange, and then adding a small amount of blue to create a brown. The industry, however, has seen the results of this as follows:

- Yellow in the mixed brown formulation fades the fastest, leaving violet.
- Red fades after yellow in the mixed brown formulation leaving blue.

Review of the formulation practices of several companies indicates when mixing organic colorants to obtain brown they commonly choose red, yellow, and black (not blue).

It is important that technicians have access to ingredient information, for instance, Color Index (CI).

Of the three traditional color theory primary colors, blue is thought to be used the least in the permanent cosmetic industry.

People in the permanent cosmetic industry sometimes refer to a formulation as having a *blue base*. This would imply the color blue is an independent ingredient. Typically the blue base referred to in this respect, is a *visual interpretation*, not an actual reference to a blue ingredient unless it is a fashion eyeliner formulation.

There is always room for exceptions, but research indicates normally people are expressing how the color appears and not an actual reference to its independent colorant formulation properties. Again, blue is not thought to be commonly used in permanent cosmetic formulations unless it is a fashion color for an eyeliner.

In practice, in order to achieve a cooler lip formulation base, manufacturers often depend on cooler colorants such as magenta, cooler reds (such as a red with a bias toward violet), ultramarine violet or pink, and other similar varieties to produce a cooler color as opposed to an independent blue ingredient.

Summary of Primary Colors:

- **TCT - Traditional Color Theory**
    - Red is designated as warm.
    - Yellow may be warm or cool.
    - Blue is cool.
- **PCCT - Permanent Cosmetics Color Theory**
    - Reds are warm if they have a bias toward orange, or cool with a bias toward violet.
        - There are reds with a less obvious bias to orange or violet when compared to other reds.
    - Yellows are warm with a bias to orange or cool with a bias to green.
        - There are yellows with less of a bias toward orange or green when compared to other yellows.
    - Blues are cool with a bias to violet or green.
        - There are blue colors with less of a bias to violet or green but blue is always cool.

As stated, all three primary colors may appear more neutral in their prospective groups when compared to other versions of the same color. For instance when comparing three different yellows, one may appear more cool with a bias toward green, one may appear more warm with a bias toward orange, and one may appear to have less of a bias and be considered more neutral of the three yellows being compared.

Secondary or Complementary Colors

The next aspect to building the tradition color wheel is creating the three *secondary colors*. These colors are placed in triangles above the corresponding primary color combination. The secondary or complementary colors are orange, green, and violet (OGV). See Figure 15-3

In **TCT**, secondary colors are two primary colors mixed together. The secondary colors are located across from, or opposite the primary colors.

TCT—Equal parts of red and yellow = orange. Orange is a secondary color that in TCT is created by mixing a red and a yellow color together.

PCCT—Permanent cosmetic formulation manufacturers have the option of mixing red and yellow colorants together to create an orange, or purchasing orange colorants. Examples of this would be an iron oxide or an organic orange.

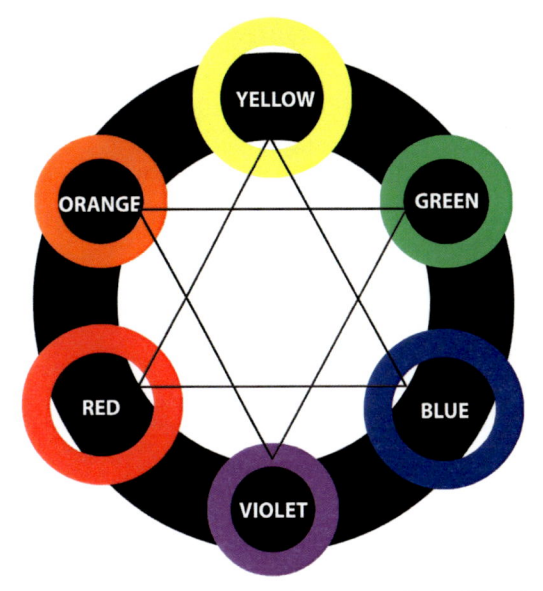

Figure 15-3: Primary and Secondary Color Wheel

Orange is a secondary color commonly used in permanent cosmetic formulation bases for eyebrow and lip formulations. Orange is also used to formulate colors made specifically for modifying the temperature of an existing eyebrow, eyeliner, or lip color to a warmer temperature. It is also used as a correction color for the colors blue, gray, and green.

TCT—Equal parts of blue and yellow = green. Green is a secondary color that in TCT is created by mixing equal parts of a yellow and a blue color together.

PCCT—Permanent cosmetic formulation manufacturers have the option of mixing blue and yellow colorants together to create green or purchasing green colorants. Examples of this would be a hydrated or chromium oxide green, inorganic metal oxides (less vibrant and appearing dull), or an organic green (bright more vibrant). Green is a secondary color that is used in bases for eyebrow formulations and as fashion colors for eyeliner formulations.

Green is also used in formulations made specifically for modifying the temperature of eyebrow and eyeliner colors to a cooler temperature. Green corrects the colors red or orange that may be seen as a residual color to aged eyebrow procedures. These green permanent cosmetic formulations are typically seen as an ash brown.

TCT — Equal parts of blue and red = violet (also referred to as purple). Violet is a secondary color that in TCT is created by mixing a blue and red color together.

PCCT—Permanent cosmetic color formulation manufacturers have the option of mixing blue and red powders together to create a violet, or purchasing unmixed violet colorants (such as inorganic ultramarine violet/manganese violet). Violet is one of the options which may be used to give a cool fuchsia color to lip formulations or fashion eyeliners rather than using the color blue.

Research indicates that violet is not used (or rarely if ever used) as a base color for eyebrow formulations but may be used as a fashion color for eyeliner colors. Because of the heavy density factor of violet, it is not a color that is used for correction (neutralizing) purposes. Although a yellow faded eyebrow is possible (there are few absolutes in permanent cosmetics) this is not often seen. If this were the case, *violet, the complementary color to yellow would not be used*. Due to the rarity of a yellow residual eyebrow, contact the formulation manufacturer or distributor for guidance.

The final step to creating the 12-step color wheel will be to add the six intermediate colors. See Figure 15-4.

Intermediate and Tertiary Colors

Intermediate Colors

TCT intermediate colors are yellow-orange, red-orange, red-violet, blue-violet, blue-green, and yellow-green (Y-O, R-O, R-V, B-V, B-G and Y-G). See Figure 15-3.

In **TCT**, these colors are created by mixing one secondary and one primary color, i.e., blue + violet = blue-violet. Three or more separate colors are mixed (one primary and one secondary— the secondary being the combination of two primaries), and in the traditional artist's color wheel, each intermediate or tertiary color being created will be an equal combination of the two colors, left and right, surrounding an open segment.

In **PCCT**, intermediate colors may be mixed by manufacturers using a combination of iron oxide, other inorganic or organic colorants,

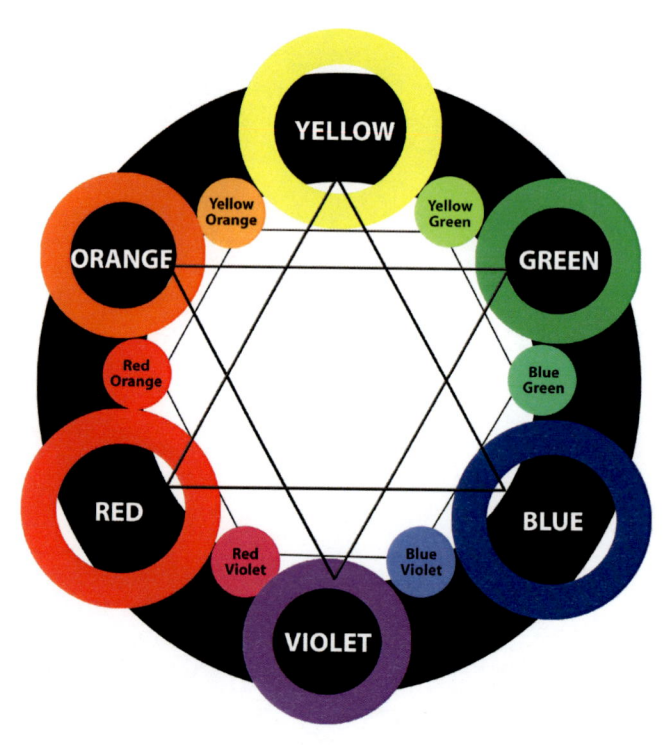

Figure 15-4: The Traditional Artist's Color Wheel – Primary, Secondary, and Intermediate Colors

or they may be purchased as independent colorants.

Yellow-orange is most often seen as a correction color for low-density gray or blue eyebrows. It is a color also used in eyebrow formulations. Red-orange and red-violet are most often seen as lip colors, although a red-orange may be the base of a very warm eyebrow color. Blue-violet and blue-green are most often seen as fashion colors for eyeliner. Yellow-green is most often seen as a correction color for red-violet eyebrows and as a base for eyebrow formulations.

There may be other uses for formulations that are not stated; each manufacturer has their vision of appropriate uses of the intermediate colors.

It is necessary to also explore the very important tertiary colors as well as the colors black and white.

Tertiary Colors

In order to avoid confusion, many reliable sources refer to *tertiary colors* as intermediate colors. Intermediate colors are the mixture of a primary color and a secondary color. The term *tertiary color* was originally coined to refer to neutral colors, those made by mixing all three primary colors. Examples of these colors would be colors such as khaki, cobalt, gold, magenta, gray, and other selective hues of brown in subtractive color theory (the behavior of dyes, inks, paints, and pigments).

Brown, Black, and White

Brown, the focus of this paragraph, is a very important subject matter to all permanent cosmetic technicians. Browns are the principal colors used for eyebrow procedures and also a color used for eyeliners. Notwithstanding that most browns used are normally acquired as ready-made formulations (not mixed by the technician in the TCT manner), it is still important to understand the formulation of browns.

Permanent cosmetic color formulation manufacturers may purchase natural inorganic brown colorants such as umber or sienna. Other sources of browns are brown colorants that are created at the powder manufacturer level by *calcining*.

Calcination is a process in which raw ore is heated until most of the easily burnt off impurities (volatile matter) are gone. This is a way of purifying the raw ore and in some cases, it changes the color. Some colorants, under extreme heat, will change color because a chemical reaction occurs that changes the ratio of atoms, or because the crystal lattice structure is altered.

Precipitation is another process. It is the formation of insoluble molecules (particulate). That reaction can be used when forming insoluble colorants from materials that begin as soluble. Other sources of brown colorants are manufacturer's mixtures of purchased colorants.

Organic colorants are also being offered in eyebrow formulations. The following was stated earlier under the primary color blue information, but applies here as well:

> *Review of the manufacturing practices of several companies indicates when mixing organic colorants to obtain brown they commonly choose red, yellow, and black (not blue). It is important that technicians have access to ingredient information, for instance, Color Index (CI).*

Black may be either inorganic (iron oxide) or organic (carbon black), or a mixture of both.

Inorganic black iron oxide is the mineral magnetite which is one of the main iron ores. It is a product purchased as a colorant and often used as an eyeliner color and a mixing color to darken other colors.

Organic carbon black is the result of the thermal decomposition of hydrocarbons. It is used for eyeliner procedures by technicians with advanced knowledge and experience. It is not advisable to use carbon black as an additive to darken other colors. Carbon black is composed of very small particles and normally remains visible in the skin longer than any color it was mixed with. Many people may associate the word carbon with the color black. *Carbon is an atom present in organic colorants*, not a color. The arrangement of a grouping of carbon atoms produces the different versions of the color black.

White used for permanent cosmetic formulations is titanium dioxide. It is a product purchased as a colorant and used moderately and appropriately at the manufacturing level as a colorant for lightening other colors or to increase opacity. *Technicians should not add white to any color independently, ever.* This is a color that is controlled at the manufacturer level. If misused, due to the large molecular size of white, it will remain visible long after the color(s) it was mixed with fades.

White or camouflage colors which contain titanium dioxide (white) should never be tattooed over another color to reduce its appearance. Titanium dioxide tattooed into another color will simply produce a third color, it is not to be used to attempt to correct misplaced or unwanted tattooing.

TCT Complementary Colors

Complementary colors are pairs of colors that are opposite one another on the TCT color wheel and provide a high contrast. The complement of each primary color (red, yellow, and blue) is roughly the color made by mixing the other two primary colors together.

- Red complements (neutralizes) green. Green is a combination of the two primary colors blue and yellow.
- Blue complements (neutralizes) orange. Orange is a combination of the two primary colors red and yellow.
- Yellow complements (neutralizes) violet. Violet is a combination of the two primary colors blue and red.

When two complements are mixed, white light components are subtracted and different hues of brown and gray are produced.

The TCT complementary pairs on the traditional artist's color wheel are:
- Blue and orange
- Red and green
- Yellow and violet

PCCT does not apply the same complementary pairing of colors like traditional color theory does. As examples:
- Orange complements or corrects (neutralizes) green and blue (includes gray) – But in PCCT, blue is not used to compliment or correct (neutralize) orange.
- Yellow complements or corrects (neutralizes) violet, but violet is not used to compliment or correct (neutralize) yellow.
- Green complements or corrects (neutralizes) orange and red, but red without a bias toward orange is not used to compliment or correct (neutralize) green.

PCCT does not use violet, blue (or any color derived from violet or blue), or red without a bias to orange, as complementary colors. Our most important complementary colors are orange, yellow, green, and intermediate derivatives of those colors.

Using Complementary Colors as Correction (Neutralizing) Colors

When using the complementary colors as correction/neutralizing color tools, the portions of the primary or secondary color being corrected must be taken into consideration. For instance, correcting an aged brown eyebrow color that shows signs of violet (cool), yellow (the complementary color to violet) would be used as a correction color. However, violet is a combination of blue and red—blue having the most depth and density of the primary colors, and red being medium in brightness and density. Unless the violet eyebrow color is quite faded (more transparent) and barely detectable, yellow, which has the least density properties of the three primary colors, will likely not correct violet in one session and may not be long-lasting.

The same example can be stated for a blue appearing lip, or a blue or gray eyebrow correction. Blue has the most density of the three primary colors. Depending on the density of color in the lip or the eyebrow to be corrected, even though orange is denser than yellow it is still less dominant than blue or gray. These examples are provided as considerations when color adjustments or corrections are necessary to restore or correct (neutralize) an existing color. An analysis of the color to be adjusted or corrected and the appropriate complementary color is necessary to prepare the client for how many sessions will be needed to achieve a favorable result.

The following formula helps to understand the strength relationships between the primary colors. This formula can be applied to color adjustment and correction procedures depending on the color being corrected, and the color being used to correct:

3Y (Yellow) = 2R (Red) = 1B (Blue)

In simpler terms, it takes three portions of yellow or two portions of red to equal the strength of one portion of blue (this applies to gray as well). These are variables that technicians must make allowances for, or if in doubt, investigate with their color formulation manufacturer or distributor. If reading this book in preparation for a fundamental class, the trainer will likely go into more depth about this subject.

PCCT Complementary Colors Used in Permanent Cosmetics Color Adjustments or Corrections

Orange as a Complementary or Correction Color

Orange complements or corrects (neutralizes) blue, gray, and green.

If an eyebrow procedure has healed or aged to a blue, gray, or green color (cool), the neutralizing color is orange or yellow-orange (both warm).

Orange is also used to correct a lip color that has healed or aged to a too cool temperature (appearing bluish or blue-violet as examples). Different mixtures of orange and yellow-orange are used to correct lip colors that appear too cool.

Yellow as a Complementary Color

Yellow complements or corrects (neutralizes) violet.

If an eyebrow procedure has healed or aged to a violet (cool) color, the neutralizing color is yellow. Yellow may be warm or cool. In some color lines, a more neutral (less of a bias toward orange or green) yellow may be offered.

To correct violet a more neutral or yellow-orange formulation would be appropriate.

Green as a Complementary Color

Green complements or corrects (neutralizes) red and orange.

The corrective process of tattooing a green based formulation would relate to eyebrows and some eyeliners that had faded to a red or orange residual color.

Green is not used to complement or correct (neutralize) a red or orange lip color. If a red or orange lip color requires a change to another color it is usually because it has healed into an unexpected color due to the undertone of the lip. Adjustments would depend on the client's color goals. Based on this knowledge, if support is needed, suggestions from the manufacturer or distributor should be requested.

TCT Complementary Colors Not Used in PCCT

Complementary colors **not** used in PCCT are the colors blue, violet and red (unless the red is a red-orange). The complementary colors blue and violet are too dense. That accompanied with the potential staining properties of both makes the use of blue and violet inappropriate colors to use as correction or neutralizing colors.

Correction/Modifier/Adjuster Formulations

Many manufacturers offer corrective green, yellow, and orange colorants (a variety of versions). Iron oxide orange is a dull color. Organic oranges are bright, vivid colors. These colors are used for corrective purposes as well as to adjust the temperature of an existing formulation to warmer or cooler. These correction/modifying/adjuster formulations have a variety of uses.

Colorant Formulations

Every color product line is manufacturer-specific as to the combination of colorants and other ingredients (such as carriers) mixed together to create their range of colors. This is the more difficult aspect of applying color theory to skin undertones, making adjustments to color at a follow-up appointment, and correcting undesirable colors. Understanding the formulations technicians ultimately use for procedures is very important.

Study support materials provided by the manufacturer. Many provide usage guidance including cool, warm, and more neutral identification for their formulations. Ask the distributor questions, and maintain photography records on how a particular formulation healed on different skin types.

Something as simple as the amount or type of wetting solution(s) (carrier) included in a formulation can make a difference when compared to another line offering a similar color. SPCP pigment supplier members are required to provide all ingredients in their formulations.

A good understanding and practical application of TCT, PCCT color theories, and formulation knowledge are critical to the outcome of procedures. Technicians can apply wonderful designs, but if the healed color isn't what was expected or appealing to the client, the design will become secondary in the client's evaluation.

Permanent cosmetic color theory (PCCT) is a complex subject to learn exclusively from a textbook. In-person classes are recommended so that an instructor is present to answer your questions. It is also a good opportunity to learn from other class attendees.

Important Elements of Permanent Cosmetic Color Theory

Notwithstanding the value of scientific support for permanent cosmetic color theory (PCCT) and its differences (and why) from traditional color theory (TCT) in the preceding pages in this section, as a novice technician the following PCCT color theory elements will compartmentalize important information.

Color Terminology:

- *Hue* identifies the color by name and distinguishes it from other colors. It is the answer to *"what color is this?"*
- The *value* of color describes the lightness or darkness of a hue created by adding black or white.
- The *saturation* of color is the relative intensity of color from vivid to dull.
- *Chromaticity* is the amount of identifiable color in a hue. Highly chromatic colors contain maximum hue (a specific color) with little or no impurities such as white, black, or grey. The less chroma in a color, the more dull and grey it will appear. An achromatic color is unsaturated or near neutral.
- *Relative temperature* of color describes the amount of warmth or coolness of a specific hue.
- *Neutralizing* color relates to the loss of vibrancy in an existing color by introducing the appropriate complementary color. As an example, orange is the complementary color to blue. By introducing orange into an existing blue color, blue loses its vibrancy and appears more neutral. This is subtractive theory at its best.

Color Perception

- The perception of color is an aspect of our visual capabilities and a psychophysical response consisting of the physical reaction of the eye and automatic interpretive response of the brain to wavelength characteristics of light above a certain brightness level.
- Eyes contain sensors that respond to various wavelengths of light.
- Eyes efficiently break down the visible spectrum into the three primary regions of color called the *primary colors*.
- A much-discussed challenge in our industry is that people see color differently. The memory of the color she or he is accustomed to seeing applied topically in the procedure area may greatly influence how the permanent cosmetic color is seen. Comments such as, *"Oh, this is too dark (or light)"* may simply be the technician's emotional translation of not being able to accept something different from what she or he is

accustomed to seeing, or it may be true even in the eyes of the technician.

Primary Colors of Subtractive Color Theory

- Primary colors are not mixed from other colors; rather, they *generate* all other colors.
  - Red
  - Yellow
  - Blue

Secondary Colors

- The secondary colors are a mix of two primary colors:
  - Green (blue and yellow mix)
  - Violet (red and blue mix)
  - Orange (yellow and red mix)

Intermediate Colors

- The Intermediate Colors are a mix of a primary and secondary colors:
  - Red-orange (red the primary; orange represents the secondary yellow and red)
  - Red-violet (red the primary; violet represents the secondary red and blue)
  - Yellow-orange (yellow the primary; orange represents the secondary yellow and red)
  - Yellow-green (yellow the primary; green represents the secondary blue and yellow)
  - Blue-green (blue the primary; green represents the secondary blue and yellow)
  - Blue-violet (blue the primary; violet represents the secondary blue and red)

Tertiary Colors

- In order to avoid confusion, many reliable sources refer to tertiary colors as intermediate colors. Intermediate colors are the mixture of a primary color and a secondary color. The term *tertiary color* was originally coined to refer to neutral colors, those made by mixing all three primary colors.
  - Khaki
  - Cobalt
  - Gold

- Magenta
- Gray
- Other selective hues of brown

Permanent Cosmetic Color Theory (PCCT) Complementary Pairs

- PCCT complementary pairs are:
  - Green is the complementary color to orange and red
  - Orange is the complementary color to blue (includes gray) and green
  - Yellow is the complementary color to violet

  Many permanent cosmetic formulation manufacturers offer corrective green, yellow, and orange colorants (a variety of versions). These correction or modifying colors have a variety of uses.

Colors Not Used as Complementary Colors in Permanent Cosmetic Color Theory

- Blue, violet, and red (without bias to orange) are generally not used as complementary colors in PCCT.

Additive and Subtractive Color Theories

- An important problem has been confusion between the behavior of light mixtures, called additive color mixing, and the behavior of paint or ink (or dye or pigment) mixtures, called subtractive color mixing. This problem arises because the absorption of light by material substances follows different rules from the perception of light by the eye.

  Light mixtures (**red, green, and blue** – additive light theory primary colors) are *added* to create white light in additive color theory, whereby materials (paint, ink, pigment, and dyes) *absorb or subtract* white light when the subtractive color theory primary colors **red, yellow, and blue** are mixed together.

- As permanent cosmetics technicians who work with formulations to be tattooed into the skin, we employ subtractive color theory.

- During the tattooing process, we are mixing a color - our color formulation, with another color -the client's skin undertone.

The Effects of Lighting on Color

- Lighting in the workplace greatly affects how color is seen through the filter of the skin. All lighting sources influence color perception to some degree. A well-equipped studio should have more full-spectrum natural lighting in order to see colors accurately.

Carbon Black

- Carbon black is the result of a grouping of carbon atoms (intentionally structured in a particular manner) which influences how black appears. It is not recommend for eyeliner procedures by technicians without proper training and experience.

- It is not advisable to use carbon black as an additive to darken other colors. Carbon black is composed of very small particles and normally remains visible in the skin longer than any color it was mixed with; similar to white if it is inappropriately or overused.

White

- White used for permanent cosmetic formulations is titanium dioxide. It is a product purchased as a powder and used moderately at the manufacturing level as a substance for lightening other colors or to increase opacity.

- Technicians should not add white to any color independently. This is a color that is controlled at the manufacturer level. If overused, due to the large molecular size of white, it will remain visible long after the color(s) it was mixed with fades.

References

1. Wikipedia the Free Encyclopedia, 01/24/08, http://en.wikipedia.org/wiki/Color_theory.
2. Wikipedia The Free Encyclopedia, 1/23/08, http://64.233.169.104/search?q=cache:rOj4p82oGx4J:en.wikipedia.org/wiki/Color_theory+A+traditon+of+color+theory+begins+in+the+18th+century&hl=en&ct=clnk&cd=1&gl=us&ie=UTF-8.
3. Elizabeth Finch-Howell, CPCP assisted with the compilation of information contained in this portion of the textbook
4. Mytia Story, BS, Biologist and Chemist, assisted with the compilation of information contained in this portion of the textbook

Section 16

Selecting Permanent Cosmetic Procedure Colorants - General Information

Learning Objectives

Introduction

Previous sections addressed Identification of Skin Undertones and Traditional and Permanent Cosmetic Color Theories. The natural progression of educational information is to apply the lessons learned in those sections to selecting an appropriate color for a particular procedure for a specific client. Tattooed color + skin undertone = healed results.

There are several variables when selecting tattoo colors. One very important variable that cannot be predetermined in a textbook is what the client prefers. There are several well-founded reasons why a client may be disappointed with the outcome of a procedure. One reason for dissatisfaction is that the color may not be as it was anticipated or desired. Listening to a client is important. Considering all the physical variables—such as skin undertone, existing eyebrow color, depth of eyelash color, how intense the coolness is or isn't in a natural lip color canvas— this is essential information to observe and consider before selecting an appropriate color.

Agreeably, changing a client's mind about a predetermined color she or he arrives prepared to ask for takes finesse. Sometimes it is simply not worth the effort unless the outcome based on the client's preference would be one the technician would not want to put their name on.

Technicians have options when working with a client to choose a color for their procedure. They can follow the client's lead without interjecting a professional opinion. This is fine, as long as the color the client desires will produce an acceptable result in the eyes of the technician. The second option for consideration is to take the lead and offer the client what is best based on professional standards and an educated opinion. Some technicians sometimes select the darker eyebrow colors without the benefit of seeing what the skin does with a lighter color. Experienced technicians are often conservative in this respect. The last option is to consider the client's desires and color expectations unreasonable, or out of the scope of your credentials and decline the business.

A guide for selecting colorants/formulations for permanent cosmetic color corrections and adjustments is provided. Permanent cosmetic technicians need to be prepared to offer these types of services. This may represent additional training to the fundamental curriculum, however, an overview is provided.

For educational purposes, all tattoo powders from which formulations are developed are colorants/pigments (both terms are interchangeable). The term ink is an informal industry word assigned for colorants/pigments, and although it has become popular and is used in the industry by many, is generally not recognized as being different from colorants/pigments in the permanent cosmetic manufacturing industry. As an end product the terms are unique to the personal preference of the manufacturer. Whether or not the term pigment/color/colorant/ink is used as a description for the end product, it is the ingredients that matters, not what it is called.

(Continued)

Because the industry uses different references for their tattoo color products (some formal and some informal) which may be inorganic, organic or a mix of both, the following section will primarily use the words colorant(s), formulation(s,) and color more than other terms. The definition of a colorant is a dye, pigment, or other substance that colors something. A formulation is a material or mixture prepared according to a particular formula, in other words, the finished product. The word pigment in this section is used when included in a definition.

Objective

Upon completion of this section, the technician will acquire the ability to conservatively assist clients with color selection and how to add warmth to a color (when appropriate), to ensure a procedure doesn't heal too cool. Always remember the formula of skin undertone + tattooed color=healed result. The technician will learn to take into account the client's overall appearance, their skin undertone, the influence of existing hair in the eyebrow or eyelash area, and the natural lip color. All of these factors affect the appearance of the healed results.

Technicians will also review and gain insight into an important aspect of our services, permanent cosmetic corrections, and adjustments..

Section 16 - Selecting Permanent Cosmetic Procedure Colorants—General Information

In Section "13", *"Identifying Skin Undertones"*, information was provided to help identify the undertones of the client's skin in the procedural area; the skin is not just one color. This section provides formulation selection information on a generalized basis.

After identifying the client's skin undertone in the procedural area, and concluding if a warmer, cooler, or more neutral procedure color is appropriate, the next step is to determine if the client desires a light, medium, or darker color. This is a good opportunity to make an important clarification. When statements are made in the permanent cosmetic industry guiding a technician to a warm or cool formulation base, keep in mind there are varying degrees of warm and cool. As an example, a brown color that appears more red-orange or orange is classified as warm. A brown with a golden base (containing a yellow-orange) is also classified as warm. Although both examples represent warm colors, the color with the golden base (yellow-orange) is less warm than the color with the red-orange (Figure 16-1) or orange base (Figure 16-2).

Figure 16-1: Red-orange

Figure 16-2: Orange

The same *different degrees of coolness* facts apply for cool colors. More neutral colors contain different amounts of yellow. If the yellow has a bias toward green (yellow-green) it is cool. If yellow has a bias toward orange (yellow-orange) it is warm. And there are versions of yellow that when compared to a warmer or cooler yellow will appear more

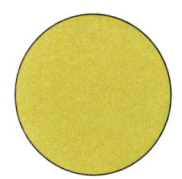

Figure 16-3: Yellow-Green

Figure 16-4: Yellow-Orange

Figure 16-5: More Neutral Yellow

neutral than ones that appear more yellow-green or yellow-orange (see Figure 16-3 thru Figure 16-9).

It is the technician's responsibility to learn the formulation line(s) they have chosen to use. Work with the manufacturer or the distributor and learn the varying degrees of the temperatures of these colors so that they may be properly selected for each skin undertone and procedure type. Manufacturers routinely offer formulations that range from the slightly warm or cool to the very warm or cool for the eyebrow, eyeliner, and lip liner procedures (includes shaded/blended lip liners – *this will not be repeated*). Technicians then have the task of recommending an appropriate color or colors (choices are always recommended) for the client to choose from for the procedure requested.

This may not prove to be as much of a challenge for the eyeliner procedure, and choices are abundant for eyebrows and lip liner procedures. Even though as the professional, a technician may know what color they would prefer to use for the procedure, by offering color options that are all appropriate, including the client in the process transfers some of the responsibility for the outcome to them.

There will be times when a client cannot choose between two different colors. A compromise might be to offer to mix the two optional colors together in varying proportions rather than an either/or choice, or just chose another color. Technicians are in control of how the color selection process plays out with a client. Some clients are easier than others to work with and they put the technician more in control of color selection after a brief description of what they prefer; other clients must feel they were very instrumental in the color selection process in order to be satisfied with the outcome.

Technicians eventually develop a preference for certain colors that serve them well for the majority of their clientele. These preferences are developed over time with knowledge of the formulations, how they perform, and how they appear healed on clientele that represents a variety of skin undertone types.

In general, color selection considerations are provided as follows:

Eyebrow Color Selection

The client's skin undertones in the eyebrow area, depth of the client's skin color (Fitzpatrick skin type), the natural hair coloring of the existing eyebrow hair (if any), and client preferences all have an influence on the color(s) selected to offer to a client for approval.

The value (light to dark) of the healed eyebrow color may heal to appear similar to the color used or darker (in degrees) if the client's skin undertone is a Fitzpatrick type IV–VI. This is due to the different degrees of possible hyperpigmentation associated with these skin types. The analysis options when selecting a color for Fitzpatrick skin types IV-VI are discussed in Section 14.

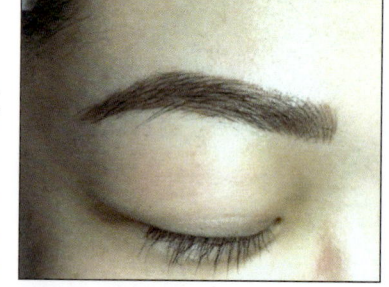

Figure 16-6: Eyebrow procedure

To touch lightly on the subject for this section, some respected professionals in the permanent cosmetics industry have indicated formulations tattooed into skin types Fitzpatrick IV–VI will appear similar to, or darker than, the color used for the procedure when healed. Others indicate they have not consistently experienced this. The tattoo technique also plays a role in how the color appears when healed. Microblading and

Section 16 - Selecting Permanent Cosmetic Procedure Colorants—General Information

machine hair stroke techniques tend to heal cooler (and at times appearing darker) than eyebrow shading techniques with the same color.

    The important thing to remember is to always be conservative. It is easier to make a color darker after it has healed than it is to try to lighten it. While we commonly work with the client based on what they ask for, the following color analysis guidance is based on the theory of *complementing* the skin undertone with an appropriate formulation base color.

The skin undertone and suggested formulation base colors below (based complementing the skin undertone color) provides technicians some options for slight color variances to offer a client while still applying complementary color theory.

Permanent Cosmetic Formulation Bases for Eyebrows

- Yellow includes:
  - yellow-green (less cool) (Figure 16-7)
  - yellow-orange (less warm) (Figure 16-8)
  - more neutral yellow (more neutral) (Figure 16-9)

Figure 16-7: Yellow-green

Figure 16-8: Yellow-orange

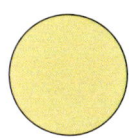

Figure 16-9: More Neutral Yellow

- Green includes:
  - green (cool) (Figure 16-10)
  - yellow-green (less cool) (Figure 16-10)

Figure 16-10: Green

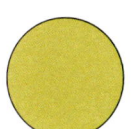

Figure 16-11: Yellow-green

- Orange includes:
  - orange (warm) (Figure 16-12)
  - red-orange (more warm) (Figure 16-13)

Figure 16-12: Orange

Figure 16-13: Red-orange

- Brown and black - different mixes of:
  - dark brown (cool) (Figure 16-14)
  - black-brown (cool) (Figure 16-15)
  - brown-black (cooler) (Figure 16-16)
  - black (coolest) (Figure 16-17)

Figure 16-14: Dark brown

Figure 16-15: Black-brown

Figure 16-16: Brown-black

Figure 16-17: Black

Skin Undertone Type, Color, Temperature and Complementing Formulation Bases

NOTE: *The skin samples are provided to give an idea of the different color/tones of the described skin - but due variations during digital capturing of the skin types and the associated difficulties with color matching in the printing process, the printed version may not be a completely accurate representation, despite the authors and publishers best attempts.*

- **Transparent skin** has violet undertones; it is cool. A yellow-based formulation can be considered. Yellow is the complementary color to violet.

- **Translucent skin** has blue undertones; it is cool. An orange-based formulation can be considered. Orange is the complementary color to blue.

Section 16 - Selecting Permanent Cosmetic Procedure Colorants—General Information

- **Rosy and ruddy skin** has red-violet undertones. Both rosy and ruddy skin types are cool. A yellow-green based formulation can be considered. Yellow-green is the complementary color to red-violet.

- **Peaches and cream skin** (more rare compared to other skin undertone types) has yellow-orange undertones; it is warm. A yellow-green based formulation can be considered.

- **Sallow skin** has more neutral (yellow) or yellow-green skin undertones tones and lacks blue or red influence. It can be either more neutral yellow or yellow-green cool. A yellow-based formulation works well. Violet is the complementary to yellow and it is one of the complementary colors we do not use in permanent cosmetic color theory. A conservative option is to be conservative and look to the yellow-based formulations (more neutral yellow, yellow-green, or yellow-orange).

- **Olive skin** has yellow-green or green undertones; it is cool. A yellow-orange or orange-based formulation can be considered. Yellow-orange is the complementary color to yellow-green. Orange is the complementary color to green.

- **Brown skin** has blue, green, or violet undertones, which are all cool. A warmer orange-based formulation can be considered. Orange is the complementary color to blue and green. Yellow can be added for those instances where a violet undertone is prominent.

- **Extreme white and black** (includes dark brown) skin more often has blue skin undertones. Both extreme white and black skin types are very cool. An orange-based formulation can be considered. Orange is the complementary color to blue.

When departing from the theory of complementing a client's skin undertone with an appropriate warm or cool color, the discussion then broadens to a specific client request.

Formulation modifiers/adjusters/correction pigments (branded under a variety of names) are provided by some manufacturers for the purpose of adding color needed to adjust a pigment color based on a client's preference and/or skin undertone, as well as for correction/neutralizing purposes. Some manufacturers may provide these pigment colors for the sole purpose of correcting/neutralizing an existing healed color in the skin. In all cases, technicians should be aware of manufacturer's directions/guidance as it pertains to using these formulations.

An example of this, is a person with darker brown skin who has blue undertones (see Figure 16-18). In order to provide contrast, the color chosen may be a formulation with dark brown, black-brown, brown-black, or black base and void of any, or any substantial amounts of orange. The orange (if needed) is added in appropriate amounts by the technician.

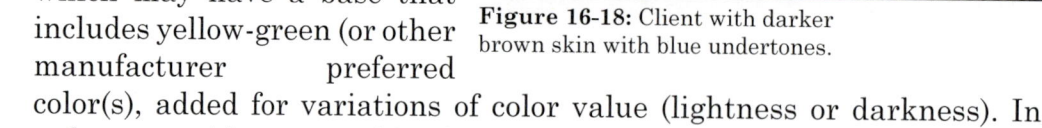

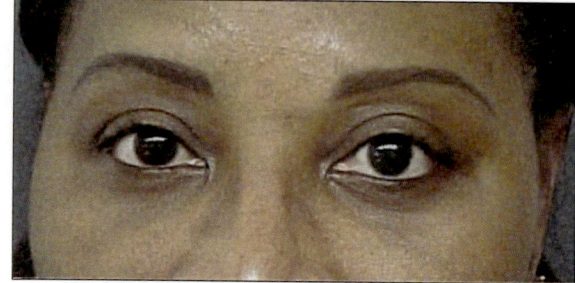

Figure 16-18: Client with darker brown skin with blue undertones.

Another example would be the color gray or taupe (see Figure 16-19 and Figure 16-20), which may have a base that includes yellow-green (or other manufacturer preferred color(s), added for variations of color value (lightness or darkness). In order to avoid a *too cool* healed result, if needed, additional yellow or yellow-orange may be added by the technician.

Figure 16-19: Gray

Figure 16-20: Taupe

Color modifiers/adjusters (and other names assigned by the manufacturer) provide technicians with the ability to choose an appropriate darker, cooler, or warmer color and then add the complementary color to their client's skin undertone in appropriate amounts if needed.

Other Eyebrow Color Considerations

In general, and there are always exceptions to general rules, using the color black alone is not recommended for eyebrow procedures unless no other color would show contrast after the eyebrow heals due to the dark color of the client's skin. It is assumed that a black eyebrow color might be considered for a person with very dark brown or black skin. Unless black is the only logical choice, a darker brown or black-brown represent the first considerations. Be conservative on the first application, as it is always easier to modify a recently healed lighter eyebrow to a darker color than it is to modify a darker eyebrow color to a lighter one.

Figure 16-21: Brown

In the example of using a dark brown (Figure 16-21) or black-brown (Figure 16-22) color on dark brown or black skin, these colors represent cooler colors. This accompanied with the coolness of dark brown on black skin can result in the eyebrow healing *too cool*. To prevent a *too cool* healed eyebrow on extreme dark brown or black skin, the dark brown or black-brown color to be used may be adjusted with orange (the complementary color to blue) to warm up the coolness of the color. This helps complement the blue coolness of the extreme dark brown or black skin undertone.

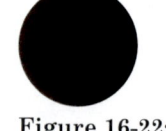

Figure 16-22: Black-brown

People with blonde eyebrows often also have light skin and light scalp hair coloring. They are often very cautious about their permanent cosmetic eyebrows appearing too

Section 16 - Selecting Permanent Cosmetic Procedure Colorants—General Information

dark. They may be accustomed to matching or coming close to the color of their scalp hair and when they arrive with their version of eyebrow design and color, and technicians may have to look hard to see a trace of the color they use with pencil or powder.

The topical makeup industry may recommend darker eyebrows for contrast and drama, but this may be a hard sell for someone who is not accustomed to seeing obvious color. Remember, there is always the follow-up visit thirty to sixty days (or as appropriate based on the client's age and health) after the initial procedure to adjust the color darker if deemed necessary.

It is recommended technicians take a conservative approach to all color selection for procedures. This point is emphasized in this section for clients with pale skin and blonde eyebrow hair. The lighter blonde colors usually prevail (see Figure 16-23).

If the client's natural eyebrow hair is very light (sometimes bordering gray or white in color), eyebrow formulations should be kept light as well.

Figure 16-23: Light Cool Blonde

A noticeable contrast of tattooed color placed behind very light eyebrow hair color results in the eyebrow hair appearing dominant, shielding or distorting the color that was placed behind it. It is recommended that light cool or warm blondes (Figure 16-24 and Figure 16-25), or a light taupe/gray (Figure 16-26) (as appropriate) be considered. Tattooing a medium or medium-dark color behind light eyebrows does not make the light eyebrow hair appear darker; in fact, just the opposite.

Figure 16-24: Light Cool Blonde

Figure 16-25: Light Warm Blonde

Figure 16-26: Light Taupe

Gray or white eyebrow hairs do little for the appearance of a natural or tattooed eyebrow. White reflects all light and subsequently, draws attention to the gray or white hairs as opposed to the nicely tattooed design work.

Some people with fuller gray or white eyebrows may not be good candidates for eyebrow tattooing if a lighter blonde or light taupe cannot be used with a good outcome.

Eyebrow tinting or eyebrow mascara are two recommended options. There will be instances where the client will commit to tinting their gray or white eyebrow hairs, or wearing eyebrow mascara after their eyebrow procedure has healed to blend in their lighter eyebrow hairs with the tattooed color.

More mature clients with transparent (violet) or translucent (blue) skin undertones may also have silver, gray or white scalp hair (some with gray hair that borders blonde). Throughout the years, some of these clients have grown accustomed to using a gray eyebrow pencil, thinking their eyebrows should closely agree with their natural scalp hair coloring.

Although a lighter blonde with a warmer base would be more appropriate to neutralize the cool violet or blue skin undertones, they stand fast on their desire for a gray eyebrow. Permanent cosmetic professionals do not always see gray as the most flattering eyebrow color, but in those instances where a gray healed color is desired, technicians must respect the client's wishes or decline the work. A suggested alternative and compromise to a gray eyebrow color is to offer a lighter taupe color (Figure 16-27).

Figure 16-27: Light Taupe

Depending on the manufacturer, taupe eyebrow colors are often characteristically more of an ash brown (cool) color which, when combined with a cool skin tone, may provide the borderline gray color the client desires without actually tattooing in gray. The skin, which is cool to some degree, cools down the appearance of the color once healed. Technicians must be well informed as to the expected performance of taupe colors. Some taupe formulations have more green, some more yellow, or yellow-green, and some have a gray cast.

Technicians can't go by a manufacturer assigned color name; they have to understand the ingredients in the formulations. Often technicians will act conservatively with taupe colors for eyebrow procedures and add a small amount of a yellow or yellow-orange modifier/adjuster in order to first determine how the client's skin undertone will affect the healed color before using a taupe exclusively. Manufacturers have formulated softer versions of gray colors that can also be offered to these clients.

Eyebrow formulation bases are red-orange or orange which are both warm, yellow (a more neutral yellow, a cool yellow-green, or a warm yellow-orange), cool green, cool dark brown, cool black-brown, cool brown-black, or cool black. There are wide selections of formulation lines from which to choose.

To speak about all the available lines and the varied formulations the manufacturers offer is impossible.

It is the responsibility of technicians to be well educated on their formulation ingredients to apply that knowledge with the skin undertone type they are working with, and apply that information as both relate to the procedure being conducted.

The Aged Eyebrow Color

Another eyebrow color scenario technicians are confronted with is *color correcting/adjusting and color refreshing* aged eyebrow procedures, some of which were tattooed by other technicians.

This is mentioned because it is not unusual for a technician to have requests for eyebrow work that was originally performed by other technicians. Technicians move or retire (as do clients), and although a client may be professionally referred to a technician, often they independently look for another technician to provide their color correction/adjustment or refresher/color boost work.

Skin undertone affects how all color appears in the skin, including how it looks when the color subsequently fades over time (as all color does). Skin undertones are subject to change (due to thinning skin) as a person ages, which affects how the original selection of color appears through the filter of the skin. As a result, what is sometimes seen are aged and faded eyebrow colors, and depending on the ingredients of the original formulation used, the eyebrow may have traces of warmer or cooler residual colors (general examples). Ideally, tattooed eyebrows would fade uniformly as they age, but the industry sees different variations of aged color.

Eyeliner Color Selection

The color and density of the client's eyelashes can influence the depth of color offered for eyeliner procedures. It is customary for topical makeup eyeliners to be dark brown, black-brown, brown-black, black, or charcoal (all standard eyeliner colors). As a result, many clients will request a color the same as or close to what they have been applying topically for many years. Consider the natural color of the eyelashes (without mascara). If the eyelashes are light, they will diminish the appearance of the darker tattooed eyeliner color. Some technicians consider a dark brown rather than other standard eyeliner colors under these circumstances.

Although a client may request a blue, green, violet, or some other fashion color(s) for an eyeliner procedure, more often than not, a large percentage of clients request dark brown, black-brown, brown-black, black, or charcoal. Using these standard eyeliner colors makes the formulation selection process somewhat easier. It is recommended that only trained and experienced technicians use organic carbon black for eyeliner procedures.

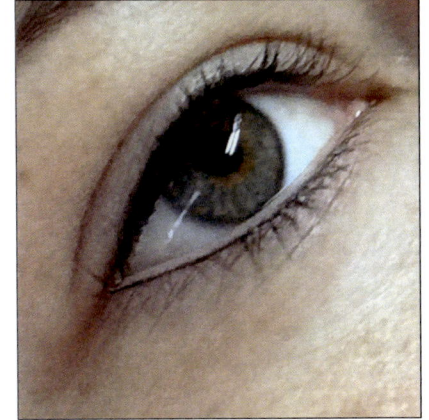

Figure 16-28: Eyelash enhancement and lower liner

Organic carbon black is the thermal decomposition of hydrocarbons; it is a smaller molecule than other black formulation types, and, if not used properly, can result in eyeliner migrations. A client may tire of a trendy eyeliner color and/or the aging process of the once vibrant eyeliner color. The color may fade to a washed-out version of what was originally tattooed and require more maintenance and upkeep.

If in agreement with this concept, consider advising clients who ask for non-standard colors that a basic dark brown, black-brown, brown-black, black, or charcoal eyeliner color may be a more versatile basic color choice. They can always apply a non-standard color topically with cosmetics over their permanent cosmetic eyeliner for special occasions.

With this said, there will be clients who are adamant about fashion eyeliner colors (see Figure 16-29). It is the technician's job to work with the client and come to a decision that both are comfortable with.

If it is agreed to tattoo a non-standard eyeliner color, consider avoiding versions of violet colors on eyelids that have blue, or violet undertones. One reason a client may have a blue or mauve undertone around their eyes is because of thinning skin (see Figure 16-30).

Figure 16-29: Fashion Color Eyeliner
Advanced procedure technique

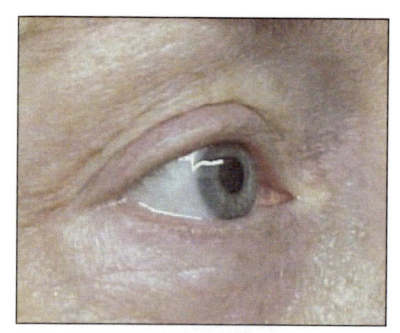

Figure 16-30: Thinning skin and violet undertones

This is more commonly seen on the eyelids of more mature clients. If one of the mentioned colors is used, a combination of a vascular system (appearing bluish, violet, or red-violet through the skin) that is close to the surface of the lids may result in an undesirable or unexpected color. Eyelids with this undertone coloring can appear tired, and the tattooed color loses its contract to the lids if the chosen color accentuates the existing bluish or mauve undertones.

Lip Color Selection

Lip liner will be addressed. Full lip color is considered an advanced procedure and is not appropriate fundamental textbook information. Lip liner training may also be considered procedures more suitably offered and learned after novice technicians are comfortable with eyebrow and eyeliner procedures. This varies between trainers, class curriculums, and the duration of the fundamental class program.

The client's natural lip color has an influence on the formulation's base temperature (warm or cool) and the value (lightness or darkness) of color chosen for lip liner procedures. More often the procedure is focused on defining the vermilion border and blending with the

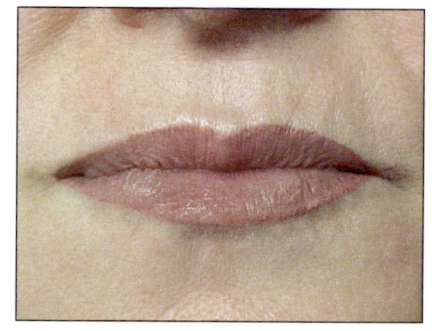

Figure 16-31: Shaded Lip Liner

Section 16 - Selecting Permanent Cosmetic Procedure Colorants—General Information

natural lip color.

Clients may request lip liner colors with the intention of altering the appearance of their natural vermilion border color. However, a color that departs dramatically from the client's natural lip tone is characteristically considered inappropriate for a lip liner. The result is a *ring around the mouth* appearance that only appears complete when the client applies other lip color products. It is advisable for technicians to consider refusing lip liner requests that would result in an extreme demarcation line of color around the mouth.

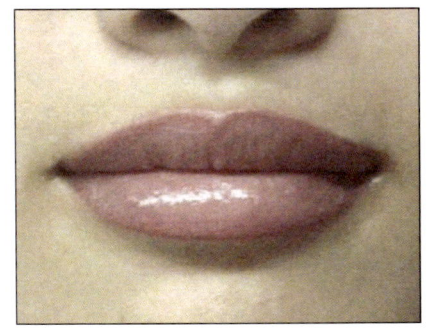

Figure 16-32: Lip Liner

It is advisable to choose lip liner colors that will closely correspond with a client's natural lip tone when healed. This is essential to achieve a soft, natural lip definition appearance when the procedure has healed.

Darker lip formulations are cooler in temperature. Darker, cooler lip colors tattooed into a lip that has strong cool undertones may produce a *too cool* healed lip. This is neither desirable nor easy to correct. Blue is not thought to be an ingredient in most permanent cosmetic formulations unless as a fashion eyeliner color. A magenta color, ultramarine violet, or a cool red are three colors often substituted to create the cool appearance of many lip formulations.

Figure 16-33: Darker Lip Color

Orange is a color often added to lip formulas as insurance to complement the natural cool (bluish appearing in different degrees) lip undertones. The complementary color to blue on the traditional artist's color wheel is orange. Even the coolest appearing lip formulations may indeed contain some degree of orange. Often this is information that is provided by the manufacturer or distributor.

Some organic red lip formulations (bright colored) may be less opaque and sheer when healed. If a sheer organic red-based formulation is used on the vermilion border of a client who has strong cool (bluish appearing) undertones, what may result is a violet or purple color when healed (blue + red = violet).

The lighter and medium lip formulations often represent the manufacturer's addition of white to the formula for opacity. As a result, the lighter and medium color lip formulations may prove to provide more coverage to slight natural lip variances than the darker formulations, which can get lost in the cooler undertones of a lip.

Technicians are *strongly cautioned* not to add additional white to lighten any formulation. White forms larger particles, is very cool, sits closer to the surface of the skin, and reflects more light.

The warmer the base of the lip formulation, the less likely it is that a lip will heal too cool.

Asking a client to bring the topical cosmetic lip liner pencil she or he may request for a permanent cosmetic lip liner color is always advisable. The additive of orange as insurance to a cool lip color does not need to be discussed with the client. This is a professional judgment call on behalf of the technician to do what is ultimately best for the client.

Adding an appropriate amount of orange to a lip color is a technique that normally acts only to absorb or neutralize the cool undertones in the client's natural lip. When used conservatively, orange does not noticeably alter the healed appearance of the target color selected.

Creating New Color by Mixing

Tattoo formulations are often mixed together by technicians. This is common in the permanent cosmetic industry and acceptable as long as it is recognized that this represents creating a completely different color than a manufacturer has formulated or tested.

Adjusting the healed results (if necessary) of a custom-made color has been proven to be more complex than adjusting the outcome of a procedure conducted with one color, or one color with the addition of a modifier. For instance, if the color did not heal as desired, which of the mixed colors needs to be adjusted at the follow-up appointment? It is recommended for novice technicians to mix no more than two colors for the reasons stated.

Mixing eyeliner colors is not a common practice due to the acceptance of standard colors used and the wide variety of selections that are available. Manufacturers also provide a wide range of eyebrow and lip colors from which to choose. The less number of colors mixed together to create a different color, the better. Ensure that any custom colors mixed are well documented on the client's chart.

Summary

Color selection for each client is unique, it's an art, and it is an integral part of a successful permanent cosmetic business. Technicians rarely ever get exactly what they see in formulations containers (or viewed on the surface of the skin) once the color has been tattooed into the skin and the procedure has healed.

The client's skin undertone influences the final healed color. The warm and lighter-to-medium lip formulations are considered conservative selections for the novice technician. The addition of orange to a cool based lip formulation is considered a good insurance technique to avoid the lip color from healing too cool if the formulation doesn't contain the orange needed. Some manufacturers add more orange to their lip colors, and some do not).

Be conservative. It is better to conduct the procedure more than once to get the desired results comfortably for the client than to produce unwanted color and be in a position of correcting or attempting to remove an unwanted color.

This section of the textbook may be challenging to technicians who are just entering the industry and have not been exposed to different brands and formulations, etc. It is not expected that technicians would try to memorize the information. It is provided primarily as an introduction to the world of skin undertones and suggested color considerations. It is a source of information to refer to.

There are many very good formulation manufacturers. Always ask for their support materials. After a few years, technicians find that they have certain selections in their inventory of colors that they would not be without.

Permanent Cosmetic Color Correction and Adjustment Guide

You may want to refresh your knowledge of Permanent Cosmetic Color Theory (Section 15) to better comprehend the following guidance. Briefly, as a refresher to the Permanent Cosmetic Complementary Colors guide:

Permanent Cosmetic Color Theory (PCCT) does not apply the complementary pairing of colors like traditional color theory does. The following applies:

- Orange compliments or corrects (neutralizes) green and blue (includes gray) – But in PCCT, blue is not used to compliment or correct orange.
- Yellow compliments or corrects (neutralizes) violet, but violet is not used to compliment or correct yellow.
- Green compliments or corrects (neutralizes) orange and red, but red without a bias toward orange is not used to correct green.

Knowledge of permanent cosmetic color correction and adjustment techniques is important. While a technician may decide not to offer correction services to people who were not their original clients, over time, it will be necessary to apply these skills to adjust and correct color that the client did not take care of properly and a host of other situations they may encounter.

The following examples require knowledge of color correction/adjustment techniques:

- Clients who request correction services as a result of a poor color choice.
- Adjustments needed due to color shifts resulting from chemical exposure (facial products), lack of sunscreen protection, or changes in skin undertone classification.
- Adjustments needed after an initial procedure has healed, and the color requires a slight modification to a warmer or cooler version.

Example 1

Correction Services on Work Previously Performed by Another Technician:

It is not uncommon for prospective clients to request corrections after they have been previously tattooed by someone other than the person conducting the correction procedure. These corrections are often the most difficult to analyze and often involve design correction as well.

Under these circumstances, the correcting technician is normally not aware of the original formulation manufacturer or color utilized for the original procedure. The technician bases their evaluation process is what they see, the client's skin undertone and an unacceptable color. This puts the technician in a position of attempting to analyze the characteristics of an unknown color and forming a plan for correcting the color to the client's specifications.

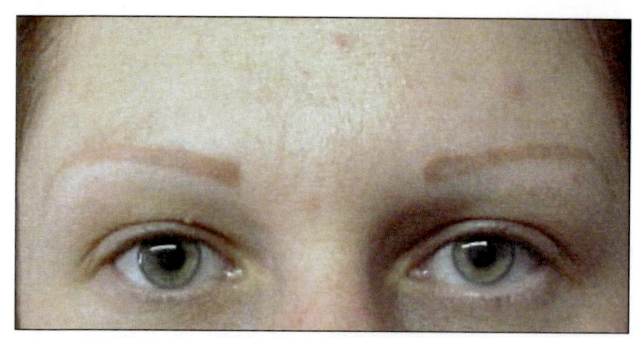

Figure 16-34: Brow that requires design and color correction

The first question to the client will be, *"Why are you not returning to the original technician for the correction work?"* This is important because the original technician has all the historic information necessary to make color correction choices easier. Many times the answer will relate to dissatisfaction on the client's behalf; they have lost faith in the original technician and refuse to return for additional work.

Be very cautious about being involved with conversations regarding a client's previous experience with another technician. Even though a disgruntled client may speak freely of their version of the previous relationship, as there is no way of knowing what transpired between the client and original technician. It may very well be that the client is as much responsible for the poor color choice as the technician although, in most instances, technicians who are well trained will refuse to follow through with unwise color choice requests. The client also may not have cared for the procedure as directed.

The bottom line is, without historical information at hand, important data needed to work with confidence on another technician's work may not be readily available. Proceed with caution, if at all.

If possible, obtain the original brand and the specific color used. Once a technician has this information the manufacturer or distributor can be contacted and important questions asked. This, accompanied with an analysis of the person's skin undertone, may reveal a lot of information as to why the color appears as it does. Unfortunately, more often than not technicians do not have the benefit of any prior color information from the client's previous technician, or what could be considered 100% accurate information from the client. They have to make a decision if they can correct the color to the client's satisfaction based on what they see.

Example 2

Adjustments Needed Due to Color Shifts Resulting from Chemical Exposure (Facial Products), Lack of Sunscreen Protection, or Changes in Skin Undertone Classification.

Color changes may occur as a result of chemical exposure (facial products as an example), unprotected procedures exposed to the sun, tanning beds, and other known contraindications of permanent cosmetics. Under these circumstances, a technician may see an undesirable or prematurely faded version of the original color.

Every individual colorant in a formulation has a life. Particular colors are mixed together by the manufacturer in anticipation they will age in a similar manner over time. Environmental stress factors can disrupt the normal aging process of a color resulting in the need for color correction work. Also for consideration is the skin's maturing personality. As the skin ages, the classification of undertones is subject to change. A peaches and cream complexion can later in life appear rosy or ruddy, for instance. The skin thins and the vascular system is more influential on the classification of skin undertone.

The client may very well have originally received the correct color choice at the time, but in concert with the maturing process, the properties of the skin composition and the classification of skin undertones may have changed. Skin undertone changes affect how the color is seen through the filter of the skin. Over time, as a client returns for subsequent refreshers and an unexpected aged and faded color is seen, technicians often fault the manufacturer of the color that was originally used.

In reality, it is possible that neither the specific color brand nor the technician's original choice of color may be the source of the problem. The shift in color appearance may very well be as a result of a change to the client's skin undertone, chemical exposure (facial products), lack of good maintenance on behalf of the client, excessive sun exposure, and a multitude of other possibilities neither the technician nor the formulation manufacturer has any control over. There are many actors in the theater of colorant and formulation behavior.

The following guide refers to correction colorants, and depending on the brand may have a specific name such as a *modifier, anti (name), adjustor,* or a variety of other descriptions. This indicates a color that made specifically for color correction or adjustment purposes. Often these specialty colors are different versions of orange, yellow, and green (PCCT complementary colors).

Eyebrow Color Corrections:

Existing color that requires correcting and color adjustments as outlined in examples 1 and 2 follow the same technique processes:

If the *eyebrow* color is warm (red or orange):
- Use a cool (green) correction colorant (there are different shades of green

including yellow-green).

If the eyebrow color is cool blue, gray, green, or black:
- Use an orange correction colorant (there are different shades of orange, including yellow-orange).

If the eyebrow color is cool violet:
- Use a yellow correction colorant (there are different shades of yellow including a more neutral yellow and yellow-orange).

It is at this juncture a decision must be made. There are two choices for consideration:
- The optimal decision would be to tattoo the correction color and allow the correction procedure to heal. At the follow-up appointment analyze whether or not additional work is needed with the correction color. If not, proceed with a choice of a color that meets the client's expectations (often referred to as a *target* color).
- The second option is to take a chance that tattooing the correction color and the choice of a color that meets the client's expectations (target color) at the same appointment will be effective. This can be a risky approach depending on the density of the procedure to be color corrected. If, when the client returns for the follow-up appointment, additional correction work is needed, this further correction is now more complex. A new color is seen as a result of the combination of correction and target colors and the skin has limits as to how much tattooed color it will effectively hold.

In the event the eyebrow color to be corrected is not dense (at times transparent), it may be adequate to use an appropriate warm, cool or more neutral based target eyebrow color (not a specific color formulated for corrections) for the procedure.

Under these same low-density color circumstances, another option is to make a pass with the correction color, and then subsequent passes with the chosen target color.

If the color is quite dense, laser or tattoo lightening/removal techniques (both are dependent on if considered appropriate for the procedure and client's Fitzpatrick skin type) should be employed prior to any subsequent tattooing. This relieves the procedure area of color particles that consume space and allows room for a more effective correction process.

Technicians must effectively analyze the density of the color to be corrected, make good decisions, and apply the appropriate technique.

Eyeliner Color Corrections

Eyeliner color corrections are not as common or as challenging as eyebrow or lip liner color corrections. Typically the eyeliner is refreshed with a black or black-brown, charcoal, or the original fashion eyeliner color, and that seems to elevate most of these type corrections.

An exception to this would be what is called *French* eyeliners where white, or some directive of white, has been tattooed over the eyeliner color to highlight it. The color white is nearly impossible to redirect to another color.

Lip Liner Color Corrections

If the lip liner color to be corrected is blue or violet:

- Use an orange-based corrective formulation. There are orange colors that are more neutral orange, red-orange, and some that are that are more yellow-orange.
- The selection must be appropriate for the lip color in question and there are many to choose from. If in doubt, contact the manufacturer or distributor for advice.
- There is the choice of tattooing only the correction color and allowing healing to take place before tattooing a target color, or proceeding with both at the same session.

The density of the lip liner or shaded lip liner color to be corrected is the deciding factor. Tattoo lightening/removal to reduce the density of color is a consideration.

Full lips are considered advanced work in most training venues and are not addressed in a fundamental textbook.

Example 3

Minor Color Adjustments at the Follow-Up Appointment

Minor color adjustments that may be needed at the follow-up visit to original work are normally the easiest to resolve after thirty to sixty days post-procedure (or as appropriate based on the client's age and health profile).

If the original color selected was appropriate for the client's skin undertone, what the client requested, and conservative in color value, in all likelihood the only change (if any) will be that the color will require an adjustment to slightly darker.

Keep in mind that the darker the formulation, the more cool properties the formulation will have by degrees (the darker the color, the cooler the color). This can be accomplished by adding a small amount of a darker color (darker than the initial color used) to the original color used. Also, take into consideration that another application of the same color will produce more depth of color. Sometimes adding a darker color is not necessary to achieve a darker version of a procedure; only deepening the same color by reapplication of the same color is needed. The more colorant particles, the more depth of the same color.

If it is decided to go over the entire procedure area with a totally different warmer or cooler color to add warmth, coolness, or for darkening purposes, ensure that all surrounding edges of the procedure area are adequately covered, or once the adjustment procedure has healed, a slight halo of the lighter color may be visible.

Altering a newly healed eyebrow or eyeliner color to appear slightly warmer or cooler can be accomplished by adding a small amount of a warm or cool color corrector formulation (these are sold under a variety of names indicating a color made specifically for correction or adjustment purposes), as appropriate, to the original color at the follow-up appointment. This allows technicians to continue to use the original color approved by the client but to alter it slightly at the follow-up visit based on the healed result.

If working conservatively and using natural appearing colors for *lip liners* and *shaded/blended lip liners* (as recommended), a minor color adjustment is likely to only involve deepening (more dense saturation) the color. That is normally accomplished by performing the procedure again with the same color, thus providing more depth of color. Full lip color adjustments are not appropriate content for a fundamental textbook. This is advanced work and requires training that focuses on color modifications.

If correction formulations (which are sold under various descriptions) are not available in the formulation line used, the manufacturer or distributor can be contacted for advice. Many times manufacturers will offer color correction advice that leads technicians to the use of a warmer, cooler, or more neutral color in their existing line as appropriate.

Color corrections and adjustments can be successfully achieved if the technician is well trained in the artistic application of permanent cosmetic color theory is knowledgeable about the formulations used, and works conservatively. Many times, color corrections and adjustments require multiple sessions to achieve the desired result.

Section 17

Basic Facial Morphology and Placement of Procedures

Learning Objectives

Introduction

Often it is asked, "Is it important to be an artist to perform permanent cosmetics?" The answer is clearly yes. The extent to which artistry is important, however, is limited to the face for the novice technician. Advanced work (breast areola complex as an example) on other parts of the body will require the benefits of specialized artistry as well. Whereby many permanent cosmetic artists are accomplished in other areas of artistry, the face is the primary canvas of permanent cosmetics and understanding basic facial morphology is crucial for a successful procedure.

The study of facial morphology is a science. The proper placement of procedure design work is the responsibility of the technician, Clients may request a technician disregard appropriate design work and placement, and while some deviation may be acceptable, unreasonable requests should not be agreed to.

Often clients will try to encourage permanent cosmetic artists to work outside the parameters of industry standards. They may ask for eyebrow placement higher than what would otherwise be appropriate. Also not uncommon is the request to make smaller lips bigger by placing the pigment far outside the vermilion border. It is evident from photos available on the Internet, or inexperienced technician websites that without a good education to the contrary, technicians can create problems for themselves, their clients, and cosmetic surgeons and other medical and beauty service providers who work with the same canvas as the permanent cosmetic artist.

Objective

Upon completion of this section, the technician will recognize the parallels between topical makeup design and permanent cosmetic design work. She or he will have a better understanding of how to recognize symmetry, asymmetry, and how the design template and subsequent permanent tattooing work can help improve upon noticeable asymmetry. The technician will learn the standard sections of an eyebrow design, proper placement of the eyebrow, eyeliner, and lip template design work in relation to the client's facial morphology and age characteristics.

Section 17 - Basic Facial Morphology and Placement of Procedures

It is important to understand the fundamentals of topical makeup artistry and to the extent possible apply these guidelines to the placement of permanent cosmetic procedures. Precise placement will create the symmetry or a better impression of symmetry, which translates to balance or proportional harmony.

Symmetry has been scientifically proven to be inherently attractive to the human eye. It has been defined not only with proportions but also with the similarity between the left and right sides of the face (bilateral symmetry).

Why all the emphasis on symmetry? Physical symmetry is associated with beauty and in general, studies indicate attractive people tend to be more intelligent, better adjusted, and more popular. This is described by some as the *halo effect*—due to the perceived perfection associated with angels. Research shows attractive people also have more occupational success and more dating experience than their unattractive counterparts.

Facial Proportions

A working knowledge of the dimensional relationship between one facial feature and another helps us appreciate the differences in individual faces; few people have perfect facial proportions, and without the imperfections that give distinction to the face, everyone might somewhat resemble everyone else.

Makeup, hairstyles, beards, and mustaches help people to compensate for small imperfections. Attractiveness is not dependent on perfect facial features to everyone and many see the value in faces with character. Some people feel uncomfortable with less than perfect proportional faces and choose to have plastic surgery to improve the proportion of some feature of their face. A rhinoplasty, (surgical remodeling of the nose), is a popular cosmetic surgery procedure for those who feel their nose is out of proportion with the other features of their face, and lip fillers are frequently used to boost the volume of lip tissue for people with lips that are not proportionate.

The horizontal diameter of the face is divided into three equal sections. The first section starts at the forehead and extends to a line that is even with the top of the eyebrows. The second section extends from the eyebrows to the tip of the nose. The third section is from the tip of the nose to the tip of the chin.

The vertical diameter of the face is divided into five equal sections. Each section is approximately the width of one eye, with space the size of one eye between the eyes. Lips and eyebrows measure slightly more than the width of one of the sections.

The eye follows the gentle lines of a symmetrical face as a whole, whereas the eye will quickly identify indiscretions in the facial lines and/or proportions. Eyes follow lines and when the flow of the line of a facial characteristic is interrupted, this translates to asymmetry or imbalance.

As an example as to how the eye accepts a balanced face as a whole, as opposed to the eye being drawn to imperfections or lack of symmetry, below are examples for study purposes (see Figure 17-1 and Figure 17-2). In each of the two sets of pictures, with the use of computer technology, the original picture of the women (original picture is the first picture) has been split and rejoined into two right sides (center picture) and two left sides (last picture) of the face. This demonstrates just how very similar symmetric faces appear and how different asymmetric people would look if they were bilaterally symmetric. Compare the perfectly symmetrical (bilaterally or mirror image perfect) to the woman's real appearance demonstrated in the first photograph.

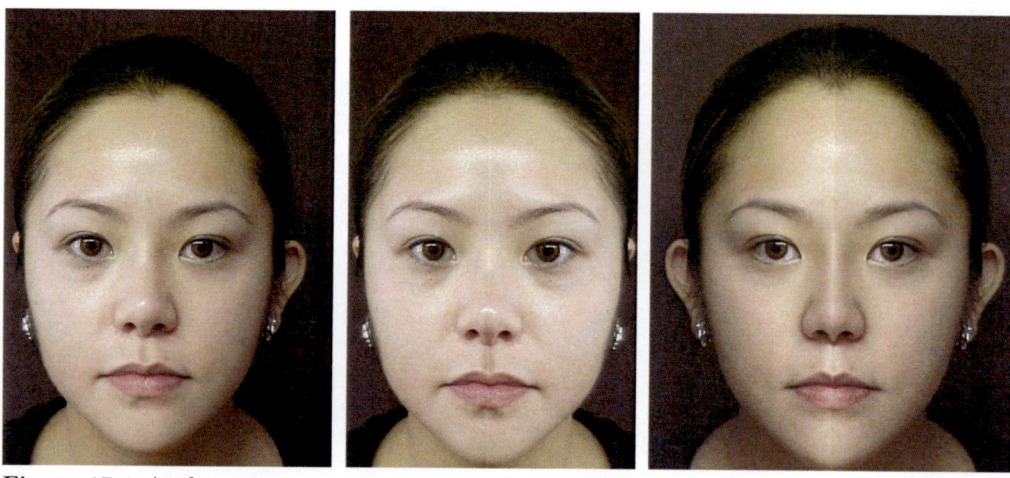

Figure 17-1: As the woman appears (left); two right sides of the face (center); two left sides of the face (right)

There are slight differences when comparing these three photographs, indicating this woman's face is more symmetric. The two right sides of the client's face when joined illustrate the appearance of more pleasant symmetry than joining the two left sides of her face.

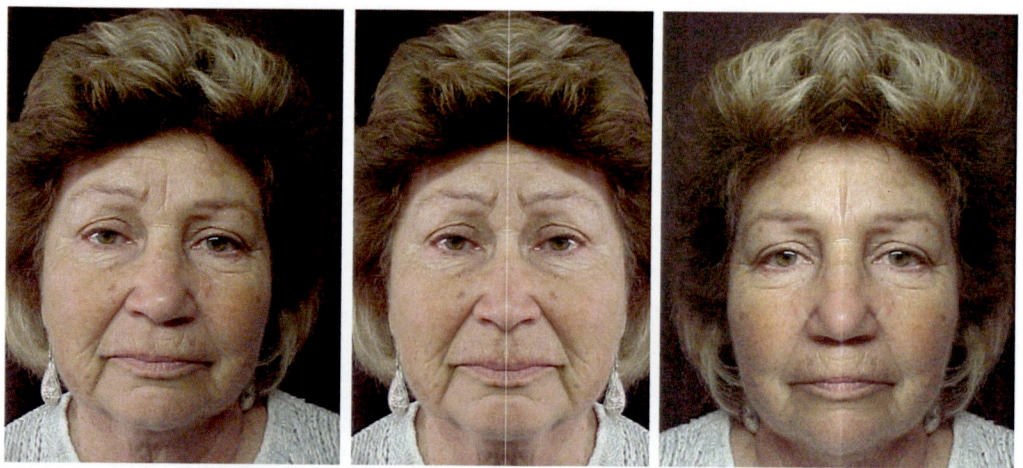

Figure 17-2: As the woman appears (left); two right sides of the face (center); two left sides of the face (right)

There are noticeable differences when comparing these three photographs, indicating

Section 17 - Basic Facial Morphology and Placement of Procedures

this woman's face is less symmetric. The two left sides of the client's face when joined illustrate the appearance of more pleasing symmetry than joining the two right sides of her face.

Creating the best impression of symmetry is part of our job as permanent cosmetic professionals.

Volumes have been written about makeup artistry, facial symmetry, and the achievement of a physically beautiful face. It is suggested if you do not have a makeup artistry background you pursue learning more about this subject through available books on the subject or enroll in a class that teaches the basics. Technicians cannot anticipate learning all there is needed to know about makeup artistry, facial morphology, and creating the illusion of balance and beauty in a permanent cosmetic class.

Nonetheless, basic information is appropriately discussed in a fundamental class for permanent cosmetics. To understand correct placement of eyebrows, eyeliner, and lip liners, technicians must have an understanding of traditional makeup artistry. In many instances, this knowledge gives insight to what cannot or should not be done with cosmetic tattooing.

The Client and Topical Makeup

Topical application of makeup addresses the immediate, more dramatic, or event-specific needs of a client often associated with seasonal trends and without the concern for potential aging skin characteristics. Tattooing pigment in the skin requires a vision of what will be appropriate now as well as in the future.

Topical makeup application theories become of great importance during the consultation and design phases of the desired procedure. The client usually arrives with a preconceived notion of what design and color selections are best based on her or his routine topical makeup preferences.

One very important aspect of a more mature client's relationship with daily makeup application is that often the client tends to apply colors and designs that looked good on her or him when they were younger, sometimes without consideration for skin undertones that have changed and the different positioning of aging skin. Eyesight and dexterity challenges may result in misplaced makeup, but it is not unusual for the client to have worn it in that fashion for so long it has become what they are accustomed to seeing. The younger client may routinely apply more dramatic designs and colors that will not stand the test of time with permanent cosmetic applications.

Permanent cosmetic technicians have their work cut out for them. Negotiating appropriate colors and designs with people who have become accustomed to their own design work and a variety of colorful topical makeup must be approached in an educational and sensitive manner. Conversations that lead to statements such as *"This is what you should consider for permanent cosmetics, and this is what you can add with traditional makeup if you wish to enhance the permanent cosmetic procedure"* are often discussions we have with clients.

Colors used for topical makeup applications that the prospective client is accustomed to applying are also at times unrealistic when considering a permanent application. Some clients will bring in a variety of eyebrow pencils and powders to show the technician the technique they use to reach that perfect color. A wide range of lipstick types and colors are presented to show technicians frosted, matt, and gloss finishes, which may be unrealistic when considering a tattooed finished lip appearance. Although topical makeup and permanent cosmetics have commonalities, the vast differences lie with the fact that topical makeup is applied on top of the skin, can be washed off, and colors are often changed based on what the client has selected for clothing to wear or a change in hair color, etc.

If technicians had the opportunity to attend a presentation of a professional topical makeup artist and permanent cosmetic professional discussing makeup suggestions for the same person, they may hear very different presentations. The differences are at times quite remarkable and strengthen the fact that they serve two different purposes.

Permanent cosmetics and traditional topical makeup can work together. Clients should be made aware that just because they have permanent cosmetics, it does not take away from their ability to apply different shades of topical makeup to an eyebrow to accommodate a change in hair color, or to apply thicker eyeliner for special events to a basic permanent eyeliner design. A subtle permanent cosmetic lip color can always be enhanced with topical lip products since people seem to like applying different colors and textures of lipstick to change the ambiance of their appearance. In order to simplify the differences between permanent makeup colors and designs that should be considered for procedures, some technicians advise their clients to consider permanent cosmetics their makeup lingerie.

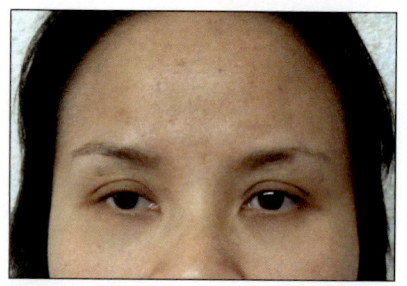

Figure 17-3: Natural Eyebrow

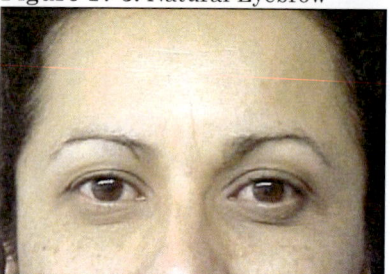

Figure 17-4: Natural Eyebrow

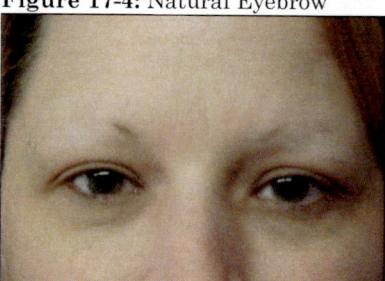

Figure 17-5: Natural Eyebrow

Eyebrows

Eyebrow procedures are one of the most popular services in our industry for a variety of reasons. The eyebrows frame the eyes and provide expression. If a person has few eyebrow hairs the eyes appear duller, and the overall presentation of the face (how a person appears to another) is unbalanced. People seem to feel entitled to eyebrows.

A healthy natural eyebrow follows the supra orbital bony structure of the curved line of the eye socket.

As designers it is somewhat easy to draw and discuss our own idea of the perfect eyebrow; however, there is another aspect that must be considered: how does the client feel they should look? This imposes a variable that becomes frustrating at times when artistically, and based on standard makeup artistry guidelines, an eyebrow should be placed in a particular manner, but the client sees things differently. Even more importantly, how do the client's natural eyebrows appear? Often they are not even, one or the other eyebrow may have more hair than the other, or the client may have little or no eyebrow hair at all. Figure 17-3 to Figure 17-5 are a few examples of natural eyebrows.

An approach that is very revealing is to ask the client to arrive at the consultation (or the appointment if a consultation is to be joined with the actual procedure timing) with her or his eyebrow drawn on as she or he typically applies it with topical makeup. Remove only one of the topically drawn on eyebrow designs and draw on a classic (standard measurements) eyebrow.

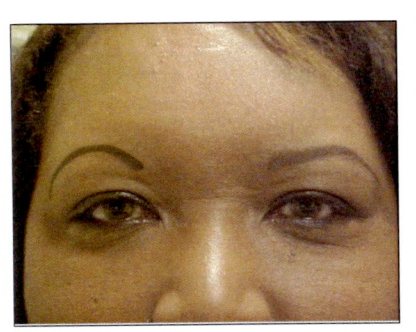

Figure 17-6: Client drawn eyebrow design on the client's right side

Rather than possibly intimidate the client, be relaxed in your approach to how, in your opinion, the eyebrow should appear; especially if quite different from how the client draws them on. Inform the client you would like to help them make a good decision about the final design based on *standard facial morphology eyebrow placement*. This standard placement will be referred to as a *classic* design.

Once the classic eyebrow has been applied, and the client is viewing the work in a mirror, cover one side of the face with a piece of paper and switch back and forth so the client can see the differences in how your drawn eyebrow appears vs. his or her version (Figure 17-6). Another option is to take a digital photo with the client's and your versions of the eyebrow design and let the client view the differences from a photo perspective.

An appealing and properly placed eyebrow is predicated on the shape of the client's face. The placement of the arch and the length of the tail of the eyebrow provide the illusion of the face appearing wider or narrower.

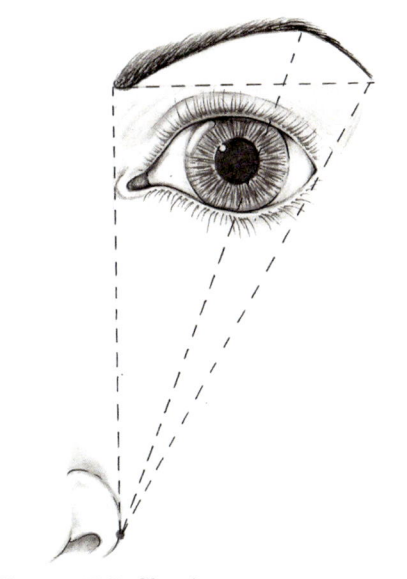

Figure 17-7: Classic Eyebrow Construction

There are four elements to a classic eyebrow construction: The *bulb* (the beginning of the eyebrow), the *bridge* (the distance from the bulb to the arch), the *arch* (also referred to as the high point by some technicians), and the *tail*, which is the end of the eyebrows (see Figure 17-7).

In addition to the standard (classic) placement guides in Figure 17-7, the following is provided:

- The bulb should not be placed dramatically lower than the tail nor the tail placed dramatically lower than the bulb.
- The bridge preferences (length) will be influenced by the arch (high point) position and may differ in client preference. The position of the bridge should coincide with the position of the bulb and arch.
- The arch height preference will vary in preference; some clients prefer a higher more defined arch, and some less defined and lower.
- Eyebrow template guides are commonly used for design placement purposes.

With the assistance of photo enhancements, different expressions will be created by different placement of the bulbs of the eyebrows.

Placing the bulbs closer together (Figure 17-8) creates the appearance of the eyes being closer set and the expression of an unhappy or more serious expression. Placing the eyebrows further apart (Figure 17-9) creates a blank expression and the illusion of the eyes being further apart as well.

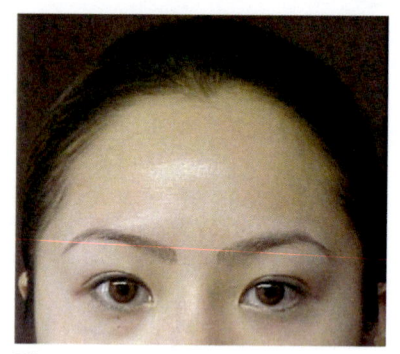

Figure 17-8: Brow Placement Closer Together

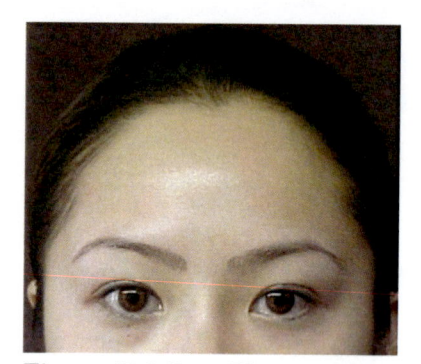

Figure 17-9: Brow Placement Far Apart

Compare the effect eyebrow placement has on how the eyes appear to be placed and the overall projection of expression (figures Figure 17-10 to Figure 17-12).

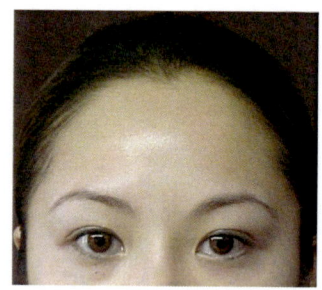

Figure 17-10: Normal Placement

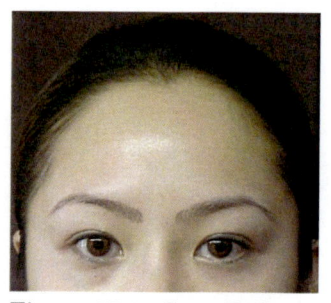

Figure 17-11: Inset Bulbs

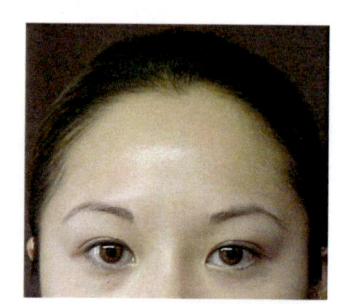

Figure 17-12: Wide-set Bulbs

Section 17 - Basic Facial Morphology and Placement of Procedures

In each of the photographs the eyes are exactly the same width apart; however, depending on eyebrow placement, they appear somewhat different depending on the beginning position of the bulb placement. This is how we create illusions with permanent cosmetics.

Shapes of the Face

There are seven basic facial shapes: oval, square, round, pear, oblong/rectangle, diamond, and heart.

1) **Oval:** The oval face is considered to be the ideal shape because of its balanced proportions. The oval face is neither curvilinear nor angular (Figure 17-13).

2) **Square:** A square face is characterized by a strong jaw line and a broad forehead. Width and length are in similar proportions (Figure 17-14).

3) **Round:** A round face has curvilinear lines with the width and length in the same proportions and no angles (Figure 17-15).

4) **Pear:** The pear-shaped face has a narrow forehead that widens at the cheek and chin areas (Figure 17-16).

5) **Oblong/Rectangle:** The oblong/rectangle face is longer than it is wide and is characterized by a long, straight cheek line (Figure 17-17).

6) **Diamond:** A cross between a heart and dramatic oval shaped face. This face shape is widest at the cheekbones and narrow equal at the forehead and jawline (Figure 17-18).

7) **Heart:** The heart-shaped face has a very wide top third and small bottom third (Figure 17-19).

Figure 17-13: Oval

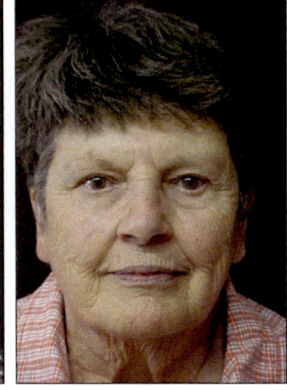

Figure 17-14: Square

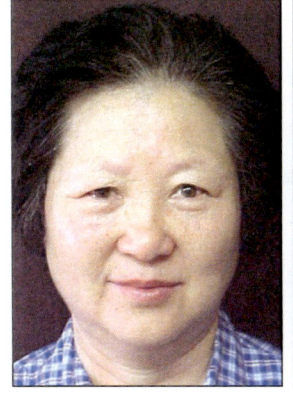

Figure 17-15: Round

Figure 17-16: Pear

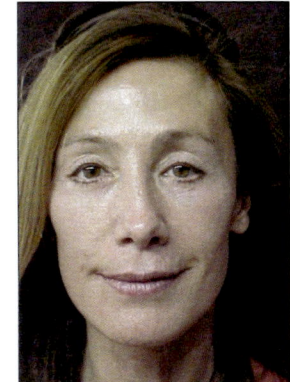

Figure 17-17: Oblong/Rectangle

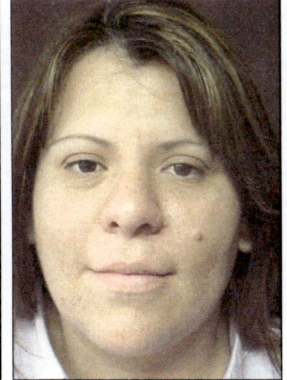

Figure 17-18: Diamond

Figure 17-19: Heart

Creating Symmetry with Eyebrows

The shape of the face has a great influence on how the eyebrow is designed.

- If the client has a wide face, slightly shorten the brow to create a slimmer appearance.
- If the client has a narrow face, slightly lengthen the brow to create a wider appearance.
- If the shape of the face is angular, the arch can be slightly rounded to give the face a softer appearance.
- If the face is very round, a more angular eyebrow will help give the face sharper lines and definition.

Work with the client until you both have agreed on the eyebrow placement design.

Eyes

Although asymmetry caused by *differences in the size of the eyes* exists, it is more common to consider eye asymmetry in relation to the way the surrounding skin affects the appearance of two eyes that would otherwise appear the same size. The tissue surrounding the eye is the thinnest on the body and changes as the body ages or in response to sun exposure.

As an example, Figure 17-20 shows the eyes of a woman who has one eye larger than the other.

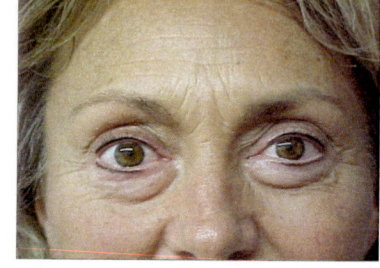

Figure 17-20: Woman with right eye larger than left

The typical eye asymmetry often seen is caused by hooded eyelids or eyes that have inconsistent lid space as shown in the examples in Figure 17-21 and Figure 17-22.

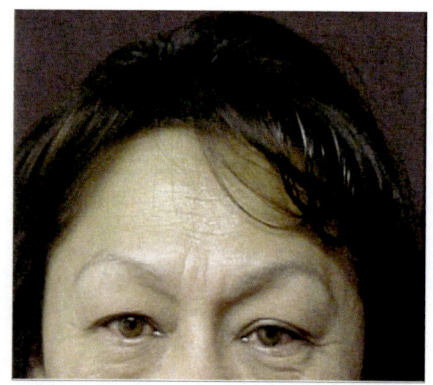

Figure 17-21:
Hooded eyes and inconsistent lid space

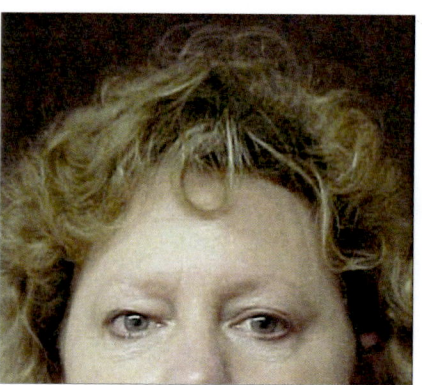

Figure 17-22:
Hooded eyes and inconsistent lid space

In reality, technicians often find that many more mature people need an eyelift (blepharoplasty) to return the eyelids to a symmetric position, which would expose the eyes to reflect a similar appearance.

Even though some feel top eyelash enhancements (see Figure 17-23) can make the eye appear smaller because of the close proximity of the dark line to the eye (depending on the shape of the eye), most clients want the appearance of a darker eyelash root line. Eyelash enhancement is a very popular service and one that the novice technician should focus on.

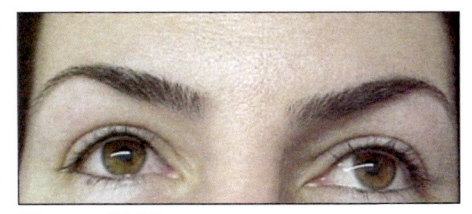

Figure 17-23: Top Eyelash Enhancement

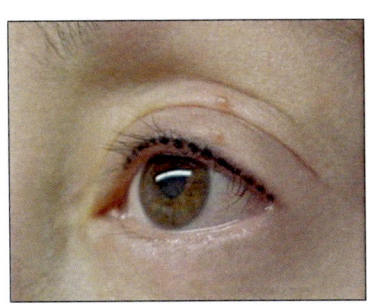

Figure 17-24: Eyelash
Eyelash enhancement dotting technique

A technique for eyelash enhancement not as frequently offered, but yet another option for consideration is the top eyelash dotting technique or pointillism (see Figure 17-24). Some think this liner technique does not noticeably create the appearance of a smaller eye. In a fundamental class, eyeliner procedures are typically limited to eyelash enhancements (narrow top liners may also be offered) and narrow lower eyeliners placed within/adjacent to the lower lash line, as in the example in Figure 17-25.

These are basic eyelash enhancement procedures. These types of procedures do not emphasize the appearance of asymmetric eyes to the same extent as wider and more dramatically designed liner procedures. Wider, dramatic eyeliner designs are advanced procedures that require students to seek out trainers who offer specialized classes specific to techniques associated with learning to create the illusion of eye symmetry with design work.

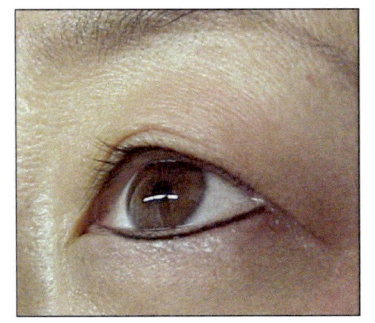

Figure 17-25: Lower Lash Liner

Lips

The points of the cupid's bow of symmetric lips are centered below the nose (see Figure 17-26).

The shape of the lip is subject to change based on the maturing process, blood flow, and hormonal changes.

There are many shapes of asymmetric lips. Some of the commonly discussed lip shape problems are the lips without a defined cupid's bow, lips with an extreme cupid's

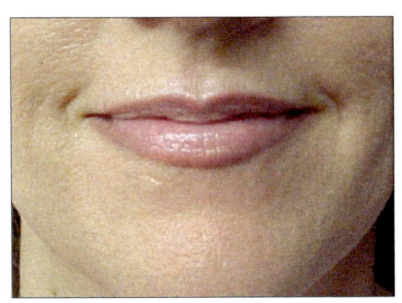

Figure 17-26: Symmetric Lips

203

bow, the wide mouth, the thin upper lip, the thin lower lip, and the small narrow mouth.

Dental problems can also result in asymmetric lips. The position of the lips is predicated on support from the teeth. Permanent cosmetics will not improve or solve the asymmetries associated with dental problems such as the absence of teeth or protruding teeth.

Asymmetric Lip Shapes

The Oval Mouth

Color the center upper lips into a slight cupid's bow. Keep the corners sharp (Figure 17-27).

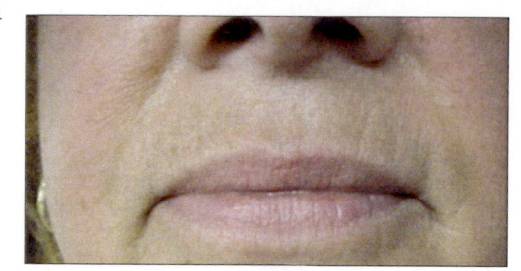

Figure 17-27: Oval Mouth

Thin Lips

Determine the natural lip line that has diminished with age. Emphasize the appearance of size by placing pigment adjacent to the outer line of the lip line with a soft recreation of the Cupid's bow (Figure 17-28).

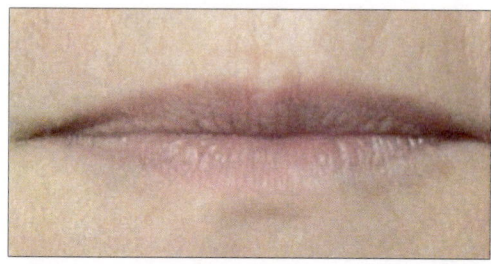

Figure 17-28: Thin Lips

Droopy Corners

Deemphasize the down-turned corners of the mouth by building up the upper lip at the corners of the mouth and slightly cutting in at the corners of the lower lip (Figure 17-29).

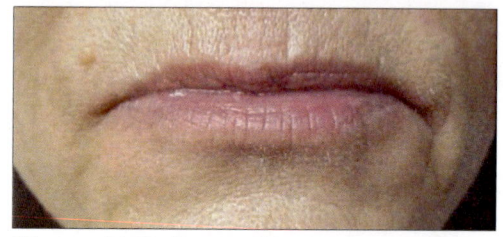

Figure 17-29: Droopy Corners

Thinner Upper Lip

Emphasize the upper lip by placing pigment adjacent to the vermilion border at the outside position, making slight adjustments to the cupid's bow (Figure 17-30).

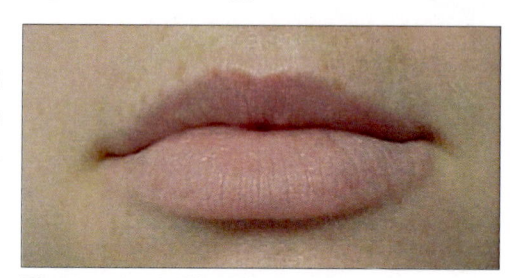

Figure 17-30: Thin Upper Lip

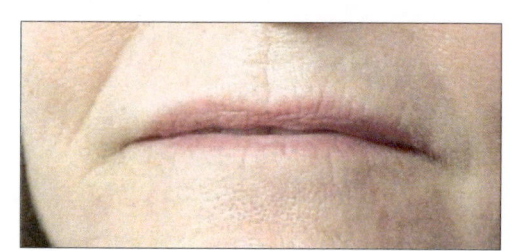

Thin Lower Lip

Place the lip line on the lower lip adjacent to the outside position of the vermilion border, slightly extending the curve of the center of the lower lip for balance (Figure 17-31).

Figure 17-31: Thin Lower Lip

It is not advisable to attempt to dramatically change the shape of the mouth. Small adjustments to the lip line can create dramatic improvements. Novice technicians should not attempt to achieve lip symmetry if this means placing pigment beyond the edge of the vermilion. Technicians who have not had appropriate training to do so, or attempt it on a client who is not a good candidate, however, often try this. In either instance, it can be disastrous for the unsuspecting client. Just because a client achieves more fullness or symmetry with topical makeup does not imply it is appropriate to do with permanent cosmetics. Figure 17-32 and Figure 17-33 show examples of inappropriately or inadequately exceeding the vermilion border.

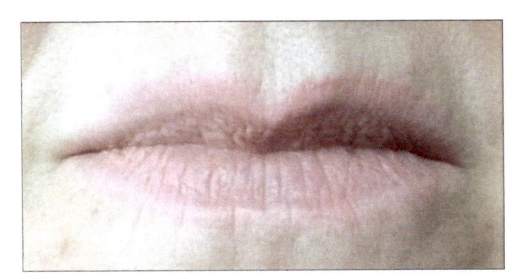

Figure 17-32: Inappropriately placed pigment

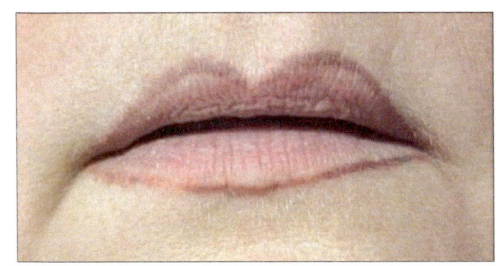

Figure 17-33: Inappropriately placed pigment

Permanent cosmetic technicians will get requests from clients who do not know any better to enlarge the size of their lips or achieve needed symmetry by dramatically exceeding the vermilion border with tattoo pigment placement. Don't agree to provide these types of services.

Larger lips are provided by the medical industry in the form of lip fillers or other cosmetic procedures, surgical and nonsurgical. It is not the job of the permanent cosmetic technician.

Not everyone is a good candidate for lip procedures. Although not an issue of symmetry, poor candidates for lips include not only those who have unrealistic expectations regarding what can be done with the shape of the lips with tattooing but also color. Darker skin Fitzpatrick types (often Fitzpatrick IV, V and VI) are typically not good candidates. The blue, blue/violet, or variegated (two-tone) natural lip coloring cannot be covered by permanent cosmetics. People with these types of lip coloring challenges are best off using topical makeup. Topical makeup can cover natural lip coloring, freckles, and inconsistent coloring, while tattooing does not. Two examples of people who are not good candidates for lip color procedures are provided in Figure 17-34 and Figure 17-35.

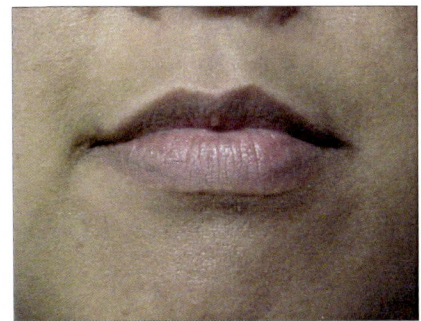

Figure 17-34: Variegated (two-toned) natural lip coloring

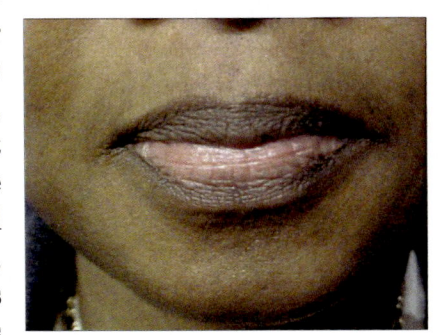

Figure 17-35: Variegated (two-toned) natural lip coloring

In Closing

Balance and symmetry are always goals. If a technician is unable or unwilling to correct or as a minimum, greatly improve an obvious asymmetry, it is best not to pursue permanent cosmetics with that client as it will only emphasize the imperfection and the technician will be credited with creating that imperfection.

Permanent Cosmetic Designs and the Aging Process

It is difficult to imagine putting facial features in fast forward in order to determine what will eventually appear differently as the face continues to mature. Future facial changes are rarely questioned by the client at the consultation for permanent cosmetics because people have the tendency to think of how they look today, not how they will appear in the years to come.

It is, however, a very important factor when offering a client design and color selections for permanent cosmetic procedures. Assuming a person has selected a well-trained technician for this service, permanent cosmetics applied today need not be a fear factor for the future.

When considering the natural progression of age and the longevity of the positive appearance of permanent cosmetics, the most important issues are proper placement, the design of the procedure, and the color of pigment to be used. If not properly placed with the future effects of gravity and thinning skin taken into consideration, procedures could very well not age as attractive as the client had hoped. Conversely, proper placement and classic designs (avoiding trendy designs and colors) can ensure clients will enjoy the pleasure of a fresh face and youthful appearance for many years to come.

Eyebrow Designs

The eyebrow design should be placed in the area where the natural eyebrows grow (no matter how sparse) or once grew. In the absence of any hair in the eyebrow area, use the brow bone as a guide. Similarly, if the client is pursuing an eyebrow procedure to enhance their own eyebrow hair that is extremely light or sparce, following the natural eyebrow placement is very important. New eyebrows or enhancements to existing eyebrow hair will then age naturally along with the skin in which it is placed. Occasionally a client will prefer to draw her or his eyebrow tails *slightly* above the brow bone. This design may or may not be proper for a permanent cosmetic eyebrow procedure, depending on whether the client would ever consider future cosmetic surgery, such as a brow lift. Slightly higher exaggerations of the tail of the eyebrows may work for those who never intend to have plastic surgery. This is not recommended if facial surgery is a consideration and it would affect the placement of the eyebrows.

Top Eyeliner Designs

When considering a permanent cosmetic top eyeliner design, a sure safe choice is pigment placed in and directly above the lash line. This conservative design also gives the most options for using topical makeup for special occasions when a more dramatic appearance is desired. Some more mature women or men may feel that wider eyeliner on the upper eyelids will compensate for the faltering effects of excess eyelid skin. This is not true or recommended; although there may be nothing wrong with this choice as long as heavy eyeliner has always been worn and most importantly if an eyelid surgery to remove the excess skin above the eyelids is not a consideration.

Surgery to remove excess eyelid tissue (aka blepharoplasty) is becoming more affordable and in some instances, if the excess skin interferes with eyesight or proper functioning of the eyelid, some health insurance companies under certain conditions may cover the associated costs. As a result, more and more people are electing to have this surgical procedure. If conservative eyeliner enhancements and top eyeliners are correctly placed adjacent to the lashes, permanent cosmetic top eyeliner should not pose any challenges for the surgeon performing a blepharoplasty.

An eyeliner design that has an increased potential of being affected by eyelid surgery is the one in which the extension of eyeliner goes beyond the last eyelash, even ever so slightly at the outer corner of each eye (usually a tapered tip design of the eyeliner). Several plastic surgery procedures change the positioning of skin around the eyes. What may give the impression of a lift in that area at the initial time of the top eyeliner procedure may in time, either from the natural aging process or surgical procedures, appear misplaced, uneven, and/or be partially or totally hidden in the excess skin at the outer canthus area of the eyes.

Wider eyeliner with extended tails (or tips) is an advanced procedure.

Lower Eyeliner Designs

The same principles apply to lower eyeliner. There are several surgical technique options that could have an undesirable effect on lower eyeliners. Keep eyeliner designs conservative and ensure that placement is through the lower eyelashes. As the skin in the area ages, or in the event the client has a lower eyelid lift, the lower eyeliner will remain in its original placement. In the event surgical removal of excess skin beneath the eye is elected, depending on the technique utilized, a touch-up may be needed to restore the integrity of the original design.

Lip Color Designs

The same thoughtful consideration must be given to lip liner placement. Professional technicians recognize that if placed properly, permanent cosmetic lip liner can actually detract from noticeable wrinkles on and directly above the lips. Although placement of the lip liner can tastefully be placed *adjacent to* the vermilion border (no space between the pigment line and the vermilion border) to slightly enhance the size of the lips, if noticeably fuller lips are desired, there are surgical and nonsurgical medical techniques available to easily achieve this effect. A permanent cosmetic lip procedure that exceeds the natural vermilion border of the lips is not the answer for a person who desires considerably larger volume lips.

Another problem associated with an exaggerated lip liner that departs from the natural vermilion border is that the texture of the natural vermilion border is thicker and more noticeable than the tissue surrounding the lip. As a result, you will likely see a lip within a lip if the lip liner is not placed on or directly above the natural vermilion border of the lip.

Permanent cosmetics are indeed the answer to many design and color related problems of the face; however, aging is a natural process that can only be improved with conservative, thoughtful, well-placed procedures and appropriate color choices.

Section 18

All About Procedures

Learning Objectives

Introduction

This section promotes safe, conservative permanent cosmetic procedure information and practical technique options.

Artistic technique will vary from trainer to trainer and technician to technician. The ultimate goal of all trainers and technicians is to produce safe permanent cosmetics that are beautiful; those that meet the client's expectations. In this section there are options offered for many examples of techniques to consider, encouraging the reader to be open to several ways of accomplishing the same task.

Often it is the practical application of the guidance of others, whether it is in a training class, information provided by a speaker at a gathering, experience sharing on social media sites, or in text format that is the has value to the technician. Occasionally, it may be something as simple as advice given about what not to do that puts complex subjects in a more straightforward and workable format.

Objective

Upon completion of this section, the technician will gain insight into overviews of industry techniques and protocols associated with the eyeliner, eyebrow, and lip liner procedures.

Overview of Procedure Techniques and Protocols

This section is dedicated to the processes of the fundamental procedures. These procedures are eyelash enhancements (which may include narrow-to-medium width upper eyeliners), lower eyeliners, eyebrows, and lip liners (includes blended/shaded lip liners). Trainers may differ in technique for each procedure and the terminology used in regard to the procedure type during classes.

There are several techniques in the arena of procedures. Differences include where to start and end the tattooing process. Another example of technique variances is how to mark the template of an eyebrow or lip procedure prior to proceeding with tattooing (some may also use single-use markers for some eyeliner work).

In regard to anesthetics, some trainers and technicians anesthetize a procedural area and then proceed with drawing on the design template, while others perform this process in reverse. There are locations where some or all anesthetics are not legal; technicians depend on stretching and other procedural techniques for their permanent cosmetic tattooing services.

Considering the variables of available sources of information after a fundamental class, it is always enlightening to discuss the subject of techniques, whether it be the use of anesthetics, drawing and marking a design template, where to start and finish the tattooing process, or aftercare preferences.

After a fundamental class, there are options for gaining additional knowledge. There is the option of attending a continuing education class, there are permanent cosmetic technique social media sources, options to participate in webinars, listening to speakers on a particular subject at a convention or conference, shadowing other technicians, or reading subject-related articles. All sources mentioned have value and provide choices for consideration.

It is important to keep an open mind; we should always be in a learning mode. From the fundamental class, technicians take the information presented and learned, and then, often through the natural process of repetitive movement, or while attending a class with a different trainer or networking, will later find a slightly different way that works better for them (or as an alternative method).

Each trainer has a policy on these subjects and will advise their students accordingly. Technicians will develop their preferences based on training and experience.

The following pages in this section of the textbook provide basic information and techniques for consideration both text and pictorial formats. If this textbook is being read in preparation for a fundamental class, the trainer will provide information and choices as to how to commence and complete each procedure type in class.

For technicians who have completed their fundamental class and are exploring supplemental information, knowledge is power, and there is much knowledge for consideration to ascertain from this section.

The Basic Table Setup

It is important to gather the supplies that will be needed for the procedure(s). Being unprepared breaks the rhythm of the procedure process.

Supplies will vary depending on the type of procedure(s) being conducted and the device being used.

Single-Use Items:

- Absorbant worktable cover
- Bed/table cover
- Cord covers and machine cover (if using a machine)
- Pigment and anesthetic holder
- Personal protection equipment
    - Medical grade examination gloves—several pairs
    - Masks—If the technician chooses to wear one for protection from body fluids
    - Apron
- Absorbent material to wipe excess pigment from the tips of machines or to remove excess pigment from the needles of a manual device (could be a sponge, tissue, gauze, etc.)
- Cotton-tipped applicators, i.e., cotton swabs or microbrushes
- Cotton pads or other absorbable material for removing product from the procedural area
- Protective covering for the client to avoid staining clothing during the procedure
- Waste receptacle (waste container liner)
- Water receptacle (cups)
- Tissues- several tissues may be needed
- Design template marking device (not needed for eyelash enhancement, optional for thin upper and lower eyeliner)

Eyeliner- Add:

- Eye products that are manufactured specifically for moisturizing or cleansing the eyes
    - Common containers must be protected with barrier film
- Eyewash container protected with barrier film or eyewash can be

transferred from a common container to a single-use cup and drawn out for use with a single-use pipette (dropper)

- Microbrushes, eyeliner brushes, or marking pencil (all single-use) if design work calls for the eyeliner to be drawn on with pigment or pencil

Eyebrows-Add:

- Single-use sharpened eyebrow pencil or single-use powder and applicator for eyebrow design work

Lips- Add:

- Single-use sharpened lip liner pencil for design work
- Two sets of cotton mouth rolls or plastic lip guards if these products are preferred

Additional Worktable Related Activities and Requirements – Add:

- Machine or manual device
  - The sterilized single-use manual device needle and handle sterilized pieces (if not a single unit)
  - Sterilized single-use machine accessories (if using a machine) **Note:** Wait until the client arrives and witnesses the removal of sterilized items from their packaging.
- Protective eyewear - **Note:** Protective eyewear is required if a mask is being worn as protection from body fluids.
- A mirror for the client - The handle of the mirror should be protected with barrier film.
- Lamps, controls on equipment power sources, non-disposable parts of machine handpieces, and any other objects that could be touched during the procedure must be protected by applying a protective barrier such as barrier film.

Client Management Protocols

During the Consultation

- Technicians should ensure they will enjoy working with people they accept as clients.
- Request that the prospective client wear their traditional makeup (if any is commonly applied) to the consultation in the same design style they expect their permanent cosmetics to appear when healed.
- Discuss any recommendations with the client regarding color or designs.
- If the client is found to be a good candidate for permanent cosmetics based

on anticipation of a good working relationship and medical related profile questions asked and forms completed, take photographs.

- Ensure that the photograph will reflect the detail necessary to adequately compare the pre-procedure photographs and permanent makeup (post procedure) designs. The consultation photographs will document how the client appeared with traditional makeup. It is common to use these photographs for reference purposes.

- Provide the client with pre-procedure guidelines.

- Discuss appropriate timing avoiding dates close to a scheduled special event and agree on an appointment day and time.

- Request the client arrive at the scheduled appointment without topical makeup applied.

Before the Client Arrives

- Assemble the appropriate supplies for the procedure. Reference *The Basic Table Setup (page 212)* for guidance. Do not open the sterilized needle(s) and machine accessories packaging (if using a machine) or manual devices until the client arrives and initials on the client chart notes that they witnessed the opening the package(s).

- Affix protective barrier product on items that are likely to be touched during the procedure such as a machine, power source adjustment controls, the lamp where it may be touched during the procedure, the handle of a mirror for the client, and other objects as appropriate such as products in common containers that may be used during the procedure. If the device to be used is a machine, the electrical cords should be covered from the point that the cord joins to the machine to the power supply.

- If the client is a return client or has completed an informed consent and client history forms at the consultation, have these forms available for review and signature prior to beginning the procedure. Existing forms should always be reviewed and re-signed on the day of the procedure. People may become aware of health issues between appointments that are important for technicians to be advised of and to document. Supporting client file forms should reflect data as of the day of the procedure, and signed/dated accordingly.

- Technicians who work in a medical environment may be required to follow an office policy regarding the forms utilized for cosmetic tattooing.

Many times when working in a medical office, clients of a permanent cosmetic technician are also considered patients of a physician. It is not uncommon for the client/patient to be required to fill out whatever office's forms are required each time a service is conducted, regardless of the short-term period between services.

After the Client Arrives

- Review the client history and informed consent forms (or medical office forms as appropriate) with the client and ensure the forms are up-to-date and signed.

- Show the client the pre-sterilized needle(s) and machine accessories (if using a machine) or manual device selected for the procedure, all of which are sealed in the manufacturer's packaging.

  For technicians that purchase non-sterile needles and sterilize in an on-site sterilizer, the packaging should be intact and the sterilization date noted on the packaging per Occupational Safety and Health Administration (OSHA) or other governing agency mandates.

- Place the package(s) on the worktable, for opening immediately prior to commencing with the procedure. Many technicians ask the client to sign on the client chart notes document that indicates they have witnessed the opening of the sterile needle(s) and machine accessories (if using a machine) or manual device (needle and handle packages if not pre-assembled) to be used for the procedure.

  If required to use medical office forms and the chart notes do not provide a space for the client to initial witnessing the opening of sterile needles and accessories, ask the physician or the office administrator about making notes on the client/patient chart to the effect that this was done.

- If the procedure is eyeliner and the client wears contact lenses, they must be removed for the procedure. During the consultation, an eyeliner client should be advised not to wear their contact lenses and to bring eyeglasses.

- Once the consultation has occurred and an appointment for the procedure agreed to, it is advisable to direct clients to arrive at the procedure appointment without makeup. The task of removing makeup immediately prior to the procedure can result in irritation. Makeup contains bacteria; it is difficult to completely remove and causes the cleansing of the area to be more intense.

- The sequence for each procedure type provided assumes there has: (1) been a consultation during which it has been determined that the client is a good candidate for permanent cosmetics, photographs with normally-applied makeup has been taken, and a color has been selected for the procedure; (2) The hands are washed and gloves donned before, during, and after the procedure as appropriate based on infection control practices; (3) Client forms have been completed by the client and the client's chart notes document will be updated with information with current procedural information.

The Eyeliner Procedure

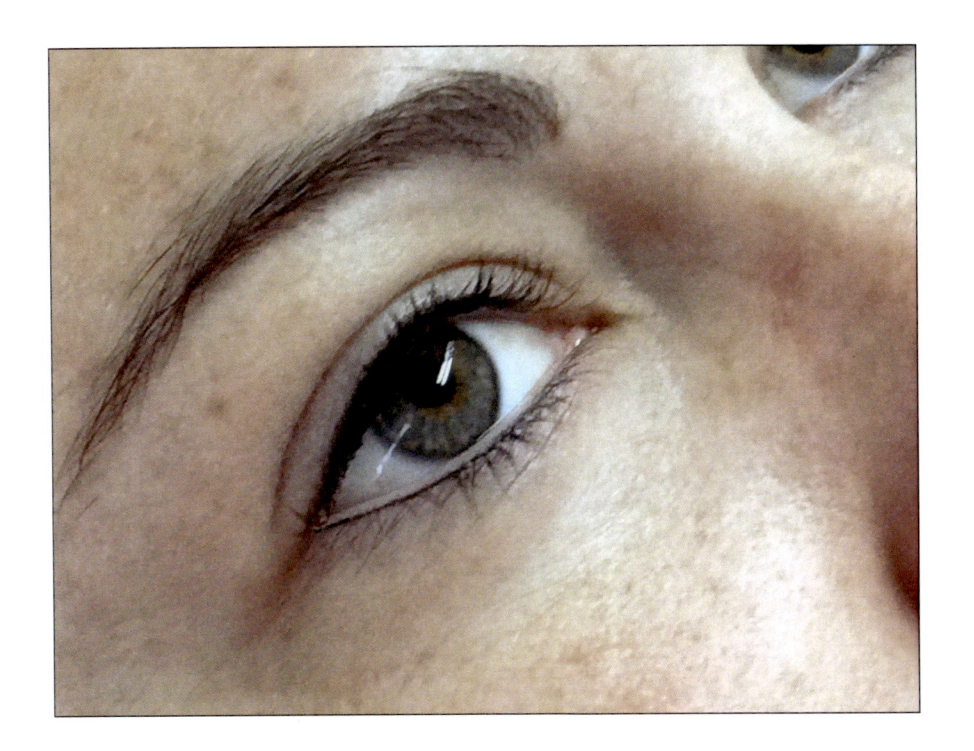

The Eyeliner Procedure Sequence

Please review the *Overview of Techniques and Protocols (page 211)* at the beginning of this section before proceeding.

There are many ways to approach eyelash enhancement and upper and lower eyeliner procedures; the following represents one or more approaches to the basics steps of the procedure processes.

During a class or as more and more eyelash enhancement and upper and lower eyeliner procedures are performed, technicians may find this sequence of the process one they use, or they may be trained differently, or develop a technique of their own that may work better for them.

Pre-Procedure

- Before beginning the procedure, cleanse the client's eyelids with a product manufactured specifically as safe for use around the eyes. Lightly massage the eyelash area with a moist cotton swab to thoroughly cleanses the eyelash bed.
- Inspect the eyes to ensure they are free from any visible abnormalities (see Figure 18-1 thru Figure 18-3).
- Even if something you see doesn't prevent the procedure from going forward, point out the irregularity to the client and make appropriate notes on the client's chart. If this was not noticed by the client before, it may come to their attention during the healing period (clients routinely inspect the area) and it's best to address it before the procedure. If you see it, say it, and document it.
- Lubricant eye drops manufactured specifically for the eyes should be used, but sparingly. Gently blot the eyelashes with a cotton pad or tissue after each use.

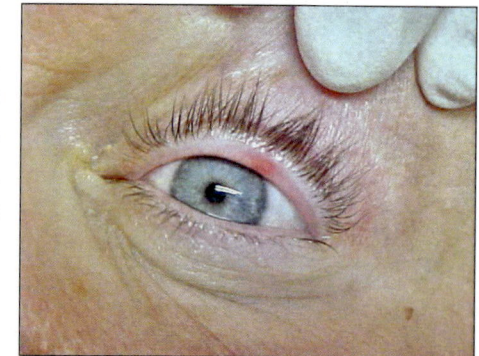

Figure 18-1: Irregularity on Tarsal Plate (Wetline)

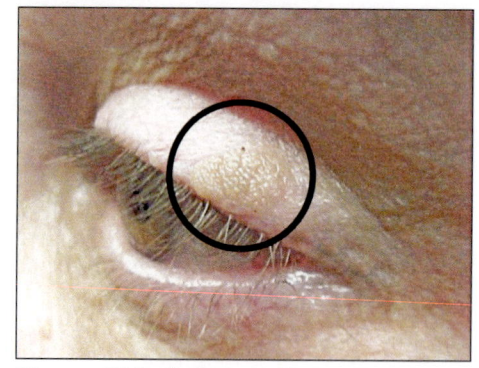

Figure 18-2: Growth on Upper Eyelid

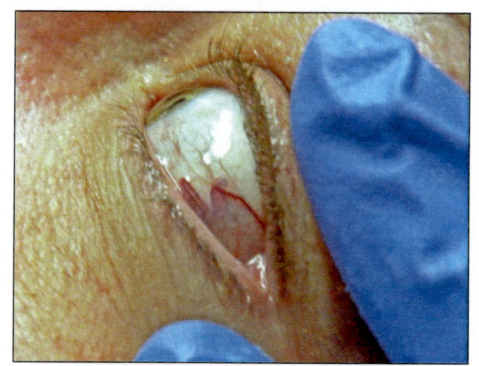

Figure 18-3: Broken Blood Vessels

Anesthetics
- If using a pre-procedure anesthetic, apply the anesthetic to the upper eyelid area in a controlled tube-like form adjacent to, or slightly above the upper eyelashes and slightly below the lower eyelashes. The melting properties of some cream topical anesthetics (if using an anesthetic with properties that cause the product to be affected by the temperature of the skin) will spread and position closer to the eyelashes during the time waiting for the anesthetics to take effect.
    - If the product has less melting properties, the anesthetic can be placed closer to the lash line. In either case, if using anesthetics for the eyeliner procedure, always apply anesthetics in a manner to keep the eyes safe. *Do not* occlude (cover with a plastic material) the anesthetic. This may cause the anesthetic to smear into the eyes or to melt quickly and can be responsible for anesthetic getting into the eyes and possibly causing a cornea burn.
- If using a pre-procedure anesthetic, wait the anesthetic manufacturer's prescribed time before removing the anesthetic, watching closely to ensure the client's body temperature does not melt the anesthetic so quickly that product would get into the eyes. Always be prepared to remove the anesthetic and rinse the eyes. Do not leave a client alone with anesthetic on their eyelids.
    - If working in a medical office where injected anesthetics are used and this is a chosen method of anesthesia, now is the appropriate time for those injections for the upper and lower liner tattooing process.
    - Injected anesthetics are considered unnecessary by industry leaders for eyeliner comfort control. The injections can cause bruising and swelling which distorts the appearance of the canvas. This bruising can remain a long time, even days after the procedure appears healed.
- If over-the-counter level topical anesthetics can be used legally, the products developed for the permanent cosmetic industry are effective. If you have questions, consult with the anesthetic manufacturer(s) and inquire about the pH of the products to be used around the eye.
- If pre-procedure anesthetic was used, remove the topical anesthetic in a controlled manner avoiding contact with the eye. Using a cotton swab or other single-use implement remove it up and away from the upper lash line and downwardly away from the lower lash line.
- Rinse the eyes thoroughly with an eyewash product.

Applying the Eyelash Enhancement and Eyeliner Design
- If performing eyelash enhancement only, an upper eyeliner design template is not applicable.
- If performing upper eyeliner (which always includes an eyelash

enhancement), some technicians elect to draw on the upper eyeliner design with pigment using a single-use instrument (brush or pencil) on both upper eyelids.

- Drawing on the eyeliner with pigment using a single-use brush or other implement is optional. If the eyeliner is narrow and *hugs* the lash line, drawn on template work is usually considered unnecessary. The exception would be for designing a fine-line thin taper or wedge at the outer canthus position.

The Eyelash Enhancement and Eyeliner Tattooing Process

- Remove the sterile needle and machine accessories or manual device from the packaging and assemble (as appropriate for the device being used).
- If an upper eyelash enhancement (see Figure 18-4) is the only procedure to be performed, proceed with the proper stretch and commence with the enhancement tattooing process. Begin at the last lash at the outer canthus of the eye and work toward the last lash at the inner canthus of the eye.
- If upper eyeliner is included in the eyeliner procedure, consider tattooing the enhancement (through the lash line) portion after the upper eyeliner has been completed. Swelling can occur during the enhancement tattooing process, causing distortion to the upper lid canvas. Fine crisp upper liners are more difficult to tattoo into swollen eyelids.

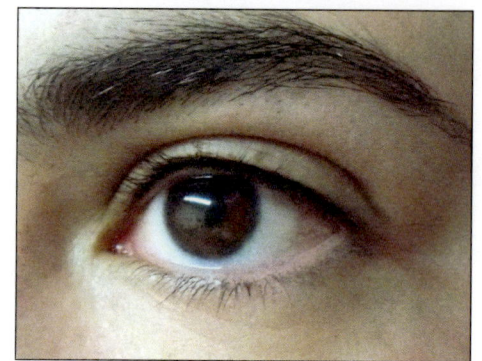

Figure 18-4: Upper Eyelash Enhancement

- Upper eyeliners that include fine-line tapers or wedges (not elongated tips) at the outer canthus position should be tattooed first on each eye before proceeding with the line across the upper eyelids.

Tapered fine-line tips (or wedges) are areas of the eyeliner design that swell quickly and may smear from tearing of the eyes. This is why it is recommended to tattoo the fine-line tapered tips or wedges first.

- If the eyeliner includes a fine-line taper or wedge at the outer canthus position and technician has chosen to tattoo the tapered portion of the eyeliner first, then proceed to tattoo the line across the lash line.

Tattoo from the outer last lash position to the inner

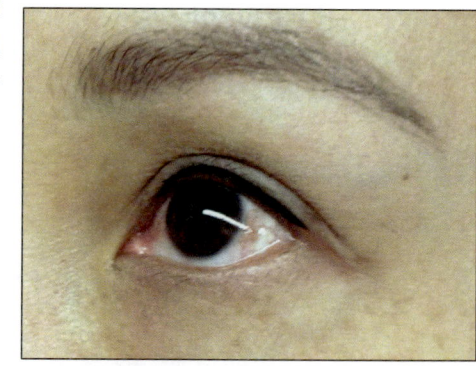

Figure 18-5: Thin Upper Eyeliner with Taper

last lash position. This is a suggested path of eyeliner tattooing. There are a variety of positions from which to begin and end.

- After upper eyeliner has been tattooed (if appropriate; some may only request an eyelash enhancement procedure or narrow eyeliner that follows the upper lashes from the first to the last eyelash) proceed with the eyelash enhancement portion of the procedure.

- Another option is to tattoo both the enhancement and the upper liner in sections by tattooing the narrow upper liner and then moving the needle down in that same section to tattoo the enhancement.

- Apply the post-broken skin anesthetic (if using anesthetics) where the initial pass was made and move to the other eye. Complete the same process; apply post-broken skin anesthetics(s) to the eyelid that has just been tattooed and return to the original eye for the additional passes.

- The number of passes is trainer and technician-specific. Repeat the final (additional) pass to the second eye, applying post broken skin anesthetics (optional) along the way as needed to keep the client comfortable.

The process of moving from one eye to the other for one pass and then back for an additional pass(es) is suggested to ensure both eyes are tattooed with equal pigment and passes.

Completing one eyeliner pass and then moving to the other eye is not an uncommon technique. If the client cannot tolerate the tattooing process in order to finish both eyes equally, this puts the technician and client in an awkward position.

By moving methodically from one eye to the other, this ensures that even if the client wishes to reschedule for the remainder of any work required, equal eyeliner has been completed on both eyes to satisfy the client. This process also allows for optimal anesthetic effect if the topical anesthetic is applied on the *waiting* eye while tattooing is being performed on the other. With this said, however, be aware that some experienced technicians prefer to remain on the same eye until it is finished and then proceed to the other eye.

- Use post-broken skin anesthetics sparingly. If used excessively, this is a practice that will ultimately dilute the pigment being tattooed. Diluted pigment can result in lighter or spotty appearing healed eyeliner.
  - ♦ If an injected anesthetic was used in a medical office, depending on how long the tattooing process takes, a topical post-broken skin anesthetic may be required to maintain client comfort and cooperation.

- After the eyelash enhancement/upper eyeliner (as appropriate) is complete, rinse the eyes thoroughly with an eyewash product.

- If lower eyeliner (sometimes also referred to as a lower lash enhancement) is included in the procedure, apply anesthetics to the lower lid area and wait the manufacturer's prescribed time before removing.

It is not uncommon for more experienced technicians to anesthetize upper and lower lids at the same time when tattooing upper and lower eyeliner is to be performed. Novice technicians with less experience may find this practice resulting in anesthetic getting into the client's eye during tattooing. Trying to avoid touching anesthetic can also adversely influence how the skin is stretched.

- Remove the anesthetics with a cotton swab, wiping down (not across) and away from the eyelashes.
- Rinse the eyes thoroughly with an eyewash product.
- If desired, a very thin line of pigment or a line drawn with a single-use pencil can be applied as a design guideline for the lower eyeliner. Draw the guideline on one eye, and then perform the lower liner procedure. Repeat the same process for the second eye.
  - This is a matter of technique preference. The pigment guideline must be as thin as the needle that will be used to tattoo the procedure and drawn exactly where the lower eyeliner is to be tattooed. This practice is often used when the client has few eyelashes to provide a natural template guide to follow. It isn't always necessary, but a choice.
- Proceed with the lower eyeliner procedure, working from the outer last lash moving across to the inner position only as far as the client indicated the line should be placed. Complete the first pass and apply anesthetic for broken skin (if used) and move to the second eye and repeat the process. The reasoning supporting moving from eye to eye on the lower eyeliner is the same explained earlier for upper enhancement and liner work. And although it is common to begin at the outer lash to the inner lash positions, there are people who may choose to work differently.
- Make an additional pass(es) on both lower eyeliners.
- Once the eyelash enhancement/upper eyeliner/lower eyeliner procedure(s) are completed (if both upper and lower liners were included), rinse the eyes thoroughly, flushing out residual pigment that may have gotten into the eye during the procedure process.

Conduct a thorough search, looking under the upper and lower eyelids for any pigment needs flushed out with an eyewash product. Flushing residual pigment out of the eye with eyewash is recommended.

If it becomes necessary to use a cotton swab, first moisten it with eyewash and very lightly draw the pigment to the moistened swab avoiding direct contact with the eyeball.

- Allow the client periodic breaks as needed during the tattooing process. It is difficult to remain lying down (if the client has been in a lying down position) for long periods of time and a short restroom or water break gives the client renewed energy to see the procedure through easily. It is also a good time to check the completed work from a different perspective.

After the Procedure Is Complete
- Cleanse the client's face.
- Once the procedure is complete, ask the client to sit up (if they were in a lying down position) and view the eyeliner procedure. Be cautious about agreeing to make any *major* changes in the design work, as the appearance of the enhancement/eyeliner(s) is likely swollen and will change during the healing process.
- Technicians may elect to schedule disposing of the needle and worktable supplies until after the client has had the opportunity to freshen up and the immediately-after photographs have been taken. The need for small detail work may be noticed by the client or in photographs that will require additional tattooing. This review should only take a few moments. Do not leave used product and needles on the worktable beyond the final evaluation period.
- Take the immediately-after pictures. Take a full-face picture of the client and a close-up one of the eyeliner area. If, through the eye of the camera, the work is considered satisfactory and the client agrees, proceed to the final steps of the session.

Final Steps
- The client may be asked to return to the procedure chair/bed and cool compresses applied on the eyelids to reduce swelling (if this is a policy to do so).
- Apply an aftercare product to the eyelids if this is a chosen practice. **Note:** The application of an aftercare product is technician specific and it must be manufactured specifically for use around the eyes.
- Review aftercare instructions and provide an aftercare products kit (if it is policy to direct the client to apply a healing product during the healing period and/or to provide the products).
- Schedule the follow-up appointment.
- Update the client's chart notes document with current procedural information.
- See "Section 4 - Safe Practices for Permanent Cosmetic Technicians" for Post Procedure Protocols (page 40).

Designing Eyeliners Tutorial

There are many different types of eyeliner procedures technicians are requested to perform. A client may or may not know the exact name of the permanent cosmetic procedure types offered. Detailed information and photo examples are often required to determine the client's exact wishes. It is wise to provide eyeliner clients with a thorough education to establish a clear understanding of what the client expects to see when the procedure is healed before proceeding.

Because often eyeliner clients are accustomed to considering all topical makeup applied to the eyelid lash areas as eyeliner, a review of the following terminology will assist with determining how the client actually anticipates the healed permanent cosmetic eyeliner to appear.

To assist with a clear understanding of client design wishes, the client can be requested to wear eyeliner to the consultation the way they would like to see the permanent cosmetic version healed. It is not, however, unusual to find it necessary to discuss these issues over the telephone when service fees are part of the conversation, so it is good to be able to accommodate design questions verbally.

Upper Eyelash Enhancement

Pigment is tattooed within (through) the upper eyelashes (see Figure 18-6). Some technicians may also refer to tattooing within (adjacent to) the lower eyelashes as an enhancement. The lower eyeliner procedure is also referred to as a lower eyelash liner. The terminology used is trainer and technician specific.

The upper eyelash enhancement procedure is very natural appearing. It produces a darkening of only the upper lash line without a tattoo pigment line above the lash line. As a result, a client will appear somewhat as if they are wearing mascara close to the root of the lash line. The upper

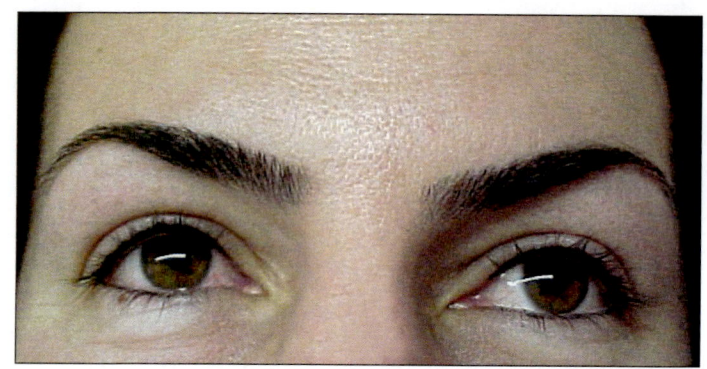

Figure 18-6: Healed eyelash enhancement

eyelash enhancement is a popular procedure for both men and women who feel they would benefit from the definition the upper eyelash enhancement provides.

There will be a number of clients who initially request an upper eyelash enhancement primarily because they feel somewhat insecure about the outcome of an upper eyeliner procedure. They may be ultraconservative in the beginning. When the procedure is healed, the client often returns for the post-procedure appointment requesting upper eyeliner be added (a line above the lashes).

Depending on the width of the upper eyeliner desired this request may represent an additional cost factor. There are technicians who will provide a small line above the lash enhancement at no additional cost at the follow-up appointment, and those who charge an additional fee. If it will be policy to charge more for a small closure line or adding narrow or medium eyeliner to the enhancement, make this clear to clients during consultations. Addressing this subject on consent forms may also be advantageous.

Upper Eyeliner

All upper eyeliners include the eyelash enhancement procedure. To conduct upper eyeliner, pigment is tattooed on the eyelid next to the upper eyelashes. The primary areas of discussion regarding upper eyeliners are width and design. This includes questions such as where the line starts and suppers, the width desired, the design placement of a dome (slightly higher section of the design - if any), and of the taper that finishes the design at the outer and inner canthus positions.

Novice technicians should focus on eyelash enhancements with thinner-to-medium upper eyeliner (see Figure 18-7) and avoid wider eyeliner designs with elongated tips, as these require expertise acquired with advanced training.

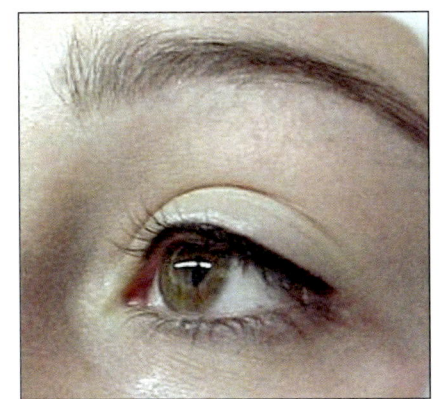

Figure 18-7: Healed medium upper eyeliner

Lower Eyeliner

To conduct lower eyeliner, pigment is tattooed through the lower lash line. Routinely, the line of the lower liner begins at the last lower eyelash at the outer canthus area of the eye and proceeds, as a maximum, to the last lash in the inner canthus eye area.

Inspect the client's eyes carefully during the pre-procedure period and ensure that a lower liner taken to the last lash at the inner canthus eye position will appear to be positioned the same on both eyes.

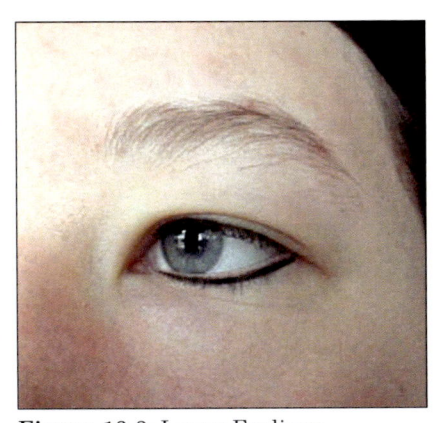

Figure 18-8: Lower Eyeliner Closure Design

Many clients have had a lower blepharoplasty and as a result, the skin positioning next to the lower lashes may be obviously different on each eye. It is less risky to finish the lower liner without including a line that appears to enclose the eye (see Figure 18-8).

Lower eyeliner that includes tattooing through the last few inner canthus eyelashes may have a tendency to provide an appearance of enclosing the eye and is not requested by all clients.

It is common to work with clients who are accustomed to applying lower eyeliner at the outer canthus location and proceeding along the lower lash line to lightly taper approximately where the iris ends when the client is looking straight ahead (see Figure 18-9). This preference will vary between clients.

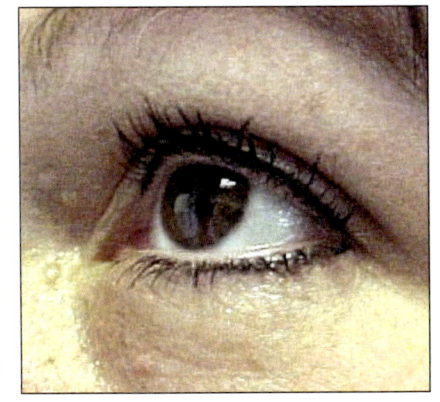

Figure 18-9: Healed Upper and Lower Eyeliner

Lower eyeliners can take on a variety of design work, most commonly in different widths. It is not common practice to join the upper and lower eyeliners at the out canthus. The skin is extremely thin in this area with a large population of blood vessels. Pigment placed in this area may migrate (spread) or may not hold at all due to the thin composition of the tissue.

Tattooing the Wetline (Also Referred to as Tattooing the Mucosa or Tarsal Plate)

Some clients are accustomed to darkening the wetline of the upper and/or lower of the eye with traditional makeup for dramatic effects.

There is a lot of discussion among permanent cosmetic technicians as to whether or not tattooing this area is a good idea or a poor one. Technicians report they routinely avoid tattooing the wetline unless they are working with an alopecia client or a client who has very few and/or sparse eyelashes. Under these circumstances, they will consider dropping down *slightly* onto the upper wetline (slightly below the upper eyelash line) during the enhancement portion of the procedure to give the appearance of more depth.

Typically, however, when working with clients with eyelashes that are easily seen and healthy, technicians report avoiding tattooing on the wetline area of the eye. This tissue is different from that of the lash line and eyelids and tattooing also places needles dangerously close to the eyeball if the wetline tattooing should encompass a wider area. There are also tiny meibomian glands at the edge of the wetline that secrete an oily substance (meibum) that protects the tear film. Medical professionals have advised that these glands may be harmed with wetline tattooing and have the potential of contributing to dry eye or associated conditions. The wetline tattooing philosophy, however, will vary between trainers and technicians. It is agreed upon that tattooing the wetline is an advanced procedure that requires specialized training.

It is important to take into consideration that healed eyeliners (upper and lower) have a tendency to appear to have lost a portion of the width line and vibrancy of the pigment after healing. This appearance of pigment loss occurs for a number of reasons.

First, after completing the procedure the area is puffy, giving it a bloated or wider appearance. Second, during the healing process sloughing of the edges of the design and pigment dehydration will normally result in a narrower design and lighter color appearance than observed immediately after the original procedure. Third, new skin heals over the tattooed area and color must then be seen through the filter of the skin.

Based on the client's skin type and the technique of each individual technician, the healed appearance will vary somewhat from client to client; nonetheless, healed upper and lower eyeliner will typically be more narrow and the color will appear less vibrant than the version of the lines originally tattooed (see Figure 18-10 and Figure 18-11).

Eyeliner Stretching Techniques

Stretching techniques are very personal and unique to each technician. There are many variables to consider:

- The technician's dominant hand (right or left)
- The size of the hands
- The device being used
- If the technician works from one side of the procedure bed or both sides
- The fit of the gloves used
- The condition of the client's skin (firm or loose around the eyes)

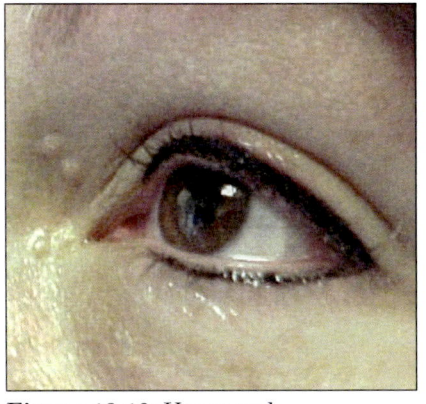

Figure 18-10: Upper and Lower Eyeliner
Immediately after

Each technician, based on their physical characteristics and capabilities coupled with the flexibility and/or limitations of the workplace environment must practice different techniques to find the stretching technique that is effective and comfortable for them to use.

Whereas one trainer will demonstrate a stretching technique for eyeliner that works well, another trainer may have a different, but equally efficient manner in which to accomplish eyeliner stretching control. Technician characteristics often affect how their stretching techniques are developed.

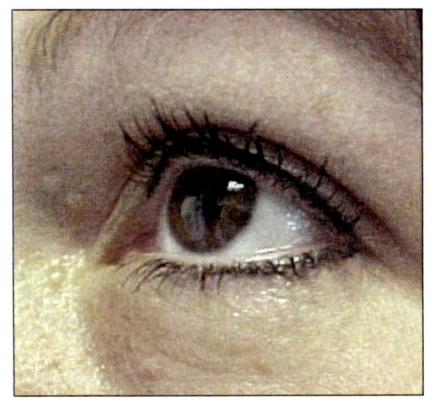

Figure 18-11: Upper and Lower Eyeliner
Healed

Eyeliners are not difficult to perform if there is a comprehensive understanding of the complexities of the functions of lids, lashes, eyes, and their role in our procedures. Stretching techniques employed during eyeliner procedures minimize client movement and enable the technician to tattoo on a smooth taut canvas.

The lids and eyelashes protect the eyes. The lid's major functions are to protect the vulnerable surface of the eye from debris, trauma, and drying. Drying of the eye can result in corneal damage. On the outermost layers of the lids, the skin is thinner than anywhere else on the body. The upper lids are more mobile than the lower lids. The eyelashes along the upper lids are normally longer and denser than lashes along the lower lids.

Depending on the activity, the average person blinks from 4 to 15 times per minute.

Each blink provides protection from trauma and is also the mechanism by which old tears are directed into the punctum, and fresh tear layers are laid down on the surface of the eyes.

Blinking is controlled by three muscles: the orbicularis oculi, which functions to close the lids, and the levator palpebrae superioris muscle and Muller's muscle, both of which are responsible for opening the lids. The Muller's muscle is under the control of the sympathetic (fight or flight) nervous system.

Simply stated, as these facts relate to our procedure, the skin requires a firm, well-formed and appropriately placed stretch that effectively controls and manages the three muscles controlling the eyelids.

Upper lids are more mobile than lower lids and contain more dense eyelashes than the lower lids. As a result, the upper eyeliner procedure may be more challenging than the lower lid for some technicians. Because the procedure requires charge over the function blinking, the eye must be kept moist. This can be achieved by providing moistening eye drops prior to and during the procedure and also allowing a composed natural blink at intervals during the procedure. Always blot off any excess eye drops so the moistness does not draw closely placed anesthetic or residual pigment into the eye.

Above all, the protection of the eye is the first priority during an eyeliner procedure. Caution must be taken to avoid all foreign materials from entering the eye. If the client experiences discomfort or excessive tearing be prepared to immediately flush the eye out with an eyewash product.

The following stretching techniques are provided as examples to assist in completing eyeliner procedures while keeping the client's eyes safe. It is suggested these techniques be practices thoroughly on a friend or family member without the added burden of a device in hand.

Directions for stretching techniques in this section are provided for right-handed technicians. The information provided may be mirrored for left-handed technicians. As demonstrated (see Figure 18-12, photos individually marked 1–10), a wooden cotton swab may be used to represent a device while practicing. Once a stretching technique comfort zone is found, technicians can then feel confident and more routine when implementing stretching techniques during an actual procedure.

Section 18 - All About Procedures

Eyeliner Stretching Techniques

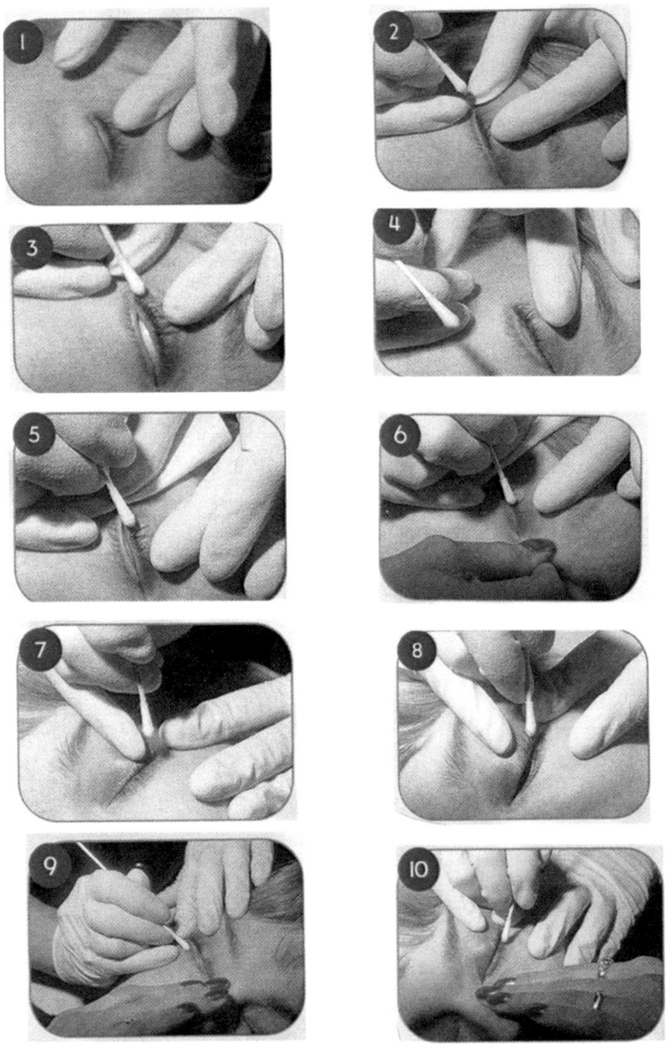

Figure 18-12: Eyeliner stretching techniques

As the suggested stretching technique directions are read, refer to the following photo collage, numbered according to the sequence of directions. This is not an active procedure. If it were, the client would be wearing gloves in an assisted eyeliner stretch.

The following stretching techniques guidance is based on the technician tattooing from both sides of the client. Many technicians work from one side only and will need to adjust their stretching techniques accordingly. There are several examples in Figure 18-14 on page 233.

Begin on either the client's right or left eye. Novice technicians should consider beginning on the side where they feel the most confident and comfortable. For the purposes of agreeing with the example photographs, the client's right side is addressed first. Begin on the right eye at the last lash at the outer canthus, moving slowly and methodically toward the inner canthus.

With the client's eye in a relaxed position, gently place the middle finger of the left hand close to the eyelashes at the point where tattooing will begin. Some technicians refer to this finger as their *rudder* finger. This is because, by adjusting its position either slightly up or down, the eyelashes follow that direction, thus giving a full view of the area to be tattooed from any perspective.

With the rudder finger of the left hand raise the excess eyelid skin up to the orbital rim and hold it in place (Figure 18-12, Photo 1).

Place the ball of the left thumb as close to the outer edge of the eye as possible and gently stretch outward. On the right eye, the thumb is the major stretching mechanism. Place the little finger of the right hand beneath the lower lashes. This provides a slight separation of the upper and lower eyelashes. The client's eye may be slightly open or closed.

Control of the client's lids has now been accomplished. (Figure 18-12, Photo 2) If the client can completely blink independently, positioning is not effective and the lid's Muller's muscle will respond to the nervous system's sympathetic fight or flight commands.

Periodically during the procedure, because control is maintained over the client's lids, plan to relax the rudder finger to allow some slack in the lid's positioning. Lower the lid gently down to allow the client to blink and moisten the eye. A good time to plan on incorporating controlled blinks for the client is when the stretching positioning is changed, or when stopping to retrieve more pigment.

With the stretching technique in place and planning complete, the procedure can begin. Ask the client to look down or toward their nose. By doing this, the orbital shape of the eyeball will fill a void in the eyelash area that might otherwise recess inward. Ask the client to maintain this positioning of their eye. If the eyeball moves, this affects the positioning of the needle. This position for the client's eye results in a firmer foundation for the tattooing process and is very effective for clients with deeply recessed eyes (Figure 18-12, Photo 3).

A section of the upper eyeliner has now been tattooed, more pigment can be retrieved, and the stretching position can now be moved to the next area. Relax the rudder finger, complete a controlled blink for the client, and move the stretch focus to the next area. (Figure 18-12. Photo 4) **Do not release the eyelid tissue**. The client may automatically squint and if allowed to do so may result in getting product into the eye. When a release of the eyelid skin is appropriate (during short breaks, for example) remind the client not to squint.

Move the rudder finger over slightly and again, place it gently, directly above the next area to be tattooed. Raise the excess skin up to the orbital rim as before. To move the ball of the thumb forward, it is recommended a material such as cotton square or round to pad the eye is used under the thumb for support. Please note that this is not a press-down motion. It is a motion of gently laying the ball of the thumb across a section of the eye and gently stretching outward. (Figure 18-12, Photo 5)

Follow this technique repeatedly moving toward the inner canthus of the eye, progressing no further than the growth of the eyelashes. At this point, the tissue is not as readily available due to the natural curvature shape of the eye. To ensure access to the proper placement in this area, one of two things can be done. Move the rudder finger slightly forward and gently *press-out* the lash line, or in a rare instance the client can be gloved up and requested pinch the sinus areas of their nose. This will provide for an added stretch that opposes the rudder finger and thumb stretches. These combined stretches clear the way for safely tattooing the inner canthus area (Figure 18-12, Photo 6).

Below is an additional close-up photograph for a stretch to tattoo the inner canthus section of the eyelash enhancement:

If the technician is right-handed, that was the more comfortable side. Now proceed to the left side, which is typically more challenging for right-handed technicians. On the left side, use the little finger of the right hand as the rudder finger. Use the index finger of the left hand as the stretching mechanism. The middle finger of the left hand serves to separate the upper and lower lashes (Figure 18-12, Photos 7 and 8).

All other techniques and eye safety precautions mentioned above for tattooing the right side are repeated.

The lower lids are less mobile and the eyelashes more sparse. The placement of the pigment design line is adjacent to (or through), the lashes and often the eyeliner design is not extended to the very last eyelash in the inner canthus area unless the client specifically

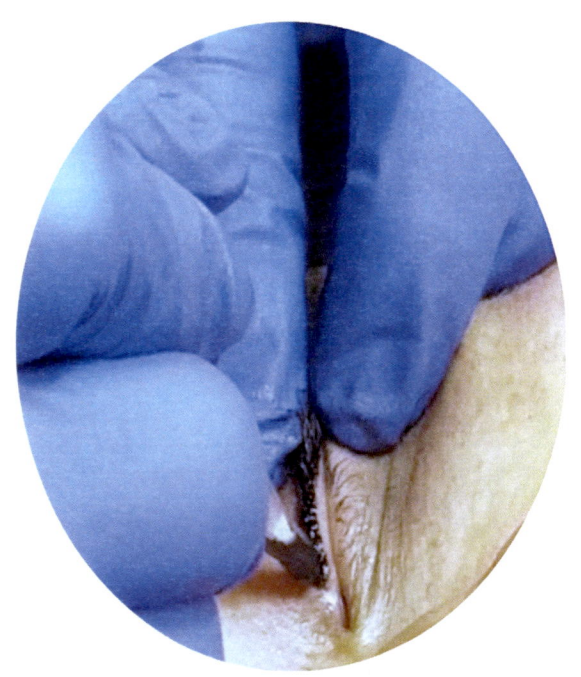

Figure 18-13: Stretching Technique for the Eyeliner Enhancement Inner Canthus

asked for this. During the consultation, design work had been discussed and was agreed upon. If the client's eyes are recessed (inset) and the tissue difficult to manage, consider the following: Apply *slight* pressure to push or pout-out the lower lash line with the finger directly under the area being tattooed.

The primary goals of good stretching techniques are twofold. First, a good stretching technique produces a taut foundation (think of the tautness of material in an embroidery hoop) for tattooing. This reduces client discomfort, gives the client the needed confidence that the technician is in control, and ensures a clean needle entry into the skin. Second, by effectively stretching in small sections that are being tattooed, small drapes/folds in the skin are not allowed to form. In rare instances, the client's assistance may be requested to achieve these goals if necessary.

Begin on the right side of the client's lower lid. Use the middle and index fingers on the left hand to form a *V* at the outer canthus corner. The middle finger serves to separate the upper and lower lashes, and the index finger serves as the stretching mechanism. Place the little finger of the right hand directly below the area to be tattooed, gently draw the excess skin toward the client's cheekbone, and hold it in place.

If this positioning accomplishes the task of a smooth canvas, then proceed. If it does not, as stated above, the little finger may be placed closer to the lash line, applying light pressure to press or pout-out the area to be tattooed to accomplish the goal of a smooth canvas. The little finger serves as the rudder finger and focuses on the area being tattooed.

If desired, in order to obtain a smooth canvas (this is sometimes necessary if the client has skin that is difficult to manage), the client may be asked to place their gloved right hand on the cheekbone and *gently tug* (this is not an exaggerated pulling motion) the skin toward the bridge of her nose (see Figure 18-12, Photo 9). Request the client to look upward or over to their nose, which fills the void in the lower lash area; this area could otherwise be recessed. This may assist in creating a smoother canvas.

When sitting on the left side of the client, the little finger of the right hand is used to separate the upper eyelashes from the lower. The index and middle finger on the left hand are used to form the *V* at the outer corner of the eye. The index finger provides the gentle stretch outward, and the middle finger serves as the rudder and focuses on the area where you are tattooing.

In rare instances, the client may be asked to place their left hand on the cheekbone and *gently tug* the skin toward the bridge of the nose. Ask the client to look upward or toward their nose, filling the void in the lower lash area. This may assist in creating a smooth canvas. (Figure 18-12, Photo 10)

In regard to the optional assistance of the client, this is presented for consideration only as some may feel asking for the client to participate is not appropriate, while others see it as an asset. Often the decision will be based on how difficult or easy the skin surrounding the eyeliner procedural area is to control without the client's assistance.

Stretching techniques are an important element of all permanent cosmetic procedures. Without an effective stretch, it is doubtful pigment will be tattooed into the upper dermal layer of the skin. There is a risk of altering the approved design and that random client movements may alter the positioning of the needles.

If eyeliner procedures are not healing to expectation, technicians can surely look to methods of stretching the skin as an element of the process that must be mastered.

Section 18 - All About Procedures

The photographs in Figure 18-14 illustrate a variety of different eyeliner stretching techniques being performed by right-handed technicians while tattooing with both machine and manual devices.

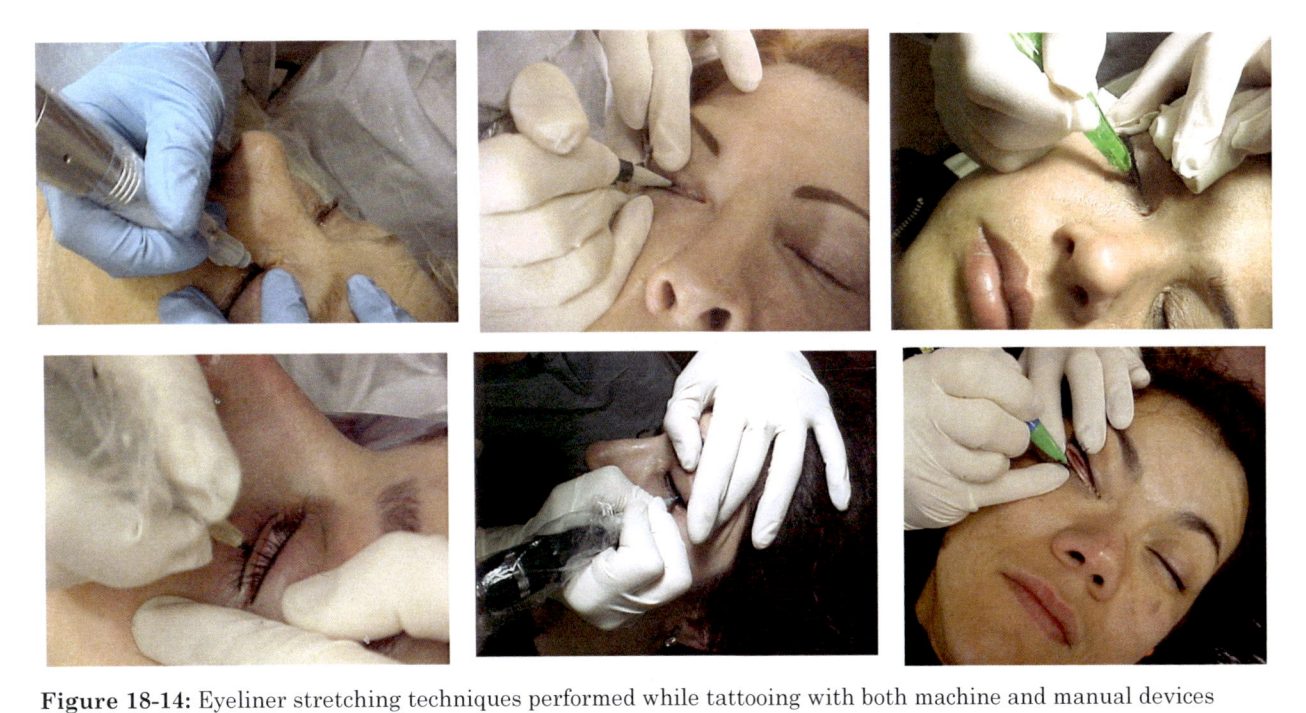

Figure 18-14: Eyeliner stretching techniques performed while tattooing with both machine and manual devices

Below is an additional close-up photograph for a lower eyeliner stretch:

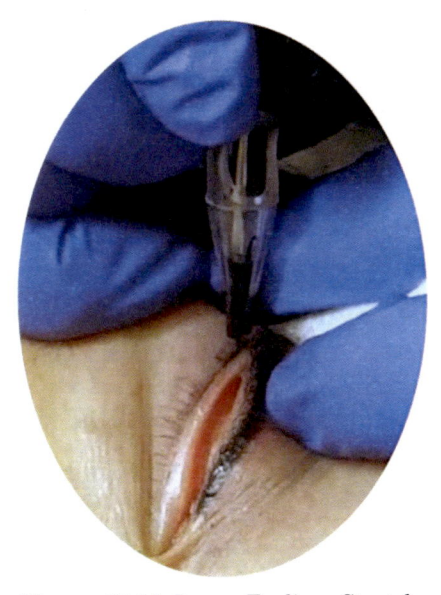

Figure 18-15: Lower Eyeliner Stretch

The Eyebrow Procedure

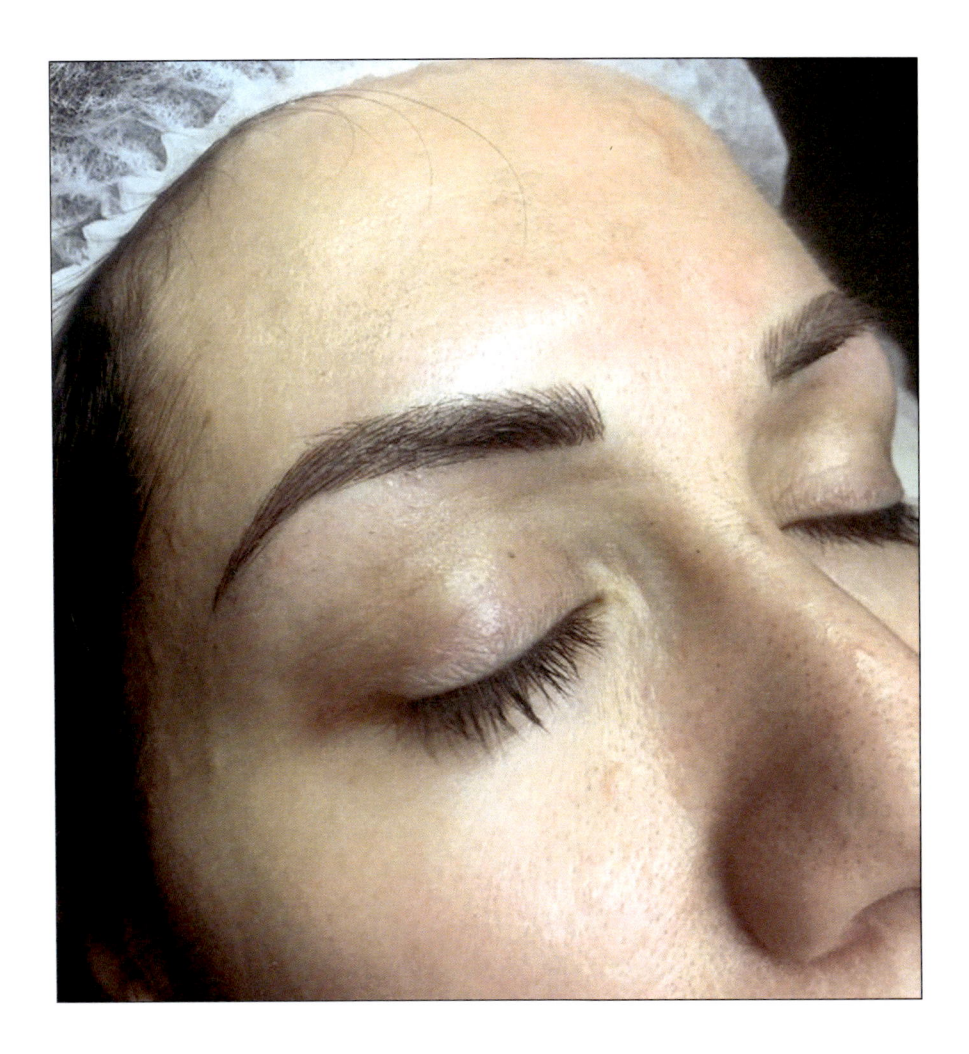

Permanent Cosmetic Eyebrow Tattoo Techniques

There are currently many techniques employed for permanent cosmetic eyebrow services, and it is anticipated others will continue to be introduced in the future. They are all tattooing techniques.

Formal training is recommended for each of the different techniques that may be of interest. To become familiar with the terminology and associated general description, an introductory overview of several popular and frequently discussed techniques is offered.

There are several reasons why different eyebrow techniques have been developed. One very important aspect of this is what the client is familiar with, including their appearance without the aid of any pencil or powder. Often we are asked to just enhance their natural eyebrow hair design or to reproduce what they have drawn on for years. Another reason to be aware of different techniques is to converse with clients about design work they have heard about, or seen in magazines and social media sites that appeal to them.

Over time, one eyebrow technique will likely not fit all the different requests voiced by clients who describe or show us what they want. Whereas one client will specifically ask for microblading or hair stroke eyebrows (machine or microblade techniques) based on their preferences, another will be more comfortable with different versions of shaded brows.

It's to every technician's advantage to become familiar with the terminology and appearance of the different types of eyebrow permanent cosmetic techniques.

Microblading

Microblading (which may be called by different names such as, but not limited to, microstroking, embroidery, etc.) is a manual device, non-machine method of creating the appearance of natural individual eyebrow hair designs (see Figure 18-16 through Figure 18-18). There are a variety of different needle configurations manufactured specifically for microblading hair stroke eyebrows. During training students are introduced to needles used during the hands-on segments of the class, and later the technician may choose from a variety of different microblading needles on the marketplace.

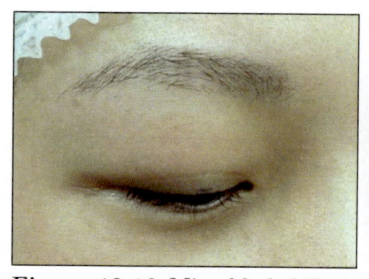

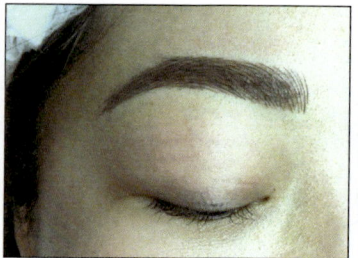

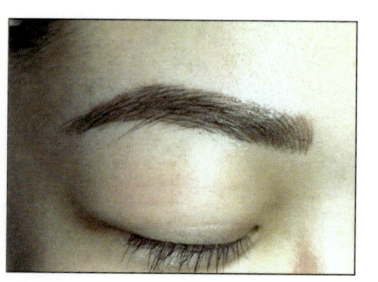

Figure 18-16: Microbladed Eyebrow
Before, Immediately After, and Healed

The technique involves a non-machine method of gliding a group of very small needles that are arranged in a line through the eyebrow design area. The needles are moved in a manner specifically with the intent of creating the appearance of individual eyebrow hair strokes in a designated design pattern.

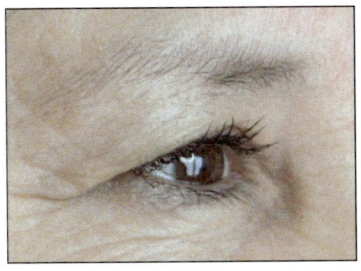

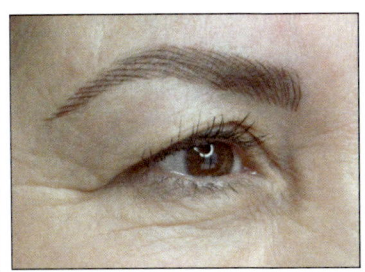

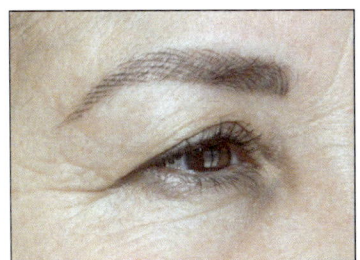

Figure 18-17: Microbladed Eyebrow
Before, Immediately After, and Healed

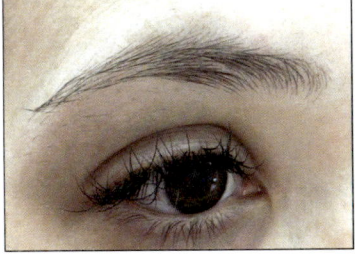

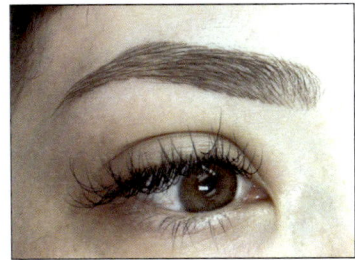

Figure 18-18: Microbladed Eyebrow
Before, Immediately After, and Healed

Machine Method Hair Strokes

Machine method hair strokes create the appearance of natural appearing individual eyebrow hair strokes in a designated design area (see Figure 18-19 through Figure 18-21). There are several needle sizes manufactured for this delicate work. The single needle of different sizes in diameter is a popular selection; however, there are others for consideration.

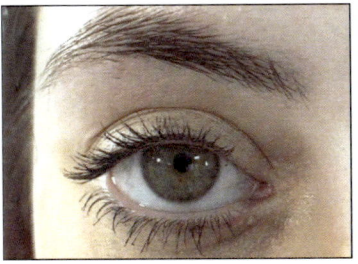

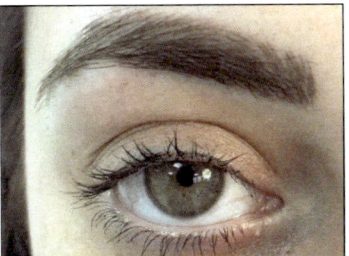

Figure 18-19: Machine Hair Stroke Eyebrow
Before, Immediately After, and Healed

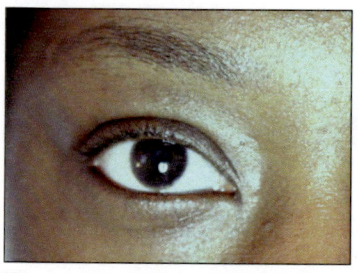

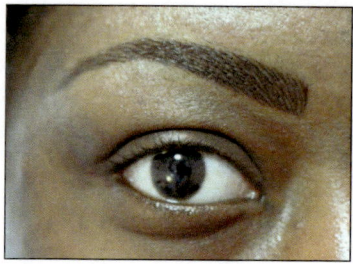

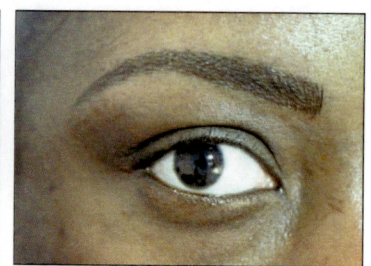

Figure 18-20: Machine Hair Stroke Eyebrow
Before, Immediately After, and Healed

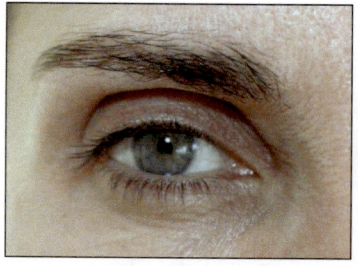

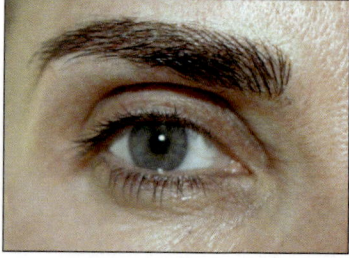

Figure 18-21: Machine Hair Stroke Eyebrow
Before, Immediately After, and Healed

Shaded Brows

Shaded Brows result in a more filled or powdery appearance of the tattooed eyebrow design. There are many technique names associated with shaded eyebrows, but ultimately, it is a design that results in all or part of the template being more filled in more than that of a machine hair stroke or microbladed appearance.

This technique may be produced with machine devices, often using (but not limited) to a shader style needle grouping. Beautiful shaded brows have also been produced with a single needle. Another device used for the shaded brow appearance is the manual device (with needle sizes and configurations different than microblading hair stroke type needle configurations), often through the use of a technique of tapping motions on the skin.

Pointillism eyebrow technique (see Figure 18-22) is a form of a shaded eyebrow as well. The more dots (pointillism) tattooed, the darker the color and more saturated the eyebrow color will appear when healed. After the shaded eyebrow has healed, hair strokes can be tattooed for dimension and texture if desired.

Figure 18-22: Eyebrow Pointillism Technique
Immediately After

The more or less passes with a machine or hair stroke microblade configuration device, or dots (pointillism) with a machine, or taps with a manual device (non-microblade hair stroke configuration) in one area of the eyebrow, the more or less density of pigment when healed. People who are accustomed after years of applying eyebrow pencil or powder may be comfortable with the shaded eyebrow technique.

Below are examples of shaded brows (Figure 18-23 through Figure 18-26). Some are a softer appearance of the shaded tattooed eyebrow, often referred to as a powder brow. The powder brow may be produced with the machine and manual devices (often using a shader type needle configuration, or by making less passes over the eyebrow design). There are also techniques to produce this appearance either with faster hand motions using smaller needle configurations such as a single needle or smaller groupings or by diluting the pigment for a softer healed appearance. There are many ways to create the appearance of a powder brow.

Some of the examples of a shaded brow below are more saturated. The final result is dependent on the needle choice and whether or not the pigment was used full strength, or diluted. The number of passes made also affects the appearance of the healed result

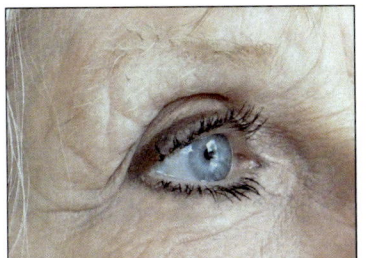

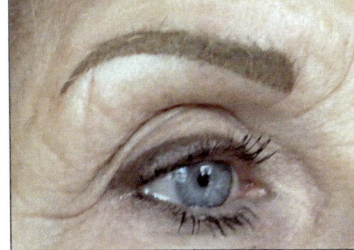

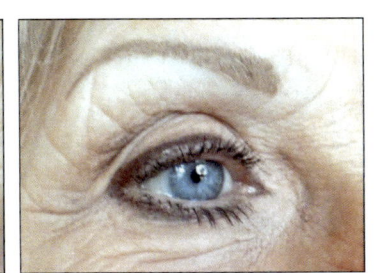

Figure 18-23: Shaded Brow
Before, Immediately After, and Healed

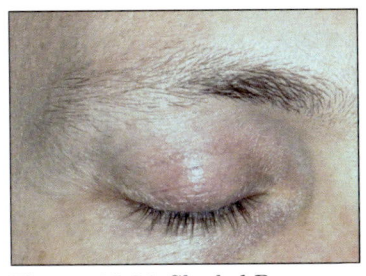

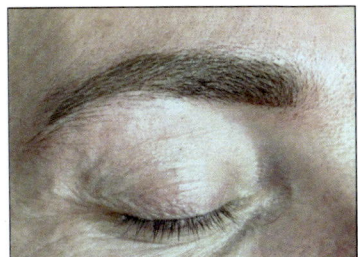

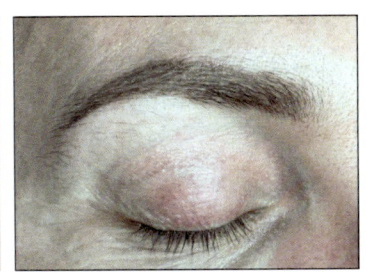

Figure 18-24: Shaded Brow
Before, Immediately After, and Healed

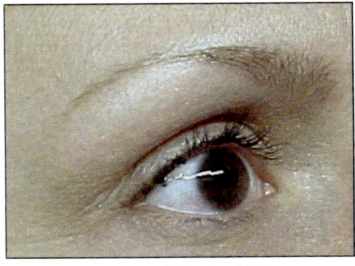

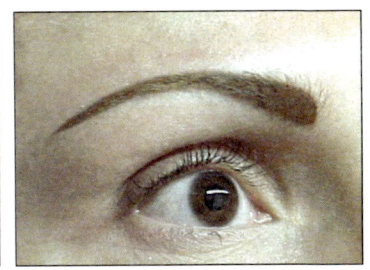

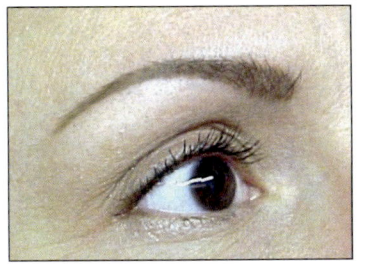

Figure 18-25: Shaded Brow
Before, Immediately After, and Healed

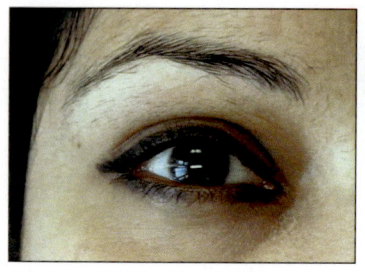

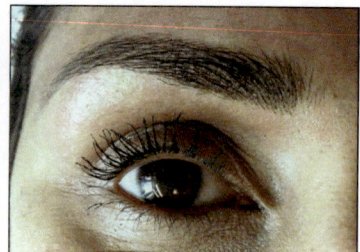

Figure 18-26: Shaded Brow
Before, Immediately After, and Healed

It is common to see combinations of techniques used for eyebrow tattooing. For instance, below is a brow technique referred to an Ombre effect eyebrow style (see Figure 18-27). The eyebrow is shaded with lighter density) in the bulb area for a graduated healed color appearance (either with tattooing technique, or dilution of the pigment).

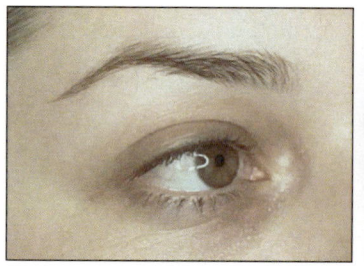

Figure 18-27: Ombre Effect Eyebrow
Before, Immediately After, and Healed

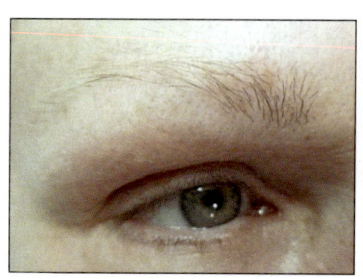

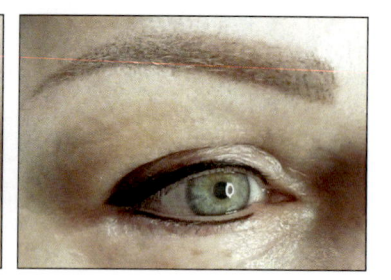

Figure 18-28: Ombre Effect Eyebrow
Before, Immediately After, and Healed

It is commonplace for technicians to combine different techniques and often different devices (machine and manual device combinations) to create their versions of the permanent cosmetic eyebrow appearance. Not every client is a good client for a particular technique. People with oily skin, large pores, or sensitive thinning skin due to age, or other skin condition related reasons, may be a better candidate for one technique rather than another.

Also, we have to consider what the client wants, and often in a more mature community of clients, it's what they've been used to seeing with the use of topical cosmetics.

Section 18 - All About Procedures

Once a person has trained in a permanent cosmetic eyebrow technique, due to a variety of client requests and exposure to different styles shown on social media, training offers a wide range of techniques to choose from for a versatile eyebrow menu of services.

Pre-Eyebrow Design Sequence

Please review the *Overview of Pre and Post-Procedure Protocols* at the beginning of Section 18 before proceeding (see page 211).

There are many ways to approach an eyebrow procedure. Technicians have techniques that work well for them which at times are subject to change as new tattooing techniques or experience provides variety to their procedure processes.

The following sequence options represent basics steps of one or more methods of accomplishing the process. As more eyebrow procedures are performed, technicians will develop a step-by-step process that works well for them. Trainers provide their students with directions during classes.

- Cleanse the client's eyebrow area and surrounding skin.

- Inspect the eyebrow area to ensure the skin is free from any visible abnormalities such as rashes or moles (see Figure 18-29).

- Although something that is seen may not prevent the procedure from going forward, take photographs and point out the irregularity to the client. Make appropriate notes on the client's chart. If this was not noticed by the client before, it may come to their attention during the healing period (clients routinely inspect the procedural area) and it's best to address it before the procedure. If you see it, say it, and document it.

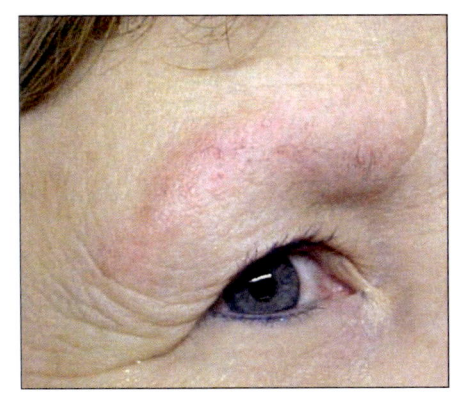

Figure 18-29: Rash in the Eyebrow Procedure Area

- If using a pre-procedure anesthetic before designing, apply an adequate amount of the chosen anesthetic to the eyebrow area. Anesthetic use for the eyebrow area before designing and at times even during the tattooing process is technician-specific (see Figure 18-30).

There is also a technique whereby the skin is cleansed, inspected, and the eyebrow template is drawn on and marked. After these initial steps, the eyebrow area is

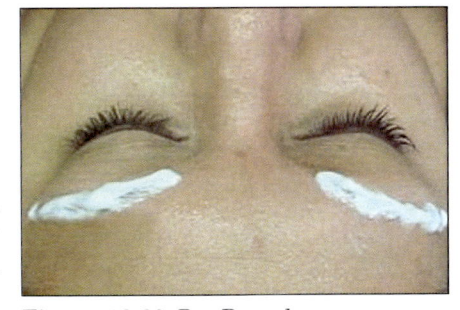

Figure 18-30: Pre-Procedure Eyebrow Anesthetics

241

lightly tattooed (or lightly scored) and at that time a secondary anesthetic may be applied. The sequence of anesthetic use (if any is used) is technician and trainer-specific.

- Pre-procedure topical anesthetic on the eyebrows may be occluded (if desired and/or if recommended by the anesthetic manufacturer) with a tented position of barrier film. Caution is recommended, however, to have the client in a position that would prevent anesthetic from melting downwardly and possibly getting into the eyes.
- Wait the manufacturer's prescribed time before removing the topical anesthetic and then cleanse and pat the skin dry.
- If working in a medical office where injected anesthetics are available and this is the chosen method of anesthesia, now is the appropriate time for those injections. The permanent cosmetic industry considers injected anesthetics unnecessary for client comfort control. Topical anesthetics developed specifically for the industry are effective.
  - There may be other sequences of anesthetic use that are trainer or technician-specific for consideration. The use (or sequence of use) of topical or injected (in a medical office) anesthetics may be predicated on the type of brow technique that will be tattooed.
- The different techniques are microblading, shaded with a machine or non-microblading manual device, machine hair stroke, or a combination of techniques (see *Permanent Cosmetic Eyebrow Tattoo Techniques,* page 236).

Designing Eyebrows and Marking the Eyebrow Template

Designing eyebrows for clients will come easier to some technicians than to others. Many technicians are in the beauty industry and their services include the designing, shaping, and/or waxing of eyebrows for their clients.

In order to effectively design eyebrows, there must be a general knowledge of facial morphology and the standard measuring techniques used by makeup artists and other beauty professionals. Refer to Section 17 of this textbook, *Basic Facial Morphology and Placement of Procedure* (page 253) for additional information on client facial proportions, the different facial shapes, and eyebrow design placements.

Expecting to begin to learn how to draw a good eyebrow design during a fundamental permanent cosmetic class is not recommended. Students should be familiar with the eyebrow designing task when arriving to class so the time can be utilized to learn how to tattoo permanent cosmetic eyebrows. That is not to say time will not be spent on this subject, but as a rule, it is not the time to begin learning about eyebrow design. Time allotted to eyebrow designing is often based on the length of the fundamental class.

Students and/or technicians who are less familiar with the task of designing eyebrows have several alternatives. One option is to take an art class at a local community college. In some locations, art stores offer lessons as well. Ideally, this should be completed before a fundamental class date. There are also books written on this subject. It is also a good practice to ask trainers for resource materials.

One exercise for consideration is to acquire beauty books such as wig catalogs and other beauty magazines that show close-up pictures of models. Many times in these close-up pictures individual eyebrow hairs can be seen clearly. As an exercise (using an extra fine tip ink pen), trace over these individual hairs. The purpose of doing this is to train your hand through repetition of movement, to develop a memory of the smooth movements required to effectively draw on an eyebrow design that flows. There are a variety of techniques employed by professionals who draw on eyebrows for their clients.

Another option is to purchase eyebrow templates. There are different brands on the market from which to choose, although these too take some time to master and the templates are not always a design type the client has in mind; the design options are limited.

Permanent cosmetic technicians provide solutions for the aftermath of a client's eyebrow fashion attack, the effect of a medical condition, or as a result of the aging process. They also provide convenience and consistency of design appearance for the person who has an active lifestyle.

If all facial shapes, client partiality to design, and existing (or lack of) hair in the brow area were all identical factors, the technician's job would be simplified. In all fairness to the individuality of all clients' facial characteristics and preferences, eyebrows should be as unique as the client for whom they are designed.

It is always comforting to a potential client to ask that they wear their eyebrows to the consultation appointment the way they are accustomed to applying them, and to bring the topical makeup product(s) used. This sends a signal that the technician is concerned about providing familiarity, which is a major concern to people who are considering permanent cosmetics. As soon as the client arrives, it becomes visibly clear what the potential client has accepted as a normal eyebrow design and color.

The longer technicians perform permanent cosmetics, the more interesting designs they will encounter. Some client brow designs are pencil thin, some are very thick, some long, some short, and some asymmetric. On the other hand, a client may not use eyebrow makeup at all and trust the technician for design work.

If the potential client normally applies eyebrow pencil/powder and arrives for the consultation appointment as they typically wear them, as requested, technicians have an immediate opportunity to ask how the design work is perceived. If the potential client has applied unflattering eyebrows and says *"I love my eyebrows like this, I just want to have them tattooed permanently"*; the work ahead is significant if the technician chooses to proceed. If the response is something to the effect that the client recognizes the design work is not flattering, the task of designing could then be considered a teamwork-oriented task. And, there are also instances when the client designs a lovely eyebrow, which could be used as a template for the permanent cosmetic work.

An important factor to remember is that the client's brain has recorded a normal vision of their appearance. Although some may say they are open to change, the fact is that they are *accustomed* to looking a particular way. A change in appearance, even a positive one, is difficult for some people to accept in a short timeframe.

A basic eyebrow design as described below may be drawn on using standard facial morphology measurements or brow guides (see Figure 18-33), and after viewing the work, the client may ask for changes that lead right back to what they arrived with (assuming the client wore makeup to the appointment). If the client is not accustomed to wearing makeup, seeing eyebrows drawn on may seem odd and take some getting used to. These are everyday occurrences in the permanent cosmetic industry.

By using an eyebrow pencil/powder color that the client is accustomed to, technicians sidestep the potential client's fear of an unwanted color, and the design alone becomes the focus. It can also be used as a baseline for helping to select a pigment color that will heal to a familiar color if an appointment results from the consultation. This is assuming the client's familiar color is appropriate.

The primary goal technicians strive to focus on is to design eyebrows based on client-unique facial morphology factors. This is the key to customizing flattering eyebrows. The eyebrow consultation aspect of the permanent cosmetic process is important. There will be people who cannot be pleased, and others who will cooperate in such a manner that it is obvious the designing task will be routine.

It is at this junction when technicians decide whom they will provide eyebrow services to, and those who will be advised that permanent cosmetics are not the right choice at this time, or that they are not the technician for the eyebrow procedure requested. For those whom technicians have accepted as eyebrow clients, on the day of the scheduled appointment, the designing process becomes the focus.

There are many techniques employed for eyebrow design work. Eyebrow guides are a very popular method for ensuring symmetry (see Figure 18-33). Ultimately, each technician finds their comfort zone when designing eyebrows.

Below is one method for applying basic eyebrow designs, based on standard facial morphology design measurements (see Figure 18-31).

Place a dot or mark at each of the standard measurement prime areas, the frontal zone (bulb area), the arch, and the exterior zone (tail). Standard measurements provide that the bulb should not be lower than the tail (this can result in an angry appearance), nor should the tail be lower than the bulb (this can result in a sad appearance). Standard arch placement is determined by using the outer rim of the client's iris as a guideline, making adjustments to the arch to compensate for high/low forehead and overall

Figure 18-31: Connect the dots (or marks made) with a light-handed stroke method creating the desired width and unique design elements.

face shape.

From the baseline created, adjustments may be made to compensate for:

Wider or Narrower Set Eyes

Move the frontal zone (bulb area) slightly inward to compensate for wider set eyes and outward for narrow set eyes. If the client has hair in the brow area, the placement of the natural hair, particularly in the bulb area, should be respected. If the bulb area is extended inward far past the natural hair growth, once the procedure has healed, it may be very apparent and contrast with where the natural hair begins. This gets tricky because many clients ask for wider and/or extended brows that are not close to the natural eyebrow hair they have. Technicians must use their judgment as to whether the healed or aged appearance of the tattooed eyebrow design will work well the client's natural eyebrow hair.

High or Low Forehead Characteristics

Arches are more flattering placed slightly higher to compensate for a client with a high forehead, and lower for those with lower forehead characteristics. This practice is assuming this can done without departing too far from any natural hair growth. Options of eyebrow arch placement are dependent upon the client's existing natural eyebrow hair and their preferences.

The Shape of the Face

The shapes of the face (round, oval, heart, oblong, diamond, and pear shapes) is also a primary consideration when determining arch, height, and tail length. Reference Section 17 (page 193) of this textbook, Bruising During Procedure (page 253) for additional information.

- **The round**—shaped face will appear more aesthetically pleasing if a more angular design is used. Avoid rounded eyebrows on a round face.
- **The oval**—shaped face is considered the most desirable face shape to work on. Utilizing the standard measurements will normally produce an eyebrow design that requires little modification.
- **The heart**—shaped face is wider in the forehead area. To balance out the top-heavy appearance, eyebrow tails should be kept slightly shorter.
- **The oblong**—shaped face requires width to offset the appearance of having a linear (long) face. Arches should be kept to a minimum so as not to enhance the linear appearance and tails lengthened slightly to provide some horizontal lines to the facial structure.
- **The diamond**—shaped face can benefit from a good balance of vertical lines achieved with the design of the arches and a well-placed exterior zone (eyebrow tail area).
- **The pear**—shaped face can benefit from minimizing the illusion of bulk

at the jawline by extending the eyebrow exterior zones (tails) slightly out for balance and raising the arches for linear effects. This is a difficult facial shape to work with.

Once the eyebrows have been drawn/powdered onto the eyebrow area show the final eyebrow design to the client. Make adjustments as guided by client preferences. A little too long? Slightly shorten the tails. A little too short? Slightly lengthen the tails. A little too thin? Add a line to widen the design, and so it goes. Client preferences must be considered and very minor changes to accommodate client input goes a long way to achieving satisfaction.

There are very important safeguards technicians may wish to consider when designing eyebrows and selecting pigment color. The first application of an eyebrow is less risky if it is more conservative in design and color. The unknown factors are (1) How the pigment will heal, so a conservative pigment color is selected. The pigment can always be darkened at the follow-up appointment. (2) How much the design appearance will change during the healing process is also an unknown factor, and (3) Given thirty to sixty days to reflect on how the client feels they appear, will the client ask for minor changes?

Some clients return and the eyebrow design appears much smaller than they did in the immediately-after photograph, while others return with a very similar if not the same design appearance. Some clients are just fine with the approved design work until they go home and have an opportunity to look at themselves in their own environment. Other clients take the input from a family member or friend as gospel and return asking for something slightly different.

As a result of these unknown factors, a conservative philosophy is also (in conjunction with pigment selection) suggested for eyebrow design work. A slightly smaller (narrower, slightly shorter, etc.) eyebrow design provides some room during the follow-up appointment for minor, but very important, adjustments for symmetry or small changes requested by the client.

The *slightly less is better* philosophy for eyebrow design work for younger clients is important as well for additional reasoning. This applies not only for possible fine-tuning needed at a follow-up appointment for minor design changes, but also because a younger client will likely need some adjustments over time to accommodate for asymmetries resulting from the aging process.

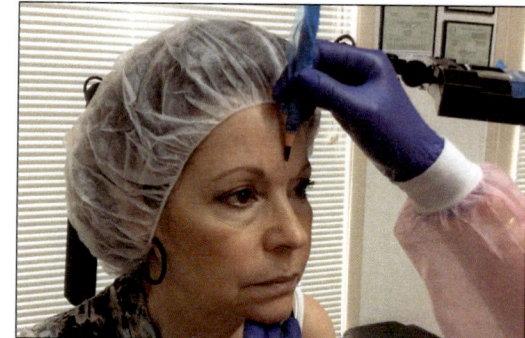

Figure 18-32: Marking for Eyebrow Design Placement

Design the eyebrow template with a single-use topical brow pencil which has been sharpened with a sharpener that has been disinfected (see Figure 18-32). Single-use powder and a powder applicator is another option

Eyebrow guides are also commonly used (see Figure 18-33)

Section 18 - All About Procedures

- Once the design is in place, provide the client with a mirror. Allow the client to review the designed eyebrow, and ask for approval. If the client indicates any changes are preferred, make those changes (assuming the technician is in agreement with the requested changes) and proceed once the client approves the eyebrow design template.

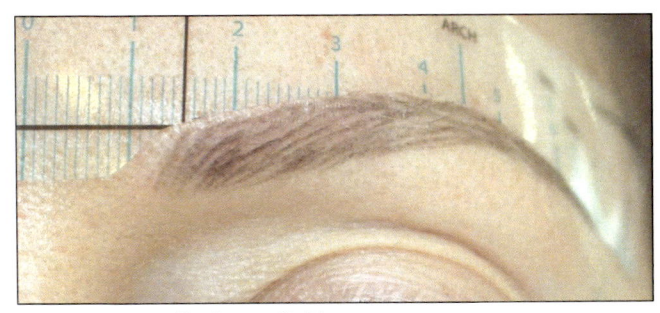

Figure 18-33: Eyebrow Guide

After the client has approved the eyebrow design, the template, which will be followed during the tattooing process, must be established.

There are several ways to secure the topical design template. The technique will vary from trainer to trainer and technician to technician. Some technicians use the chosen needle configuration to lightly sketch the design into the epidermal layer of the skin around the eyebrow.

This technique requires a skilled hand and knowledge of the appropriate depth of tattooing that novice technicians may not feel comfortable with at first. It is important that the pigment used in this particular sketching technique only be tattooed *superficially* into the skin (into the epidermal layer). These guideline marks are not intended to be permanent. This is referred to as creating a *bloodline around the design*.

Another technique to consider is to dot systematically around the eyebrow design with a single-use nontoxic marker, proceeding only when the dots reflect the exact topical design that the client approved (see Figure 18-34).

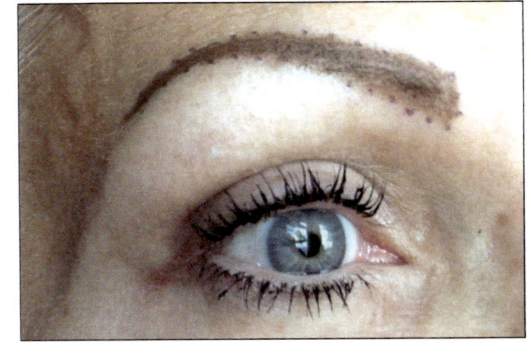

Figure 18-34: Dotting Around the Eyebrow Design with a Single-Use Dotting Pen

Another technique is to draw lines around the brow template with dark and/or white single-use marking pencils (see Figure 18-35).

If this textbook is being read in preparation for a fundamental class, the trainer will demonstrate the manner in which eyebrow design templates will be secured for application on models in the class. There are optional techniques for consideration

Once the eyebrow design has been approved by the client and the design template secured (marked), proceed to the tattooing process.

Figure 18-35: Marking Lines around the Eyebrow Design with a Single-Use Marker

The Eyebrow Tattooing Sequence

- Remove the sterile needle and machine accessories (if using a machine) from the packaging and assemble (as appropriate for the device being used).

- Where a technician begins the eyebrow procedure is a matter of personal preference and training. Some technicians prefer to begin in the tail area, slightly up from the tip and move toward the arch and then to the bulb.

    Others prefer to begin in the bulb area or midway in the brow design. There are many techniques for tattooing eyebrows. Training, and ultimately personal preferences will dictate the beginning point that is most comfortable and effective for each technician.

- If using anesthetics, apply post broken skin anesthetic(s) to the eyebrow after the initial pass is complete and move to the other eyebrow. Complete the same process; if using anesthetics, apply post broken skin anesthetics(s) to the eyebrow just tattooed and return to the original eyebrow for an additional pass.

- Repeat an additional pass to the second eyebrow, applying anesthetics along the way only as needed to keep the client comfortable. This is only one example of the eyebrow tattooing process. Another option is to complete one eyebrow entirely before moving to the other eyebrow.

- Use post-broken skin anesthetics sparingly. If used excessively, this is a practice that will ultimately dilute the pigment being tattooed, resulting in a lighter or spotty appearing healed eyebrow procedure.

- Allow the client periodic breaks as needed. It is difficult to remain in one position for long periods of time and a short restroom or water break gives the client renewed energy to see the procedure through easily. Breaks are also a good time to check the progress of work from a different perspective.

After the Procedure Is Complete

- Thoroughly remove any residual pigment from the face.

- Ask the client to view the completed eyebrow procedure. Determine at this juncture (with the client's input) if there are any minor changes to be made. Be cautious about agreeing to make any major changes in the design work, as the appearance of the eyebrows will change during the healing process.

- Technicians may choose to wait until the client has had the opportunity to freshen up and the immediately-after photographs are taken before proceeding with cleaning up the worktable. During this period, the need for small detail work may be noticed that will require additional tattooing. This review should only take a short time. Leaving used product and needles on the worktable is not permitted beyond the final evaluation

period.
- Take the immediately-after pictures. Take a full-face picture of the client and a close-up of the eyebrows. If, through the eye of the camera, the work is considered satisfactory and the client agrees, proceed to the final steps of the session.

Final Steps

- Eyebrows do not show the effects of tattooing as evidently as lips or eyeliner. As a result, applying cool compresses is a matter of preference, not necessity.
- Apply an aftercare product to the eyebrows if this is a chosen practice.
- Review aftercare instructions and give an aftercare products kit (if it is policy to direct the client to apply a healing product during the healing period and/or to provide the products).
- Schedule the follow-up appointment.
- Update the client's chart notes document with current procedural information.
- See "Section 4 - Safe Practices for Permanent Cosmetic Technicians" for Post Procedure Protocols (page 40).

Eyebrow Stretching Techniques

Stretching techniques are very personal and unique to each technician. There are many variables to consider:
- The technician's dominant hand (right or left)
- The size of the hands
- The device being used
- If the technician works from one side of the procedure bed or both sides
- The fit and texture of the gloves used
- The condition of the client's skin

Considering the variables that are unique to each technician, there can be no such thing as the only way to stretch the skin for an eyebrow procedure. Each technician, based on their physical characteristics and capabilities coupled with the flexibility and/or limitations of the studio environment must practice different techniques to find the best stretching technique to achieve basic goals.

As an example of how difficult this may initially seem vs. how easily stretching techniques will ultimately become, recall how awkward it was when first beginning to type on a keyboard. Once letters were typed over and over, typing quickly and accurately became automatic. The same analogy applies to stretching techniques. It simply takes practice and repetitive movements are required. If this textbook is being read in preparation for a fundamental class, the trainer will provide specific directions.

Regardless of the method in which technicians mark, stencil, or draw the pattern of the client's desired eyebrow design, the initial common goal is always to maintain the pattern intact until sufficient pigment has been tattooed into the eyebrow template and the topical markings are no longer required. Although the ideal stretch for any procedure is a short span stretch, initially technicians may have to be satisfied to start with a wider span stretch so as not to disturb the markings.

In order to accomplish this stretch, initially, minimum contact with the topical markings is recommended. Until a permanent image is obtained on at least a portion of the eyebrow design, a stretch from the tail to the bulb is an option. Another stretching option is an offset stretch adjacent to the area that is being tattooed. In either instance, keep the skin taut, tugged upward onto the brow bone and anchored in place while making the initial pass within the markings.

Once any portion of the eyebrow has been successfully tattooed and the topical markings are no longer needed in that area to maintain the design, the stretch can then be shortened and one of the stretching fingers can be placed on the tattooed portion of the eyebrow, bringing the next section closer to be tattooed. This shortening of width span for the stretch continues until the first pass is completed over the entire eyebrow and the design is completely visible without the aid of initial markings. The objective is to always keep the skin taut and in-place in the area that is being tattooed. Figure 18-36 shows commonly used eyebrow stretching techniques.

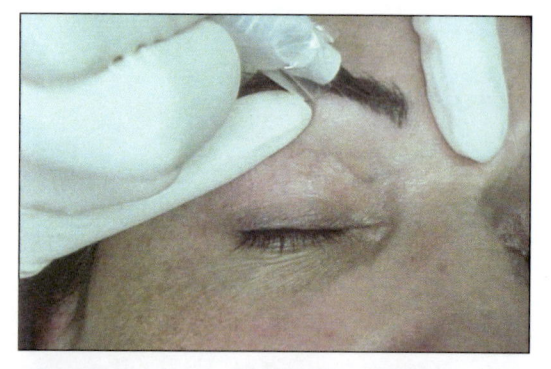

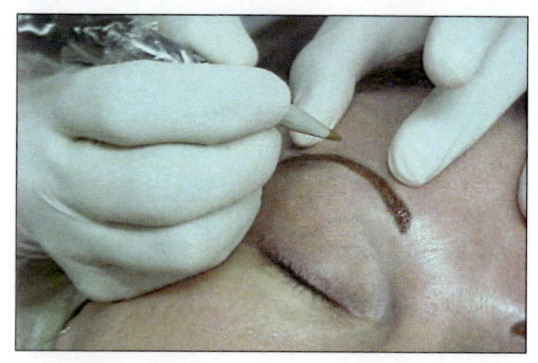

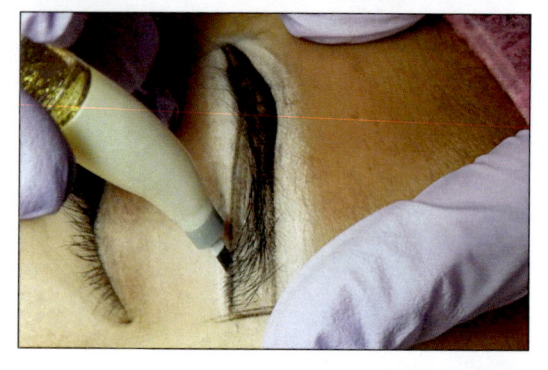

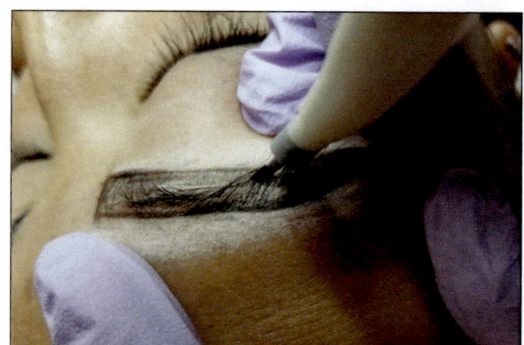

Figure 18-36: Commonly used eyebrow stretching techniques.

Lip Color Procedures

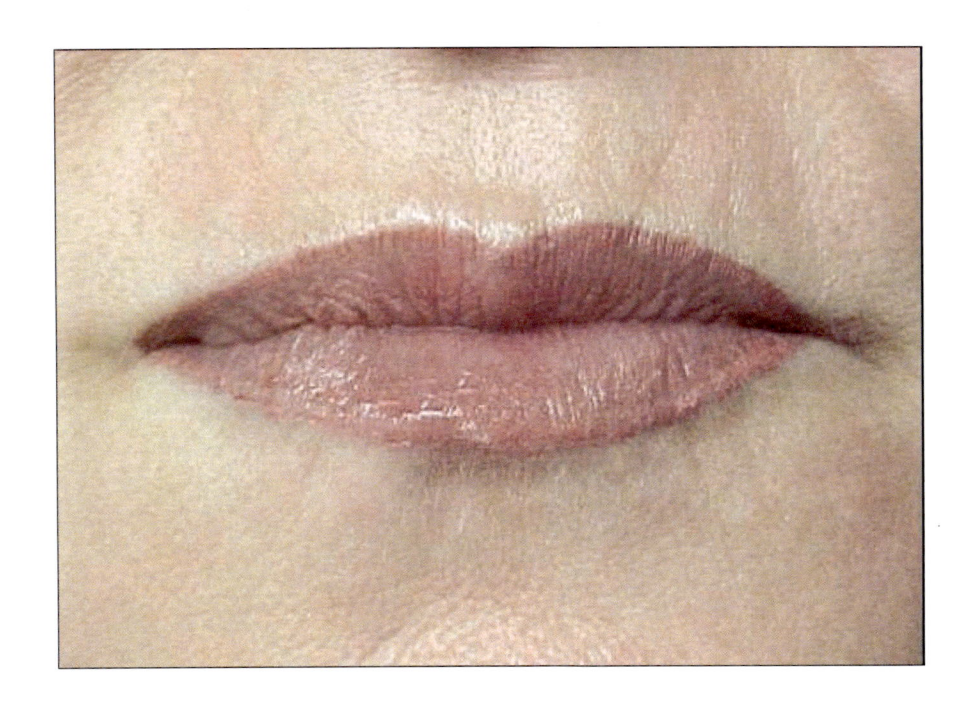

The Lip Liner and Shaded Lip Liner Tutorial

Please review the Overview of Pre and Post-Procedure Protocols at the beginning of Section 18 before proceeding (see page 211).

Whether lip liners and shaded lip liners are appropriate procedures to offer during fundamental training is specific to each trainer. Lip color procedures are reported to be more challenging to many novice technicians.

More contrasting and vibrant lip colors used for the procedures are obvious if a minor mistake is made. Some laser tattoo removal professionals will not (or may be hesitant) to attempt to remove lip liners with a laser because of the possibility of white (titanium dioxide) ingredients. A lip pigment color that contains white may limit the type of laser that can be successfully used, or may add a layer of treatment to the removal process.

The lip canvas is not always symmetric and often requires delicate design corrections. The majority of lip procedure clients look to the service as a cure for unattractive lips when in reality, the results of tattooing may not be able to fully meet the client's expectations. Expectations are an important part of the consultation. This information is not intended to detour new technicians from training for lip procedures, only words of caution to consider the appropriate timing for lip procedure training; confidence is important.

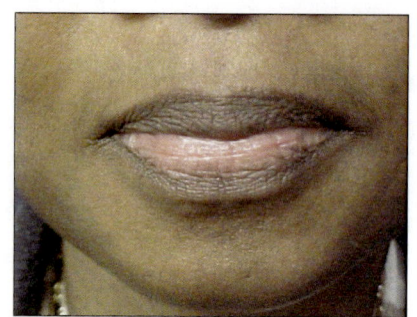

Figure 18-37: Darker Variegated Lips

Expectations of what can and cannot be achieved with a permanent cosmetic lip procedure are common subjects between clients and technicians, often based on what the client commonly achieves with traditional cosmetic lip products. Clients will present their technician their expectations regarding design and color. If a client has a history of cold sore breakouts, this can also add an element of a precautionary requirement such as needed anti-viral medication when appropriate. The darkness or evenness of color in the natural lip can also be a determining factor when deciding if a person is a good candidate for lip procedures.

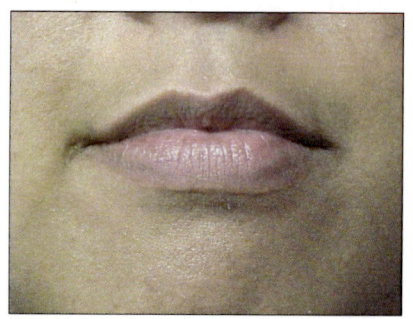

Figure 18-38: Cooler (Violet) Variated Lips

As discussed in Section 17 *Basic Facial Morphology and Placement of Procedures*, a person with darker or very cool natural lips and/or variegated (two-tone) lip coloring is not often a good candidate for permanent cosmetic lip procedures (see Figure 18-37 and Figure 18-38).

Lip liners and shaded lip liners typically concentrate on the restoration of the appearance of a lip by shaping and defining the vermilion border of the lips with a pigment color that very closely matches the client's natural lip color. If a color is requested by the client that does not closely agree with the client's natural lip color, this can produce a *noticeable demarcation line* of lip pigment vs. the natural lip color that requires a cosmetic lip color product to appear finished.

Filling in low circulation areas of the lip adjacent to the vermilion border is a part of the shaded lip liner procedure. Lip liners and shaded lip liners may vary in color depending on the client's natural lip coloring and preference. Technicians have the choice not to accept clients who insist on a color that would produce a noticeably contrasting line as a lip liner.

Full lip color addresses both the vermilion border and all the skin of the lip vermilion right up to the inner lip mucosa (see Figure 18-39). This mucosal tissue begins just beyond the closed lip.

Full lip color is considered an advanced procedure that should not be attempted without the continuing education training necessary to perform the procedure well.

Offering lip liners and shaded lip liners decrease some of the inherent risks associated with full lip color procedures. The more tissue that is being tattooed (i.e., full lips), the higher the risk of a fever blister (cold sore) outbreak, color distortions, client discomfort, and in many instances additional (two or more) procedures are necessary to reach the client's goals for color intensity. The following is a profile of the lips:

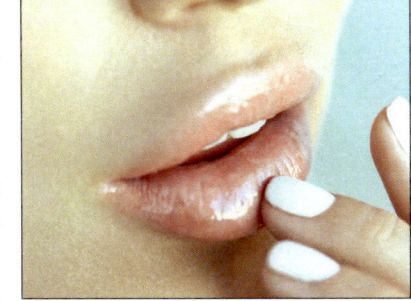

Figure 18-39: Lip Vermilion & Inner Lip Mucosal

The natural lip color is cool (some cooler than others) based on vascular and hormonal activity. Some lips may have obvious hyperpigmentation (darker areas of the lip color) or broken blood vessels that appear as darker blue spots/areas. To add to the complexity of permanent cosmetic lip procedures, many clients seeking lip color services have high and low circulation areas on and/or within the vermilion border. Irregular natural lip color affects the appearance of shape and the overall presentation of the lips.

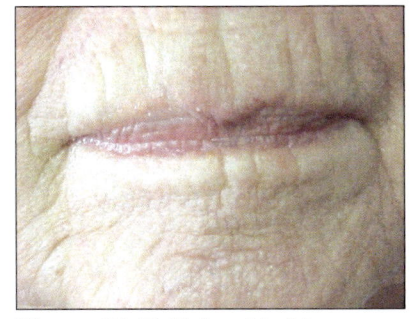

Figure 18-40: Before Lip Liner

Due to a decrease in vascular and hormonal activity, often a characteristic of the more mature person's lips, it is not unusual for clients to say that as they have aged they feel as if their lips have decreased in size. More mature people with fragile skin may bruise during a lip procedure. This is not uncommon for this age group (see Figure 18-40 and Figure 18-41). The bruising subsides during the healing process. It is not uncommon for lip clients to exhibit a loss of collagen in either or both the upper and lower lip, some more severe than others. The loss of collagen results in loose, less manageable lip tissue during the lip procedure.

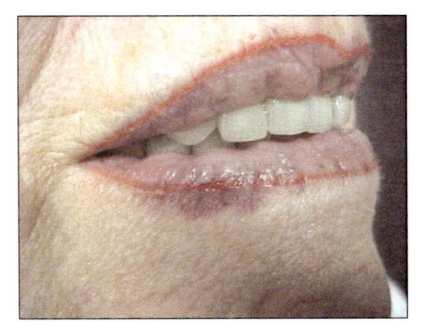

Figure 18-41: Bruising During Procedure

Lip liner procedures are generally not the answer to making a person's lips appear physically larger. It is recommended that novice technicians not consider placing a permanent cosmetic lip line outside the client's natural vermilion border to the point that there is skin showing between the permanent cosmetic lip line and the client's vermilion border. Many technicians have done this only to realize that the result is the appearance of a *lip within a lip* because the vermilion border lip tissue is different from that of the skin above and inside it. Irregular color or a blurred appearance may be apparent after the lip procedure has healed or during the lip aging process. As the procedure heals and ages, often without more frequent touch-up procedures to keep the color consistent, an obvious departure from the vermilion may be seen (see Figure 18-42).

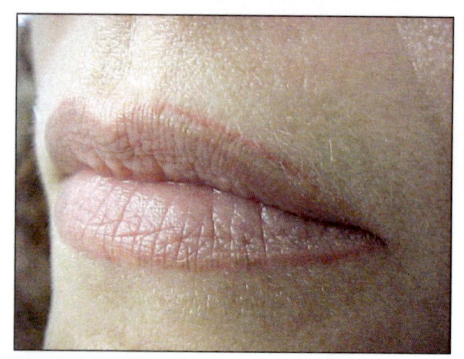

Figure 18-42: Tattooing outside the Vermilion border

This can also occur unintentionally due to the inflammation of the skin while tattooing the lip liner, causing the area to turn pink. This can lead the technician to believe it is lip skin not requiring additional tattooing.

If a client is seeking a permanent cosmetic lip procedure only to dramatically increase the size of their lips, they should consult with a medical professional.

Lip liner and shaded lip liner clients will often bring a cosmetic sample of lipstick or lip liner pencil that they feel they want to see as a healed color. This sample color is somewhat misleading because topical lip color rarely remains as it appears in the container after being applied to the lips. Cosmetic lip color is affected by oils and acids in the lip tissue, the pressure that a person exerts when applying it, and the numerous finishes/glosses incorporated into the formula or those which are applied over it. Lipstick and lip pencils also have dynamics. They are applied on the surface of the lips providing texture, often disguising natural flaws such as freckles, discoloration, etc.

Pigment that is tattooed into the lips is greatly affected by the natural color of the lips. It is not always effective at disguising discoloration flaws and is dependent on a light source reflection for seeing the maximum depth of color. It is recommended that a client is offered pigment lip liner or shaded lip liner colors that will look natural and attractive with their natural lip color, avoiding dark/cool colors that provide high-contrast to the client's natural lips. Clients should be advised that the color of their natural lips will have an effect on the permanent cosmetic pigment tattooed chosen.

The loss of pigment during the exfoliation phase of the healing process can be up to 50 percent on the vermilion border, and up to 75 percent within the lip. Depending on the properties of the pigment and color used, the client may require *at least* two appointments (the original and a follow-up visit as a minimum) to achieve the desired results.

There are many ways to conduct a permanent cosmetic lip procedure. The following sequence represents the basic steps and options of the process. As more and more lip procedures are performed, technicians will develop techniques that they are comfortable with. If this textbook is being read in preparation for a fundamental class, and lip procedures are part of the curriculum, the trainer will give specific directions.

Pre-Lip Procedure Design Sequence

- Cleanse the client's lips and surrounding skin.
- Inspect the lips to ensure the skin is free from any visible abnormalities that may have not been noted during the consultation.

    Although something minor that is seen may not prevent the procedure from going forward, take photographs and point out the irregularity to the client.

    If an irregularity was not noticed by the client before, it may come to their attention during the healing period (clients routinely inspect the procedural area) and it's best to address it before the procedure. Make appropriate notes on the client's chart including any information the client provides that may have the potential of affecting the outcome of the procedure. If you see it, say it, and document it.

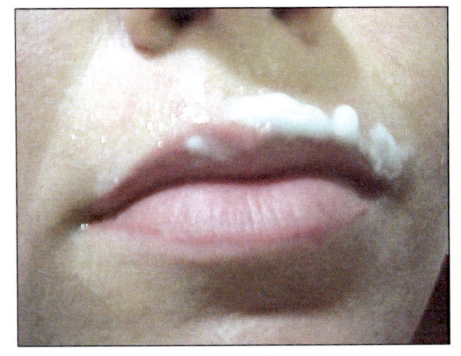

    Figure 18-43: Melting lip pre-procedure topical anesthetic

- If topical anesthetics are used, now is the appropriate time to pre-numb the lips.
- Remind the client not to talk while anesthetic is on their lips; the anesthetic will melt from the warmth of the skin and can enter the mouth and throat (see Figure 18-43).
- Wait the manufacturer's prescribed time before removing the topical anesthetic.
- Ensure the lips and surrounding skin is dry before designing the lip liner template.

Designing Lip Liners and Shaded Lip Liners

Lip Liner and Shaded Lip Liner Designs

Lips have a natural design although minor changes may be needed for symmetry purposes. Every client has lips, some more symmetric than others, some fuller than others, some with more consistent color than others, but they all have lips. The permanent cosmetic technician's designing job is focused on creating a natural design that is more color-consistent and symmetric. If this cannot be reasonably accomplished, the work should be declined.

However minimal the lip liner design may be, it is essential to provide symmetry. The goal is to ultimately create an appearance of a symmetric flattering lip line that will heal to the desired result without any significant departure from the natural lip line.

Lips are not always symmetric in natural design, although very small changes make a very big difference. The lip liner instrument used for applying the design guideline should be single-use, and one that is or can be sharpened to a fine-tip so that the width of the drawn-on guideline is not wider than that of the needle configuration that will be used to apply the pigment.

Permanent cosmetic technicians may safely draw the permanent cosmetic template line on the vermilion border to maintain the client's natural lip shape, or directly above (adjacent to) the vermilion border to create the appearance of a slightly larger lip while maintaining the integrity of the natural lip line. If a space of skin can be seen between the line drawn on with topical lip liner pencil and the client's vermilion border, the line has been drawn too far outside the vermilion border to conduct a procedure that will appear natural when pigment is tattoed and the lip procedure heals and ages. *Note:* There are some very experienced technicians who, under ideal circumstances, can depart from the natural vermilion border with success; this is an advanced procedure. This notation is provided because there are no absolutes in the artistry of tattooing. This textbook, however, is geared to the new technician and advice is given accordingly.

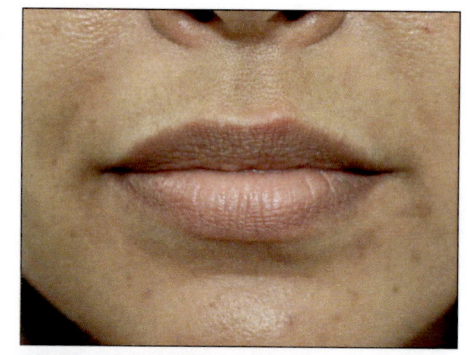

Figure 18-44: Before Shaded Lip Liner

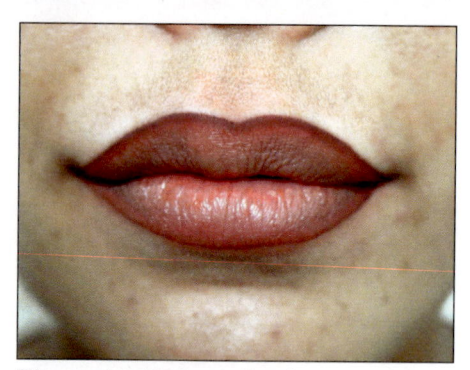

Figure 18-45: Immediately After Shaded Lip Liner

If the client desires a slightly fuller appearance of their lips, the line of the design may be placed *directly bordering (adjacent to) the outside line of the vermilion border*, making minor adjustments for natural irregularities (no skin should be apparent between the design adjustments and the vermilion border). Lips framed with a darker/cooler color lip liner (not recommended) will appear smaller and the color obvious unless finished with the use of a topical cosmetic lip product. Use a color similar to the client's inner lip tissue natural coloring to increase the appearance of lip fullness.

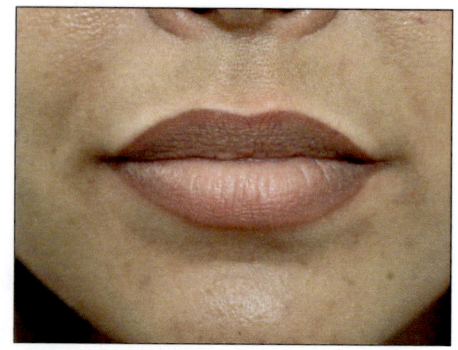

Figure 18-46: Healed

The vermilion border is a different tissue than the vermilion tissue. As a result, this area will naturally appear to lose less pigment, approximately up to 50 percent (as opposed to the inner lip area which will appear to lose up to 75 percent of the applied color, this varies), during the healing process and may appear slightly more prominent than the lip shading. (see Figure 18-44 through Figure 18-46).

Section 18 - All About Procedures

Applying the Design Guideline

- The position the client is in while the lip line guideline is applied is specific to each technician and trainer. Apply the lip design with a single-use marking device that is smear-resistant (see Figure 18-47).

- Apply the lip line design with a narrow line that does not exceed the width of the needle configuration that will be used. If the lip line design is applied wider than the needle to be used, a technician may tattoo on the guideline, thinking they are right on target with the design line, only to wipe it off later and observe the line is distorted.

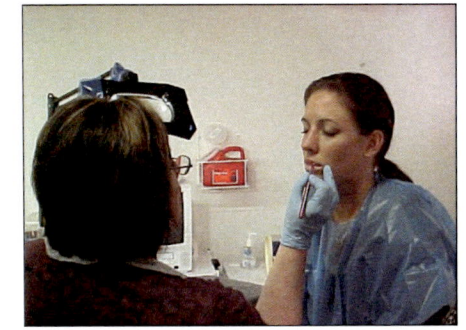

Figure 18-47: Applying the Lip Template

- Once the lip liner template has been drawn, make any necessary adjustments to ensure the shape is symmetric. Provide the client with a mirror and ask for approval of the design line. Make agreed upon changes (if any).

The Lip Procedure Tattooing Process

- Technicians and trainers vary in opinions on the next step. There are technicians who prefer to insert lip support products (cotton lip rolls or lip guards as examples – both single-use products) before beginning the procedure, others do not use either of these aids until the lip line has been tattooed, using only a taut measured stretch during the procedure. Others do not use lip support products at any time. All represent options for consideration.

- Remove the sterile needle and accessories (machine or manual device accessories) and assemble the machine or manual device components.

- Where a technician beings the lip procedure is a matter of preference:

  ♦ The tattooing process can begin at the far corners of the mouth, working the lip in quarters from the corner to the Cupid's bow on the top lip (sections one and two) and from the corners of the mouth toward the center of the bottom lip (sections three and four). Working the lip from the corners toward the center of the top and bottom lips will allow for movement of the device used to systematically proceed from the outer corners to the center on both sides of the top and bottom lips (see Figure 18-48).

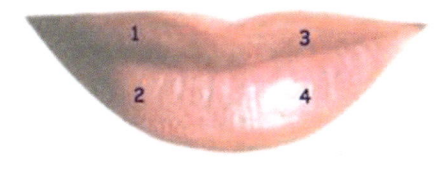

Figure 18-48: Lip Tattoo Process

- Another technique is to begin at the center of the Cupid's bow working down toward the corner of the mouth and on the bottom lip beginning at the center point and work toward the corners.
- Another option is to proceed from one corner of the upper lip across to the further corner and then move to the lower lip corner across to the furthest corner.

There are many techniques for tattooing the lip liner and shaded lip liners. If reading this textbook in preparation for a class, the trainer will give specific directions. Techniques learned in class, and ultimately personal preferences, will dictate after having completed a few lip procedures.

- If topical anesthetics are used, apply the post-broken skin anesthetic and allow it to take effect for several minutes before proceeding. A good indicator the post-broken skin anesthetics are working well is the appearance of the client's blanched natural lip color if using a product containing epinephrine.
- If injected anesthetics are to be used in a medical environment, consider this a recommended appropriate time to ask the physician to conduct this service. It was important to secure the lip line design template before injections, which can cause swelling and/or bruising.
- Once the anesthetic has taken effect and this is evidenced by the blanched lip color (if the product contained epinephrine), technicians who elect to use support aids during the lip procedure consider this an appropriate time to insert a lip support product. The use of some single-use cotton rolls or mouth guards under the lips to provide support for a good stretch is specific to each trainer and technician.

The lip support material may be inserted into the mouth for the lip (top or bottom) that will be tattooed first, or support may be inserted in both (top and bottom lips) at the same time. Some clients have such small mouths that putting both lip cotton rolls (mouth guards are typically one piece), in at the same time results in discomfort for the client and may require frequent interruptions of the procedure in order to adjust the material used. Many prefer to use support material during the lip procedure, stating the following reasons for this preference: (1) they provide a solid cushion between the lip and teeth. This firmer surface will allow for a more solid stretch pressure in order to minimize the effects of a possible quivering lip; and (2) if using a cotton material, the cotton absorbs saliva. A drier mouth may reduce the need for the client to interrupt the procedure in order to swallow.

- Proceed with additional passes on the lip line if this is necessary to ensure the lip liner is secured.
- Stretch in small increments along the lip line while tattooing. **Note:** The number of passes a technician makes on the lip line is dictated by the intended healed appearance, how well the client's lips accept pigment, and how well the first guideline pass was tattooed. Some clients need

fewer passes than others. The number of passes required is evaluated on an individual basis. It is important to not overwork the skin by making unnecessary passes.

- If the client has requested a shaded/blended lip liner procedure, once the lip liner has been satisfactorily tattooed, proceed with the shading/blending portion of the process.

- If choosing to use the technique of lightly abrading/opening the lip tissue that will be subject to the shading procedure, now is the time to do so. Some technicians feel that this is a good technique to open the skin in order to prepare it to quickly accept the gel or liquid anesthetics (if using topical anesthetics) for the shading process.

There are a number of ways of accomplishing the abrading/opening process prior to tattooing pigment into the lip if this technique is used. Some use the same needle used for the lip line tattoo, slightly grazing the skin to open it for the shading process. Others report they open a new sterilized needle configuration because the shading needle is different from the liner needle used.

In either instance, lightly abrade/open the lip tissue within the lip line that has just been applied; then apply post-broken skin anesthetic to the area. Wait the manufacturer's prescribed time for the anesthetic to take effect before proceeding.

- Some technicians prefer small circular motions for the shading process, others continue with a linear line across the lips, while others use an up and down (zigzag) motion. It is not unusual to employ one or a combination of these techniques.

- If using topical anesthetics, use only as needed to keep the client comfortable during the procedure. Do not apply anesthetics just because it is necessary to stop tattooing to retrieve more pigment, or during short client breaks. Excessive application of an anesthetic agent can dilute the lip pigment being tattooed and result in a lighter than expected or spotty healed result.

- If an injected anesthetic was used, depending on how much time the shading process takes, it may be necessary to apply a topical gel or liquid anesthetic to keep the client comfortable.

- Allow the client periodic breaks as needed. It is difficult to remain in the same position for long periods of time and a short break gives the client renewed energy to more easily cooperate during the procedure. It is also a good time to check the progress of the lip procedure from a different perspective.

After the Procedure Is Complete
- Cleanse any residual pigment from the face and mouth areas.
- Once the procedure is complete ask the client to sit up (if the client has been in a lying down position) and view the lip procedure. Be cautious about agreeing to make *any major changes* in the design work. The appearance of the lips immediately after the procedure is distorted from the tattooing process.
- Technicians may choose to wait until the client has had the opportunity to freshen up and the immediately-after photographs are taken before proceeding with cleaning up the worktable. During this period, the need for small detail work may be noticed that will require additional tattooing. This review should only take a short time. Leaving used product and needles on the worktable is not permitted beyond the final evaluation period.
- Take the immediately-after pictures. Take a full-face picture of the client and a close-up of the lips. If, through the eye of the camera, the work is considered satisfactory and the client agrees, proceed to the final steps of the session.

Final Steps
- The client may be asked to return to the chair/bed so that cool compresses can be applied to the lips to reduce swelling (if this is customary to do so).
- Review aftercare instructions and give an aftercare products kit (if it is policy to provide the products).
- Schedule the follow-up appointment.
- See "Section 4 - Safe Practices for Permanent Cosmetic Technicians" for Post Procedure Protocols (page 40).

Lip Procedures Stretching Techniques

Stretching techniques are very personal and unique to each technician. There are many variables to consider:
- The technician's dominant hand (right or left)
- The size of the hands
- The device being used
- If the technician works from one side of the procedure bed or both sides
- The fit of the gloves used
- The condition of the client's skin (firm or loose around the lips)

Each technician, based on their physical characteristics and capabilities coupled with the flexibility and/or limitations of the workplace environment must practice different techniques to find the stretching technique that is effective and comfortable for them to use.

Considering the variables that are unique to each technician, there can be no such thing as the only way to stretch the skin for a lip procedure.

As an example of how difficult this may initially seem vs. how easily stretching techniques will ultimately become, recall how awkward it was when first beginning to type on a keyboard. Once letters were typed over and over, typing quickly and accurately became automatic. The same analogy applies to stretching techniques. It simply takes practice and repetitive movements are required. If this textbook is being read in preparation for a class, the trainer will provide specific directions.

The lips are very buoyant and tend to bleed more than the eyebrow or eyeliner procedures. They represent a larger area of skin to tattoo than the eyeliner or eyebrow procedures, and they are more likely to draw an observer's attention.

Lip stretching techniques that involve holding one finger on each of the two sides of the mouth of the upper or lower lip normally cannot ensure the focused taut stretch needed for precise placement of pigment and stabilization of lip tissue, especially if the lips are larger.

Due to the buoyancy of the lips, this type of an *end-to-end* stretch is not recommended for the initial pass of the lip line design. Although there are always exceptions, if this type of stretch is employed, the lip tissue may move forward against the pressure of the moving needle and a misplaced lip liner may result. Normally lips are tattooed with sectional stretches.

To maintain the lip line design for the initial pass, many trainers and experienced technicians recommend lightly tracing or sketching on the topical makeup lip liner template with a single-use nontoxic, semi- permanent red marker pen (other pen types are available), in order to allow placing the fingers carefully on the lips to employ a taut stretch (see Figure 18-49).

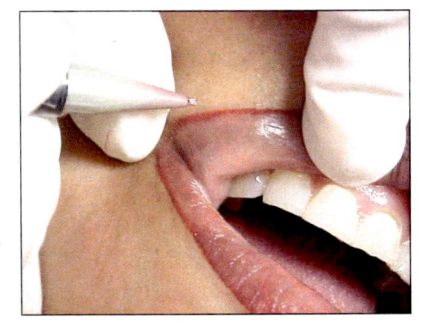

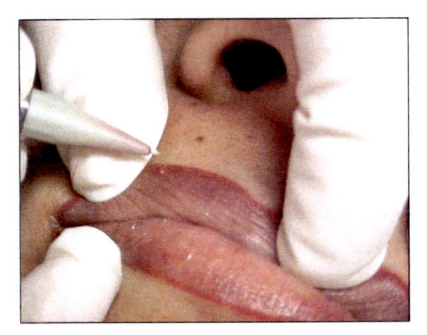

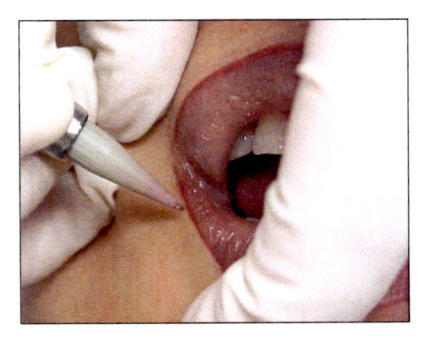

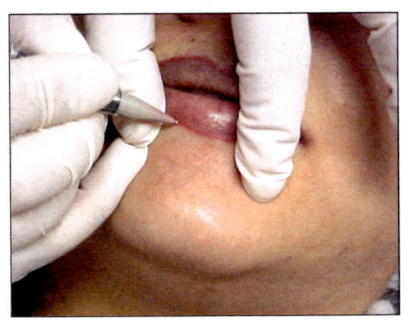

Figure 18-49: Lip Stretching Techniques

Although the gloved fingers may be placed directly on the lips, marker pen lines can be distorted. To avoid smearing and line distortion, use a *position the fingers on and lift off* motion each time a stretching position is changed.

Others who do not use the single-use nontoxic, semi-permanent marker technique will avoid pressing directly *on* the topical cosmetic makeup lip liner template for the first pass. Otherwise, the topical makeup guideline is easily smeared.

It is suggested the technician press on the lip tissue directly above where tattooing with the middle and index fingers. Stretch backward away from the lip with the thumb

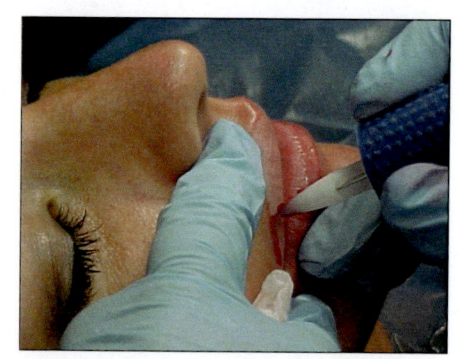

Figure 18-50: Stretching Technique

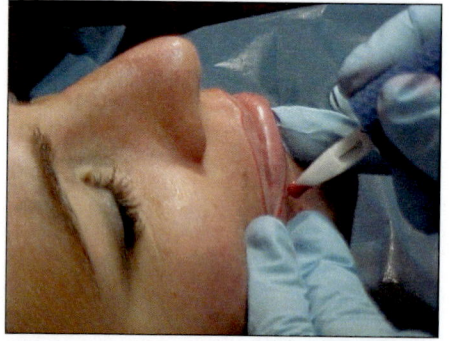

Figure 18-51: Stretching Technique

(for top liner), index, and middle fingers (for lower liner) directly behind the area that is being tattooed (optional stretching positions (see Figure 18-50 and Figure 18-51). This calculated stretching technique pushes the vermilion border of the upper lip upward and causes the skin to become more stressed and taut in the area being tattooed, while the stretch outwardly with the thumb tugs the skin in more of a straight line.

Technicians may begin the lip procedure at the outer corner of the top lip, stretching as indicated above through to the middle of the Cupid's bow area and then tattoo lower lip on the same side from the outer corner to the middle of the lower lip. Or, technicians may elect to reverse this technique and stretch and work from the center of the Cupid's bow downward toward the corner of the mouth per section on the top and from the center to the corner of the mouth per section on the bottom lip.

Change positioning to the opposite side of the client if this is preferred and an easier position to work from and tattoo the lip tissue from that side in the same manner. If it is preferred to remain on the primary side (right or left), establish a taut stretch from that position and tattoo toward, not away from yourself (see Figure 18-52; this is a machine device technique).

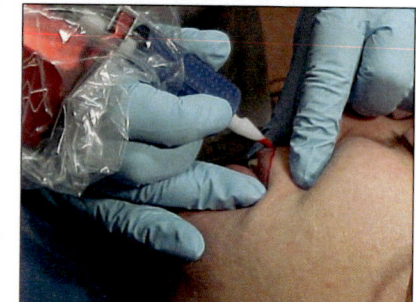

Figure 18-52: Lip Stretching Techniques

Working from one side for lip procedures is not a common technique for technicians who use the manual device, and they typically must switch from side to side as they work. There are times when positioning of the procedure bed (and the availability to work from both sides) dictates which position tattoo and managed stretching techniques are used.

By working the skin in identical directions from the outer corners toward the center of the mouth (or in reverse) in four sections, there is less probability of loose skin moving (see Figure 18-53).

If the lip line has not been marked with a single-use nontoxic, semi-permanent marker, once the lip line has been tattooed and the topical cosmetic guidelines, which were required for the initial pass, are no longer needed, the stretching fingers can then be laid directly on the lip without fear of loss of guidelines, applying short-span stretches directly on the area of the lip that is being tattooed.

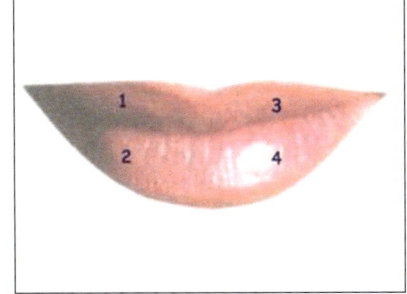

Figure 18-53: Working in four sections

If shading is included in the lip procedure being conducted, once the lip line has been tattooed successfully, the stretching fingers may be placed directly on the lips in short stretch spans for the shading process.

There are many effective lip procedure stretching techniques. The techniques presented in this section are examples for consideration.

Ultimately each technician will customize lip stretching techniques that are based on their unique requirements and preferences. The concept to master is to employ a stretch that keeps the fingers off the drawn-on topical makeup guideline as much as possible until the lip line is tattooed.

How Will I Look?

How people look to others is always subjective. Many people tend not to notice permanent cosmetic procedures that have been tattooed on co-workers, partners, or family members unless they have been previously advised of the event. Lip procedures may be the exception; they draw attention, whereas eyeliners and eyebrow procedures may escape notice. On the other hand, there are some people who notice even minor changes and are not shy about inquiries.

If a client returns to work or has a social event soon after, feedback from clients indicate their female coworkers sometimes noticed that something was different, but the exact source of the change was not obvious to them. Women seem to be much more curious about changes in other women than men are. Just imagine overhearing John ask Steve, *"Hey Steve, I really like your new hair color, what brand did you use this month?"* Or..."*Steve, I know you have done something to yourself that makes you look so rested and aesthetically pleasing, come on, tell me what you have done?"* It just doesn't seem to routinely happen between men as much as women, and when it comes to a man asking personal questions of a woman, this is even less likely to happen. This is characteristically a woman-to-woman or woman-to-man issue that technicians have to help their clients deal with.

How clients feel they look is also very dependent on whether they normally applied topical cosmetics before the permanent cosmetic procedure(s). If they typically wore makeup, they may not see much of a difference between how they looked with makeup on and how they look immediately after the permanent cosmetic procedure, with the exception of localized skin irritation. Often this is dependent on the client's skin type.

On the other hand, if the client ordinarily did not wear any makeup, the new look may take a few days to consider the new appearance *familiar*. If a client is very sensitive to comments or opinions from others, is a person that did not previously wear topical cosmetics, if they are socially active, or work outside the home, appointments should be timed so they have a few days for the appearance of the procedure(s) to calm.

The color of skin, the color of the pigment used for the procedure, the extent of the procedure, (i.e., the width of eyeliner, and the different types of lip and eyebrow procedures), and whether the client tends to swell from small injuries all play a role in the *immediately after* the procedure appearance.

For instance, if a person of color has an eyebrow or eyeliner procedure, there may not be much of a difference between how they looked with topical cosmetics and how they look immediately after the procedure. A person with lighter skin may see a greater difference in the topical cosmetic look vs. their new permanent cosmetics for a few days. The contrast of the pigment with lighter skin and any associated skin irritation produced by the tattooing process may be more noticeable to others than if the procedure were performed on a person of color.

Eyebrow procedures cause very little if any swelling, so the primary focus is on the change of color in the eyebrow area and any skin irritation that may be obvious on some lighter skin types. At the appointment, care should be taken to provide an eyebrow client with the choice of pigment colors that will result in a natural appearance based on their skin tone and natural eyebrow hair (if the client has eyebrow hair).

Working conservatively (a safe mode) also enables clients to become accustomed to their new eyebrow color. Some technicians routinely give a new brow client a wash of pigment color (diluted pigment). If they untimely want more color, this can be achieved at the follow-up visit. It's considered better to have a client return asking for more color at a follow-up appointment than for them to report they felt it necessary to take off work for a few days or cancel social engagement(s) because the color they left with was so bold they were uncomfortable with their appearance.

Clients with lighter skin will show the lightest of color tattooed more dramatically than the person with darker skin shows the darkest of color that has been tattooed. Why? Because lighter skin shows the effects of inflammation from the tattoo process more predominantly and even the lightest of colors provides a greater visible contrast.

Figure 18-54 and Figure 18-55 show before and immediately-after photos of two women, one with Fitzpatrick Type I skin with a light color pigment applied and one with Fitzpatrick Type V skin.

Figure 18-54: Eyebrows - Fitzpatrick Skin Type I
Before and immediately after

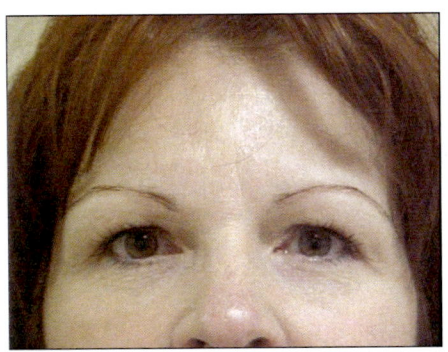

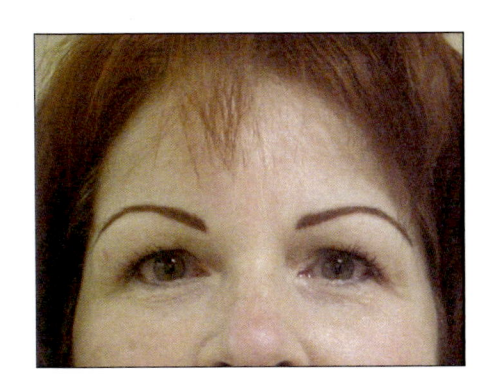

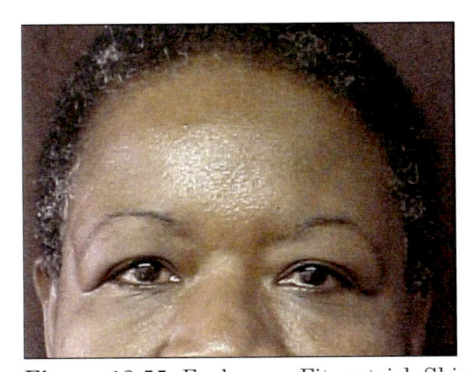

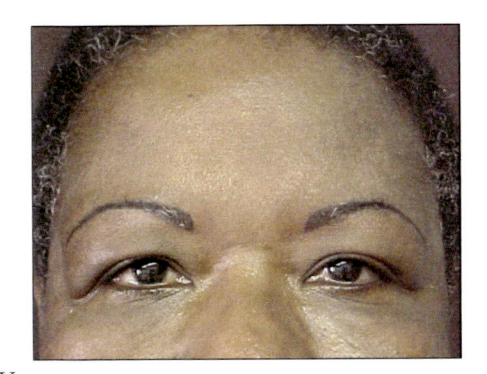

Figure 18-55: Eyebrows - Fitzpatrick Skin Type V
Before and immediately after

Eyeliner procedures produce some puffiness; however, eyelash enhancement procedures with small upper eyeliners produce a look similar to that of someone with environmental allergies.

People with lighter skin can appear more irritated from eyeliner procedures than people with darker skin. Even the slightest swelling appears more apparent on the person with light skin.

The wider the top eyeliner design tattooed, the more swelling and inflammation a person may expect; however, even the most extreme design work routinely only results in puffiness that affects the normal appearance of the eye tissue for a few days. There are exceptions to every rule so the best technicians can offer eyeliner clients is a portfolio of pictures of before, immediately after, and healed procedures. Technicians will find great value in the immediately-after photos because they provide a visual answer to the unknown, *how will I look?* Clients who have the opportunity to see a variety of photos of people who have just had eyeliner work performed are usually pleasantly surprised and relieved.

Permanent cosmetic procedures rarely produce significant (if any) bruising of the affected tissue; however, if there is going to be an opportunity for slight bruising, it will normally happen on the wider upper eyeliners. ***Note:*** Bruising may occur on a lip procedure especially if working on mature thin skin, but more predominantly if bruising occurs it is on the thin tissue of the eyelids. The good news is that this bruising is characteristically so subtle it appears somewhat like eye shadow over the liner that has just been tattooed. Clients with lighter skin color show the effects of any minor eyeliner bruising far more than those with darker skin.

The first two examples of eyeliner are noteworthy (see Figure 18-56 and Figure 18-57). Two women came in for eyeliner, one immediately after the other. Both had the same anesthetics, similar width (medium) top eyeliner, and the same device and needle configuration was used in both examples. One is a Fitzpatrick skin type I and the other is a Fitzpatrick skin type III. The difference in how the two women appeared immediately after their procedures is quite noticeable.

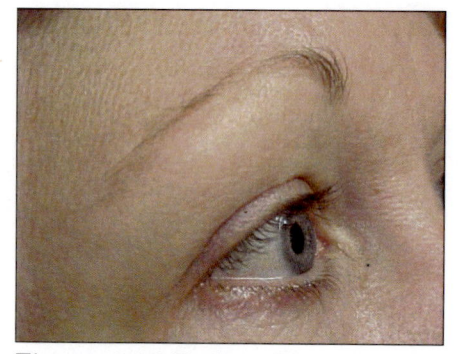

Figure 18-56: Eyeliner -Fitzpatrick Skin Type I
Before and immediately after

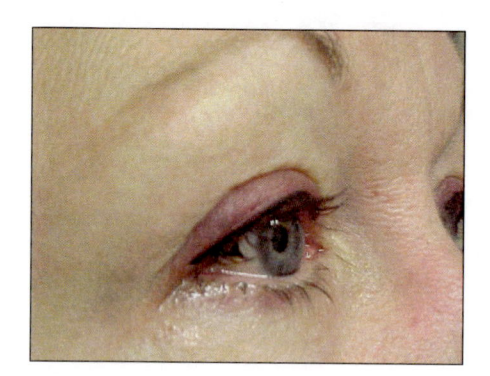

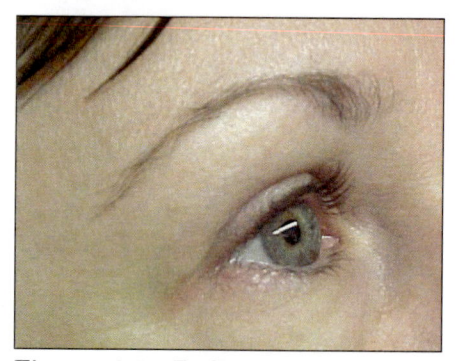

Figure 18-57: Eyeliner -Fitzpatrick Skin Type III
Before and immediately after

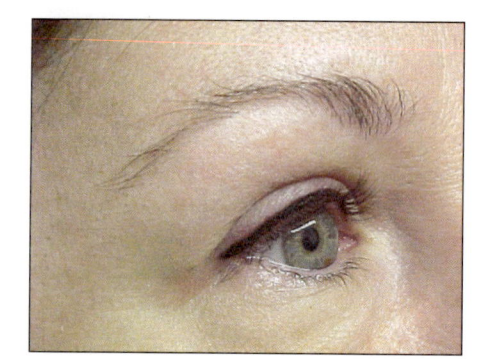

The width of the eyeliner to be tattooed and size of the client's eyes (determining how much tissue is tattooed) also can be an indicator of how a person may expect to look. Eyelash enhancements (pigment tattooed in the lash line) normally appears less irritated than when accompanied with small, medium, or wider width eyeliners. Although the amount of irritation and inflammation that results from an eyeliner procedure is specific to the client's skin type, the eyeliner width design is also a factor can contribute to any irritation and swelling.

Section 18 - All About Procedures

The eyeliner procedure types range from a lash enhancement to a lash enhancement accompanied by wider eyeliner (see Figure 18-58 through Figure 18-61). As seen, the eyelash enhancement and more narrow eyeliners, result in less swelling and irritation.

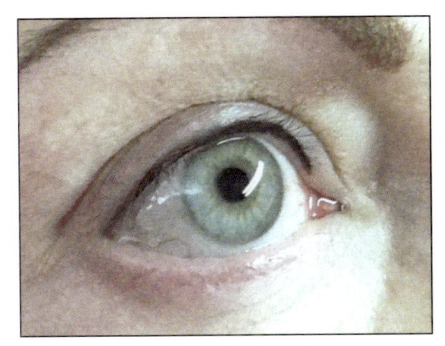

Figure 18-58: Eyelash enhancement

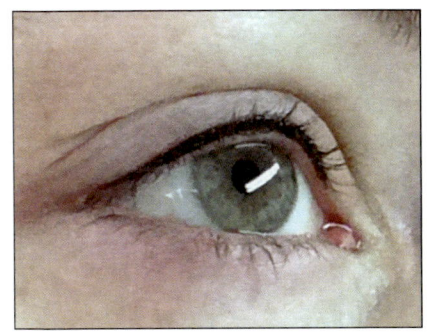

Figure 18-59: Narrow width eyeliner

Figure 18-60: Medium width eyeliner

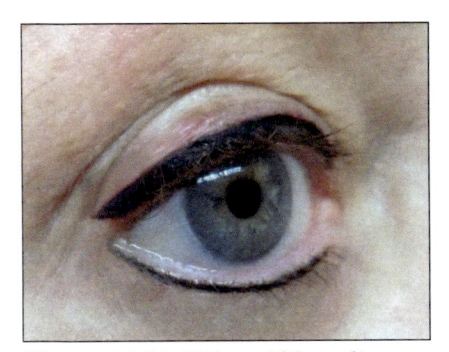

Figure 18-61: Wider width eyeliner

Note: Eyelash enhancements, narrow width eyeliners, and lower eyeliners are normally considered appropriate for technicians during and after their fundamental training class. Medium widths to wider width eyeliners are advanced work. Pictures of this advanced work are provided in this section for visual comparison purposes only to show the effects of different eyeliner widths on different skin types. Do not attempt advanced work without training.

Lower eyeliner rarely produces noticeable swelling. The design line is typically very narrow. See Figure 18-62 and Figure 18-63.

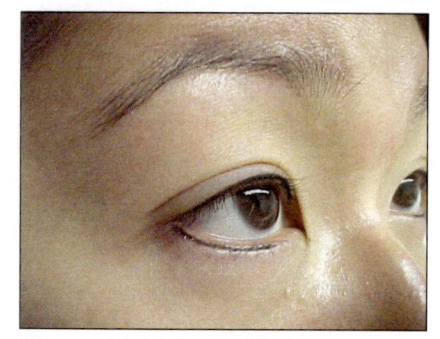

Figure 18-62: Lower Eyeliner Immediately after

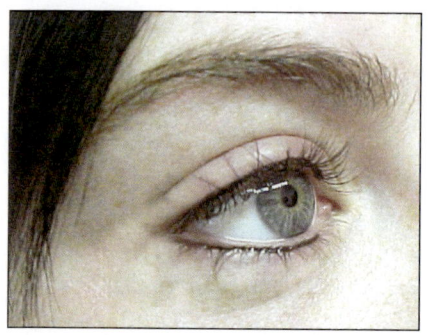

Figure 18-63: Lower Eyeliner Immediately after

Lip liners and shaded lip liners produce slight swelling and clients will appear as if they have applied a cosmetic lip liner. Some onlookers may suspect that a lip filler product is responsible for the appearance of fullness. Advanced full lip procedures can produce an intensity of color and swelling that is noticeable to others for several days. There is no getting around the fact that a full lip procedure was performed. See Figure 18-64 to Figure 18-66 for the immediately-after appearance of the lip liner, shaded lip liner, and full lip procedures.

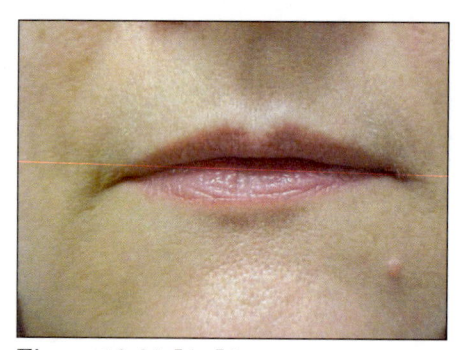

Figure 18-64: Lip Liner
Before and immediately after. The lighter inner lip is due to the effects of anesthetic with epinephrine, a vasoconstrictor.

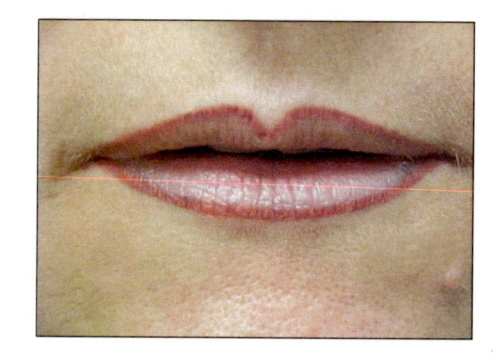

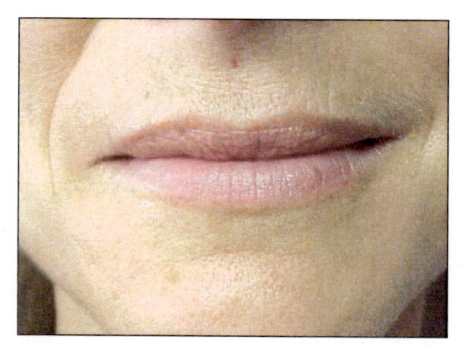

Figure 18-65: Shaded Lip Liner
Before and immediately after.

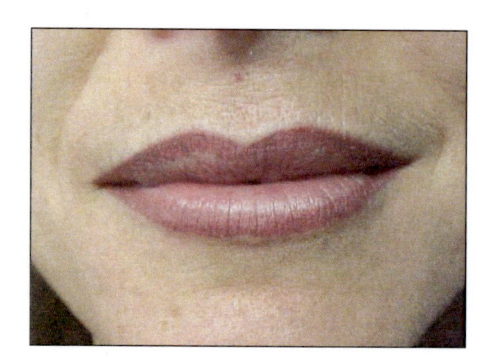

Figure 18-66: Full Lip Procedure
Before and immediately after.

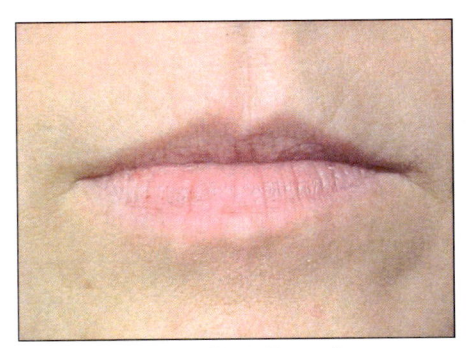

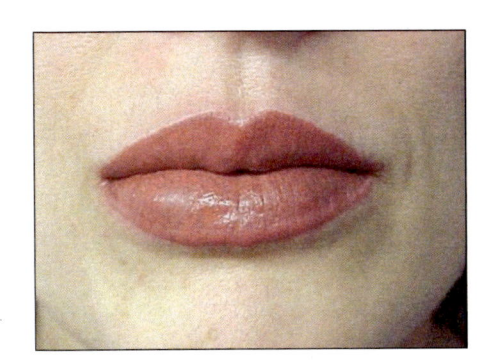

Note: Lip liners and shaded lip liners may be (this is trainer specific) appropriate for technicians during and after their fundamental training class. Full lips are advanced work and some trainers, depending on the length of the class, may feel all lip work should be postponed until the eyebrow and eyeliner procedures have been perfected by the novice technician. Pictures of advanced work are provided in this section for visual comparison purposes only to show the additional irritation and swelling to be expected. Do not attempt advanced work without training.

The best approach to a client's question *how will I look*, is an honest response to the client which is based on an evaluation of the procedure type, the skin type, the color selected, and the agreed-upon design. How clients will look immediately after a procedure and for how long is based on the client's unique characteristics and procedure specifics. Photographs are very helpful to make important points. It is safe to state that clients with lighter skin will show the indication of eyebrow and eyeliner tattooing more so than clients with darker skin and clients with minimal work performed; however, one can never predict just how much more. Many times it is wise to remind clients that in today's social environment it's not uncommon to see women and men with swollen or red skin and/or stitches, etc., resulting from appearance improvement services.

Can This Procedure Be Saved?

The title of this section sounds somewhat like the name of a soap opera or advice column segment, doesn't it? The process of attempting to save a poorly applied permanent cosmetic procedure can reflect the similar drama one would expect from either of these examples.

Similar to a soap opera, the poorly tattooed procedure presented to a technician for correction plays out like a story. It has a beginning, and then the poor aspects of the procedure represent the building of drama and emotional indignation, a corrective action is developed, and then there is a conclusion. Once the client is advised of their options they may be resigned to accept the procedure *as is*. If corrective actions are agreed to they may agree to accept the results modifying the aspects of the procedure that represents the problem. In either event, there will indeed be a conclusion.

All technicians have been or will be, presented with problem procedures that represent the beginning of how the story will ultimately unfold. Even though the end of the story is usually an unknown factor, technicians must be aware of the elements of the impending drama. The technician's role in this story may ultimately be one of a hero, a technician with good intentions who made things somewhat better, or a one who was not successful. In any case, the last technician to work on a client owns the work and the client's perception of their role in the correction story. Not all clients will see the correction process through to a positive conclusion.

Unfortunately, technicians will not always be able to initially judge the client who ultimately may tell a technician who is attempting to correct a problem that they have had enough. An initial visit with a client seeking help will typically be a pleasant one. They are seeking help and are hopeful that the technician they are consulting with is the one who can solve their problem. As the relationship with the client unfolds, caution must be exercised in order to monitor the temperament of the client as options are offered.

A client with an open mind and who is willing to work with a teamwork attitude is one a technician may be able to assist without a change of attitude about what is entailed for the process of corrective procedures. Conversely, a client who speaks of their anger toward the original technician and cannot let go of the unfortunate circumstances in order to accept help is one who must be monitored closely, or declined for correction services. It serves no useful purpose to rehash the past. Don't take premature steps to attempt to help a person until convinced they are a willing and temperamentally sound participant. Small steps toward a positive ending are recommended as opposed to drastic steps that may place the helpful technician in professional harm's way.

Several articles have been written on this subject, often suggesting technicians refrain from getting involved in problems created by other technicians. However, in the best interest of variation and realization that technicians with the best of intentions do indeed get involved, the following guidelines are designed to help lead to a successful end for both the client and the technician.

Rule 1: Analyze, Analyze, Analyze.

There are many ways to approach corrections. Analyze and investigate the options associated with the particular task at hand.

- How much of the existing procedure can be utilized in a modified version of the design?
- Can the color of the procedure easily be modified (corrected) by utilizing good permanent cosmetic color theory and corrective color procedures? Or, should the density of the existing undesirable color be lightened first and be allowed to heal before tattooing a corrective or target color? This can require multiple tattoo lightening sessions by a trained technician or in

some instances, laser treatments.

- What is the overall attitude of the client? Are they threatening legal action against the original technician (even if is you)? If a client threatens legal action against you, contact your insurance representative or legal representative in the absence of insurance coverage before any further action is taken.
- How *high profile* is the client's business or social exposure? This may influence the extent of involvement. The timing of corrective procedures may also be affected by this factor.
- Why is this client not returning to the original technician?
- When was the initial work performed? How old is the tattoo?
- Has the initial work been exposed to client, physician, or another technician's attempts to correct or modify the problem areas? If so, is there any resulting scar tissue? Is there any indication that another technician used flesh-tone pigments in an attempt to cover-up the undesirable work?
- Lastly, since the goal of being in business is to make a profit, what will be charged for corrective services and on what basis?

Within this group of inquiries, the most important question of all is: *Why is this client not returning to their original technician?* It is important to explore that particular question. There are people who request unrealistic procedure designs and/or color, then after realizing their mistake, move on to another technician for correction procedures.

Imagine that a client has convinced an inexperienced technician who needs more training to tattoo an inappropriate design or color and then changes their mind. This situation is a calamity for both the client and the technician. Ask who performed the procedure. It might prove helpful to contact the original technician and discuss the events surrounding the request the client is making. This option doesn't appeal to everyone. No one likes to hear their work was not acceptable to a client, regardless of the circumstances. On the other hand, the original technician may shed some light on circumstances the client did not disclose. As the author, I recently experienced this. I was able to contact the original technician and our conversation was very helpful. Technicians have a right to know what kind of situation they are stepping into. Investigate the surrounding circumstances as much as possible.

A more positive and understandable reason why clients do not return to their original technician is because their original technician is not available. Technicians retire or change locations and sometimes are not available to all their prior clients.

The answers to the questions in the Rule Number 1 (analyze, analyze, analyze) section will have a bearing on the process of if, when, and how to proceed. When a prominent cosmetic surgeon was asked how he decided if he would be willing to get involved with patients needing cosmetic surgery corrections, he responded, "*I have to be 95 percent sure that I can make an improvement the client will view as satisfactory, otherwise, I'm jeopardizing my business*". Permanent cosmetic technicians should consider this approach when deciding on whether to proceed with corrective procedures on work performed by other technicians.

It is always recommended that as a minimum, the client is advised that corrective work can make things *better but not perfect*. Under these circumstances, the client has been properly advised that they cannot expect the appearance of reversing the original procedure. It is impossible to reverse the original procedure and go back in time before mistakes or bad decisions were made. All client conversations in regard to expectations and what can and cannot be accomplished must be documented before proceeding.

With pigment lightening products and techniques being a proven successful option in many instances (see *Section 26 - The Principles of Tattoo Lightening and Removal*), our technical choices for successful modification of poor procedures have increased significantly. Under the right conditions, we can now realize significant lightening of undesirable areas as a viable method to attain corrective goals. Modifications of existing designs are somewhat easily achieved as long as the corrective measures don't include making an existing design significantly smaller, and remember, very small changes make very large differences. What may be perceived by the client as a very annoying or distressingly big problem may actually be resolved with a minor correction process, in the hands of a well-trained permanent cosmetic professional.

If deciding to proceed with a corrective procedure, analyze the job before committing.

Rule 2: Corrective Procedures Options

- Color-correct without attempting to lighten pigment when possible. It requires less patience on behalf of the client, and it provides as close to instant gratification as can be expected to be achieved in this situation.

- If reducing the density of unwanted color is deemed necessary on an entire design area before tattooing a corrective color and/or a new desired pigment color, carefully manage the timing. This usually involves the appearance of noticeable crusting and a longer healing period before additional color can be tattooed. Some clients do not deal well with unattractive conditions (crusting) or have the patience for multiple tattoo lightening procedures.

- If the old design is quite faded, it may be possible to put a design within a design without any tattoo lightening of the faded pigment. For instance, if a faded wider eyeliner design is presented as being too wide for the client's taste, consider tattooing a thinner eyeliner design within the old one, leaving the faded portion above (or below the lash line liner) as a smudged or shadowed effect.

Some clients with eyebrow designs that are very faded (transparent) will accept a slightly different new brow design leaving just minimal areas of the faded old design. Although this is not ideal, the new brow, because of its crisp new color, will draw attention away from small discrepancies of the faded old design work. Again, this is not ideal; however, often this is far more agreeable to a person who does not consent to pigment lightening attempts by a permanent cosmetic technician or removal attempts by a laser professional. There have to be some options for corrections that are acceptable in order to go forward.

- Evaluate the overall shape and appearance of previous work before proceeding even if the client is not displeased with what they have. The brows, for instance, could have originally been placed nicely, but if the procedure is several years old, the client may have some facial asymmetry that would result in placement adjustments.

Technicians must choose their successes and avoid getting involved with problems they do not feel qualified to solve. Exercise the following precautions:

- Conduct detailed consultations with a client seeking corrective services so they know what to expect.
- Always obtain signed intake office forms prior to proceeding.
- Don't work outside the parameters of insurance coverage if 95 percent assurance of success cannot be honestly predicted. Speak with your insurance agent about the appropriate way to refer prospective clients to others.

Always remember, a good story generally ends with a satisfying ending and every technician wants to be viewed as a hero.

What Not to Do

Many articles have been written and advice given about *how to* perform permanent cosmetic procedures. These instructions have resulted in volumes of written data, videos, social media posts, and photo examples of good and bad photos shared in convention presentations. This shared information is usually advantageous; it is how technicians learn and grow. This information also encourages the development of new products that support our every-changing permanent cosmetic industry. Another approach for technician growth is to list the basics of *what not to do*. The following list is a summary of some of the things to avoid in our industry.

Specific Procedure Don'ts

Eyebrow Don'ts

- Don't chase around expressions when designing eyebrows. Have the client close their eyes and relax their face to ascertain whether the eyebrow design is symmetrical.

- Don't expect the client to be able to see everything you are seeing from the vantage of a mirror. Some clients can't see that well and when they put on their glasses, it obscures the eyebrow design. Take a picture of the design work and view it together with the client (with their glasses on if needed). Creating a third person situation while both of you look at the eyebrow design on the computer makes critiquing eyebrow design less personal and more objective.

- Don't design eyebrows *while tattooing*; no one is that good at eyeballing brow design and the canvas will change as the area becomes irritated. Swelling, although usually ever so slight may occur during the procedure.

- Don't proceed with the eyebrow procedure without properly marking the eyebrow design template. There are several techniques for accomplishing a template of the design before beginning to tattoo.

Eyeliner Don'ts

- Don't allow the client's eye to remain open for long periods of time. Every client has a specific need to blink (some more than others) and disallowing this need can result in injury to the eye.

- Don't assume that pigment has not drifted into the eye during the eyeliner procedure. The smallest amount can cause irritation or injury. Rinse the eye frequently during the procedure and check the eye carefully for any residual pigment.

- Don't allow the client to wear mascara and eyeliner to the appointment on the day of the procedure. Both of these topical cosmetic products can contain bacteria. Even cleansing the area minutes before beginning the

procedure may not ensure that all the bacteria has been adequately removed and the cleansing process can cause irritation before the procedure begins.
- Don't allow the client to move their eye in random motions during the procedure. Eyeball movements change the positioning of the skin surrounding the eye. Verbally guide the client to where they should look during the procedure.

Lip Don'ts

- Don't assume the appearance of all asymmetric lips can be corrected with a permanent cosmetic lip procedure. Some asymmetry is caused not only by lack of blood flow (diminished color) but also by dental irregularities such as a protruding or missing tooth (or teeth). Medical conditions may also affect skin texture or muscles in the face, resulting in a mouth that appears different on one side or the other.
- Don't schedule medically administered lip anesthetic injections at least before the lip line has been successfully tattooed. Injected lips swell unevenly and can lose valuable color, which is essential as a guide to a properly placed lip line.
- Don't fall into the trap of a client's desire for larger lips if this can't be accomplished by placing the lip line adjacent to the outside of the vermilion. There are only a few very experienced technicians in this industry who can accomplish this procedure on selected clients without creating a *lip within a lip* appearance. Producing lip volume is more often better accomplished with medically administered lip fillers. The job of novice technicians is definition and color, not volume. **Note:** Whether or not lip liner/shaded lip liners are appropriate procedures for training during a fundamental class is specific to each trainer and often also based on the length of the class. Full lips are considered advanced procedures.
- Don't overwork the lip tissue; doing so may result in scarring. Overworking the lip tissue is most often seen when the technicians have performed procedures on lips that have been anesthetized with medically administered anesthetic injections.
- Don't provide lip services for clients with a history of Herpes Simplex I (cold sores/fever blisters) unless they have contacted their physician and obtained an antiviral medication and have taken it prior to the appointment as directed by their physician. There may be regulations in place that dictate the conditions under which technicians may proceed if the client indicates they have a history of herpes.
- Don't attempt to change natural bluish, violet, or brown lips to a lighter color. Attempting to go from dark to light is normally futile and not appropriate work for novice technicians under any conditions. This color characteristic is most prevalently seen on Fitzpatrick V, VI and some IV

skin types.

Anesthetic Don'ts

- Don't expect over-the-counter (OTC) level anesthetics to work instantly. Allow anesthetics to work as directed by the manufacturer.

- Don't overuse gel and liquid anesthetics. Many technicians develop a habit of applying a post-broken skin anesthetic repeatedly without determining if more than one or two applications are even necessary for controlled comfort. Excessive application of anesthetic causes the pigment being tattooed to become diluted, resulting in a lighter version of what is expected (or spotty) when the procedure has healed. If using post-broken skin anesthetics, apply them in moderation, allow them to work, blot off the skin, and then proceed to tattoo.

- Don't suggest to clients that they should take prescription medications without consulting with their physician. If topical over-the-counter level anesthetics do not work on a specific client or if they express concern about pain during the consultation, advise the client to consult with their physician and discuss obtaining appropriate medication. If a client takes a prescription medication to help manage discomfort during the procedure, they will need to make transportation arrangements to get to and from the appointment safely home.

- Don't expect one anesthetic to work the same on all clients. If anesthetics are used, there are a variety of anesthetic products that have different ingredients and carriers. Keep a few different OTC types of anesthetics on hand for clients who are more challenging to anesthetize.

- Don't use anesthetics that have expired. Dispose of expired anesthetics.

Aftercare Don'ts

- Don't assume clients know how to care for their procedure during the healing process. Before a client leaves, demonstrate what is expected of them in regard to a maintenance process for cleaning and applying aftercare products (if a product is used). Written aftercare instructions should be provided to all permanent cosmetic clients. If the client is responsible for obtaining their own products, this information should be provided prior to the procedure appointment date.

- Don't suggest any medication-type aftercare products. Although they may be available over the counter, unless the technician is a physician or working under the direction of a physician, it is only appropriate for tattoo artists to recommend non-medicated over-the-counter products.

- Don't dip into a common container and put a product into an unlabeled smaller container to give to clients for aftercare. If supplying aftercare products ideally, purchase them in single-use packaging and ensure they are properly labeled.

All Procedure Types Don'ts

- Don't overwork the skin; this can result in scarring. There's always an opportunity to do more at a later date.
- Don't ever attempt to correct or hide misplaced pigment with lighter (camouflage) pigment color. It doesn't work and makes things worse.
- Don't push the client past their comfort zone. This normally applies to eyeliner and lip procedures.
- Don't use products that are not intended or appropriate for tattooing.
- Don't assume clients are your friends; they are clients and although a friendly relationship is needed, one that includes personal information and discussions is discouraged.
- Don't overwork yourself. Work within the boundaries of being at your best.

Each technician should begin a what not to do list of their own. Technicians can develop habits that at some point may be a contradiction to their overall professional goals.

Section 19

Pain and Anesthesia

Learning Objectives

Introduction

The anticipation of pain is a sensitive subject. The decision as to whether a prospective client schedules an appointment may very well hang in the balance of whether or not the procedure will hurt. It is accepted that pain is manufactured by people and that each client we work with will have a different threshold of tolerance to the tattooing process.

There are anesthetics that are formulated specifically for our industry to minimize procedural discomfort. They are nonprescription strengths anesthetics referred to as over-the-counter, OTC levels. The legal use of anesthetics for permanent cosmetics is geographically specific; however, in the USA anesthetics must be manufactured and cannot be made by formulating pharmacists.

In this section, technicians will also learn to assist a client to cope with whatever level of discomfort they may experience. The proper use of topical anesthetics is important. However, the mind over matter distraction and relaxation techniques employed to support the effects of anesthetic agents (if they are used) that are presented are equally as valuable.

Objective

Upon completion of this section, the technician will have a sound understanding of the different types of anesthetics employed by the non-medical and medical industries if they are legally allowed to use anesthetics in their locality. Technicians will have learned how topical anesthetics work and how to apply topical anesthetics on sensitive areas of the face. In conjunction with the use of anesthetics, the technician will have a greater understanding of employing distraction and relaxation techniques that assist clients to easily endure a reasonable level of discomfort during a procedure.

Section 19 - Pain and Anesthesia

Pain serves an honorable purpose: to keep us safe.[1] Pain can be real or imagined, but it feels all the same to the person experiencing it. Thousands of receptor nerve cells sensing heat, cold, light, pressure, and pain act as the neurological regulator over our body, telling us when something is wrong. Whether a nuisance type pain such as a mild tension headache or overwhelming pain brought on by illness or serious injury that requires immediate medical intervention, pain is a part of our body's security system.

Some undetermined amount of pain or slight discomfort is considered normal during permanent cosmetic procedures, and the degree of pain or discomfort is always client-specific. More importantly, the anticipation of pain is one of the reasons many people may not pursue permanent cosmetic services. Why wouldn't everyone want the convenience and the confidence of looking their best at all times? One of the reasons is likely because they fear an unknown level of pain they will encounter, plain and simple.

The prospective client's pain-educated brain produces a warning that may result in declining the opportunity for the benefits of permanent cosmetics. Three often uttered words from a client during a consultation are *will it hurt*? To tell a client they would not experience any discomfort would mean you are a mind reader or most likely ultimately will prove to the client that you have intentionally not told the truth, the whole truth, or at best, you are an inaccurate mind reader.

Ultimately, technicians have to break the news to clients that in all likelihood without the benefit of medically injected anesthetics (and even then you can't be sure, and the injections alone may be painful) they will experience some degree of discomfort. Eyebrow tweezing and brushing the teeth is painful to some people. People don't look forward to pain but on the other hand, know they can tolerate a certain level without much trouble. Our body produces endorphins to assist with the tolerance of minor short-term pain, and that is exactly how to define the pain associated with permanent cosmetics.

Figure 19-1: Client's Anxiety

Regardless if you choose to use anesthetics or not it is always good to know about products that produce anesthesia. Certain drugs called *anesthetics* are able to cause complete or partial loss of feeling. The loss of feeling they produce is called *anesthesia*. Some definitions of anesthesia include total or partial loss of sensation, and artificially induced unconsciousness or local or general insensitivity to pain. Before the discovery of anesthetics in the late 19th century, surgery was performed only in extreme emergencies and often resulted in death from shock. With the onslaught of beauty services that involve different degrees of discomfort, topical anesthesia has become a focus of attention in the beauty and medical industries.

Anesthetic compounds may be composed of a single entity drug such as lidocaine or a combination of drugs such as lidocaine and benzocaine or tetracaine, and some contain epinephrine as a vasoconstrictor to enhance the action of the anesthetic. There are many different methods to deliver the medication to create a localized, regional, or general anesthetic effect. These range from intravascular, epidural, or localized injection, inhalation of medication in gas form, and topically applied creams and gels.

Below are the different types of medically administered anesthesia by a physician or, in some cases, other medically licensed personnel such as a nurse anesthetist. There are four broad categories that can be used:

Local anesthesia usually involves the injection of an anesthetic drug with a needle to cause the loss of sensation in a small area.

Regional anesthesia involves the injection of local anesthetic drugs in a manner that causes a larger number of nerves to be blocked. This is similar to local anesthesia but takes advantage of certain attributes of the body in order to have a larger effect. Depending on the part of the body that needs to be affected, a small amount of drug can affect a large number of nerves. For instance, a spinal involves local anesthetic drugs injected into the fluid surrounding the spinal cord. The drug is able to spread in this fluid and therefore affect a larger number of nerves. Similar techniques are used on other parts of the body to affect larger regions of nerves.

Sedation implies the use of medications to make patients drowsy in an effort to make them more comfortable. It does not result in complete unconsciousness.

General anesthesia implies that medications are used to affect the brain in a way that causes unconsciousness. As a result, the patient becomes unaware of stimulation and pain and after recovering from the general anesthesia does not remember the procedure (amnesia).

Over-the-Counter Anesthetics

Given that the higher prescription level of anesthetics is limited to the medical profession, nonmedical professionals offering services that could be best completed with the aid over-the-counter (OTC) levels of anesthetic drugs (nonprescription levels) in cream, gel, and liquid form(s). Applications of these OTC drugs produce a localized anesthetic effect on the skin it is applied to.

The eyebrows are located on one of the thickest areas of skin on the face (the chin being another). The nerve receptors are more recessed in the area where color will be deposited. As a result, the eyebrow procedure generally is less uncomfortable whether using anesthetics or not, and many experienced technicians indicate they do not. Some consider the use of anesthetics for eyebrows non-productive use of precious time as it only takes a few minutes to make the first pass on an eyebrow and apply a post broken skin anesthetic (if at all). There are also reports that pre-anesthetizing before designing an eyebrow results in slickness to the skin which causes designing to be more difficult. On the other hand, there are others who would not consider proceeding without pre-numbing the area and applying a post broken skin anesthetic during the procedure.

Many technicians who provide eyebrow microblading and machine hairline stroke eyebrow procedures have indicated they do not pre-anesthetize the skin before designing.

The comfort of the client during an eyeliner procedure does have far-reaching implications beyond just keeping the client comfortable. Well-numbed skin tissue on the eyelids also serves to ensure some degree of control, cooperation, and lack of involuntary reactions of the client to the prickly sensation around the eyes. Uncontrollable flinches can put the client in harm's way as well as prevent a perfectly executed procedure.

In earlier years of our industry when occasionally a technician would have clients anesthetized by their dentist prior to a lip procedure, many of the poorly conducted lip procedures seem to result from the effects of injected anesthetics. Several of these anesthesia medications included lidocaine and epinephrine. Epinephrine acts as a vasoconstrictor. Once the blood vessels are constricted, color in the lips is diminished and the lip vermilion border is more difficult to ascertain.

Many times, due to the injections the lip swells unevenly before the process of tattooing is underway. Another consideration is overworking the skin. This is a recipe for a poorly conducted lip procedure and a displeased client possibly requiring removal and/or corrective services.

Some technicians who work in a medical environment develop a compromising protocol for lip services. The technician applies an OTC anesthetic cream, applies the topical lip liner guide, conducts the lip liner procedure, and then, the physician injects anesthetics for the remaining full lip procedure. This compromise is worth consideration when a client feels entitled to prescription-level injected anesthetics because more was paid for the procedure to be conducted in a medical environment.

There has been documented concern regarding the liability and ethics associated with a medical professional such as a physician or a dentist who would provide lip injection anesthetic service and then allow the client to leave his or her office to have the cosmetic lip procedure conducted at another location. There may be geographical laws that address this practice. Check with the American Dental Association in the United States (or a comparable association in other countries) for specifics.

It is the opinion of many industry leaders that the use of OTC anesthetics is good and injected anesthetics are not only unnecessary for the low-level discomfort produced during permanent cosmetic procedures, but also can also result in a procedure being overworked by a novice technician who does not have the benefit of the client vocalizing reports of discomfort.

Overworking the skin can result in scarring. *The voice of discomfort is an important one.* The client will tell a technician when they have had enough and that is usually about the time when the skin has been worked to the point that it is appropriate to stop.

In regard to the use of OTC post-broken skin gel and liquid anesthetics, *these are hydrated products*. Use these aids sparingly and only as needed based on each client's comfort needs. When they come in contact with the color being tattooed into the skin, they can have a diluting effect if used excessively or not blotted off before tattooing, much as one would see if they put a few drops of color (pigment) in a pigment cap and added a drop of liquid. Technicians who apply anesthetics habitually see the results of this in the form of the healed procedure appearing to have lost more pigment than anticipated. Once the applied post- broken skin gel or liquid anesthetic has been applied and has taken effect, blot the excess anesthetic off the skin before proceeding to tattoo.

The industry has several Society of Permanent Cosmetic Professionals (SPCP) supplier members to thank for the anesthetics they have formulated for use during permanent cosmetic procedures.

Technicians who have been in the business for years can recall when there was nothing much to offer in the way of product pain management. OTC level anesthetics now are effective, but there will still be some clients who do not respond well to anesthetics of any kind, topically applied or injected by a medical professional. These clients will have a high metabolism rate and may metabolize any anesthetic well before the procedure is completed. These people are considered *fast acetylators*. They will require more time and special handling to keep them comfortable and possibly more applications of anesthetics during the procedure.

The legalities of OTC levels of anesthetic are geographically specific. It is important to know and comply with the laws in the workplace locality as this is a subject that varies from location to location.

If anesthetics are not legal, or preferred, technicians rely on the tried and true pain reducers; the professional stretching techniques and distracters such as counting, to perform their work.

Effective Use of Anesthetics

Before and During Permanent Cosmetic Procedures

All technicians who are not physicians, or work in a physician's office where prescription strength anesthetics are legally administered by a medical professional, know the value of techniques associated with anesthetizing procedural areas. This is accomplished with over-the-counter (OTC) strength topical anesthetics if, in their locality, this practice is legal and they elect to do so.

There is usually no such thing as a discomfort or pain-free procedure, even if only minor or pressure related. Regardless of the level of anesthetic strength, the client's enzymes go to work right away to degrade the effectiveness of the anesthetic. Whether anesthetics are applied topically or injected (appropriate for those technicians working with a physician in a medical environment), people who are difficult to anesthetize pose a challenge for all providers who depend on anesthetics to complete a service.

Many factors affect the comfort of a client other than the quality or duration of anesthetics. Fear and anxiety are certainly responsible for imagined discomfort and those fears and anxieties must be put to rest before beginning a procedure. Some clients will be more comfortable than others under any conditions; they just simply have a higher threshold of pain.

OTC anesthetics that are produced exclusively for our industry are effective when used according to the manufacturer's guidelines. Many contain a combination of anesthetics such as lidocaine, tetracaine, and epinephrine, a vasoconstrictor which, when applied properly and allowed to work for the prescribed time, decreases the amount of body fluids which may be produced during a procedure.

How much anesthetic and what brand to use is often client-specific information. The age, weight, general discomfort tolerance level, and overall state of mind of clients are all factors that contribute to how easily they respond to anesthetics, and for what period of time the anesthetic is effective.

In order to understand discomfort and the use (or not) of applicable anesthetics, the procedure that is being conducted is a mitigating factor. Eyeliner skin is the thinnest skin on the face. Eyes are a vital organ that the body works hard to protect. Perceived or real discomfort is usually a safety concern for clients considering eyeliner. Lips are plentiful with nerve endings and are quite sensitive to the touch.

Eyeliner Anesthetics

The eyeliner procedure involves thin sensitive skin. Also, the eyes are a vital organ that the client's body will work hard to protect. Many clients experience involuntary movements because of discomfort. It may be in both the technician's and the client's best interest to apply anesthetic before the procedure begins and during the procedure as needed for managed comfort. Even though the procedure normally involves a small to medium line of color deposit, without anesthetics a client may be less cooperative when asked to control their desire to shy away from the device being used for tattooing and as a result, respond to the discomfort by involuntarily squinting. On the other hand, there are many technicians who cannot legally use OTC anesthetics and employ stretching and client management techniques that result in a completed procedure without incident.

There is normally very little show of body fluids (blood) associated with eyeliner. This will vary between clients, some of whom take daily doses of aspirin or other prescribed blood thinning medication. Slight swelling may be a factor and if the post-broken skin anesthetic contains epinephrine, this does assist with controlling body fluids and has some positive effect on the swelling factor.

With the use of unbroken skin anesthetics and anesthetics for broken skin, often the client reports only the sensation of pressure while the eyeliner procedure is being conducted. Extreme care must be exercised when applying and removing anesthetics from the eyelids. If the anesthetic gets into the eyes, the client may react by reporting a burning sensation and their level of anxiety will mount until the eyes have been effectively rinsed with eyewash and are free of anesthetics. Failure to cleanse anesthetics from the eyes, depending on the eye's tearing properties to dilute the anesthetic to tolerable levels, can result in a chemical burn that causes pain, sensitivity to light, excessive tearing, dilated pupils, and the need for immediate medical attention.

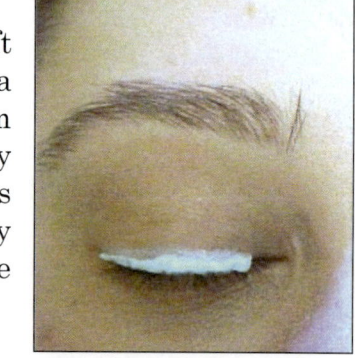

Apply eyeliner anesthetics carefully to the lash line (see Figure 19-2) with a single-use microbrush or cotton swab, leaving a bead of anesthetic across the upper lash line and immediately below the lower lash line.

In order to avoid any opportunity for the anesthetics to drift (melt) into the eye, it is suggested that the top eyeliner area is anesthetized, the procedure performed, and then the bottom eyeliner areas anesthetized approximately fifteen to twenty minutes before beginning the bottom eyeliner procedure (or as directed by the anesthetic manufacturer). This may seem overly cautious, but better to err on the side of being conservative around the eyes.

After anesthetic is applied, the client can be advised to close their eyes as if they were resting and not to open the eyes until the anesthetic has been removed. Depending on the product, eyeliner anesthetics may be more or less stable (stay put in place) when in contact with warm skin. If the technician feels this is necessary to keep the client's eyes safe it's a good practice.

Figure 19-2: Upper liner Anesthetic

Always remain in the room close to a client who has anesthetics on their eyelid areas and be prepared to rinse the eye out with an eyewash solution specifically formulated to cleanse the eyes. Remove the anesthetic carefully, working away from the eyes (see Figure 19-3). Rinse the eyes thoroughly and blot the skin dry before proceeding to tattoo.

Eyebrow Anesthetics:

Many technicians do not offer anesthetics for the eyebrow area; others only use anesthetics for the eyebrow procedure on broken skin. They make their first pass or prick the skin before tattooing the procedure on each eyebrow and apply anesthetics only as needed for client comfort.

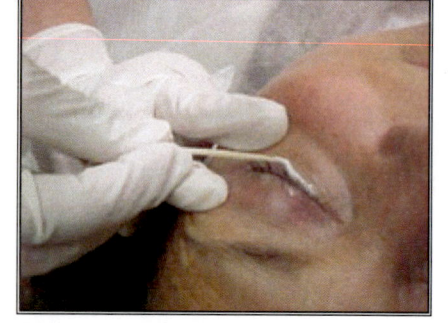

Figure 19-3: Remove anesthetics away from the eye

Another reason voiced by microblading technician experts for not applying anesthetic before the design phase of the procedure is that pre-anesthetic causes the skin to be slick and affects the drawing on of the template.

The application of eyebrow anesthetics (if pre-procedure anesthetics are used) on unbroken skin should be applied in ample amounts to do the job intended without harm to the client (see Figure 19-4).

Section 19 - Pain and Anesthesia

Unbroken skin is semi-permeable, which means it will accept some molecular substances. By applying anesthetics much like icing on a cake, the client's body temperature will have a melting or warming effect on the anesthetic and allow the skin to absorb it in layers during the allotted time it remains on the skin.

Too little anesthetic applied to the area is counterproductive to the goal of effectively numbing the area. In regard to eyebrows, some technicians apply an anesthetic after the brows are drawn on. Appropriate amounts will vary considering the design must remain in place after the anesthetic is removed.

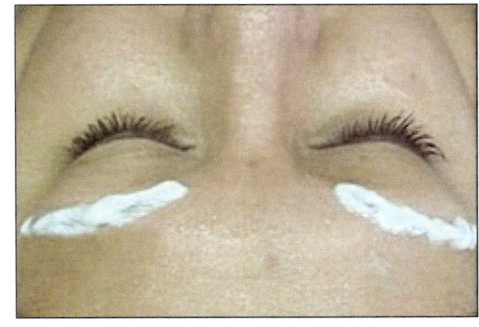

Figure 19-4: Eyebrow Anesthetics

Below are examples of eyebrows marked for microblading. A pre-anesthetic was not used. Once the eyebrow design template is drawn and marked, the skin is scored, or the skin lightly pricked with the needle, a secondary (liquid or gel) anesthetic is dabbed on with a single-use cotton swab (see Figure 19-5). Once the anesthetic takes effect, the excess anesthetic is blotted off (see Figure 19-6) and design markers checked (see Figure 19-7).

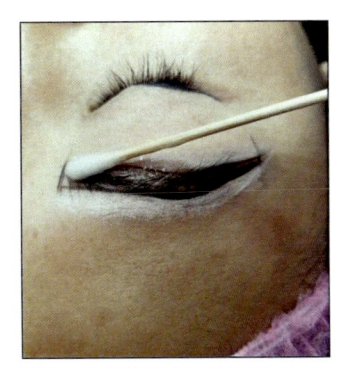

Figure 19-5: Anesthetic is applied to lightly pricked skin

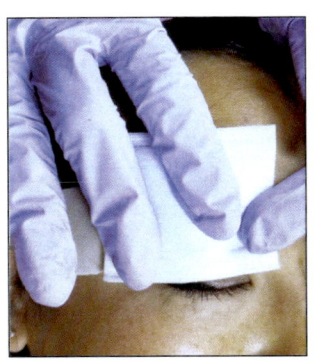

Figure 19-6: After taking effect, the anesthetic is blotted off

Figure 19-7: The blotted design area is checked to ensure design markers remain in place

Lip Liner Anesthetics:

Anesthetics for lip liners and blended (shaded) lip liners should be applied in ample amounts to do the job intended (see Figure 19-8, page 288). Anesthetics melt into the semi-permeable skin. While applying the anesthetic purposely to the lip liner area, anesthetics melt and often drift into the full lip area. Some technicians intentionally apply anesthetics to the entire lip even though the procedure is a lip liner.

While tattooing a lip liner, the sensitive lip tissue is stretched and anesthetic on lip tissue that is not intended for actual tattooing doesn't do any harm. Ask the client not to talk during this time as anesthetics can get into the mouth and throat. This is a quiet time for clients.

Anesthetics formulated for broken skin should be used during the procedure only as needed. There is limited room in the skin being tattooed for color deposit. When technicians continually apply hydrated substances such as anesthetics, gel or liquid form (if used) they must be applied with managed caution. Gel and liquid anesthetics, if not blotted off after taking effect, are essentially lessening the concentration level of the tattooed color that the anesthetic comes in contact with.

During a procedure, technicians have the choice of keeping the color formulation at full strength, or continually covering the area with anesthetics and risking diluting the concentration of the color. Secondary (post-broken skin) anesthetics should be blotted off the skin before proceeding to tattoo to decrease the possibility of tattooed color contact dilution.

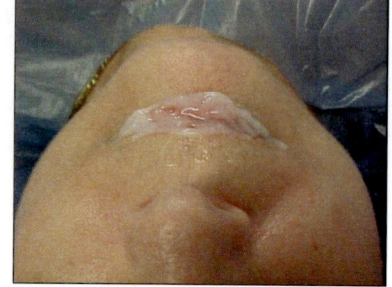

Figure 19-8: Anesthetizing Lips

There will be clients who indicate they plan on seeing their physician for a relaxant or prescription strength pain management medication in order to be more comfortable through the procedure. It is highly recommended that those clients are advised to arrange for a driver to return home after the procedure. It is not ever suggested that after a client takes prescription strength medications for relaxation or pain management purposes that they drive an automobile afterward. This is a client safety and liability issue that must be taken into consideration.

Another word of caution relates to OTC pain relievers or antihistamine products. You may hear of technicians advising their clients to take these medications. Do not advise clients to take any medications, OTC or otherwise, if you are not a medical doctor. Benadryl® is frequently mentioned as an OTC medication that assists with swelling; however, it is also a medication that can cause drowsiness and should not be recommended to clients. Most clients drive themselves to and from procedures and principled technicians do not want to be involved with suggesting anything that would prevent a client's safe drive to their permanent cosmetic appointment or home.

If technicians manage the skin during procedures properly, employing good stretching techniques, use OTC anesthetics as directed, and do not overwork the skin, there is normally only minor discomfort and swelling associated with permanent cosmetic procedures.

Over time, experience with OTC levels of anesthetics and developing good stretching techniques for procedures will enhance effective management of client discomfort. Technicians must be realistic regarding how long a client can sustain even minor discomfort and allow short breaks in order for the client to regroup or rest for a few minutes before proceeding.

In addition to the use of anesthetics and developing good stretching techniques for procedures, there are many forms of distraction and control methods utilized that result in an effective and comfortable procedure experience.

Section 19 - Pain and Anesthesia

Mind Over Matter

The client's cooperation is essential for a successful permanent cosmetic procedure. Technicians must maintain control over clients, and clients must also be willing to give their technician the needed control.

Ways to Encourage a Client to Release Control

Set the Scene

- Smile as clients are greeted when they arrive. Professionals are expected to have pleasant personalities (see Figure 19-9).
- Ensure that the climate in the workplace is pleasing to clients and not extreme.
- The workplace should be orderly and the décor pleasant (see Figure 19-10).
- Offer the client a comfortable chair while discussing the procedure and/or filling out forms.
- Music should be generic and background volume level.

Figure 19-9: Be friendly and greet clients

Figure 19-10: Clean and orderly workplace setting

Encourage Trust

- Provide a level of confidence that is viewed as being worthy of control.
- Wash your hands at appropriate times; clients notice this practice even if they do not mention it.
- Make the client the only concern. Don't answer the phone or allow others not involved with the procedure in the area while in session with a client (see Figure 19-11).
- Use a calm, quiet voice when conversing with a client.
- Never offer a discomfort or pain-free procedure. If the procedure is completed with minimal discomfort, feel fortunate. Levels of discomfort are unpredictable. Don't promise something that cannot be delivered!

Figure 19-11: Stay off the phone

Stress Discovery

- Inquire about how the client manages stress (see Figure 19-12).
- Does the client practice mental stress techniques?
- Does the client have physical conditions or special requests that must be considered for positioning during the procedure?
- If clients indicate they are nervous, ask questions that will assist in putting those fears aside. Why are you nervous? If it is fear of design work, let them know their approval of the design work is necessary before proceeding. Is it fear of discomfort? Advise clients that techniques and anesthetics (if anesthetics are used) and stretching techniques will be used that are very effective in the control of discomfort.

Figure 19-12: Manage stress

Preparation for the Procedure—Prepare the Client with Information

Inform the client that they will experience a variety of physical sensations and sounds during the procedure such as:

- The sensations and pressure produced by the required procedural stretching techniques
- The coolness and temporary sensation of topical anesthetic application
- The dampness of pads dipped in cool water used for wiping and cleansing the procedural area
- The sensation of moistening and cleansing the eyes with OTC eye products
- A machine's vibration sensation
- The Velcro sound of a manual (non-microblading) device when in operation

Advise clients that conversation during the procedure will be limited to directions and occasional inquires about their comfort. They will appreciate the focus on the work that is being performed.

Control Techniques During the Procedure

- Stretching techniques are the client's measurement of who is in control. Stretching technique speaks volumes about a technician's confidence and control level. Keep stretching techniques firm but not intrusive to soft tissue.

- **Proper breathing techniques** are good control techniques the client can practice during a procedure. Do not encourage deep breathing, only normal, regular breathing. Breath holding excites the client's nervous system and puts the body on guard.
- **Voice levels** should be kept calm and that of one in control when speaking to clients during the procedure.
- **Positive control reminders** are helpful when given the opportunity such as: *breathe, relax your legs and arms, relax your hands on your chest, etc.*
- **Positive statements and actions** are excellent motivators, such as:
  ◊ *You are doing great.*
  ◊ *Thanks for your patience.*
  ◊ *That stinging sensation is just temporary, very soon the area will be more numb.*
  ◊ *How about a break, would you like to sit up for a minute?*

Keep directions, input, observations, suggestions, and questions upbeat and positive in nature.

- **Observe the client's body language** to determine when breaks are required. Don't wait for the client to ask for one. Squinting eyes, clenching jaws, fisting of the hands, leg crossing, and holding of breath are all signs of stress. If a change in the client's comfort level is noticed, suggest a break.
- **Avoid planting negative seeds** such as conversations with the client that utilize the words *hurt, pain, tired, sore, blood,* or *needles.*
- *Change the focus of any discomfort* by changing the area that is being tattooed in a systematic manner; i.e., consider one pass on one eye, eyebrow, top lip, and then switch to one pass on the other eye, eyebrow, and bottom lip. Repeat passes as needed until the procedure is complete.
- This suggestion is not provided to alter the methodology in which procedures are performed. They are offered for consideration and at times may only be needed to assist with completing a procedure on a client who is very sensitive.
- **Keeping clients informed** during the procedure lets the client know the status of the procedure process:
  ♦ *I'm almost ready to stop and apply more anesthetic.*
  ♦ *I'm laying the device down now; we are going to take a break for a few minutes.*
  ♦ *I think you need to sit up and stretch for a few minutes.*

All these status related statements keep the client informed.

- **Reward clients** for time spent by letting them look at the progress of the procedure during a break. Assuming clients will like what they see, this form of reward and gives them a reason to continue to cooperate and follow directions.

  This practice can be time-consuming and the client is often looking at an incomplete procedure. Not all technicians feel this is a positive technique for clients, but it one for consideration if deemed a positive client management technique.

- **Counting** is one of the most distracting methods there is to take the client's mind off any discomfort they may be experiencing. Temporarily counting aloud while working on a sensitive area has proved to be a wonderful distracter. Or, request the client to mentally count from 1 to 200 by 5's or other such distracting counting suggestions during work on sensitive areas.

- **Communication.** Technicians should lay the ground rules for how clients are expected to communicate during a procedure. Technicians use various methods. Be cautious that whatever is suggested as a means of communication to advise a break is needed does not result in movement of the procedural area.

When Conventional Techniques Fail

Conventional techniques do not work on all clients for a garden variety of reason. When extreme measures are necessary consider the following actions:

- STOP and determine the reason that the client is more sensitive.
  - Is there any biological reasoning for the sensitivity?
  - Did the client disregard initial instructions and have strong or large amounts of caffeine?
  - Did the client disregard initial instructions and have alcohol?
  - Is the procedure being performed a follow-up procedure that was scheduled too soon after the initial work? Possibly the initial procedure has not had time to properly heal and the client is overly sensitive for that reason.
- If the source of sensitivity cannot be resolved at this visit, finish as much of the procedure as possible to make it presentable to the client and reschedule an appointment under more ideal conditions.

Addendum—Be Aware: Clients Who Enjoy Drama

- Some clients see pain as a badge of courage; the more drama the better (see Figure 19-13).
- Efforts to minimize discomfort are a form of attention that some clients crave and strive for.
- Some clients see pain as an opportunity to suffer and then to tell their friends of their sacrifice.

Figure 19-13: Drama

References

1. Kate Ciampi Shergold RN, CPCP assisted with the compilation of information contained in this portion of the textbook

Section 20

The Healing Process

Learning Objectives

Introduction

Not unlike other beauty services, cosmetic tattooing must heal before the client sees the final results. Clients need to be informed as to what to expect and be provided with reasonable timelines during which the natural changes of the appearance of their new permanent cosmetics progress in conjunction with the body's healing process.

Technicians who are well informed about the healing process, those who understand the cellular renewal process and the effects of that process on the procedure area, have clients who are emotionally prepared for those changes and will care for their procedures in a manner that prevents infection.

Objective

Upon completion of this section, technicians will understand the body's biological healing process for minor wounds and what is normal in regard to the appearance of the permanent cosmetic procedure inherent to the progression of healing.

Section 20 - The Healing Process

It is important for technicians to understand the healing process associated with permanent cosmetic procedures.[1] How the procedure area is seen immediately after being tattooed changes in appearance to what is seen several days or weeks later. By becoming acquainted with the healing process technicians will become a better informed and as a result, they are good advisors to their clients.

After the initial tattooing of color into the skin, the procedure site may appear blotchy, or inflamed in appearance. Bruising is not common, but possible, especially when performing eyeliner or lip procedures. The body's healing process begins when a wound is inflicted. The tattooing process creates a small wound with the needles used during a procedure.

Once the body detects the wound, it begins the healing process by rapidly sending healing blood cells to the tattoo site to prepare for the rebuilding of the damaged skin tissue and to ward off any bacterial invasion.

Inflammation of the area may last up to 48 hours, depending on the location of the procedure site and the amount of assault inflicted on the tissue. This estimated inflammation period may vary.

Immediately after tattooing, pigments remain suspended until such time they adhere to or are encapsulated by skin cells (see Figure 20-1).

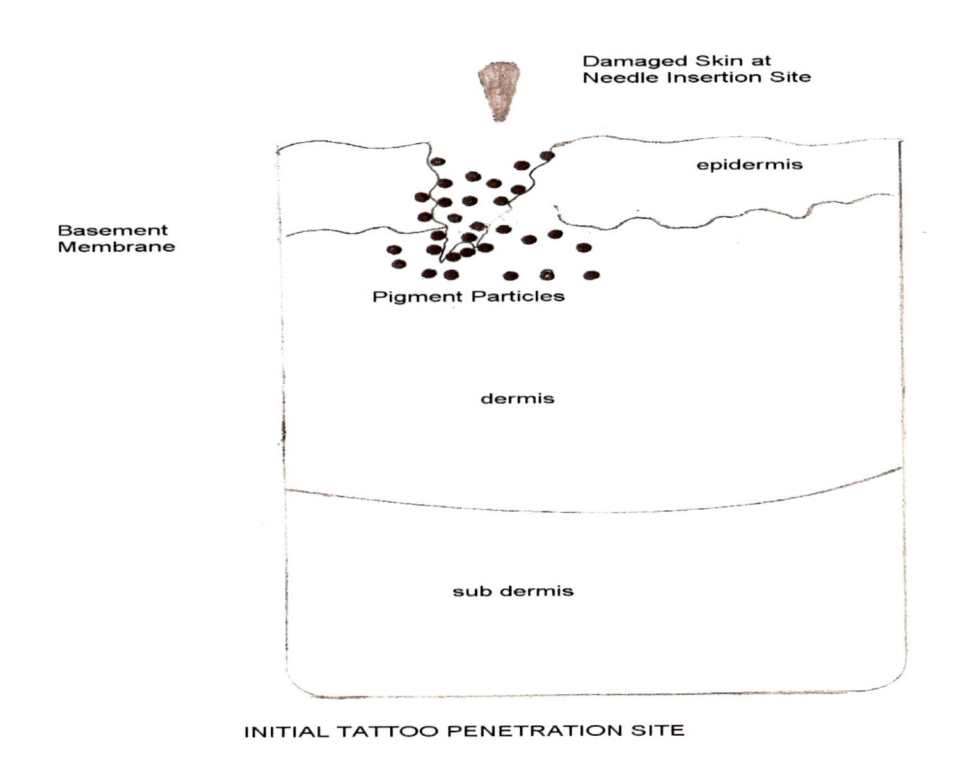

Figure 20-1: Initial tattoo penetration site
Drawing by Liza Sims.

Freshly tattooed sites must be protected from the sun (UV rays) and bacteria (dirty hands, dust, etc.). A healing agent (typically an ointment) may be applied sparingly throughout the day as (or if) directed by the technician, for approximately a week to ten days (or until the flaking is complete). If a healing agent is used for eyeliner, it should be one that can safely be used around the eyes.

The tattooed site will lose moisture for the first 24–36 hours and care should be taken to not allow moisture to become trapped under the ointment. Previously applied ointment (if used) may be removed carefully with a clean, moist (cool water) cotton swab, gauze, or well-moistened cotton pad (no lint) and the area should be allowed to air dry before reapplying ointment. The tattooed area should appear only slightly shiny after the ointment is applied and excess ointment may be removed by a damp (cool water) cotton swab or lightly blotted off with a clean material such as gauze or well-moistened cotton pad. The procedure site will require more frequent cleaning/ointment applications during the first two days to ensure the seeping body fluids do not become trapped under the ointment.

The client should be clearly instructed not to apply too much ointment as moisture can become trapped underneath it, causing the tattooed site to take on a bubbly appearance. The bubbled areas of skin will form scabs and will result in poor color retention.

There are three phases to the healing process:
- The inflammatory phase
- The proliferation phase
- The maturation phase

The Inflammatory Phase

While in the inflammatory phase, there are two main activities taking place:

Hemostasis

- Stopping blood loss from damage to capillaries and small vessels. The immediate vascular reflex causes vasoconstriction and diminishes the loss of blood.
- The exposed collagen (resulting from the damaged tissue) will cause the blood platelets to stick to it.
- The platelets will release serotonin-rich granulated cytoplasm, which is also a vasoconstrictor. This process is known as clotting.

Inflammation

- The body calls for more immune cells to migrate to the wound site to stabilize the wound, limit the injury, and prevent bacteria from gaining access to the vulnerable underlying skin layers.
- Neutrophil cells are dispatched to the wound site for decontamination by

the scavenging of debris and bacteria.

- Macrophage cells (large yellowish cells with arm-like projections whose job is to ingest bacteria) are in wound healing. The macrophage cells arrive and secrete enzymes and cytokines. This produces new collagen by stimulating fibroblasts (the scaffolding support structure for tissues and organs) and keratinocytes (protein cell and building block of the epidermis).

- Tattooed colorant particles are initially taken up by keratinocytes, fibroblasts, macrophages, and mast cells (part of the immune system and present in almost all tissue containing blood vessels).

- As inflammation subsides with the development of new fibroblasts and keratinocytes, the next phase of healing begins.

The Proliferation Phase

- The covering of a wound with epithelial tissue (epithelium covers almost all external and internal body surfaces as an uninterrupted layer of cells). This occurs early in the process of the body's wound repair mechanism. If, as in tattooing, the basement membrane remains intact, epithelial cells move (migrate) upward toward the surface in a normal process.

- New capillaries are formed and deliver nutrients to the surrounding cells for tissue reformation and granulation.

- Fibroblasts separate and first form a ground substance, then collagen. The normal layers of the epidermis are primarily restored after about three days in the proliferation phase.

- The cosmetic tattoo procedure site will begin to flake, similar to what is experienced after sunburn in about three to seven days (this may be client and procedure-specific). This process should not be interfered with. The client must be instructed not to pick or scratch the area during this phase.

The Maturation Phase

- The wound contracts with the formation of scar tissue. Wounds reach their maximum strength in three months to one year, depending on surface area and depth.

- Collagen continues to be deposited for some months, but the main collagen deposition completes its cycle in about 28–35 days. In this phase, the basement membrane (epidermal/dermal junction) is in active reformation and the tattooed colorant particles and are still contained in the basal layer of the epidermis as well as the upper layers of the dermal papillary layer.

- The tattooed colorant is still being desquamated through the epidermis through migrating skin cells (see Figure 20-2).

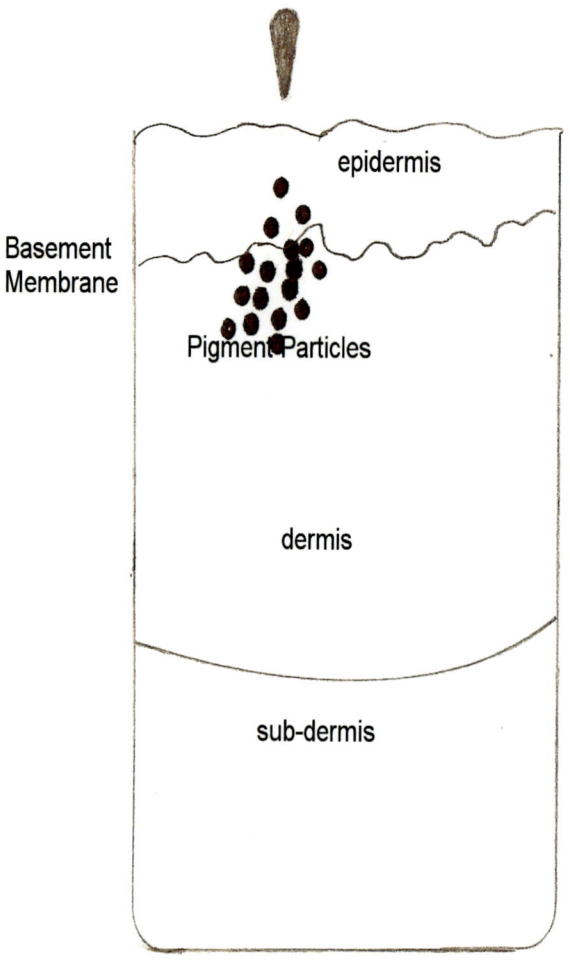

Figure 20-2:
Tattoo needle penetration site at about 28 to 35 days
Drawing by Liza Sims.

- At fifty to ninety days, the basement membrane has completed its reformation cycle and further color loss through the epidermis will no longer take place. The remaining color resides in and around the dermal fibroblasts at the papillary level. (see Figure 20-3).

Healing involves a complex interaction of cellular function and activity and is augmented by proper home care and good hygiene. Well-explained and detailed home aftercare instructions are important to clients' understanding and compliance.

Ideally, permanent cosmetics should always be completely protected from sun exposure. This is not always possible, but clients must be warned that sun exposure will cause the color to fade. Sunglasses should be worn over permanent eyeliner and sunscreen with an SPF of at least thirty should cover permanent eyebrows and lips when sun avoidance is not possible.

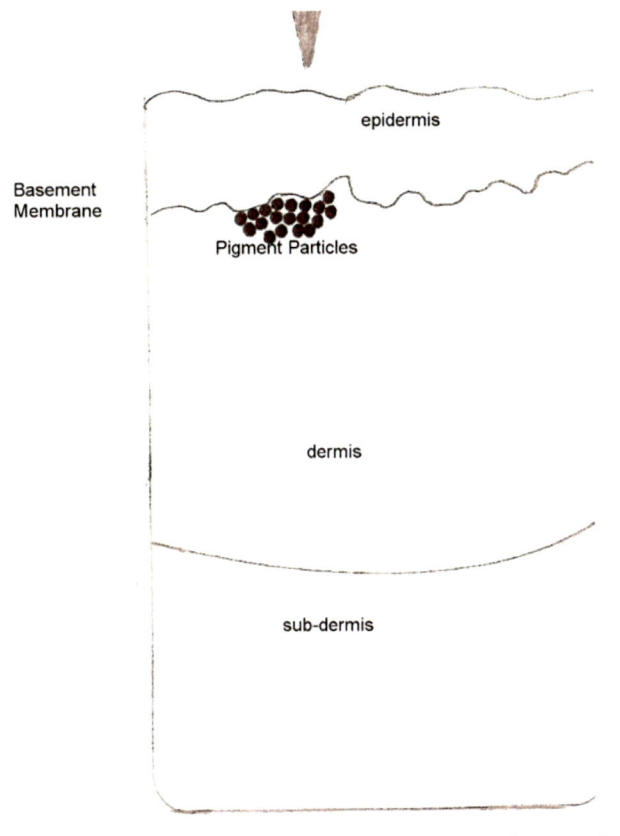

Figure 20-3: Tattoo needle penetration site at about 90 days
Drawing by Liza Sims.

Understanding the Changes in the Procedure Appearance

Clients are not likely to be interested in scientific details of the healing process; however, they do need a simplified explanation of what to expect and why. Knowing what is taking place and what changes to expect allows the client to participate in a healthy aftercare program and enables her or him to explain the darker appearance of the procedure to friends and family.

In all likelihood many uninformed clients have panicked after returning home with very dark eyebrows, swollen eyes or lips and unsuccessfully tried to remove the tattooed color they felt was too dark, or appeared larger than expected (due to swelling). The best investment is to provide information they can easily understand.

The client may ask:

Why does the procedure area appear larger than the design I approved?

Answer: Because of swelling, the procedure area appears larger or thicker than the design you approved. The swelling will subside in a few days and the design area will appear smaller.

Why is the color so dark? It didn't look that way when we selected the color.

Answer: Wounds create irritation (inflammation) and irritation may add to the appearance of a darker procedure color. The irritation will subside in a few days.

When the irritation subsides in a few days will I see the final color?

Answer: No, there is excess tattooed color trapped in the epidermis (top layer of the skin), which will desquamate (shed) during the healing period. The loss of color that occurs during the desquamation process results in less color saturation and ultimately has a lightening effect on the appearance of the procedure. Once the healing process is well underway, new skin cells form over the tattoo and provide a veiling of the procedure area, which also contributes to a softer appearance.

Lip color begins to bloom on about day 15 and the final color may be seen on about day 30 to day 45. Truer brow and eyeliner colors will be seen on about day 28 to 35.

The client's age and health contribute to the appropriate timing for a completely healed procedure. Ultimately, when the healing process is complete, on the average, for Fitzpatrick I & III skin types, eyebrow and eyeliner procedures may appear up to two shades lighter than what is seen immediately after the procedure. As provided in Section 14, Fitzpatrick skin types IV-VI may see similar to, or one to two shades darker than the color used for the procedure due to hyperpigmentation.

Lips shed the most tattooed color during the healing process. On the average, up to 50 percent of lip color may be lost on the vermilion border and up to 75 percent from the vermilion.

Explaining the changes in procedural appearances in simple terms, or even better, providing an estimated schedule of what to expect per procedure on written aftercare directions is in your best interest as a technician. Knowledge is power, and if clients are empowered with information, she or he will work with their technician and care for the procedure as directed, educate others who may be inclined to be critical of the appearance of a new procedure, and be prepared to provide educated status reports for their technician when they are called in a few days to check on their procedure healing progress.

For additional information about the healing skin process and dry and moist wound healing see "The Principles of Tattoo Lightening and Removal" on page 357.

References

1. This section was provided by Liza Sims.

Section 21

Solar Care and Prevention of Premature Permanent Cosmetic Color Fading

Learning Objectives

Introduction

Once a procedure has been safely performed, it has healed, and the client is well on her or his way to enjoying the benefits of permanent cosmetics, as technicians we have one more task to complete: to advise the client how to maintain the pristine appearance of their procedure.

To overlook this important part of our services would be a disservice to the client, possibly resulting in a client's dissatisfaction with her or his permanent cosmetics, and prevent a client from talking about the benefits of your services to others.

Referrals are our lifeline in the permanent cosmetic industry. So what does this entail? The number one enemy to cosmetic tattooing is sun exposure. It is not unusual for a client to pursue permanent cosmetic services in preparation for an upcoming sun-filled vacation. Technicians must be prepared to advise their clients how to avoid as much sun exposure as possible.

Objective

Upon completion of this section, the technician will understand the importance of counseling clients to avoid sun exposure. They will learn the importance of procedure timing and the use of sun protection products that are advisable after the procedure has healed.

Section 21 - Solar Care and Prevention of Premature Permanent Cosmetic Color Fading

It is a well-known fact that exposure to the sun's ultraviolet (UV) rays results in premature fading of permanent cosmetic procedures. All color is subject to fading. If the sun did not have an adverse effect on all color, houses would never require painting, paint on automobiles would never oxidize, and clothing washed repeatedly and/or dried in direct sunlight would never fade to a lighter color.

According to reports, exposure to the sun's UV rays is the primary cause of skin cancer and premature signs of aging, freckling, skin discolorations, and a multitude of other skin related conditions. Reports indicate that tanning beds are certainly no safer than direct sun exposure and result in the same medical and skin conditions.

Nonetheless, there are people who are willing to take their chances in several health and beauty related arenas and go into the sun with their skin unprotected. Intentional tanning seems to be a normal pastime for some people during the summer months. All a person has to do is to take a look at the beaches in summer to find hundreds of people that disregard all warnings of the hazards associated with sun exposure. There is no such thing as a healthy tan that was obtained by self-sacrifice to the rays of the sun.

In respect to permanent cosmetics, exposure to the sun accelerates the degradation of permanent cosmetic colorant (pigment) formulations and results in not only a lighter (faded) color, but also may result in undesirable color shifts (one or more colorants in the formulation used for the tattoo fades prematurely).

Lightfastness is a characteristic of all colorants tattooed into the skin. Lightfastness ratings are an indication of each colorant's resistance to fading from light exposure. UV light and light in general, is known to alter color by breaking the colorant's chemical bonds. This is known as *photodegradation*. It is important that clients recognize how they care for their permanent cosmetics plays an important role in how soon they may return for a color refresher procedure.

Excessive sun exposure is counterproductive to the permanent cosmetic maintenance program. Incidental exposure, i.e., riding in a car, outdoor sports, and gardening can also take its toll over time.

It is impossible to expect that clients will not ever be exposed to UV rays from the sun, or subject their procedure to facial maintenance products that contain chemicals and exfoliation properties that have not been formally studied as to how they may affect permanent cosmetics.

During a consultation, it is not unusual for clients to ask how long it will be after the procedure that they might require a color refresher. This is dependent on many factors such as the color and technique used for the procedure, if they consistently use a sun protection product on the procedure area, any medical conditions and their treatments, facial maintenance ingredients, professional cosmetic treatments, and of course the most important element, unprotected exposure to the sun. The timing of a color refresher is very client-specific.

Clients should be advised that they will require a color refresher (also called touch-ups, color boosts, and other similar descriptions, etc.) at some point in the future. Predicting the timing of color refreshers is, at best, an estimate without specific lifestyle information from the client and factoring in tattoo color and technique information.

There may be questions relating to the level of sun protection products that should be applied over the procedure area to protect it. Some clients have a favorite brand that they use (if they use a sunscreen product at all). Technicians will be hard pressed to convince clients to change from a favorite sun protection product just because their permanent cosmetic technician feels they may need a product containing a higher SPF than what they are currently using.

Broad or full spectrum sunscreen products protect against UV-B rays and UV-A exposure. UV-B rays (shorter wavelengths) penetrate the top layers of the skin. UV-A rays (longer wavelengths) penetrates the deeper layers of the skin, causing premature aging. Both damage the skin and can cause skin cancer.

Clients who advise that there is a certain SPF in their foundation makeup are inadequately covered. Normally clients do not cover their eyebrow, eyeliner, or lip areas with foundation makeup; and if they do, the procedure color looks more opaque and cool, so this should be discouraged. The sun protection product has to be one that is applicable for putting on the procedure area, not around it.

Understanding Sunburn Protection Factor (SPF)

SPF (sun protection factor) is a measure of how much solar energy (UV radiation) is required to produce sunburn on protected skin (i.e., in the presence of sunscreen) relative to the amount of solar energy required to produce sunburn on unprotected skin. As the SPF value increases, sunburn protection increases.[1]

There is a popular misconception that SPF relates to the amount of time of solar exposure. For example, many consumers believe that if they normally get a sunburn in one hour, then an SPF fifteen sunscreen allows them to stay in the sun fifteen hours (i.e., fifteen times longer) without getting sunburn. This is not true because SPF is not directly related to the amount of *time* of solar exposure but to *amount* of solar exposure. Although solar energy amount is related to solar exposure time, there are other factors that impact the amount of solar energy. For example, the intensity of the solar energy impacts the amount. The following exposures may result in the same amount of solar energy:[1]

1) One hour at 9:00 a.m.
2) Fifteen minutes at 1:00 p.m.[1]

Generally, it takes less time to be exposed to the same amount of solar energy at midday compared to early morning or late evening because the sun is more intense at midday relative to the other times. Solar intensity is also related to geographic location, with greater solar intensity occurring at lower latitudes. Because clouds absorb solar energy, solar intensity is generally greater on clear days than cloudy days.[1]

In addition to solar intensity, there are a number of other factors that influence the amount of solar energy that a consumer is exposed to:

- Skin type
- Amount of sunscreen applied
- Reapplication frequency[1]

People with fair skin (Fitzpatrick I-II) are likely to absorb more solar energy than people with darker skin (Fitzpatrick IV-VI) under the same conditions. Fitzpatrick III skin types can fall into either category based on their skin type and their sun exposure experience. The melanin in darker skin serves as a natural defense against UV rays. The amount of sunscreen applied also impacts the amount of solar radiation absorbed because more sunscreen results in less solar energy absorption.[1]

Because sunscreen products wear off and become less effective with time, the frequency with which they are reapplied is important to limiting absorption of solar radiation. The reapplication frequency is also impacted by the activities that consumers are involved in. For example, consumers who swim while wearing sunscreen need to reapply the sunscreen more frequently because water may wash the sunscreen from the body. In addition, high levels of physical activity require more frequent reapplication because the activity may physically rub off the sunscreen and heavy sweating may wash off the sunscreen. In general, more frequent reapplication is associated with decreased absorption of solar radiation.

Because of the various factors that impact the amount of solar radiation, SPF does not reflect the amount of time in the sun. In other words, SPF does not inform consumers about the time that can be spent in the sun without getting sunburn. Rather, SPF is a relative measure of the amount of sunburn protection provided by sunscreens. It allows consumers to compare the level of sunburn protection provided by different sunscreens. For example, consumers know that SPF 30 sunscreens provide more (but only slightly) protection than SPF 15 sunscreens.

Technicians should periodically conduct research to determine what the medical community and/or government agencies suggest as adequate SPF protection if they plan on advising their clients of the latest information on this subject.

> *Sunscreens that pass the broad spectrum test can demonstrate that they also provide UVA protection. Therefore, under the label requirements, for sunscreens labeled "Broad Spectrum SPF [value]", they will indicate protection from both UVA and UVB radiation. To get the most protection out of sunscreen, choose one with an SPF of at least 15. If your skin is fair, you may want a higher SPF of 30 to 50.*[2]

Common complaints from clients about sun protection products include the white pasty color of the product, the greasy feeling that it may leave on the face, and that some products cause the eyes to tear. As a result, many people avoid using sun protection products or refuse to apply them around the eyes (which may be appropriate depending on the product direction provided). Sunscreen manufacturers have made progress to reduce the pasty appearance of their products.

Some reports indicate that more frequent application is an effective approach to better protection; however, considering the busy lifestyles of people today, and that people do wear foundation makeup and other cosmetic products, it is doubtful that a person can be convinced that sunscreen must be applied two to three times a day.

The day-to-day regime of sunscreen and sun block applications will normally occur in the morning before the day has begun. There are products that appear less white and pasty, people just need to shop around and find the one that suits them for everyday use.

Clients with Fitzpatrick skin types IV–VI may be the hardest to convince they require sun protection. Their skin is darker than Fitzpatrick skin types I-III and they may feel more immune to the effects of the sun.

One element of concern regarding permanent cosmetics and sun exposure is the timing between the procedure and any subsequent exposure to direct or extreme (more than incidental) sun exposure and heat conditions. It is not uncommon for a prospective client to indicate that she or he is interested in permanent cosmetics because of a planned vacation shortly after the procedure. This is ill-advised timing if the vacation destination includes sun related activities or swimming.

First of all, no one should time permanent cosmetic procedures around an important event. Refraining from activities conducted in direct or extreme sun exposure for a minimum of two weeks is recommended and preferably four is optimal. Much of the timing of this recommendation is contingent upon the age and health of the client in relation to healing.

These instructions and the knowledge of the adverse effects of the sun certainly do not imply that once clients have permanent cosmetics that they will never enjoy the pleasure of hobbies or tasks that expose them to sunlight. Hats, sun visors, and sunglasses help shield the face from sun exposure.

Section 21 - Solar Care and Prevention of Premature Permanent Cosmetic Color Fading

Clients need to be made aware of these issues and encouraged to use good judgment if they wish to provide maximum protection for their investment over a long period of time. The good news is that the media and medical professions are giving similar advice regarding unprotected sun exposure in an attempt to prevent skin cancer and premature aging.

On the other hand, clients can only be advised of what they should do to protect their permanent cosmetic procedures. Ultimately they make the final decision regarding the daily use of sun protection products.

If some clients have an aversion to wearing sun protection products or sun-shielding accessories, all a technician can do is to let them know that they will require color refresher procedures much sooner than they would if they applied sunscreen to the procedural area on a daily basis.

References

1. U.S. Food and Drug Administration [FDA] (2017). Sun Protection Factor (SPF). Retrieved from https://www.fda.gov/aboutfda/centersoffices/officeofmedicalproductsandtobacco/cder/ucm106351.htm
2. U.S. Food and Drug Administration [FDA] (2017b). Sunscreen: How to Help Protect Your Skin from the Sun. Retrieved from https://www.fda.gov/drugs/resourcesforyou/consumers/buyingusingmedicinesafely/understandingover-the-countermedicines/ucm239463.htm

Section 22

Herpes Simplex and Permanent Cosmetics

Learning Objectives

Introduction

Herpes is a sensitive but necessary subject to address with clients. Not only can an outbreak of this condition affect the results of a lip procedure's final appearance, but also the lesions produced are painful and unattractive. Herpes outbreaks have also been the source of legal challenges in the permanent cosmetic industry. Precautions are advisable by requiring Informed Consent forms to be completed by the client. In regard to the oral Herpes Simplex Virus 1 (HSV-1) clients who have a history of breakouts should be advised that they must acquire an antiviral medication through their health care provider before having a lip procedure conducted.

Objective

Upon completion of this section, the technician will have a working knowledge of the oral l herpes simplex viruses (HSV-1), how to advise the client regarding the need to pre-medicate with a physician prescribed antiviral medication, and which client completed forms help protect against a possible legal challenge if a breakout occurs.

What Is Herpes?

Herpes dates back to the time of the ancient Greeks, which explains why its name comes from the Greek word herpein, meaning *"to creep" or "to crawl."* The specific causes of recurring outbreaks of herpes remain a mystery to the medical industry. Today herpes has become a widespread infection that doesn't discriminate between gender, social, or economic classes. There are reports citing varied statistics representing how many people have herpes, and within those reports, a breakdown as to the number of people who have herpes 1 and herpes 2 (further explained in the next paragraph). In order to keep this section current, no specifics will be quoted but in general, the numbers quoted are in the high multimillions.

There are many known types of herpes virus, but to date, only a few are known to cause disease in humans. The most common are herpes simplex virus 1 (HSV-1) and herpes simplex virus 2 (HSV-2). Oral herpes (cold sores or fever blisters) is called herpes simplex virus type 1 (HSV-1) and genital herpes (genital sores or sores below the waist) is called herpes simplex virus type 2 (HSV-2). Medical information available indicates these viruses appear identical under the microscope, and either type can infect the mouth or genitals. Most commonly, however, HSV-1 occurs above the waist and HSV-2 below the waist. Other common herpes infections include chickenpox (varicella-zoster virus-VZV) and shingles (herpes zoster), which is the reactivation of the VZV later in life.

The immune system is the body's natural defense. The herpes virus represents an attack on the immune system resulting in the body fighting back. As the fight between the body's immune system and the herpes virus becomes more extreme, both experience profound losses. This results in the body being more vulnerable to attacks from other viruses. For this very reason, a herpes patient is often advised to keep the virus under control at all times. When addressing a herpes history with a new permanent cosmetic client during the consultation phase, it would not be uncommon if a person recalled if at one time or another she or he had experienced a herpes outbreak. An outbreak may be isolated to one blister or may consist of many blisters, all of which are

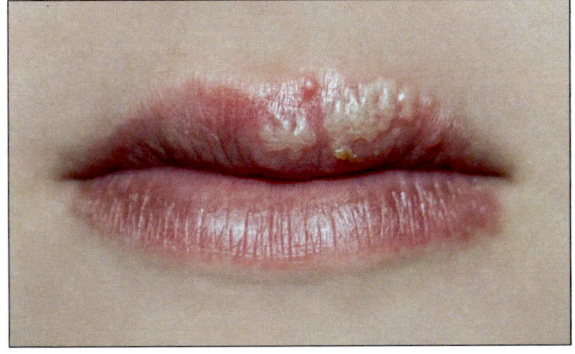

Figure 22-1:
Herpes Simplex Virus Type 1

painful and unsightly. Because of the common association between HSV-1 and HSV-2 and the ability to acquire HSV-2 through sexual contact, many clients may be reluctant to answer *"yes"* to the client history form question: Do you have a history of cold sores or fever blisters? (see Figure 22-1)

For the purposes of this section, herpes simplex virus 1 will be addressed as it has a direct relationship to permanent cosmetics, specifically the lip procedure that causes trauma to the affected area. It should be noted as a matter of educational information, however, that HSV-1 and HSV-2 can be spread from one location to other body parts from direct contact, i.e., touching the infected site (most commonly genital/oral contact) and then touching other parts of the body, including the eyes. Because the virus can be spread from one location to another, a technician who is scheduled to conduct a lip procedure and another procedure on the same client at the same appointment should never use the same needle, machine accessories, or the procedure tray setup that was used during the lip procedure on any other procedure. Everything used for the lip procedure should be properly disposed of. The risk of spreading a herpes virus or other bacteria that are common to the mouth and saliva is great. It is strongly advised to do the lips last during a multi-procedure session.

In the Beginning

At the onset of the herpes virus infection, the virus escapes the body's immune defenses by entering nerve endings and traveling to the central nervous system (CNS) or ganglia. The CNS is made up of nerve cell clusters. In the CNS the virus is inactive and it causes no harm to the body or the nerve cells where it resides. Periodically (and the timing differs from person to person) the virus can be reactivated. Once the virus is reactivated, it travels back down the nerve to the surface of the skin, multiplying, which results in an outbreak. Recurrences are often reported to develop at or near the original site of infection. During a first episode, the immune system helps ward off infection more quickly and efficiently. As a result, there may be fewer sores that heal faster, and less pain may be experienced.

Symptoms

The initial symptoms that may appear during an HSV-1 outbreak can include any or all of the following sensations:

- Burning at a specific site(s) on the lips
- Tingling at a specific site(s) on the lips
- Itching at a specific site(s) on the lips

It should also be noted that these sensations may also be experienced not only on the lips but around the mouth or nose.

This first sign of the outbreak is also known as the prodromal stage. Within a varied period of time, often within a few hours to days, these initial symptoms will progressively become obvious with the appearance of the site becoming reddened and the development of small fluid-filled blisters. It is not unusual for several small blisters to join together, ultimately forming one large blister.

Contagiousness

Both herpes simplex viruses, HSV-1 and HSV-2, are contagious and may be passed from person to person by contact with herpes sores or blisters. HSV-1 may be passed in the saliva of persons with cold sores.

Examinations or Tests for HSV-1

Diagnosis of cold sores is determined by medical examination. In many instances, people with cold sores have a history of similar episodes in the past. Furthermore, there is then usually no need for laboratory testing except for people with weakened immune systems, for whom the risk of spreading is greatly increased. Special tests may be performed on samples of fluid taken from the sores if the diagnosis is unclear. These are all medical determinations made by a client's physician.

What Causes a Recurrence?

Herpes infections have different patterns in different people. Any one or combination of the following factors may activate an outbreak: skin irritation (such as sunburn), friction, surgery, fatigue, illness, stress, diet, or menstruation. There has been much written on recurring outbreaks affected by consumption of certain foods, beverages, vitamins, and medications.

Since the recurrence pattern of herpes is varied (different people have different experience patterns), those who suffer from recurring outbreaks normally take precautions to keep the virus in remission. They know, based on their specific and unique body reactions to recurrence triggers, what precautions they must take to avoid an outbreak. For some it may be keeping stress under control, for others it may be avoiding exposure to strong sunlight, and for others still, making sure they do not get over fatigued or eat too much of a specific food group. There is no one set of rules that fits all.

Herpes and Permanent Cosmetics

Why would such an unpredictable, client-specific, medical condition such as cold sores/fever blisters cause fear in the hearts of permanent cosmetic technicians? A good reason it is an embarrassment for our clients and can be quite painful. It is also negative advertisement for our services. In regard to procedure specifics, with a significant herpes outbreak, the color can sometimes heal into areas beyond the natural lip vermilion. If a client who is excited about having had their lips tattooed and later they report the outbreak of unsightly sores on the mouth, the first reaction has got to include wondering what all their friends, family, and co-workers (all potentially referral clients) are thinking about the permanent cosmetic lip service.

Another reason is that people have actually filed legal challenges against technicians over this uncontrollable condition. There are precautions, however, as professionals, we can take to ensure that each client in our care has been advised of the possibility of an outbreak and that they have taken prescribed precautions before we go forward with a lip procedure if they have a history of HVS-1.

Full Disclosure Consent Forms

Each permanent cosmetic professional should address the possibility of a cold sore (or fever blister) outbreak (HSV-1) if a client is having a lip procedure performed. A client's signature or initials acknowledging this possibility on an informed consent form is a technician's best front line defense if this should unfortunately occur. Some localities may have laws that govern offering permanent cosmetic services to people who have a history of herpes. Know the tattoo laws in your geographical area where you offer permanent cosmetic services.

Antiviral Medication Requirement

In conjunction with full disclosure and the client's acknowledgment in writing that an outbreak is possible when having a lip procedure performed, it is industry standard, and also may be required by your insurance carrier, to ask lip clients who have a history of HSV-1 to obtain an antiviral medication in preparation for a lip procedure. Technicians should review their insurance policy or contact their agent to be well-informed on their coverage and any exclusions that may apply.

There are many different antiviral medications and products, prescription strength and homeopathic available. In the prescription form, some according to reports Acyclovir (generic for Zovirax), Famciclovir (generic for Famvir), and Valacyclovir (generic for Valtrex) are used to treat the majority of HSV-1 cases.

In the homeopathic arena, L-lysine seems to lead the list of hundreds of products marketed to the public, each touting their formulations to either prevent or rapidly heal herpes outbreaks. It is important to recognize that L-lysine and other related homeopathic products are reported to provide little if any protection for clients from HSV-1 outbreaks resulting from permanent cosmetic lip procedures. Technicians should not recommend any products even though these products may be available over-the-counter. This is not in the scope of our work. Physicians prescribe or recommend medical products to their patients for specific conditions.

If a prospective lip procedure client has a history of HSV-1, she or he should be advised consult with a physician to obtain a prescription for an antiviral medication. The medical community is normally cooperative and will provide an antiviral medication and if so, sufficient quantities to support two lip procedures and healing sessions are advisable.

If the physician declines and will not or cannot (based on preventative prescription policies) provide proper medication for those clients who have a history of HSV-1, it is advisable to turn down the work. Or, whether the prospective client has a history of HSV-1 or not, if the client expresses concern about the possibility of an outbreak, although not recalling having had an outbreak in the past, this should be a discussion the client has with a physician before going forward with a lip procedure. For additional information on this subject go to www.spcp.org and obtain the Society of Permanent Cosmetic Professionals (SPCP) Medical Issues Book to read more on this subject.

What Happens if My Client Experiences an Outbreak?

If a call comes in to report an outbreak on a newly conducted lip procedure, many technicians mentally think back to the consultation and either find they went forward with a risky procedure by not requiring the client to consult with their physician and request a prescription strength antiviral medication, or recognize they have done all they could do professionally to prevent this occurrence.

Informed consent form(s) are signed with full disclosure of the inherent risks, the client contacted their physician and obtained an antiviral medication, and the medication, according to the client, was taken as directed. So what now? Now the client has an unsightly painful blister or series of blisters to contend with, which may very well ultimately affect how the lip procedure appears when the lip procedure and the cold sores have healed.

Do not direct a client to the drug store to obtain over-the-counter (OTC) medication for the cold sore. If asked what to do by a client, the best and actually only option (unless you are a physician) is to direct them to pursue medical guidance.

A physician may indeed advise the client to use an OTC product, (at least one popular medication for cold sores that was previously a prescription has been released for OTC use). Or, the physician may call in a prescription to see the client through the healing period of the cold sore(s).

HSV-1 is a medical condition and no matter how much a technician may feel they know on the subject, medical conditions are the business of medical professionals. The physician may also be asked how much time should be given before the touch up is performed (generally it is best to double the time period) and also asked to prescribe an antiviral medication for the follow-up appointment(s).

In summary, it is part of our jobs as permanent cosmetic professionals to know about potential adverse consequences of our services. Knowing about HSV types 1 and 2 is part of the general knowledge technicians are expected to have acquired during training.

Knowledge enables us to advise our client with accurate information within the scope of our work.

References

1. Kate Ciampi Shergod RN, CPCP assisted with the compilation of information contained in this portion of the textbook.

Section 23

Medical Conditions and Permanent Cosmetics

Learning Objectives

Introduction

A client's medical condition(s) can bring an abrupt halt to scheduling a procedure that can be conducted safely. This is an area where nonmedical technicians must be knowledgeable, but should also tread lightly.

Whereby it is important to the client's health status for a technician to be able to identify a contraindicative condition (to the tattooing process), only a very small percentage of technicians are physicians who can legally diagnose. The goal is recognizing serious medical conditions that would prevent normal healing or put the client's health in jeopardy and acting in a responsible manner in the best interests of clients.

Objective

At the completion of this section, the technician will be well educated on commonly documented client medical conditions, what this means in regard to the tattooing process, and when further physician counsel is advisable for the client. This subject also requires technicians to thoroughly know their local and state level regulations as they relate to medical subjects and tattooing.

Client medical conditions play a role in the permanent cosmetics process.[1] The majority of permanent cosmetic technicians do not have medical credentials, so it is important for everyone performing an invasive procedure to be aware of those conditions that may be contraindicative to tattooing and identify when it is appropriate to make a referral to a physician before proceeding.

Primary concerns regarding some medical conditions and permanent cosmetics are allergy issues, conditions that affect the client's ability to heal, and medical conditions that may have the potential of worsening and resulting in a more serious condition from the tattooing process.

In order to prevent redundancy, when a client has been required to consult with a physician prior to proceeding with a permanent cosmetic service, the physician's written opinion on office stationery that was provided to the client should be included in the client's official client history files. If you are willing to take the word of the client who has made a phone call to their doctor and obtained a verbal opinion or direction, ensure this conversation between you and the client about the doctor's input is well documented on the client's procedure chart.

Below are medical conditions that frequently have the potential of affecting or being affected by cosmetic tattooing. This information is presented for educational purposes only since non-medical technician cannot diagnose.

Mitral Valve Prolapse (MVP)

What Is Mitral Valve Prolapse?

Also called: Barlow's syndrome, Floppy Valve Syndrome, and Mitral valve prolapse (MVP). Mitral valve prolapse occurs when one of the heart's valves doesn't work properly. MVP is one of the more common heart valve conditions. Most often, it's a lifelong condition, and a person is born with the propensity to develop problems with the valve as they get older. Many people with MVP have no symptoms or problems, need no treatment, and are able to lead normal, active lives.

MVP puts a person at risk for infective endocarditis, a kind of heart infection. To prevent it, doctors used to prescribe antibiotics before dental work or certain surgeries. By today's standards, this is more uncommon, but as a non-medical technician, it is appropriate to inquire about this condition on a client history form.

Symptoms of MVP Syndrome[2]

- Sensation of feeling the heartbeat (*palpitations*)
- Chest pain (not caused by *coronary artery disease* or a heart attack)
- Hard to breath after activity

- Fatigue
- Cough
- Shortness of breath when lying flat (orthopnea)

Permanent Cosmetics and MVP (also applies to clients with implants)

Since non-physician technicians cannot diagnose, even if they are to be made aware of these symptoms and recognize the possibility of a MVP heart condition, we depend on clients to know what their condition is, and provide the information on their client history form. This and other conditions are important to inquire about so that the client can seek proper medical advice and treatment (as deemed appropriate by their physician).

If clients pursuing permanent cosmetic services indicate they have MVP, or on their client history form, advice from their physician should be sought. This also applies to clients who have implants (prosthetics). In some instances, their physician may advise them they must take antibiotics prior to a tattoo procedure. By today's standards, this is more uncommon, but as a non-medical technician, it is appropriate to inquire.

Latex Allergy

Nitrile (non-latex) gloves are commonplace in the permanent cosmetic industry, however, a review and history of latex allergies is provided.

Allergy to latex was first recognized in the late 1970s. Since then, it has become a major health concern as an increasing number of people in the workplace are affected. Healthcare workers and other professionals who are exposed to latex gloves or medical products containing latex are especially at risk. It is estimated that 8 to 12 percent of health care workers are latex sensitive.

Latex refers to the natural rubber latex (NRL) manufactured from a milky fluid that is primarily obtained from the rubber tree (Hevea brasiliensis). Some synthetic rubber materials may be referred to as latex, but do not contain the natural rubber proteins responsible for latex allergy symptoms.[3]

Symptoms of Latex Allergy

Latex allergy can be mild or severe, with symptoms such as:
- Itchy, red, watery eyes
- Sneezing or runny nose
- Coughing
- Rash or hives
- Chest tightness and shortness of breath

Section 23 - Medical Conditions and Permanent Cosmetics

- Shock

"Some people who wear latex gloves get bumps, sores, cracks, or red, raised areas on their hands. These symptoms usually appear twelve to thirty-six hours after contact with latex. Changing to non-latex gloves and paying more attention to hand care can help relieve these symptoms. The obvious solution is to wear non-latex gloves (nitrile)."[4]

A latex-sensitive person can also have a life-threatening allergic reaction with no previous warning or symptoms."[4]

Figure 23-1 shows a photograph of a person during a permanent cosmetic procedure being performed by a technician wearing latex gloves. The client had no previous reaction to the use of latex gloves on her skin. During the eyeliner procedure (notice the hand pattern on the face where the technician rested her hand during the procedure), irritation on the face was observed and the technician changed to nitrile gloves.

Figure 23-1: Latex Allergy Reaction

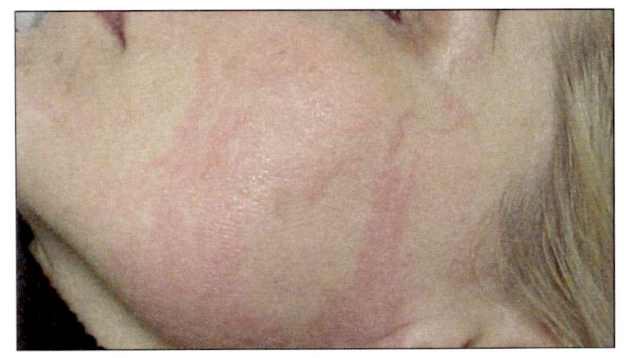

In this particular situation, the incident did not result in serious health consequences.

Permanent Cosmetics and Latex Allergies

The potential for serious reactions to latex exists and represents a prime reasoning for inquiring about this issue on the client history form. It is now common for medical, government, and beauty professionals to use nitrile gloves for their services.

Vitiligo

What Is Vitiligo?

Vitiligo (vit-ill-EYE-go) is a disorder in which white or depigmented patches of skin appear on different parts of the body. This happens because the cells that make pigment (color) in the skin are destroyed. These cells are called melanocytes (ma-LAN-o-sites). Vitiligo can also affect the mucous membranes (such as the tissue inside the mouth and nose) and the eye[5]. (See Figure 23-2)

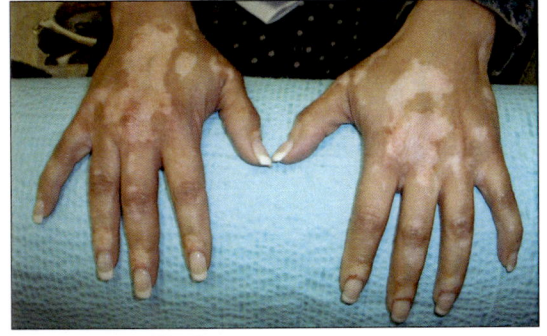

Figure 23-2: Vitiligo

Symptoms of Vitiligo

"White patches on the skin are the primary sign of vitiligo. These patches are more common in areas where the skin is exposed to the sun. The patches may be on the hands, feet, arms, face, and lips. Other common areas for white patches are:

- The armpits and groin (where the leg meets the body)
- Around the mouth
- Eyes
- Nostrils
- Navel
- Genitals
- Rectal areas

People with vitiligo often have hair that turns gray early. Those with dark skin may notice a loss of color inside their mouths.[5]

Vitiligo and Permanent Cosmetics (camouflage techniques)

Camouflage tattooing techniques (attempting to match surrounding skin color to improve the appearance of scar tissue or hypopigmented skin patches) are not recommended for people with vitiligo.

Although camouflage is a specialized service and not appropriate for fundamental training, it is not uncommon for a novice technician to look forward to the time when they can help people who have medical conditions such as vitiligo. One might be surprised, considering this may seem a prime opportunity to help those with few other options to improve the appearance of this condition, that camouflage for the vitiligo client has not been proven to be an optimal procedure by industry leaders in the permanent cosmetic industry.

Vitiligo is a medical condition, one that represents skin that is not healthy and is volatile. It has been suggested, however not proven through formal studies, that tattooing these white patches could even contribute to a worsening of this condition. Offering camouflage services to a person with vitiligo usually gives false hope. Although camouflage techniques may diminish the appearance of white, the healed color result is very unpredictable, typically does not provide an exact match to the surrounding skin, and the longevity is not predictable.

In many cases, there is a hyperpigmented (darker) ring around the areas of depigmentation, so even if a technician tattoos the depigmented areas, the darker rings will still be prominent and are impossible to adequately color correct.

Another reason for refraining from offering camouflage services to people who have vitiligo is that medical advancements may at some point offer a cure or relief from the condition and if the area has been tattooed, it is unknown how that may affect treatment possibilities.

It is the consensus of those individuals involved with vitiligo support organizations that the only appropriate area to try to correct with permanent cosmetics would be the lips.

Alopecia

What Is Alopecia?

"Alopecia areata is an autoimmune condition, in which the immune system (which is designed to protect the body from foreign invaders such as viruses and bacteria) mistakenly attacks the hair follicles, the tiny cup-shaped structures from which hairs grow. This can lead to hair loss on the scalp and elsewhere."[6]

"In most cases, hair falls out in small, round patches about the size of a quarter. In many cases, the disease does not extend beyond a few bare patches. In some people, hair loss is more extensive. Although uncommon, the disease can progress to cause total loss of hair on the head (referred to as alopecia totalis) or complete loss of hair on the head, face, and body (alopecia universalis)."[6]

Symptoms of Alopecia

The symptoms of alopecia are hair loss and balding. This may occur on the head, eyelash area, and on the entire body depending on the type of alopecia (see Figure 23-3 for an example).

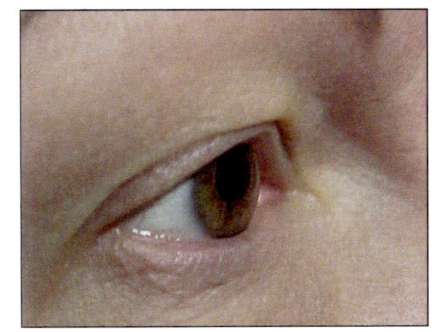

Figure 23-3: Alopecia

Permanent Cosmetics and Alopecia

Permanent cosmetics can be a blessing for those who suffer with long-term alopecia. Even though there is always the potential of the regrowth of hair, those who have the burden of dealing with this condition often look to permanent cosmetics as a solution to the loss of eyebrow hair and to provide definition to their eyes due to loss of eyelashes.

Permanent cosmetic technicians generally see an alopecia client at a time when the client has come to understand the condition fully and has somewhat adjusted to it. The daily routine of eyebrow and eyeliner application becomes too burdensome. The technician must take care to choose colors appropriately; there can be a tendency for the colors used to pull a bit cooler than usual. It is always best to take a modest approach in color and shape decisions and add to it appropriately at a future visit.

Diabetes

What Is Diabetes?

Diabetes means your blood glucose level (often called blood sugar) is too high. Your blood always has some glucose in it because your body needs glucose for energy to keep you going. But too much glucose in the blood isn't good for your health.

Glucose comes from the food you eat and is also made in your liver and muscles. Your blood carries the glucose to all the cells in your body. Insulin is a chemical (a hormone) made by the pancreas. The pancreas releases insulin into the blood. Insulin helps the glucose from food get into your cells. If your body doesn't make enough insulin, or if the insulin doesn't work the way it should, glucose can't get into your cells. It stays in your blood instead. Your blood glucose level then gets too high, causing pre-diabetes or diabetes.

People can get diabetes at any age. There are three main kinds.

Type 1 diabetes, formerly called juvenile diabetes or insulin-dependent diabetes, is usually first diagnosed in children, teenagers, or young adults. With this form of diabetes, the beta cells of the pancreas no longer make insulin because the body's immune system has attacked and destroyed them. Treatment for type 1 diabetes includes taking insulin, making wise food choices, being physically active, taking aspirin daily (for some), and controlling blood pressure and cholesterol.[7]

Type 2 diabetes, formerly called adult-onset diabetes, is the most common form of diabetes. People can develop type 2 diabetes at any age—even during childhood. This form of diabetes usually begins with insulin resistance, a condition in which fat, muscle, and liver cells do not use insulin properly. At first, the pancreas keeps up with the added demand by producing more insulin. In time, however, it loses the ability to secrete enough insulin in response to meals.[7]

Being overweight and inactive increases the chances of developing type 2 diabetes. Treatment includes using diabetes medicines, making wise food choices, being physically active.[7]

Some women develop **gestational diabetes** during the late stages of pregnancy. Although this form of diabetes usually goes away after the baby is born, a woman who has had it is more likely to develop type 2 diabetes later in life. Gestational diabetes is caused by the hormones of pregnancy or a shortage of insulin.[7]

Symptoms of Diabetes

The signs and symptoms of diabetes are:[7]
- Thirst
- Frequent urination
- Feeling very hungry or tired
- Losing weight without trying
- Having sores that heal slowly
- Dry, itchy skin;
- Tingling or loss of feeling in feet
- Having blurry vision

Diabetes and Permanent Cosmetics

Because it is the consensus that those with diabetes may have difficulty healing, it is important for clients to consult with their doctor to see if they are good candidates for permanent cosmetic procedures. In our industry, we are generally dealing with the face, an area that is usually not compromised by poor circulation, which could occur with locations such as the feet and ankles that would be affected more by traditional tattooing.

Hypertension

What Is Hypertension?

Hypertension is the medical term for high blood pressure. Blood pressure readings are measured in millimeters of mercury (mmHg) and usually given as two numbers. For example, 140 over 90 (written as 140/90).

- The top number is the systolic pressure, the pressure created when your heart beats, creating force against the arterial walls.
- The bottom number is the diastolic pressure, the pressure inside blood vessels when the heart is at rest.
- Blood pressure measurements are the result of the force of the blood produced by the heart and the size and condition of the arteries.

Many factors can affect blood pressure, including how much water and salt there is in the body, the condition of the kidneys, nervous system, or blood vessels, and the levels of different body hormones.

High blood pressure can have a negative effect on one's being. You have a higher risk of high blood pressure if there is a family history of the disease. High blood pressure is more common in African Americans than Caucasians. Most of the time, no cause is identified. This is called essential hypertension. High blood pressure that results from a specific condition, habit, or medication is called secondary hypertension."[8] (see Figure 23-4)

Blood Pressure Chart

BLOOD PRESSURE CATEGORY	SYSTOLIC mm Hg (upper number)		DIASTOLIC mm Hg (lower number)
NORMAL	LESS THAN 120	and	LESS THAN 80
ELEVATED	120 – 129	and	LESS THAN 80
HIGH BLOOD PRESSURE (HYPERTENSION) STAGE 1	130 – 139	or	80 – 89
HIGH BLOOD PRESSURE (HYPERTENSION) STAGE 2	140 OR HIGHER	or	90 OR HIGHER
HYPERTENSIVE CRISIS (consult your doctor immediately)	HIGHER THAN 180	and/or	HIGHER THAN 120

Figure 23-4: Blood Pressure Range as recommended by the American Heart Association[9]
Note: This chart is for information purposes only. Decisions regarding medical treatment should coordinated with your physician.

Symptoms of Hypertension

"Most of the time, there are no symptoms. Symptoms that may occur include, but are not limited to:[8]

- Confusion
- Chest pain
- Ear noise or buzzing
- Irregular heartbeat
- Nosebleeds
- Tiredness
- Vision changes

Hypertension and Permanent Cosmetics

Clients who indicate they have high blood pressure may be taking medications that will result in thinner blood. Ideally, bleeding is kept to a minimum during a procedure. If there is blood present, this acts to dilute the pigment the technician is attempting to tattoo pigment into the dermal layer of the skin.

Also during healing, those who bleed more than others have the potential of heavy scab formation as a normal body response to bleeding. Because of the force exerted on even the tiniest vessels, those whose hypertension is not controlled well may also bleed more during the permanent cosmetics procedure.

Trichotillomania (TTM)

What is Trichotillomania?

Trichotillomania is hair loss caused by compulsive pulling and/or twisting of the hair until it breaks off. The hair may be lost in round patches or diffusely across the scalp. The effect is an uneven appearance. Other hairy areas may be plucked, such as the eyebrows, eyelashes, or body hair.[10]

Symptoms of Trichotillomania

The symptoms of trichotillomania include:
- "Constant tugging, pulling, or twisting of hair
- Increasing sense of tension is present before the hair pulling
- Sense of relief, pleasure, or gratification is reported after the hair pulling
- Hair pulling leads to an uneven appearance.
- Bare patches or diffuse (all across) loss of hair
- Hair regrowth in the bare spots feels like stubble.
- Some individuals may develop a bowel obstruction if they eat the hair they pull out.
- Other self-injury behaviors may be present.
- People suffering from this disorder often deny pulling out their hair."[10]

Trichotillomania and Permanent Cosmetics

It is important the technician is aware of this condition before offering permanent cosmetic eyebrow or eyeliner (if the eyelashes are affected) procedures to clients with trichotillomania. If a technician chooses to do so, trichotillomania may be listed on the client history form although it is not a well-known medical condition and likely if it is on the form, every client who fills out the form will ask what it means.

Regardless, if there is suspicion of this condition, a discussion should ensue. Quite possibly clients may not even realize there is a name for it. Some clients may present technicians with not only the absence of eyebrow hair, but also pronounced irritation in or near the area to be tattooed.

Clients with this condition have acknowledged using various implements to remove even the tiniest tip of hair showing on the surface of the skin. Usually a visual inspection of the area that yields suspicion will prompt technicians who are well informed to ask the right questions to determine if a client has this condition.

Some technicians find it helpful to the client to tattoo the brow area, for instance, and then the client may elect for electrolysis for the removal of any hairs considered stray or outside the area defined by the eyebrow application. With time, because the area is tattooed and the hairs blend in with that color, some clients with trichotillomania may find the hair-pulling episodes subside.

For technicians who choose to proceed with an eyebrow or eyeliner procedure on a client who has trichotillomania, it is imperative that the skin be healed and intact before conducting the procedure.

Glaucoma

What Is Glaucoma?

"Glaucoma is a group of diseases that can damage the eye's optic nerve and result in vision loss and blindness."[11] Glaucoma occurs when the normal fluid pressure inside the eyes slowly rises. "However, with early detection and treatment, you can often protect your eyes against serious vision loss."[11]

Symptoms of Glaucoma

"At first, there are no symptoms. Vision stays normal, and there is no pain. However, as the disease progresses, a person with glaucoma may notice their peripheral (side) vision gradually failing. That is, objects in front may still be seen clearly, but objects to the side may be missed.

As glaucoma remains untreated, people may miss objects to the side and out of the corner of their eye. Without treatment, people with glaucoma will slowly lose their peripheral vision. They seem to be looking through a tunnel. Over time, straight-ahead vision may decrease until no vision remains. Glaucoma can develop in one or both eyes."[11]

Glaucoma and Permanent Cosmetics

This subject bears dialogue for and against the practice of offering eyeliner services to a client that has glaucoma. Other procedures such as eyebrows and lip color services are normally not a matter of concern for the client with glaucoma.

On one hand, it seems the perfect solution for a person that suffers from failing eyesight due to glaucoma to have their eyeliner or eyelash enhancement applied permanently. The person with this disease may not see well (depending on the progression of the condition). If the glaucoma is under control with surgery and/or medication, the client may be able to obtain a release from their ophthalmologist to have the permanent cosmetic procedure performed.

On the other hand, there are potential liability risks that must be considered. Notwithstanding legal challenges that may arise that may not necessarily supported by fact, the person with glaucoma may actually feel their eyesight is not as good as it was before the eyeliner service.

Under the stress of concern or fear, people can imagine all sorts of conditions that may not be real. An eye doctor may conduct examination and testing to determine if the permanent cosmetic procedure could have resulted in a change in visibility. Still, the client's input during these tests may have substantial merit in testimony during a legal challenge.

The choice belongs to each technician. The eyes are vital organs. Loss of vision or the suggestion that tattooing has worsened a vision related medical condition may carry risks of liability.

As a minimum, technicians are recommended to require the client with glaucoma to consult with their ophthalmologist and ask for the doctor's written opinion (on medical office stationery) as to whether the client is a good candidate for permanent cosmetic eyeliner. This does not necessarily prevent a technician from being named in a legal challenge, but it does document that the technician took responsible actions to ensure the client's eye doctor considered the procedure safe.

Skin Cancer

What Is Skin Cancer?

"There are several types of skin cancer. Skin cancer that forms in melanocytes (skin cells that make pigment) is called *melanoma*. Skin cancer that forms in basal cells (small, round cells in the base of the outer layer of skin) is called *basal cell carcinoma*. Skin cancer that forms in squamous cells (flat cells that form the surface of the skin) is called *squamous cell carcinoma*. Skin cancer that forms in neuroendocrine cells (cells that release hormones in response to signals from the nervous system) is called *neuroendocrine carcinoma* of the skin. Many skin cancers form in older people on parts of the body exposed to the sun or in people who have weakened immune systems."[12]

Symptoms:

"Most basal cell and squamous cell skin cancers can be cured if found and treated early.

A change on the skin is the most common sign of skin cancer. This may be a new growth, a sore that doesn't heal, or a change in an old growth. Not all skin cancers look the same. Skin changes to watch for (see Figure 23-5 to Figure 23-9).

Sometimes skin cancer is painful, but usually it is not."[12]

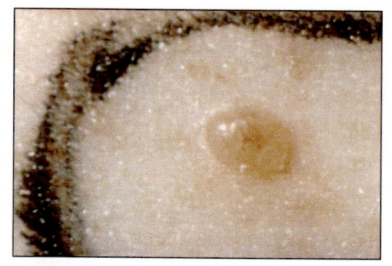

Figure 23-5: Small, smooth, shiny, pale, or waxy lump

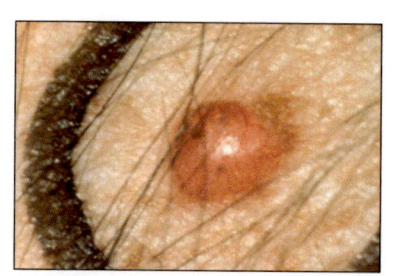

Figure 23-6: Firm, red lump

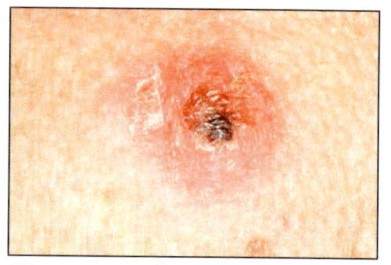

Figure 23-7: Sore or lump that bleeds or develops a crust or a scab

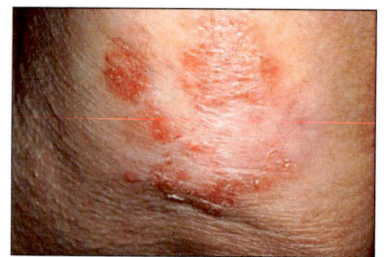

Figure 23-8: Flat red spot that is rough. dry, or scaly and may become itchy or tender.

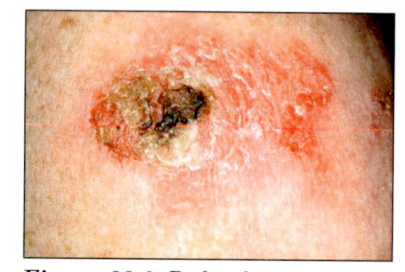

Figure 23-9: Red or brown patch that is rough and scaly

Skin Cancer and Permanent Cosmetics

Skin in the procedure area should be checked during the consultation, and on the day of the procedure, to ensure that the skin appears healthy. If you observe any unhealthy appearance, the procedure should be postponed until the client consults with her or his physician, a diagnosis made, treatment (if any) completed, and the physician does not disapprove of the tattooing process on the affected skin.

Other Conditions

Psoriasis, Dermatitis, Rashes, and Abnormal Skin Textures

All of these skin conditions represent unhealthy skin and if they preside in the area of the requested procedure, should be diagnosed and treated by a medical professional prior to proceeding. Since the majority of permanent cosmetic technicians are not physicians, even if a technician recognizes a particular condition, it is unlawful for her or him to diagnose it. The client should be advised to consult with their physician and the procedure postponed until the condition has been properly diagnosed, treated, and it no longer poses a contraindication. See Figure 23-10 for an example of dermatitis.

Figure 23-10: A rash diagnosed by a physician as dermatitis

Pregnant or Nursing

If a woman is pregnant or nursing, permanent cosmetic procedures should be postponed until after the baby has been delivered and is no longer nursing. Discussions supporting the postponement of services include the following issues:

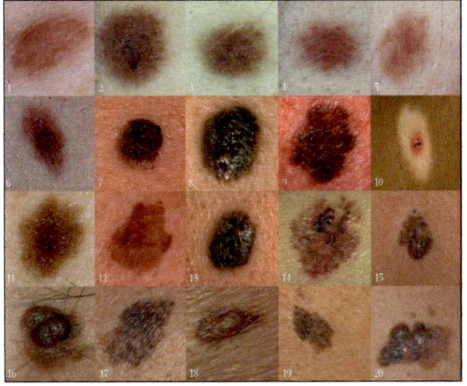

Figure 23-11: A few examples of different types of skin abnormalities.[13]

- If the baby delivers early or is born with abnormalities, the parents will surely look to any events surrounding the actions of the mother that may have contributing factors.
- The mother's immune system is low during pregnancy and nursing, and the risk of infection is higher.
- Anesthetics and other products used during the procedure are absorbed into the skin and can pass to the child.

Moles, Skin Lesions, and Abnormalities

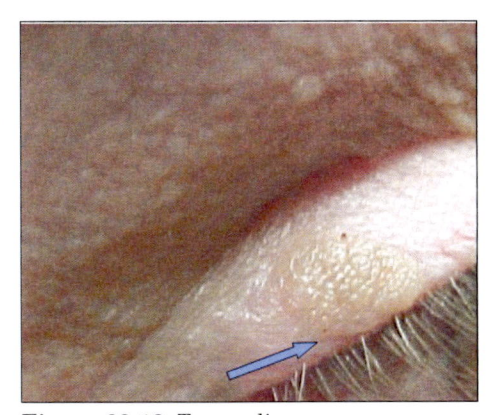

Figure 23-12: Top eyeliner was not conducted due to the abnormal condition of the eyelid skin. The client was advised to see her physician.

A permanent cosmetic technician should not tattoo over moles, medically undiagnosed skin lesions (some may be diagnosed as harmless), or any skin abnormality (see Figure 23-11).

Do not tattoo over skin that has unhealthy characteristics (see Figure 23-12, page 333). Refer clients to their physician for a solution or advice prior to proceeding.

Summary

This section of the textbook addresses some of the more frequently presented medical conditions and how those conditions relate to offering permanent cosmetic services. There are many medical conditions that may cause a person not to be considered a good candidate for one or more services. When in doubt, require the client to consult with their physician before proceeding.

References

1. Kate Ciampi Shergold RN, CPCP assisted with the compilation of information contained in this portion of the textbook.

2. U.S. National Library of Medicine - Medline Plus (2016). *Mitral valve prolapse: MedlinePlus Medical Encyclopedia*. Retrieved from http://www.nlm.nih.gov/medlineplus/ency/article/000180.htm.

3. U.S. Department of Labor - Occupational Safety and Heath Administration [OSHA] (2008). *Safety and Health Topics | Latex Allergy | Occupational Safety and Health Administration*. Retrived from http://www.osha.gov/SLTC/latexallergy/index.html

4. American Academy of Family Physicians - familydoctor.org (2016). *Latex Allergy - familydoctor.org*. Retrieved from https://familydoctor.org/condition/latex-allergy/

5. U.S. Department of Health and Human Services - National Institute of Arthritis and Musculoskeletal and Skin Diseases (2016). *Vitiligo | NIAMS*. Retrieved from https://www.niams.nih.gov/health-topics/vitiligo

6. U.S. Department of Health and Human Services - National Institute of Arthritis and Musculoskeletal and Skin Diseases (2016). *Alopecia Areata | NIAMS*. Retrieved from https://www.niams.nih.gov/health-topics/alopecia-areata

7. U.S. Department of Health and Human Services - National Institute of Diabetes and Digestive and Kidney Diseases (2016). *What is Diabetes? | NIDDK*. Retrieved from https://www.niddk.nih.gov/health-information/diabetes/overview/what-is-diabetes

8. U.S. National Library of Medicine - Medline Plus (2015). *High blood pressure: MedlinePlus Medical Encyclopedia* Retrieved from https://medlineplus.gov/ency/article/000468.htm

9. American Heart Association (2018). *The Facts About High Blood Pressure*. Retrieved from http://www.heart.org/HEARTORG/Conditions/HighBloodPressure/GettheFactsAboutHighBloodPressure/The-Facts-About-High-Blood-Pressure_UCM_002050_Article.jsp

10. U.S. National Library of Medicine - Medline Plus (2016). *Trichotillomania: MedlinePlus Medical Encyclopedia*. Retrieved from https://medlineplus.gov/ency/article/001517.htm

11. U.S. Department of Health and Human Services - National Eye Institute (NEI) (2015). *Facts About Glaucoma | National Eye Institute*. Retrieved from https://www.nei.nih.gov/health/glaucoma/glaucoma_facts

12. U.S. National Institutes of Health - National Cancer Institute (2008). *What You Need To Know About Skin Cancer - National Cancer Institute* Retrieved from http://www.cancer.gov/cancertopics/wyntk/skin/page6 [old link].

13. Photo example of moles is an excerpt from *Segmentation of Skin Cancer Images* by L. Xu, M. Jackowski, A. Goshtasby, C. Yu, D. Roseman, S. Bines, A. Dhawan, A. Huntley. Photo used with permission.

Section 24

MRI and Permanent Cosmetics

Learning Objectives

Introduction

Magnetic Resonance Imaging (MRI) is a commonly prescribed test for a myriad of suspected or confirmed medical conditions. Because there is the possibility of colorant (pigment) interaction with the strong magnetic force of MRI equipment, it is important to understand this subject well.

Objective

At the completion of this section, the technician will have a general understanding of the technical properties of MRI, how permanent cosmetics may interfere with accurate reading of test results, and that there is a potential of causing discomfort during testing.

Section 24 - MRI and Permanent Cosmetics

Magnetic Resonance Imaging (MRI) is the process used for creating pictures or images of the inside of our bodies in the form of very thin slices.*1* The images created are used to diagnose more obscure medical maladies such as multiple sclerosis, infection of the brain or spine, tendonitis, and even the early stages of stroke, to mention just a few.

MRI is one of the advanced tools in diagnostic imaging. It produces detailed images of the human body without the use of X-rays. These images are created using a powerful magnet, radio waves, and a computer system to process data. Procedures using MRI are painless and don't involve ionizing radiation. The contrast used in MRI is not radioactive and does not contain iodine.

Due to the magnetic nature of the imaging process, a detailed medical history is taken from every patient prior to being scanned. Each patient is required to complete a safety screening form in order to verify the presence or absence of any potentially damaging items such as clips, sutures, tattoos, stents, or other medical devices. Many of these items may not be deemed as problematic, but the MRI technologist must evaluate them.

One MRI scanner machine design is a short cylinder that's open at both ends (Figure 24-1). A person lies on a motorized bed that's moved inside the scanner. The patient enters the scanner either head first or feet first, depending on the part of the body being scanned.

There are other MRI equipment designs that allow the patient to sit or stand in different positions. Technology is always changing. In a more simplistic presentation: An MRI machine functions by creating a powerful magnetic field with radio frequency pulses, which used together send signals from the MRI machine to our body and then back to a computer, which then converts mathematical data into an image.

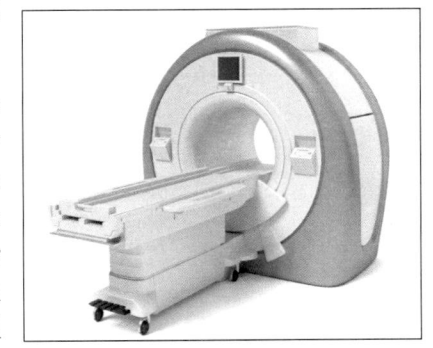

Figure 24-1: MRI Machine

It is the powerful magnetic force that has created concern, not only to those who are tattooed, but also to anyone with metal objects in his or her bodies such as implants (dental or otherwise), pacemakers, or even metal fragments. Even small metal objects such as paper clips or keys can become projectile weapons if left in an MRI room during a scan.

We now have an abundance of information provided to our industry about the composition of inorganic and organic colorants (pigments). Notwithstanding that available information, MRI and tattoos continue to provide somewhat inconsistent results.

A professional source of information is www.MRIsafety.com where Dr. Frank Shellock Ph.D., FACR, FISMRM, FACC, speaks about how decorative tattoos have presented more of a problem during MRI than permanent cosmetics. He also speaks about how permanent cosmetics and tattoos may cause artifacts and minor, short-term coetaneous reactions. The complete article can be read at the following link (http://www.mrisafety.com/SafetyInfov.asp?SafetyInfoID=228):

In the United States, the Food and Drug Administration (FDA) has provided the following information in regard to MRI and tattoos:

> *MRI complications. There have been reports of people with tattoos or permanent makeup who experienced swelling or burning in the affected areas when they underwent magnetic resonance imaging (MRI).*
>
> *This seems to occur only rarely and apparently without lasting effects. There have also been reports of tattoo pigments interfering with the quality of the MRI image. This seems to occur mainly when a person with permanent eyeliner undergoes MRI of the eyes. However, the risks of avoiding an MRI when your doctor has recommended one are likely to be much greater than the risks of complications from an interaction between the MRI and tattoo or permanent makeup. Instead of avoiding an MRI, individuals who have tattoos or permanent makeup should inform the radiologist or technician.*[2]

There may be government agencies in other geographical areas of the world that provide information on websites or in publications.

It is always advisable to stay abreast of technology that may have a bearing on our permanent cosmetic procedures, however, MRI technology is subject to technical changes and protocols, and the medical community is the best source at any given point in time to give up-to-date information.

Giving medical advice or opinions is not in our scope of work. Technicians may, however, inform clients in general about permanent cosmetics and MRI on an Informed Consent document, indicating that there is a possibility of MRI artifacts or physical sensations. Below is an example that is not intended to be acceptable or entirely inclusive of direction that may be received from an insurance or legal source. Always consult with your insurance and legal representatives about language on consent forms.

> *I understand that tattoos may cause Magnetic Resonance Imaging (MRI) artifacts and that there may be a warming, tingling, or a painful sensation in the permanent cosmetic procedural area during an MRI. I accept these risks and understand that I should consult with my physician regarding any associated risks and/or advise my physician that I have permanent cosmetics (a tattoo) in the event an MRI procedure is prescribed.*

Each technician who chooses to provide cautionary MRI information should contact their insurance or legal representative for wording that is appropriate. Our consent forms, which are signed by each client, provide confirmation that important information has been made available, has been reviewed by the client, and is acceptable.

Section 24 - MRI and Permanent Cosmetics

Although no scientific studies have been conducted, within the permanent cosmetic community it has been discussed that a procedure should be fully healed before an MRI. If a client has an MRI scheduled soon after the permanent cosmetics appointment, it's recommended the permanent cosmetic procedure(s) be postponed to another date. This alone, however, is no guarantee the client would not experience complications during MRI. The MRI patient and their medical team should discuss all options and any associated risks.

References

1. Reprinted with permission from Yale-New Haven Hospital, 1/23/08, 6/18/2017 Site is no longer active. http://www.ynhh.org/patients/diagnostic radiology/mri.html

2. https://www.fda.gov/cosmetics/productsingredients/products/ucm108530.htm 11/26/2016

Section 25

Psychology and Permanent Cosmetics

Learning Objectives

Introduction

Permanent cosmetic technicians are routinely in close contact with clients of different age groups, backgrounds, and personalities. Successful businesses are built on not only the technician's technical skills but also how well they manage prospective and existing clientele.

There are many elements of permanent cosmetic services that we must aspire to perfect in order to meet the demands of our trade. One of those elements is the ability to develop a good rapport with the varied personalities we encounter and also to recognize behavioral patterns that may be contraindicative to a long-lasting healthy relationship.

Objective

Study of this section will give insight to personalities from two perspectives, Marjorie Grimm and her experiences with clients since 1992, and Greg Shergold, who has a Masters in Clinical Psychology and is also Licensed Professional Counselor.

The objective is to provide technicians the ability to recognize behavioral traits of many different personality types, including those who may be more challenging to manage.

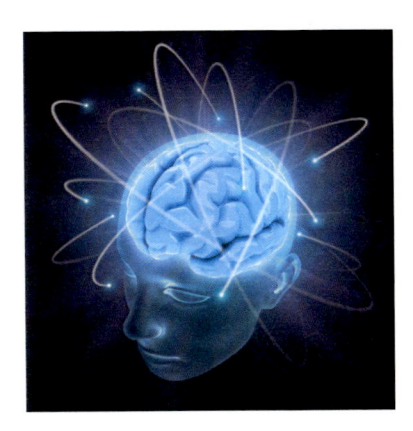

Consumer Behavior

According to Peter Noel Murray, PH.D, author of *Inside the Consumer Mind*, "for almost all consumer behavior, rational decision-making is the exception rather than the rule. Our purchase decisions are far more likely to be the result of unconscious motivations and processes. The rational process of making objective purchase decisions is undermined by social, cognitive, emotional and other forces that influence behavior".

The reason why prospective clients may choose one technician over another in the same general vicinity may be influenced by how the technician appears on their website, client testimonials posted, and reviews given on social media; etc. Credentials and technical skills (usually shown as examples of a technician's work on websites) are considered the most important, but there are often other factors in play that sways the final decision.

While it is common for technicians to provide before and after pictures as examples of their permanent cosmetic work, or written testimonials reflecting satisfied clients, often technicians do not specifically target an emotional force to influence behavior. Effective marketing includes the ability to include information presented in a manner that appeals to others on a *non-rational basis*.

Technology now provides our industry with the ability to reach out to potential clients in more personal visual formats. In addition to before and after examples of procedures and written testimonials, consider video testimonials and ads that provide the ability to include sentiment, passion, and interaction with the viewer; connect with the emotional element of the purchase decision making. Videos provide the personal *I'm talking to you and only you* aspect of communication that is sometimes lost with text testimonials or photographs.

Some of the reasons people look to permanent cosmetics are explored below:

The *Need* for Restoration or Considerable Change
- In today's society, we have a *fix it* solution for just about everything.
- The *anticipation* of considerable change is often the driving force behind

beauty services.

The *Desire* for Convenience

- We are a society of convenience and people are accustomed to a solution to whatever they consider tiresome or difficult.

Restoration

Restoration is often challenging. The client looks to the permanent cosmetic technician to restore what once was. Clients pursuing permanent cosmetics for restorative purposes have often been through a life-changing event that resulted in emotional or physical trauma, or both.

Restoration (tattooing a scar and/or the breast areola complex as examples) procedures are very rewarding services but not without their challenges. The client's expectations must be managed to develop a clear understanding of the anticipated outcome. Fortunately, in most instances, we can make things much better; but turning back the hands of time to a point where reversing the appearance of an incident that ultimately left its mark on the body, as if it never happened, is not within our scope of work.

Technicians must be aware of their own feelings and reactions. Take care not to project personal feelings and reactions onto the client. Acknowledge the condition or event, but don't make it the focus. Consider a conversation along the lines of, *"Is there anything I should be aware of when working in this area so this will be a good experience for you"*? By addressing the client in this manner, their trauma is acknowledged, but they are not forced to share or re-experience it.

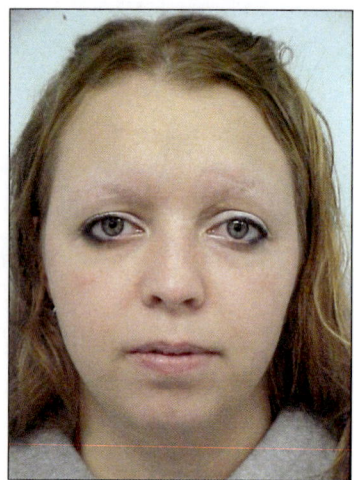

Figure 25-1: Forehead skin trauma from an animal attack

Considerable Change

Request for considerable change may stem from more mature people who are now involved with social events or dating services who have experienced a recent life changing event; for instance the death of a loved one or a change in living accommodations.

Partaking in new social circles or on social dating network sites can be intimidating. Whether or not a client voices it or not, they want their technician to make them look younger. People are subject to certain predetermined biological and genetic dispositions that permanent cosmetics can certainly improve and enhance, but not completely change. Age and appearance are important elements in many social circles. In this instance, the client is requesting, not resisting, significant change.

Often this means turning back many years to appear younger to fit an acceptable social profile. Photographs are often provided by the client as an example of how they want to look after their permanent cosmetic service(s); sometimes those photos are not even of the person themselves, but of a movie star or a person from a magazine.

It is not unusual for photographs to be unrealistic based on the client's age or other physical characteristics shown in the photograph. Clients don't seem to realize that their facial characteristics have changed with the aging process. Or, that the movie star or model in the photo they are showing as an example of what they want bears no resemblance to them in any way.

Society highly values a youthful appearance and can be much harder on people who are more mature. This is described as *Ageism* (discrimination/oppression based on age or perceived age). This feeds social expectations, therefore (in the client's mind) *I don't want to get or look older*. This can lead to clients seeking the younger version of themselves or the movie star or model example.

Convenience

Clients who tire of the process of putting on traditional makeup frequently pursue permanent cosmetics for convenience. These clients often express exactly what they want; they just want to be relieved of the chore of doing it for themselves. The term *natural* is often used as a verbal description of their expectations. The definition of natural is *present in or produced by nature.* (see Figure 25-2)

Given that our clients are seeking a change to their natural appearance, they create their own definition of the word natural as it relates to the permanent cosmetics they want. As a result, what is natural to one person will not represent natural to another. It's important to have a conversation to determine just what the client views as natural.

Figure 25-2: An example of natural as defined by nature

As an example, the author provides a true life example:

> My client was an 82 year-old woman who did not do a very good job at drawing on her eyebrows with a cosmetic pencil. I thought that a nice hair stroke brow technique would thrill her because she had said she wanted natural appearing eyebrows. I tattooed a subtle hair stroke brow; they were symmetric, nice color and shape. I had drawn on the eyebrows and received her approval, but we did not discuss technique.
>
> After the hair stroke eyebrow was tattooed, I handed her the mirror, fully expecting praise and was surprised when she said *"Well that doesn't look very natural, fill in those spaces"*. I had to laugh because in my mind they looked natural; in her mind, natural was a shaded brow. It's the technician's job to determine what the term natural means to each person they work with.

Often the term *natural* may be construed to mean something others may not notice as a change to their appearance (as they appear with traditional makeup). People who ask for *natural* are often relieved with less rather than more tattooing. Put the client in charge of any departure from what they may perceive as *natural*.

Once the *less is better* new appearance becomes familiar, they may be back for more.

The following are a few examples of the type of convenience clients we encounter. There are clients who like what they draw on with topical cosmetics, and do not want or need any artistic adjustments for the permanent cosmetic service (see Figure 25-3 & Figure 25-4).

- Using the client's design - Often the client's design can and should be used; it's *familiar*. Using the client's design work is not a sign of technician inability. The technician *always* gets credit for the total procedure regardless of who drew on the design template.
- If the design is acceptable to the technician, and the client likes it; there's nothing wrong with using it.

Technicians also encounter clients who don't like how they apply their eyebrow makeup and are open to change (see Figure 25-5 & Figure 25-6).

- Draw on an eyebrow design example; while leaving one of the eyebrows on as the client drew it. Let the client make the decision if they are open to the recommended changes.
- Technicians encounter clients who like what they have. They need artistic adjustments but are afraid of change.
- Depending on the mindset of the client, it may be productive to draw a design example for the client to leave with. Let the client decide if they are open to artistic change without pressure.

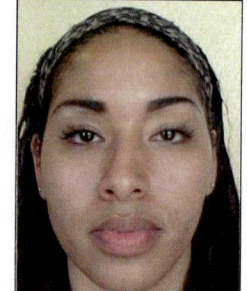

Figure 25-3: Client drawn eyebrows

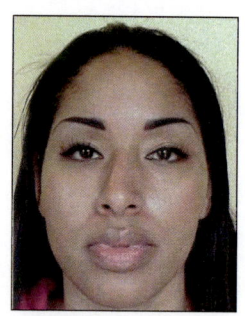

Figure 25-4: Tattooed eyebrows

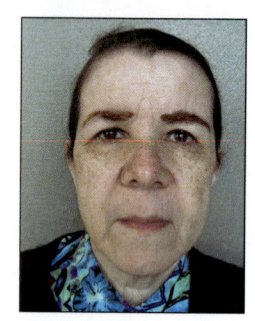

Figure 25-5: As the client drew on her brows

Figure 25-6: Tattooed eyebrows

Why People Sometimes Resist Change

Humans are pleasure and familiarity seeking creatures. We expend maximum effort to avoid pain and stress. Any sort of change is stressful; hence we have the basic innate drive to avoid it. Personality theorists believe that personality traits are more fixed and tend to vary little over the course of one's lifetime.

The *Big Five Personality Model* (or sometimes called the Five

Factor Model), breaks down the personality into five domains:

- Openness
- Conscientiousness
- Agreeableness
- Extroversion
- Neuroticism

Openness (being the relevent trait for this discussion) is the dichotomy of inventive/curious vs. consistent/cautious (polar opposite). There are people who will fall somewhere on the continuum between these two extremes.

People with the more consistent/cautious traits will likely be more resistant to change, while others may be more willing to try new and novel things. It's not that the *resistant to change* clients are trying to be difficult; they are emotionally wired to be consistent and cautious.

Change can cause people to feel that they've lost control over their territory. If change feels risky, people will often resist. People are often satisfied with the status quo rather than to consider or accept the unknown.

Without time to accept something new, change is often resisted. Change is meant to bring something different, but how different? Humans are creatures of habit. Change typically is about entering the realm of the unknown.

From an evolutionary perspective, the unknown usually would mean danger. In prehistoric times, known areas/people/animals that were familiar resulted in less danger. Danger in those times most likely would include loss of life, hence, there was a very adaptive and self-preservation tendency to avoid and fear what was unknown.

Even though we have evolved much since those days, the instinct tends to still exist within us. This can be used to explain why we seek pleasure and avoid pain/anxiety on an instinctual level.

The Eyebrow Procedure

Importantly, what is the client used to seeing? If working with a mature client, it only takes a moment to do the math to understand familiarity. Using the ages of forty to sixty; if a client has been applying a certain makeup design once a day for ten years, the brain has recorded that image 10,950 times.

If a person sees themselves thousands or even hundreds of times looking a particular way, it has likely in their mind become the way it is supposed to be. If a client's appearance is *familiar* to the degree of looking

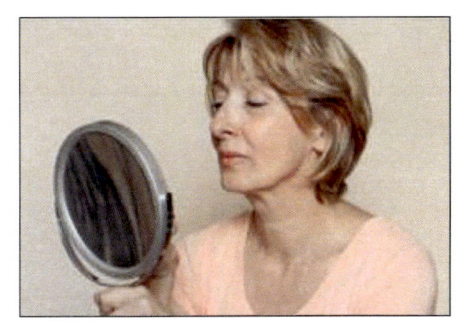

Figure 25-7: The Brain Records Repetitive Image

the same or similar for years, departing from familiar can be stressful.

This all adds up to the need to effectively deal with some clients who are familiar with their appearance and believe they look good (or at least acceptable), regardless of how others may feel or advise. The words *familiar* and *unfamiliar* are very important in the permanent cosmetic industry.

Depending on the mindset of the client, it may be productive to draw a design example for the client to take home. Let them decide if the change being proposed is acceptable without pressure. Why go through the process of preparing the client for the procedure unless it is for certain they can be pleased?

A younger client may have a mindset of how they want to appear, and it may be difficult to encourage them to accept change from a person they have just met. If a technician meets with considerable resistance to change, it's best to advise the prospective client they should seek their services with another technician, or reconsider having the procedure done altogether.Working with Anxiety

Anxiety may be triggered by stress. An outside force is a common source of anxiety; change is an outside force.

In the example of working with a person who has very little or no eyebrow hair and doesn't use cosmetics to supplement the brow hair they do have (if any), the client is not accustomed to seeing color in the eyebrow area. Even if they use an eyebrow pencil, it may be a very light color, or minimally applied. As a result, the intensity of the freshly tattooed eyebrow the first few days may cause anxiety. *Less is better*; more can be added at the follow-up appointment if needed.

The Familiarity of Design and Color

A technician who is working with a client who draws on their eyebrows with topical cosmetics will have more of a chance of pleasing the client if at least one of two things are similar (familiar) to what has been seen for years – the design and the color.

If both these elements are too *unfamiliar* to the client, this may pose an emotional problem until they become more accustomed to the changes.

Figure 25-8: The Anxiety of Change

The Eyeliner Procedure

Clients normally are reluctant (cautious) to allow technicians to tattoo around the eyes; eyes are a vital organ and our instinct is to protect them. If the client is not comfortable, don't attempt to push them past their comfort zone.

At the next appointment the client will have developed a sense of trust that they are not in harm's way and they will be more cooperative. There is comfort and confidence in knowing what to expect.

What style of liner has been requested? Consider developing an eyeliner menu. There are many benefits of showing different eyeliner designs in a menu format (several side-by-side photographs of healed eyeliner styles).

- By showing a menu of eyeliner designs the client gains confidence that the technician is truly an artist capable of many design accomplishments.
- Physiologically in the client's mind, the technician becomes an eyeliner expert.

The Lip Liner or Shaded Lip Liner Procedure

Evolutionary perspectives believe that humans tend to prefer facial features that are symmetrical. Within our context, it could be logically and non-scientifically concluded that lip procedures perhaps contribute to creating a more noticeable symmetrical face.

Lips, especially immediately after a procedure, are simply more noticeable, when compared to eyeliner/eyebrows procedures. It could also be, that lips are more sexual in nature (i.e., kissing) than eyebrow or eyeliners.

The healing process for lips can produce high anxiety and doubt. Clients may feel tempted to get rid of the evidence or to irritate the healing procedure area to see what's beneath the pigment's surface.

What to Expect

Most appearance altering business sites have a Consumer's Guide section that supports information for their services. This information is somewhat expected considering that many consumers do their research homework on Internet websites. Be prepared to advise the client of the changes to expect; preferably with photographs.

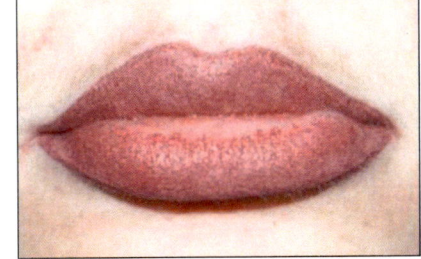

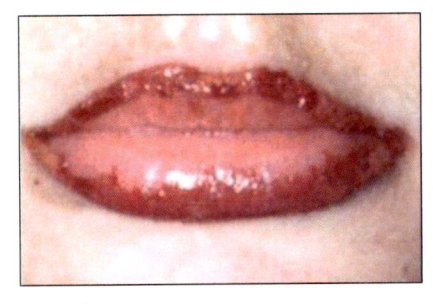

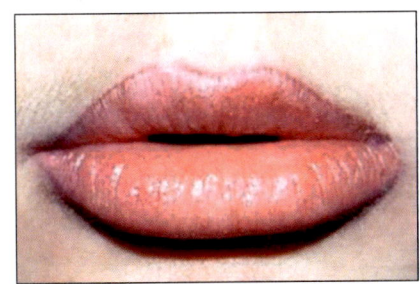

Figure 25-9: The Lip Procedure Healing Process

Words that Cause Client Concern

Concern words to avoid during a procedure:
- Hurt
- Pain
- Sore
- Bleeding
- Uncomfortable

Each of these words causes the mind to focus on that word alone, even if included in a full sentence. Find another way to convey a message or question of concern when communicating during a procedure: As examples, questions such as, *"Are you comfortable?"*, *"Do you need a short breather?"* Both questions convey concern but represent more of a positive approach. Use encouraging words and reinforcement techniques.

Personality Disorders

Being aware of the characteristics of personality disorders enables the technician to recognize certain aspects of the service that may cause stress, or explain behavioral patterns. A review of several of these personality disorders is provided below.

Avoidance Personality Disorder (APD)

People who are preoccupied with their own shortcomings and form relationships with others only if they believe they will not be rejected.

Dependent Personality Disorder (DPD)

Is characterized by a pervasive psychological dependence on others to meet their emotional and physical needs.

Body Dysmorphic Disorder (BDD)

The affected person is overly concerned with body image. This is manifested as excessive concern about and preoccupation with a perceived defect of their physical features.

Obsessive Compulsive Personality Disorder (OCPD)

The affected person has a pervasive pattern of preoccupation with orderliness, and perfectionism. This person demonstrates mental and interpersonal control at the expense of flexibility, openness, and efficiency.

OCPD should not be confused with *Obsessive Compulsive Disorder (OCD)*. *OCD* is an anxiety disorder, described by intrusive thoughts which produce anxiety (fear, worry, apprehension, etc). It also includes compulsions which are behaviors (repetitive hand-washing, nervous rituals, etc.) intended to reduce the produced anxiety.

Early Signs of a Potential Challenge

The Younger Client Who Has Been Overly Influenced by the Media.
- Younger clients often have done their best to look like beauty/appearance experts have conveyed via written material or on related TV shows. They've been programmed to value model or movie star traits.

The Client Who Arrives with Their Family or Friends for Support.
- There could be a dependency (linked to Avoidance Personality Disorder, or Dependent Personality Disorder), requiring approval of family, spouse, friends, etc.
- It could represent cultural differences; collective vs. individualistic. Collective cultures tend to do things as a family.
- It could be simply logistical (the client needed a ride to the studio and the family had to come along).

Figure 25-10: Media Influence on Appearance Expectations

The Client Who Stares in the Mirror Looking for Something Wrong.
- It could be someone who is very critical, or a sign of Body Dysmorphic Disorder.
- If tending towards the too critical end, it could possibly be related to Obsessive Compulsive Personality Disorder; a need for perfection.

The Client Who Is Obsessed About Time; They Become Frustrated If They Have to Wait a Few Minutes for Their Appointment.
- A person affected with Obsessive Compulsive Personality Disorder will schedule the day down to the minute and become extremely anxious if the plan is not followed.

The Client Who Measures (Visually or with an Instrument) Their Eyebrow Design.
- It could possibly be related to Obsessive Compulsive Personality Disorder; a need for perfection.

The Client Who Wears Excessive Amounts of Topical Makeup.

- It could be that there is a desire to wear a mask and not allow others to see the real person.
- It may be a manifestation of an Avoidance Personality Disorder; a preoccupation with their personal shortcomings.
- Or, it could simply be, that they were never taught how to wear makeup and don't know any better.

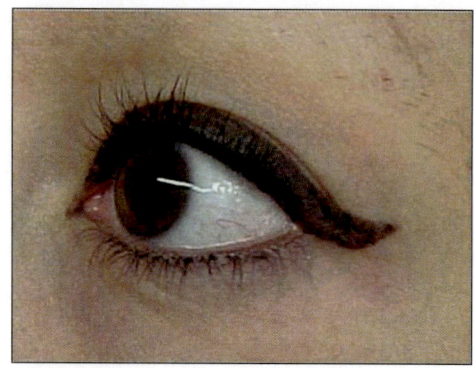

Figure 25-11: Disproportionate Eyeliner

The Client Who Asks Too Many Personal Questions; Including If the Technician Carries Insurance.

This could be something as simple as trying to get to know their technician, but at the same time, it could be a red flag. It's best to steer away from conversations that lead to a more personal relationship with clients. Technicians only need to know so much about their clients to do a good job, and clients only need to know so much about their technician to trust them with their permanent cosmetic procedures.

The Client Who Bad-Mouths Another Technician or Reveals They Would like To, or Is Suing Them.

This may be about power and dominance. On the other hand it may be a preview of what to expect from a person who may not be able to be pleased. It depends a lot on what is seen that is the source of the disapproval of another technician.

The Client Who Says, "I Don't Want My Partner to Know I Did This."

This may be an indication of:

- a power differential within the relationship;
- disapproval of the nature of the service (tattooing) for religious or cultural reasoning;
- an indication of who controls the finances within the relationship;
- the concept that it's easier to beg for forgiveness than ask for permission;
- a client who indicates they do not want their partner to find out may present a potential safety issue.
    - What are the consequences of when (not if) the partner recognizes that tattooing has been performed?

The Client Who Claims to Be Allergic to Everything Could Represent Hypochondriasis.

- It would be important to know if this is medically diagnosed, or self-diagnosed.
- Any distortion of skin color or swelling may be construed as an allergic reaction.

What the Body Is Saying

When we communicate, only a small percentage of what is communicated is from the words spoken. Studies have reported the verbal component to be a low as 7% and as high as 35%. Even at the highest reported, it would suggest at best, 65% percent of communication falls in the domain of non-verbal communication.[1] So it can be very important to understand the non-verbal aspects of communication to better communicate with clients.

As with most things, especially with regards to communication, it is important to understand there are no absolutes and there are a great number of factors that come into play. As an example, looking someone directly in the eye while talking to them is highly valued in many western cultures, while in other cultures it would be considered extremely rude. So keeping these potential variables in mind, one needs to look at the whole communication process and how non-verbal actions fit within the overall context.

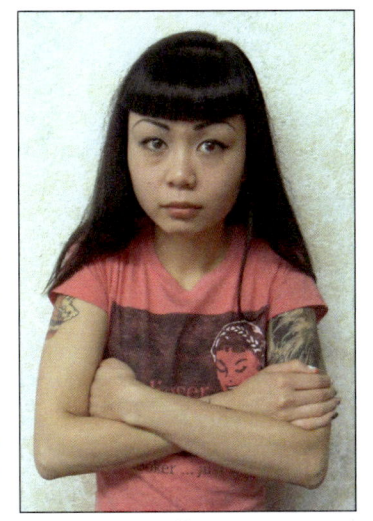

Figure 25-12: Torso Shield position

Body Language

The Torso Shield

- People who shield their torso with crossed arms feel insecure, nervous, or cautious.

Crossed Legs

- If the crossed leg points away from a person it often signifies disinterest in or a perceived threat from that person.
- Body language signs are more indicative when people first sit down and they adopt initial positions in relation to other people who are present.

Figure 25-13: Crossed Legs

Compressed or Disappearing Lips.
- This indicates stress or anxiety. This may be normal considering they are in a new environment. The technician's approach to calming initial stress and anxiety is important.

Pursed Lips.
- Pursed lips indicate the person is in disagreement with something. They are thinking of a possible alternative to something you have said or shown to them.

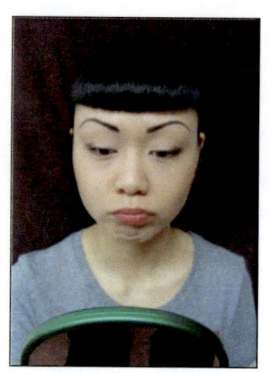

Figure 25-14: Compressed Lips

Figure 25-15: Pursed Lips

The Two Handed Handshake.
- John F. Kennedy commissioned an entire study to determine the most effective handshake.
- The use of two hands with strangers is seen as intrusive, and too personal.
  - This handshake should not be used until a more personal relationship has been formed with a client.
  - In certain cultures, the use of two hands is prefered and considered a sign of respect/graciousness.

Figure 25-16: Two Handed Handshake

Figure 25-17: The Friendly Handshake

- A light touch on the arm or shoulder during a handshake is friendly, but not as personal as using both hands.

First Contact Analysis

When the client arrives take note of:
- Traditional makeup color choices – familiarity with color choices (if any).
- Traditional makeup design work - appropriate or inappropriate design(s).
- Openness to change; observe body language and listen closely.

Consultations or first-time meetings are equivalent to speed dating. Technicians have a very short window of time to determine if they want to be in a relationship with a prospective client.

Summary

People have issues; some are more easily managed, some are more problematic. A permanent cosmetic technician cannot *cure* a dysfunctional client. It is out of the scope of our practice and training for the permanent cosmetic professional.

Recognizing potential problematic personality traits and reading body language allows for more effective client management. There will be times when a problematic personality trait is simply too much for a technician to effectively manage, and other times when these traits are quite manageable.

The important question technicians must ask is: ***"Can I work with this person (prospective client) and develop a healthy relationship on a long-term basis?"***

References

1. Adler, R., Rosenfeld, L., Proctor II, R. (2007). *Interplay: The process of interpersonal communication.* Oxford University Press:NY.
2. Navarro, J., Karlins, M. (2008). *What Every Body's Saying: An ex-FBI agent's guide to speed reading people.* HarperCollins Publishers:NY
3. Peter Noel Murray, PH.D - Doctor of Psychology - Consumer psychology practice in New York City; providing consulting and market research to corporations.
4. Contributions to this section were also made by Greg Shergold, MA, LPC.
5. Contributions to this section were also made by Amanda Le, Permanent Cosmetic Technician and professional model.

Section 26

The Principles of Tattoo Lightening and Removal

Learning Objectives

Introduction

The information provided in this section of the textbook is not intended to be a replacement for training. However, the subject of tattoo lightening and removal (hereafter referred to as tattoo lightening) is commonly discussed on social media sites, at training and permanent cosmetic events, and among technicians. It is good to gain insight early-on to the principles and information associated with this type of procedure, and at an appropriate time, decisions can be made to evaluate if it is a service to include in a business profile. This section will also benefit technicians who currently offer tattoo lightening.

Objective

At the fundamental level, only minor adjustments to a technician's own work should be performed. Anything beyond this is considered advanced work and industry experience and advanced training is needed. The examples shown in this Section are advanced work that was performed on the work of others and are only provided as an introduction to future service procedure types after experience and training has been achieved.

Section 26 - The Principles of Tattoo Lightening and Removal

For educational purposes, all tattoo powders from which formulations are developed are colorants/pigments (both terms are interchangeable). The term *ink* is an informal industry word assigned for colorants/pigments, and although used by many in the industry, ink is generally not recognized as being different from colorants/pigments in the permanent cosmetic manufacturing industry. Whether or not the term pigment/color/colorant/ink is used as a description, it is the ingredients that matter, not what it is called. The term pigment will be used in this section to describe color that has been tattooed into the skin for tattoo lightening and removal.

The procedure of tattoo lightening in itself is not technically complicated for an experienced tattoo artist. Trained technicians tattoo pigment into the upper dermal layer of the skin when they perform a tattoo procedure. Tattoo lightening is a tattoo procedure, which targets unwanted pigment in the dermis with a chosen tattoo lightening/removal solution, resulting in a decrease of pigment particles through epidermis during the healing process.

Although the procedure is not technically complicated, knowledge of skin types, appropriate choice of a needle, the management of clients, what to expect, and how long to consider waiting before the next appointment are aspects of the procedure that are important to learn.

The other option is laser tattoo removal, or in some cases, clients have elected to endure the natural color fading process. Lasers break down the pigment particles within the body with short pulses of light and depend on the body's immune system to dispose of all or partial portions of the pigment. The color's natural fading process can take several months or years depending on the type and density of the color. This option is not a popular one with clients who have unwanted pigment, especially if they go to the trouble of covering it up with cosmetic products.

The effect of tattoo lightening products or laser is the reduction of pigment particles in the dermal layer of the skin. Fewer pigment particles result in less color density and a faded appearance compared to the density of color before the procedure. In either instance, how many procedure appointments will be needed to reach the intended goal of the technician and client is based on an educated estimate by trained professionals. A good philosophy on educated estimates is to under promise and over deliver.

Liability Coverage

A technician should research and determine if tattoo lightening services are permitted within their scope of work in the locality where their business is licensed. If so, is insurance coverage required by law, or preferred by the technician? In today's social environment, insurance coverage for all aspects of business services is commonplace, whether or not required by law. A legal representative once advised that during legal challenges, one of the elements considered *is if the business owner* had *properly capitalized their business*.

The person seeking tattoo lightening services has pigment in their skin they want to be lightened or removed. The client may be dissatisfied with the permanent cosmetics that they have, the tattoo pigment may have aged to an undesirable color, or they may have changed their mind about a design or color factor. A technician may see the need for pigment adjustment of their own work from time to time.

Insurance coverage and options may vary from one insurance company to another. Technicians should read their tattoo lightening and removal insurance policy to determine if there are any skin type(s) exclusions or areas of the body where the tattoo lightening would be performed. Contact an insurance agent for specifics.

Considerations

It is imperative that technicians know the ingredients in any product they plan on using for tattoo lightening and the possible effects on the skin.

Notwithstanding that experienced technicians can follow product directions and tattoo a pigment lightening product into the skin to target unwanted pigment, there are many equally important considerations that carry equal weight to the tattooing lightening process other than product or the tattooing process alone. These considerations are as follows:

- Overall goal and objectives
- Lightening of minor areas to accomplish symmetry or correct a minor mistake
- Total removal of a design area
- Lightening of pigment density to prepare for additional tattooing with a different color
- Skin type and age
- Skin condition
- Pigment location and design pattern
- Pigment type, color, and density
- The age of the tattooed design
- If the procedure area has been subject to laser prior to tattoo lightening with product
- Needle choice
- Aftercare
- Time allotted between tattoo lightening procedures
- Client expectations

A Brief Review of Considerations

Overall goals and objectives must be discussed at the consultation so that realistic expectations can be discussed. Having photographs of prior tattoo lightening work representing the before, immediately after, and healed procedure, helps a prospective

Section 26 - The Principles of Tattoo Lightening and Removal

client make good decisions. If their expectations are not realistic, it is recommended to advise the prospective client accordingly. Technicians should be aware that if they are not planning on performing the tattoo lightening work, let the prospective client leave without further recommendations. Technicians have no control over the actions of others. If in doubt discuss your plan to refer to others with your insurance agent.

- Skin type and age of the skin plays an important part in the tattoo lightening process. Fitzpatrick skin types IV-VI may produce hyperpigmentation or hypopigmentation when the skin is wounded. Fitzpatrick III may also have these tendencies. More mature clients may heal at a slower pace than younger clients, and longer times between procedures may be advisable for clients with health conditions that may result in a slower healing agenda.

- The condition of the skin is important. Sun damaged skin, or very thin, fragile skin may prove to be challenging to work with.

- The pigment type (organic, inorganic, or a mix of the two) and specific brand color is often an unknown factor when working with a prospective client who comes to a different technician than the one who performed the original work. Technicians can always ask the client to acquire this information but often that isn't available information.

- Based on reports from experienced tattoo artists, older tattoos prove to be more challenging than newer work that requires tattoo lightening.

- Tattoos that have been lasered prior to tattoo lightening procedures have been reported to be more challenging and possibly less effective. If a combination of laser and tattoo lightening procedures are a consideration, it is recommended to perform the tattoo lightening procedures first, and at some point, when or if, it appears that no further improvement can be achieved, laser removal would be the next option for the remaining pigment.

- The needle choice is client-specific. Many choices are available as options, but the condition of the skin and the design area both are considerations when choosing the appropriate needle configuration.

- Aftercare is discussed further in this section. Often tattoo lightening product manufacturers will give directions.

- Time allotted between tattoo lightening procedures is discussed throughout this section with associated time-based photographs. Ultimately, the skin type, the design area, location, the age of the tattoo, and the health profile of the client will influence how much time is allotted for healing before another procedure (if needed) is scheduled.

- Client expectations are so important. Some clients seem to arrive at their consultation with the mindset that tattoo lightening is immediate and that they will not need than one procedure to realize complete success.

How Does Tattoo Lightening Work?

In the article *Getting Rid of Old Tattoos,* Whitney D. Tope, MD, a dermatologist, stated: "In over tattooing, the tattoo artist will dip the machine's tip in saline or another nonpigment solution and will tattoo over the existing pigment.

Over tattooing creates a perforating disorder in which the epithelium grows down around the pigment fragments, picks them up, and eventually extrudes them."

The Consultation and Pre-Testing

During a consultation, it is recommended to advise the person that one of their options is to return to their previous technician for a solution. Although many times this is an opportunity that is not acted upon, it should be mentioned so that as a minimum, the client realizes that important historical details are not available to a new technician.

Information such as pigment brand and color, number of times the procedural area has been tattooed, and any chart notes regarding the needle configuration and technique used are not a matter of a new technician's records if they did not perform the original procedure. Indicate on their chart notes that the client elected not to return to the original technician if that is the case and that historical data is unavailable.

In practicality, the new technician becomes a front-line customer service representative for a service that more often than not, they did not originally provide. It becomes their responsibility to manage the frustration of a customer who is requesting a change to their tattoo appearance. This is not to be taken lightly.

An important aspect of offering tattoo lightening services is to evaluate the mannerisms and attitude of the person who will be in a service relationship with their new technician that is quite different from that of the relationship of providing permanent cosmetics.

Depending on the saturation level (density) and design of the pigment, a technician may see the client multiple times with weeks or months in-between appointments to accomplish the desired goals initially agreed upon during the consultation. The client may leave each appointment with renewed hope that this will be their last tattoo lightening procedure. In reality, the success of the tattoo lightening procedure cannot be determined until an appropriate time has passed, the procedure has completely healed, and only then can an assessment can be made if further work is needed.

The appearance alone of the procedure during the healing process is a visual reminder that something went wrong with the client's original decision to get a tattoo. The *wrong* aspect may be as a result of an error on behalf the client who originally requested a trendy design or insisted on an inappropriate color, or it may have resulted from trusting an inexperienced technician. During the aging process, the skin changes and symmetry may become a problem. The tattoo doesn't appear properly proportioned as it did when the client was younger. The lists of the *wrongs* technicians are asked to improve upon are numerous.

Choose tattoo lightening clients carefully. They must recognize that patience on their behalf is a required part of the process. Unlike during the healing process of permanent cosmetic services, clients are not usually instructed to discourage crusting of the tattooed lightened area. When tattooing permanent cosmetic procedures or body art, clients are advised that within weeks they will have nice eyebrows, eyeliner, lips, or a treasured artistic body art design that they will appreciate and enjoy for long periods of time.

When lightening tattoos, the crusting is an important element of the healing agenda to encapsulate pigment through the epidermis. The client or other people in their social or family circles may be critical of their appearance during this time and affect how the client physically and emotionally manages the wound during the healing period. For this reason, the timing of the procedure will be important to many clients seeking this service.

Tattoo pigments are challenging to remove, some more than others. If a technician were to investigate the average number of laser removals required to diminish or eliminate the appearance of tattoos they would often find that guarantees are not made. Often multiple laser treatments are required with weeks or months between sessions to make an impressionable difference.

Technicians often share success tattoo lightening stories with before and after photographs, many of which are quite impressive. What transpires in-between the before and after photographs are where valuable lessons are also found.

If the tattoo color to be lightened is larger in area, technicians may elect to conduct a test area on a smaller portion of the design and ask the client to return in 6-8 weeks (or if the area is quite dense 12-18 weeks). At that time the technician can determine how effective the procedure and product will be based on how it performed in the smaller test area. This also gives the client an indication of how the skin in the design area will appear and provides the technician with valuable information after the procedure area has healed for several weeks. Often technicians have waited longer than 8 weeks, with the client's approval, because they have seen that a longer period between appointments often results in a better outcome. With that said, there is also value in checking in with the client or seeing them in person to analyze the progress. Keeping the client involved and interested in pursuing additional procedures if needed is part of the service.

Tattoo Lightening Forms

Ensure all client history and informed consent forms are completed, and that the client is a good candidate for an invasive procedure. Review the ingredients of the product that will be used to ensure the client does not have known allergies to any of the ingredients and that the ingredients are suitable for the tattoo lightening procedure.

This is the same assessment technicians require for permanent cosmetics or body art tattoos. The client must be a person who will heal well without complications due to a condition beyond a technician's control. An insurance company may request to review (or have on file) the forms to be used for coverage purposes.

Aftercare directions should be provided verbally and in writing.

Common Procedure Tray Products

The tattoo lightening procedure tray and device setup in accordance with bloodborne pathogens standards is the same as if performing a permanent cosmetic or a traditional body art procedure. If any directions in this section conflict with directions of an over-the-counter tattoo lightening/removal product or insurance protocol directions, contact the associated representatives for any related questions. All items listed are single-use.

- A tattoo lightening/removal product of choice, one that is not in conflict with insurance requirements or any geographical laws that govern tattoo lightening.

- A container to hold product. A finger ring may not be a good selection if the product is more fluid than creamy.

- New sterilized needles/tubes/manual device with appropriate size needles for the work to be completed. Please note that a microblading device manufactured for the purpose of tattooing eyebrow hair strokes into the skin is not recommended for tattoo lightening procedures. The small needle size of microblading devices with needles arranged (soldered) in a row is not considered effective for tattoo lightening of areas of pigment that are larger than the needle size. Hair strokes initially tattooed with a microblading device may exceed the width of the original microblading needle formation.

- Cotton swabs to apply product onto the skin.

- Cotton products to clean the procedural area and to wipe product during the procedure.

- Microbrushes – If gently massaging the solution into the area of the unwanted pigment. microbrushes are often ideal to use when applying product on small design areas such as hair stroke patterns.

- Anesthetic – The area may be pre-numbed to diminish discomfort for tattooing if legal to do so in any specific geographical location. Ideally, post-broken skin anesthetic (if used) would not contain epinephrine. The body's first response to a wound is to send blood and lymph fluids to the wounded site to *flush out* the wounded area of debris. Epinephrine used in over-the-counter level tattoo anesthetic products is intended to act as a vasoconstrictor. Unlike when tattooing pigment into the skin for a permanent cosmetic procedure, bleeding or the showing of body fluids for tattoo lightening/removal procedures is not managed in the same manner.

- An appropriately sized bandage if the procedural area is a body tattoo that is a large design area, or one that may come in contact with clothing.

- A protective covering for the client's eyes when working above or close to the eye area.

- Aftercare instructions and product if a healing agent is included.

Tattooing Lightening Needle Guidelines

Needle size selection is unique to the area being tattooed, the device being used and guidelines set forth by a tattoo lightening product manufacturer or trainer. Tattoo lightening product directions may call out a specific needle to be used. If not, it is recommended that to ensure good penetration to the target pigment area, the needle size should be selected based on the design area size, location, and the condition of the skin.

In general, number 3-round liners or shader configurations are common machine device needles effective for small areas and hair stroke designs; up to number 8-round liners or shaders, or up to 11- magnums may be common for larger design areas, although there are some classes that have introduced even larger configurations. The needle size in configurations is also important generally which range from .20 mm to .35 mm. In general manual device (non-microblading hair stroke type manual devices) single or multi-row configurations are common for small and larger design areas. These are wide-ranging suggestions, and each client will present the technician with needle size and configuration decisions to be made. Tattoo lightening training classes often provide suggested needle sizes and configurations for different circumstances.

Tattoo Lightening Technique Guidelines

There are several tattoo motion techniques; three of the commonly used techniques are:

- **Pointillism motion**
    - The pointillism technique (up and down needle movements, as if creating dots), covers the selected procedural area in small dots.
    - Pointillism is often recommended for dense or smaller pigment designs, skin types that are more fragile, or that scar easily from minor wounds.

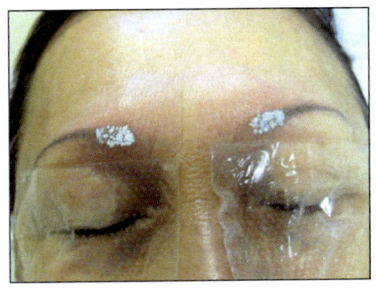

Figure 26-1: Pointillism

- **Circle/loop tattooing motion**
    - Tattoo over the area of the unwanted pigment as you would as if you were tattooing pigment in a shading technique using appropriate size circle or loop type movements.
    - Use tight or loose movements as appropriate for the design area. Tight circles are not recommended for skin

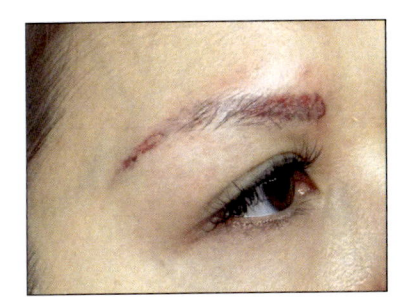

Figure 26-2: Circles

types that are fragile or that scar easily from minor wounds. This is a common movement for larger design areas.

- Back and forth motions (commonly called etching), or a motion that follows the direction of a hair stroke.

Etching Pattern stroke pattern   Hair Stroke Pattern

The back and forth or etching motion are common technique when lightening or narrowing the width size of misplaced design pigment. When lightening hairline strokes, follow the tattooed lines targeting the misplaced stroke(s).

Once the first pass or second pass has been made using the chosen product, and the skin has been compromised (opened), allow the body fluids to rise to the surface of the skin for several minutes. Whether or not multiple passes are made, or if the product is used during passes to open the skin, or only laid on after the skin has been opened, is product-specific and training-specific.

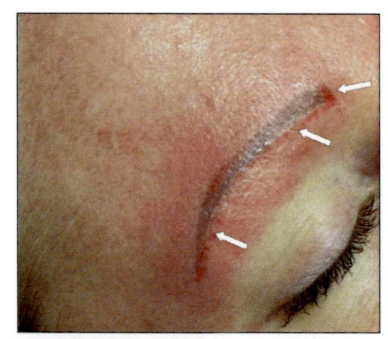

Figure 26-3: Back and forth motion

With the exception of lightening/removal procedures for eyeliners (when often sterile saline is used unless product directions indicate differently), follow the product's specific directions. Ensure the eyes are covered and protected from products when working above or around the eyes.

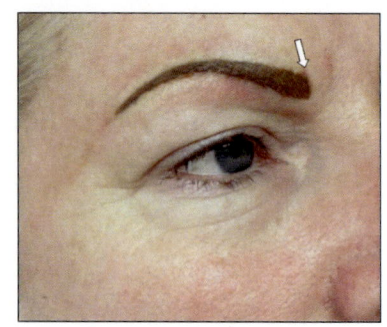

Figure 26-4: Following the direction of a hair stroke

Body Fluids and Stretching

A similar degree of body fluids, as if you were tattooing pigment into the skin, will be seen regardless of the device or the technique used. Technicians may not be accustomed to seeing what actually goes on under pigment when they are tattooing permanent cosmetic procedures, so don't be alarmed when body fluids and wounded skin are seen, the missing product is pigment which normally covers and hides this visual aspect of tattooing.

Stretching the skin is equally as important when tattooing a pigment lightening product into the skin as when tattooing a permanent cosmetic procedure. The skin must remain taut during tattooing.

Discoloration of Tattoo Lightening Products

In the early period of product development of tattoo lightening formulations, when discoloration of fluids was seen when the product was tattooed into or applied to the open skin area of an eyebrow, many reported this represented *pigment pouring out of the skin*. That phrase is provided because that is how the product was marketed at the time.

Section 26 - The Principles of Tattoo Lightening and Removal

As time passed and chemists were approached with this occurrence, it seems this was likely not just pigment (if at all) that was seen. There are other considerations based on chemistry as described by Mytia Story, B.S., who is a Biologist and Chemist:

> "Many tattoo lightening products utilize pH differentials and oxygen to lighten pigment in the skin. The colored discharge or foam (often different shades of brown and sometimes a brown-green or green color – this may vary between products used) seen once the product is tattooed into or applied to the broken skin may have some colorants in it, but the discoloration seen is mainly due to the reaction of blood with the removal product and oxygen.
>
> As blood is oxygenated it goes from red to rust-colored, to brown. The discoloration appearance seen may also be as a result of a reaction involving the pH of the product and the pH of body fluids. The color change may be the evidence of this reaction."
>
> *Mytia Story, B.S, Biologist and Chemist.*

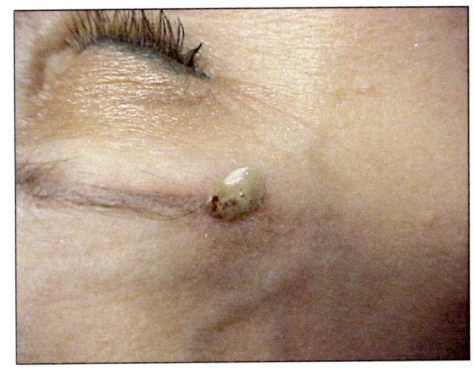

Figure 26-5: Discoloration appearance of product and body fluids

To test this information, a technician purposely cut their finger and produced a small amount of blood. An acid-based tattoo lightening product was applied to the open wound. Without a drop of pigment in the area that had been cut, the liquid shifted to a brown color. This was later repeated with an alkaline-based product and it turned green.

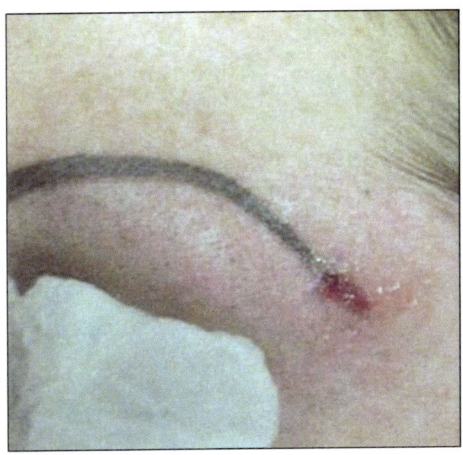

Figure 26-6: No discoloration of salt-based product and body fluids

Below is another example of how the appearance of a product can differ depending on the ingredients and pH level of the product.

The skin was then cleansed and a product with a different pH was applied.

Also, lip colored (pink, red, coral, etc.) liquid/foam is not normally produced when performing tattoo lightening procedures on lips.

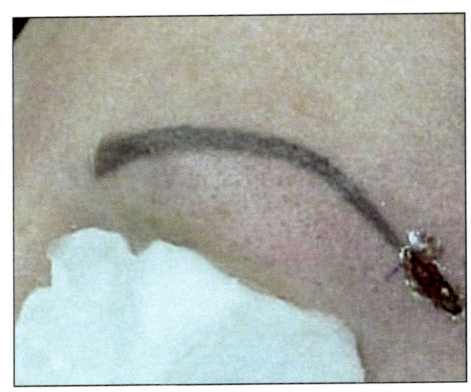

Figure 26-7: Application of a product with different ingredients and pH

What to Expect and When to Reschedule

The timing for tattoo lightening is important. Clients will need to manage their social and personal calendar due to the appearance of inflammation and crusting during the different phases of the healing process. If it is a body tattoo, the design may be one that comes in contact with clothing and precautions must be taken to protect the area during initial healing.

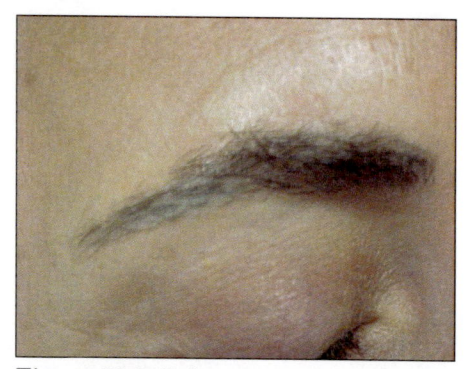

Figure 26-8: Before

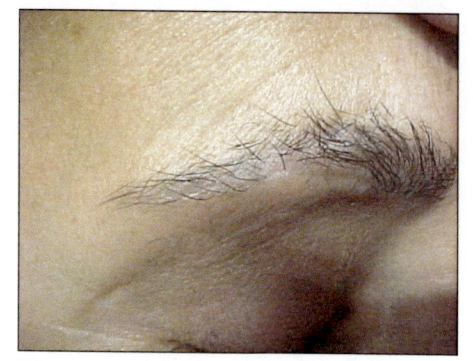

Figure 26-9: Nine months later

If given the opportunity to have clients check in during the healing period it would be unusual to see a tattoo lightening procedure that did not leave some short-term or long-term visible evidence of the tattoo lightening process in the skin. This indication is typically a pink or reddish appearance which often represents inflammation. Seeing the inflammation would depend on when the technician sees the client after the tattoo lightening procedure. Inflammation eventually subsides.

Normally it takes several weeks, months, and sometimes longer for the effects of tattoo lightening to diminish. This is specific to the client's skin type, health profile, and the tattoo pigment and design being lightened. In the case of lightening a tattoo for a Fitzpatrick IV-VI skin type (if the technician chooses to work on these skin types and there are no insurance policy exclusions) there may be a hyperpigmented appearance. In a few instances, there have been reports of hypopigmented results regardless of the skin type.

The photographs above (Figure 26-8 and Figure 26-9) is indicative of hypopigmentation. The client's main means of transportation was a motorcycle. Frequent exposure to the sun and elements may or may not have had any bearing on the slight hypopigmentation as seen nine months after the procedure, but it may have contributed.

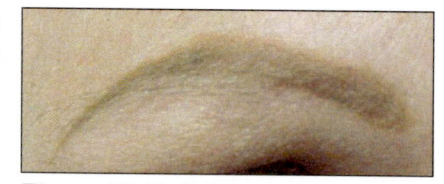

Figure 26-10: Before

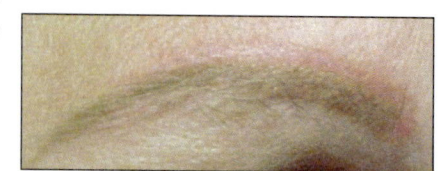

Figure 26-11: Eight-week progress check

Figure 26-12: Twelve weeks after original procedure

The next set of photos (Figure 26-10 thru Figure 26-12) is an example of the appearance of tattoo lightening on a person with lighter skin. Notice how inflammation from the wound and healing process translates through the skin in the second photo after the crusts have dried up and fallen off. Over time the pinkness and appearance of inflammation will dissipate and appear more similar to the surrounding skin as shown in the third photo.

Section 26 - The Principles of Tattoo Lightening and Removal

The following is another example (Figure 26-13 thru Figure 26-16). The eyebrow tattoo design which was placed higher than the client's brow bone area and had aged to a pinkish color. This particular client indicated that she had no natural eyebrow hair at the time the eyebrows were tattooed. When her natural eyebrow hair grew back, the misplacement was obvious.

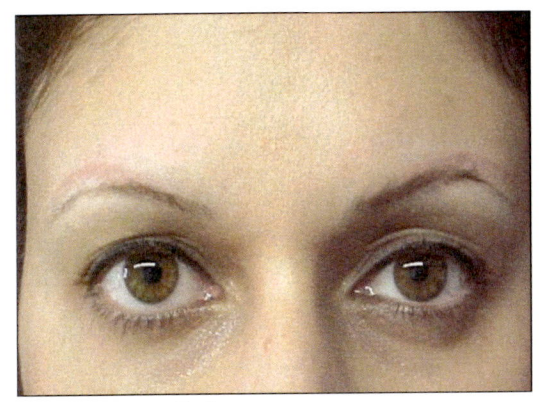

Figure 26-13: Before

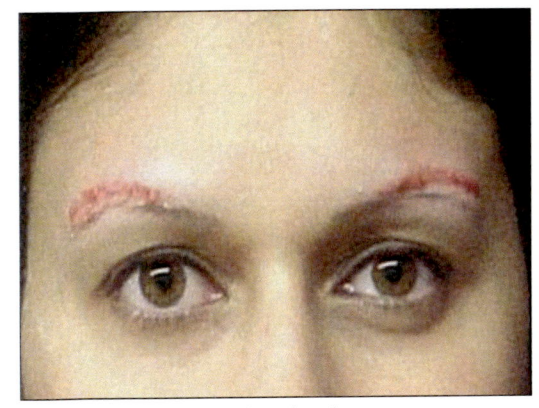

Figure 26-14: Immediately after

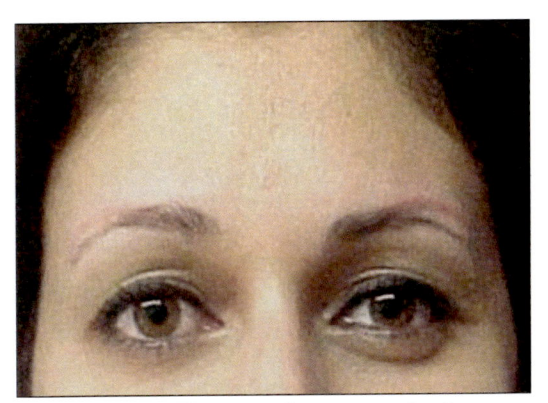

Figure 26-15: Three-week progress check

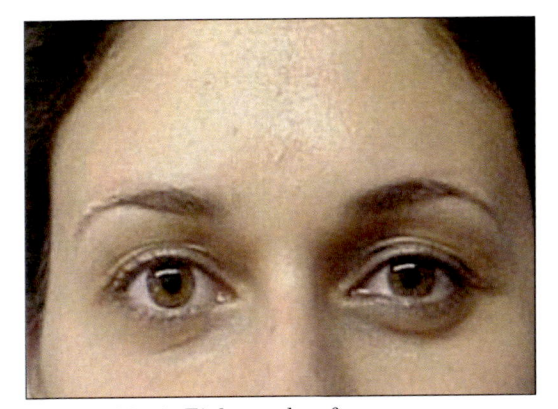

Figure 26-16: Eight weeks after the original procedure

As seen in both examples, the appearance of inflammation (pinkness) resolved with time.

The following example below does not reflect inflammation (pinkness) during the healing process. This client scheduled procedures up to six months apart and any pinkness that likely was seen during the healing process had already resolved each time additional work was performed.

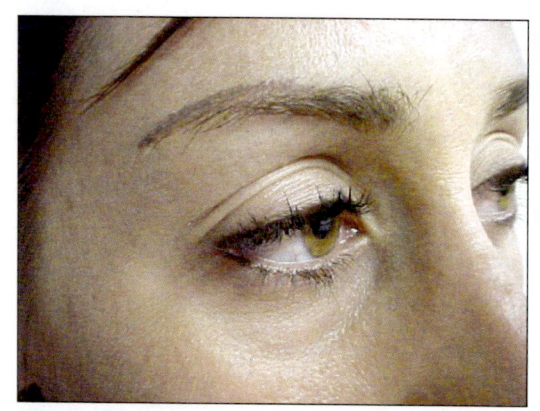

Figure 26-17: Before

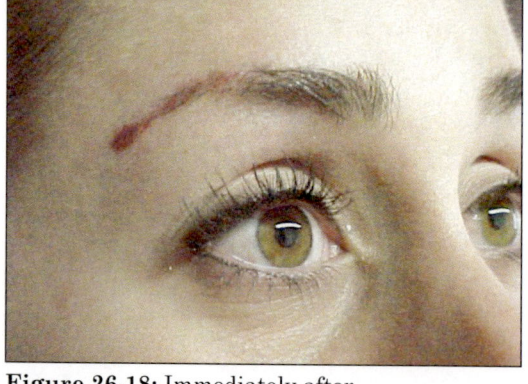

Figure 26-18: Immediately after the first lightening procedure

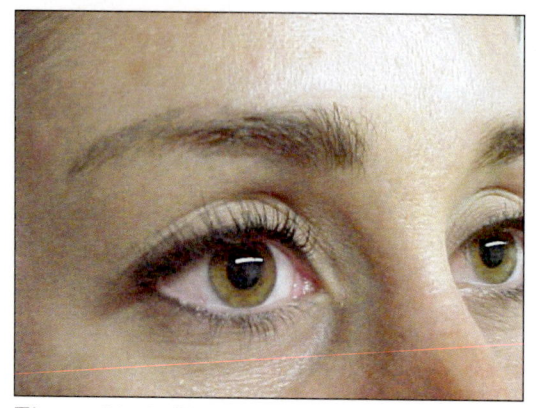

Figure 26-19: Six months after second lightening procedure

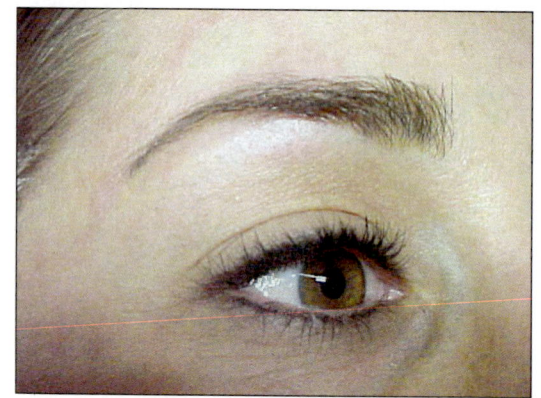

Figure 26-20: Six months after third lightening procedure healed, and after light touchup on the brow arch and tails.

The pinkness that is seen on lighter skin types becomes more problematic for lip color lightening procedures. Many lip pigments are red or pink colors and it may prove difficult to determine if, after several weeks, the color that remains is residual pigment or the appearance of inflammation from the tattooing procedure.

Clients seem to eventually accept that there is nothing that can hasten the body's natural healing process after they have experienced how the procedure area appears during the different phases of healing.

It is also been documented that the longer (within reason) that a lightening procedure is allowed to heal, the better the results. There are instances where people came from long distances and it was months, and in some cases, over a year before they were seen again. People are busy; they work, they travel, and to set time aside for tattoo lightening procedures and setting time aside for healing is often not a top priority.

The following example is a client who traveled a long distance who was kind enough to provide progressive healing photos. This is an early-on tattoo lightening client who, with the support of the progress healing photos, set in motion the fact that if she had lived closer additional lightening procedures within the six-month period may have been unnecessarily performed. With the distance involved, the initial procedure was sufficient and there wasn't a need for additional work.

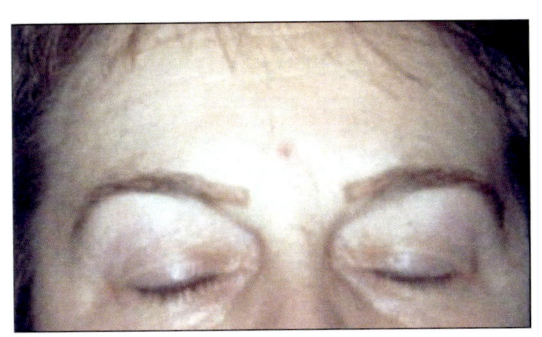

Figure 26-21: Before

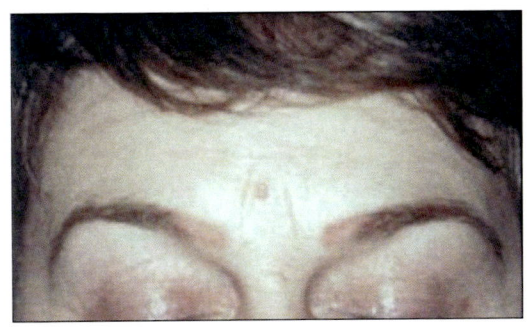

Figure 26-22: Two-month progress photo sent

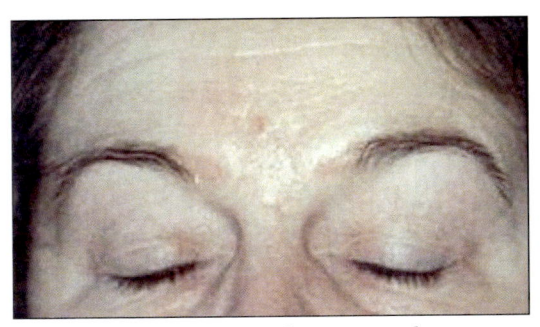

Figure 26-23: Four-month progress photo sent

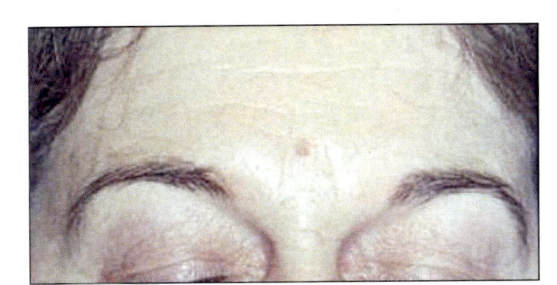

Figure 26-24: Six-month photo sent

These experiences are what initially led the industry to realize that the longer the body has to heal and for inflammation to subside, the better the results (within reason and often due to client availability). Clients who have had a substantial area lightened are not recommended for an additional procedure work in less than two-four months.

The client can return sooner in order to check on their progress and keep them actively interested in pursuing additional procedures if need be, but the longer the time between tattoo lightening procedures can stretch out, often the better the results.

During progress checks often there is a question based on the appearance of the skin where the tattoo lightening procedure was conducted. Does the pink/reddish appearance represent remaining pigment or lingering inflammation that will subside over time? There is a reliable manner to determine the answer to this question; stretching the procedural area.

The following is an example of a person who had a tattoo lightening procedure several weeks before consulting about further work. The client felt little had been accomplished and questioned the reddish coloring seen in her left (right looking at the photo) brow. A second opinion was sought out and during the consultation, she was requested to stretch the brows tightly while the appearance was photographed.

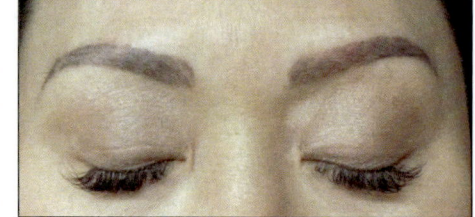

Once the client stretched each brow, the appearance changed, minimizing the inflammation seen during the healing process and to reflect the amount of pigment left in the skin that had not yet had time to fully heal and lighten to its greatest potential. Granted, there may be another lightening procedure or two needed to meet expectations, but this would be evaluated after a minimum of twelve weeks. If the design is substantial in area size and especially on the face, why put the client or the client's skin through the inflammation, crusting, possible scarring, and healing process any more often than necessary for a good result? Depending on the area of the body and the design involved, tattoo lightening can result in an appearance that is challenging for the client to manage.

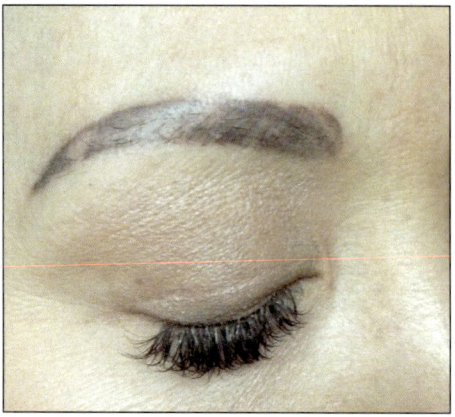

Figure 26-25: Both brows

Figure 26-26: Right brow

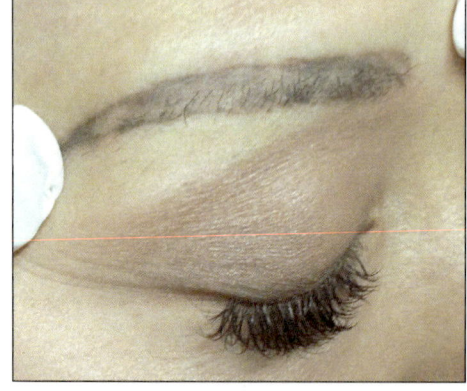

Figure 26-27: Right brow stretched

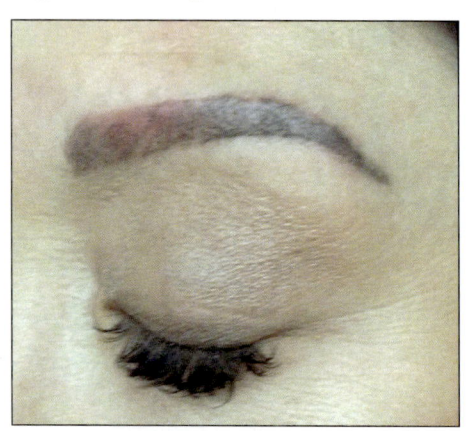

Figure 26-28: Left brow

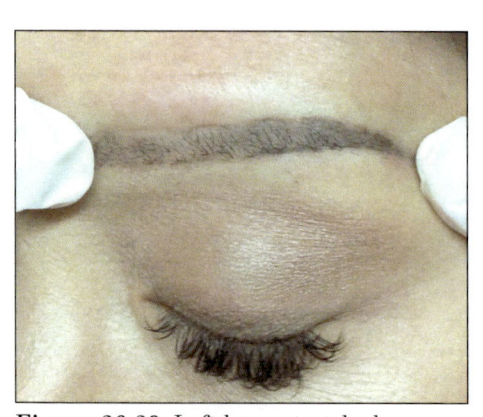

Figure 26-29: Left brow stretched

Section 26 - The Principles of Tattoo Lightening and Removal

The following is an offering from Shanan Zickefoose, BSN, RN, CPCP regarding re-tattooing the skin too soon for removal or re-pigmenting the skin.

> "All wounds go through an inflammatory process, including cosmetic tattoo wounds and wounds that introduce lightening solutions. The entire process can take anywhere from a few months up to two years to completely heal.
>
> The phases are a cascade that begins with the initial wound. It begins with an inflammatory phase that will last up to 6 days after the injury. Among many cells available during this phase, macrophages assist in providing debris clean up, or phagocytosis. It is important to note that macrophages have a very long-life span and can continue cleaning up and this can last a few months.
>
> The inflammatory phase is followed by the proliferation (epithelialization and granulation) phase which begins 4-5 days after injury and lasts up to three weeks. During the proliferative phase, approximately a month after the skin is broken, rough scar tissue is laid down and the skin is very susceptible to additional trauma.
>
> The final phase of healing is the remodeling phase and can take approximately twelve weeks to two years. During this time, the rough scar tissue is reorganized and the scar tissue will shrink and become pale. During this time, the original wound will change become white in color.
>
> With the timeline of wound healing as it relates to cosmetic tattooing, it is optimal to wait as long as possible to re-introduce a wound in the same area. By choosing to allow the skin to go through the remodeling phase, long-term scar formation is minimized. If the wound healing is disrupted before completion, abnormal healing can occur resulting in the formation of scar tissue.
>
> ### *Inflammatory Response Phases*
>
> **Inflammation:** Begins immediately and lasts 4-6 days
>
> **Epithelialization and Proliferation:** Begins 4-5 days after wound and continues up to 21 days
>
> **Remodeling:** Begins approximately 21 days after wound and will last up to two years.
>
> If adequate healing time and proper aftercare protocol is followed, the scar formation is greatly reduced. The strength of skin will only return to 70-80% of original strength under the most optimal conditions. It is advised to allow the skin to go through all phases of the inflammatory process before re-introducing the wound by either placing pigment in the skin or removal solutions in the skin."
>
> *Shanan Zickefoose, BSN, RN, CPCP*

The primary challenges with proceeding conservatively, which is in the person's best interest, are usually influenced by the client. Often people expect better results sooner than is reasonable. With the exception of minor alterations/corrections of a design area, or one where only lightening in preparation for additional tattooing is planned (reduction of existing pigment density), people may lose interest if asked to wait very long periods of time between procedures. They may begin to cover what pigment remains with makeup and/or wait out the natural fading process. That's why periodic check-up appointments are recommended. This keeps the client actively involved in the process, allows technicians to note progress information on the client's chart, and provides solid information to determine the best timing for an additional procedure if needed.

The easier procedures are those that are performed to lighten a tattoo in preparation for additional tattooing at a later date. This is common in the traditional tattoo body art industry. Below is a lower back tattoo that was lightened in four sectional procedures in preparation for a new tattoo design.

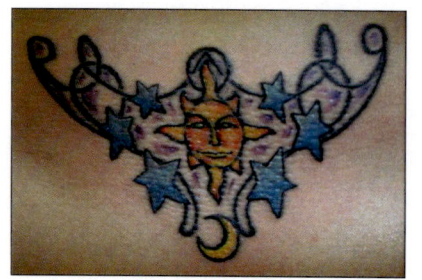

Figure 26-30: Before

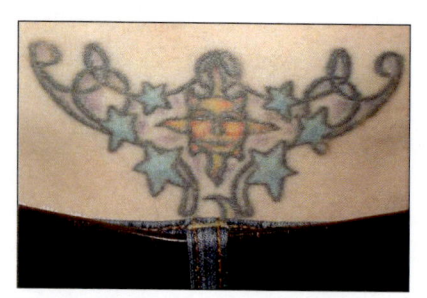

Figure 26-31: Healed after four sectional lightening procedures

Figure 26-32: New cover-up tattoo

Tattoo lightening procedures performed on areas other than the face are less stressful for a client to contend with. Below are examples of finger tattoos that were lightened after only one session on a young person. The procedure was quite effective and only saline and sea salt mixed together was used as the product. It is doubtful that crusting on the fingers represented much stress for her at all during the healing period.

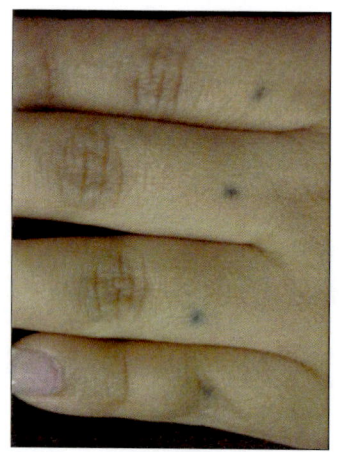

Figure 26-33: Before

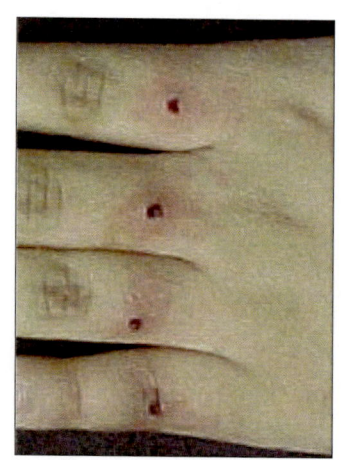

Figure 26-34: Immediately After

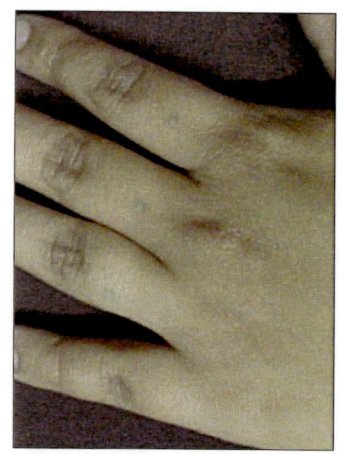

Figure 26-35: Healed two months later

Scarring and Procedure Location

Lightening procedures on areas below the knee should be carefully considered. The age of the client, the size and age of the design, and any medical conditions that may affect blood circulation are all important. Also, technicians need to be aware of any exclusion to body areas or skin types in their insurance policy.

Below is an example of a mid-calf test area. Considering the location of the tattoo, a test area to determine if healing would be problematic was conducted. The results were not positive; it appeared there was not adequate circulation for proper healing and scarring could be a factor, No further work was performed.

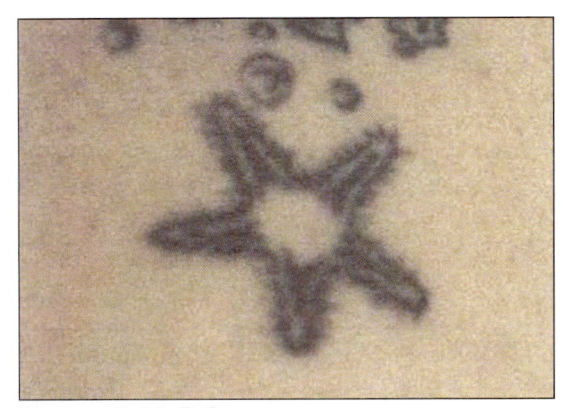

Figure 26-36: Before

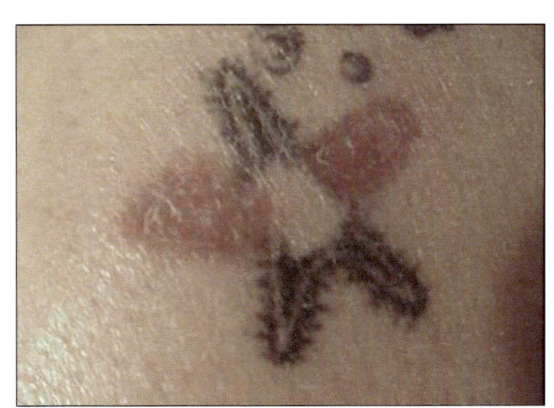

Figure 26-37: Test areas six months later

Below is another example of a test area on a lower leg tattoo. After seeing how the test area healed, and the potential for scarring, or as a minimum a very slow healing processing, no further work was performed.

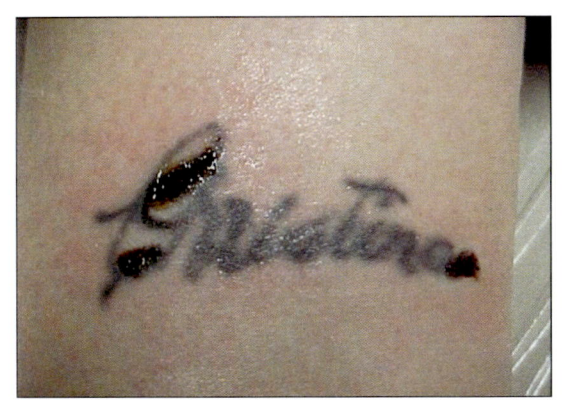

Figure 26-38: Test area

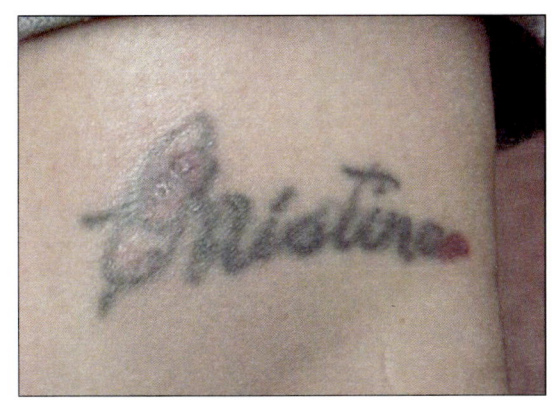

Figure 26-39: Test area two months later

Also ensure that your policy and/or your geographical location regulations allows for tattoo lightening of body art tattooing within your scope of work.

Challenging colors

Predictability of the lightening of particular colors or pigment types (inorganic or organic) is not a science. With that said, titanium dioxide (white) and colors made with a high percentage of white can be solidly stated as being very challenging if not practically impossible to totally remove. There may be an occasional success story, but it certainly is not something seen or heard of often.

The color white (titanium dioxide) forms large particles and although repeated attempts can be made to diminish its density, the appearance of complete removal is not common. Time doesn't even seem to make a substantial difference if natural fading is elected.

This is one of the many reasons technicians are cautioned to not use camouflage colors in an attempt to cover a mistake or to add white to other pigments to lighten a color to be used for permanent cosmetic procedures. Tattooing white into another color in the skin usually only produces a third color. Doing this also may put the client in a position of being turned away for laser treatments.

Below is an example of a brow lightening procedure that included a titanium dioxide

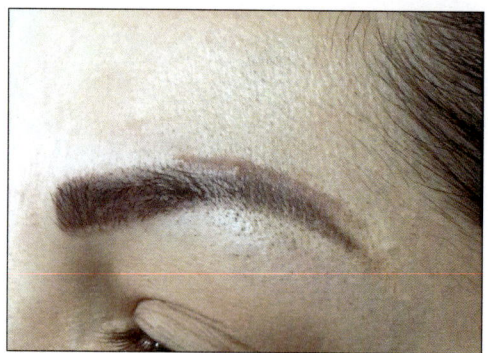

Figure 26-40: Before

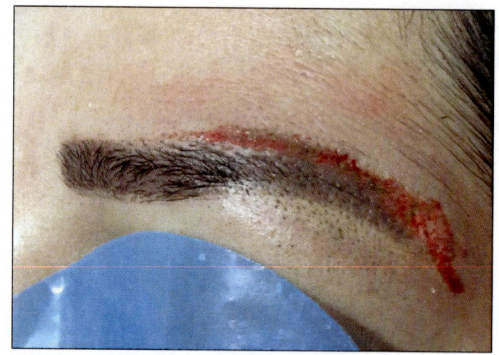

Figure 26-41: Immediately after. Notice the chunky appearance of the titanium dioxide at the tail

Figure 26-42: Eight-month progress check

Figure 26-43: Thirteen months after the procedure

(white) that was used in an attempt to coverup misplaced pigment. The white pigment was tattooed at the end of the line shown above the brow.

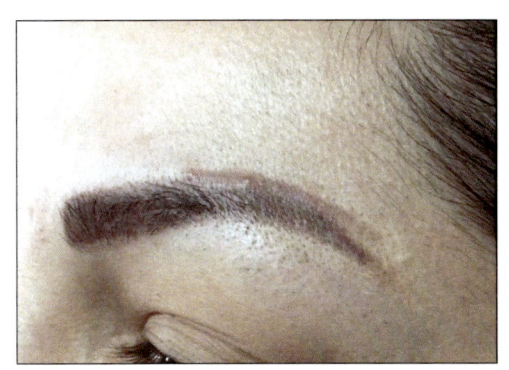

Figure 26-44: Comparison of before and thirteen months later

Using eight or twelve weeks as a guide, several additional tattoo lightening procedures could have been performed within the thirteen-month period. Ultimately the client realized the same or similar results, with no scarring or hyperpigmentation just by being patient, keeping in touch, and monitoring her progress.

There are often extenuating circumstances that support more or fewer frequent tattoo lightening sessions. The age and location of the tattoo, the density of the color, skin type, and condition of the skin has influence over whether more or less sessions will be needed for a successful procedure, and the appropriate timing between sessions. What has been realized by many technicians is that once the client realizes the appearance of tattooing with a lightening product, they often welcome less frequent sessions.

Procedure-Specific Successes

Eyebrows

The skin is thicker in the eyebrow area than other parts of the face. More stubborn pigment and larger designs may take longer to realize success, but if a client is comfortable with makeup, they often are accustomed to covering the unwanted design area after healing and before then next lightening procedure.

The following example (Figure 26-45 thru Figure 26-47, page 378) is before and after four lightening procedures and two color corrections. The white (titanium dioxide) that had been tattooed around and under the bulb area limited a significant change in design placement.

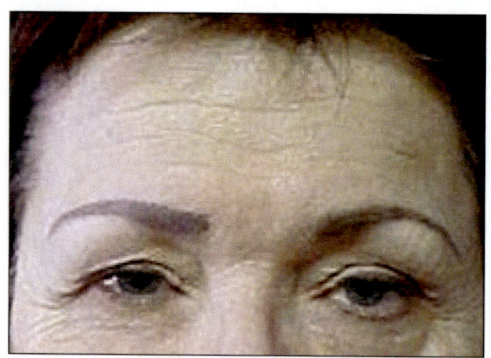

Figure 26-45: Before

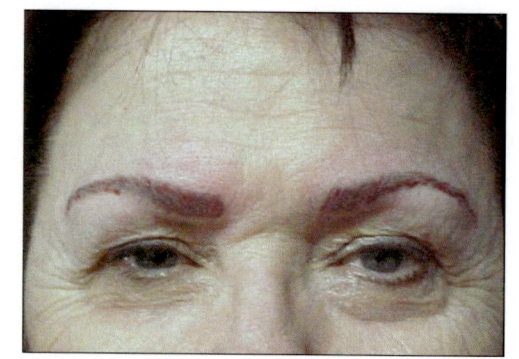

Figure 26-46: Immediately after

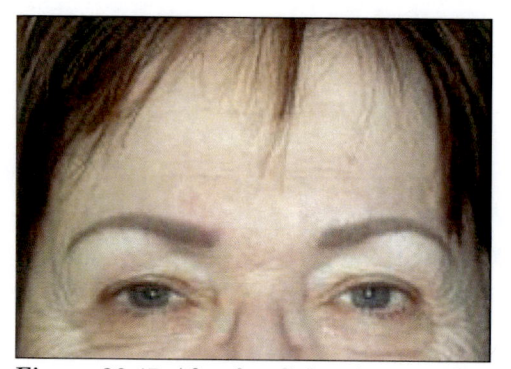

Figure 26-47: After four lightening procedures and two color corrections

Eyeliners

The eyes are a vital organ and the product manufacturer may have directions and/or provisions that indicate whether their product is appropriate for eyeliner lightening procedures. The eyelids also represent the thinnest skin on the face.

Depending on the placement and width of the eyeliner, complete eyeliner removal is time- consuming (if possible at all) and the eyes tend to swell to some degree from the tattooing process. This alone may influence whether a client wants to pursue the service. The timing of an appointment is very important.

Section 26 - The Principles of Tattoo Lightening and Removal

Misplaced smaller areas and tips of the top liner and lower liners are more available for success.

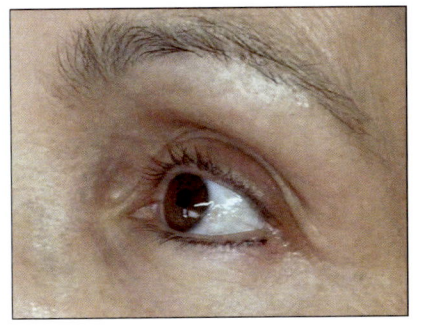

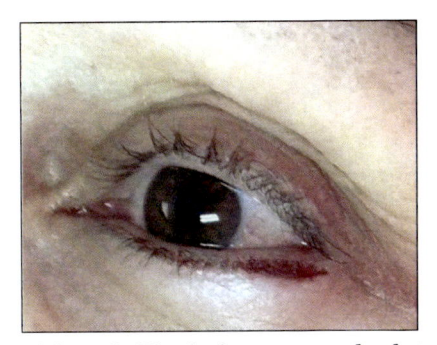

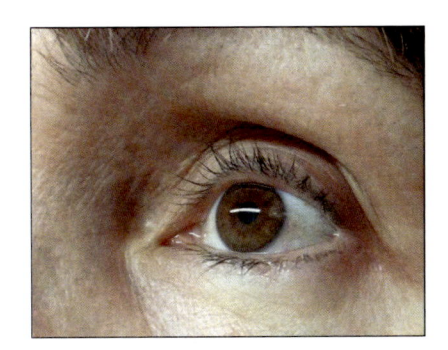

Figure 26-48: Before, Immediately After & Healed two months later

Experience indicates that eyeliner pigment migrations are usually best left to the laser community.

Lips

Full lips often represent larger tattooed areas with pigment that may be formulated to be more long-lasting. Lip pigments are also frequently cool red or pink-based colors and progress may seem slow because of the appearance of inflammation (red or pink) for periods of time. The client may feel there hasn't been the improvement they expected until the inflammation subsides.

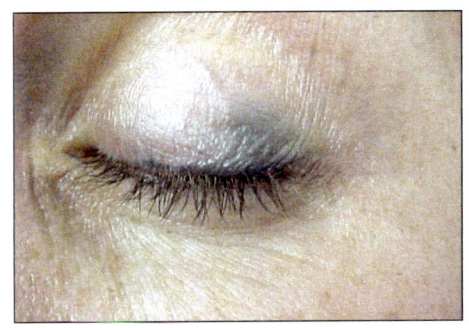

Figure 26-49: Migration of eyeliner

Below is an example of a lip liner lightening procedure with outstanding results. This was accomplished with the cooperation of a client who had been turned away by medical

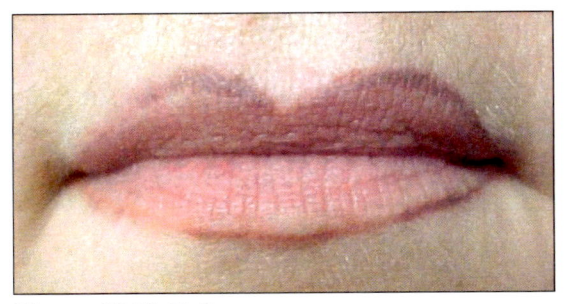

Figure 26-50: Before

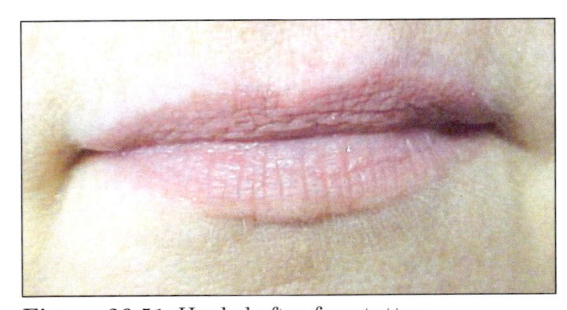

Figure 26-51: Healed after four tattoo lightening procedures six months apart

laser professionals. They laser tested a small test area in the corner of the lower lip and the color shifted to a darker color, assumedly because of the titanium dioxide in the lip pigment formulation.

Although the lips are vascular and often respond reasonably well to the lightening procedure, this was not a task without challenges. The top lip liner design placement departed substantially from the vermilion. It took several appointments to reach the final goal set, which was as close to complete removal as possible.

The tattooing was uncomfortable for her, and progress was slow but positive each time. To the client's credit, she patiently waited six months between appointments.

Aftercare: Dry Healing vs. Moist Healing

Aftercare is dependent upon the product's directions. Dry healing or an occlusive healing agent may be directed. This is usually product-specific unless sterile saline or saline mixed with salt is used, and there are good discussions about both aftercare direction types.

There is the discussion that a dry healing process may produce better results. However, on the other hand, an unprotected wound may prove to be a portal to infection. There may also be laws that override product directions that dictate the application of an occlusive dressing to tattooing (whether or not the tattooing is with pigment or a lightening product).

A healing agent used as a protective barrier from the environment and germs may prove to be important to discourage environmental bacterial exposure and infection. Always inquire about the client's normal environment. People who work in public areas such as schools, hospitals, nursing homes, grocery stores as examples, are more susceptible to germs and bacteria.

- In lieu of specific regulatory requirements, insurance policy provisions, or product directions, good judgment must be used in regard to the location of the procedure conducted, the person's health profile, and the environment the client will be in during the healing process. It is educational to use the search words *Wet or Dry Wound Healing* on the Internet and read the information provided.

The following is an offering from Shanan Zickefoose, BSN, RN, CPCP regarding her position on dry healing versus moist healing (with references provided).:

Dry Healing versus Moist Healing

Managing cosmetic tattoo wounds should be targeted at restoring functional integrity (or purpose) of the skin as quickly as possible and at the same time achieving adequate aesthetic quality of our permanent cosmetic procedures.

In 1962, a research study was conducted by Dr. Winter in which he studied wound healing and his results revealed, 'healing is enhanced by a moist wound environment compared with wounds simply exposed to air' (Winter, 1962). Additional studies continue to support Dr. Winter's research regarding wound healing in a moist environment. 'Good hydration is the single most important external factor responsible for optimal wound healing. Moist wound conditions not only accelerate the healing process and to reduce pain, but possibly also to have a significant effect on residual scarring' (Korting, et al., 2011).

What is important to note for the tattoo wound healing is moisture is necessary for all wound healing, including tattoo wounds. Moisture is necessary as the epithelial cells require moisture to cover the wound bed. Without moisture, the epithelialization (restoration of the epidermis) cannot occur. Moisture promotes migration of epidermal cells across the wound surface. A moist wound environment decreases the amount of time it takes for the body to make the crust that forms over dry wounds more soluble. Moist wound healing reduces wound pain. Moist wound healing also reduces scar formation.

It is also important to note that proper balance of moisture is necessary to promote proper wound healing while protecting the tattoo wound and promoting adequate color uptake in the healing process of the tattoo procedure. Choosing appropriate barrier dressings is important.

Our goal as providers is to provide a barrier that will provide adequate moisture barrier without being too dry or too moist. An overly moist wound bed will cause excessive exudates (lymphatic drainage) to accumulate causing the wound bed to become water logged and the tissue will become macerated (broken down tissue). An overly moist wound bed can cause color loss. An overly dry wound will inhibit migration of epidermal cells delaying the wound healing and increasing the risk of scar formation (Zickefoose, 2017).

References

Korting, H. C., Schöllmann, C., & White, R. J. (2011). *Management of minor acute cutaneous wounds: importance of wound healing in a moist environment*. Journal Of The European Academy Of Dermatology & Venereology, 25(2), 130-137. doi:10.1111/j.1468-3083.2010.03775.x

Winter, GD. *Formation of the Scab and the Rate of Epithelization of Superficial Wounds in the Skin of the Young Domestic Pig*. Nature. 1962;193:293-294.

Zickefoose, SR. (2017) *Wound Care in the Permanent Cosmetic Industry* (PowerPoint slides from SPCP Presentation).

Repigmentation of Lightened Procedure Areas:

It has been observed and recorded that areas of previously lightened pigment that has been re-tattooed may need touchup (color boosts) more frequently. The theory behind this statement coincides with case studies of the effects of lightened pigment observed over a longer period of time.

The tattoo lightening procedure has had a very positive impact on the permanent cosmetic industry. It has solved a multitude of problems and provided positive solutions for both technicians and clients.

The information and examples provided in this section are provided to encourage technicians to pause and analyze each client's needs and goals thoroughly. Equally important is to comply with any applicable regulations that govern tattooing in their geographical area, to comply with insurance policy provisions, and adhere to product directions so that the success of each procedure is more probable and represents less risk to the technician and the client.

Contributors

1. This section contained contributions from Mytia Story, BS, Biologist and Chemist.
2. This section contained contributions from Shanan Zickefoose, BSN, RN, CPCP.

APPENDIX A

Works Referenced/Works Cited

Section 1 - Facts About Permanent Cosmetics

Section 2 - Permanent Cosmetic Devices

Section 3 - Tattoo Needle Information

Portions of this section was contributed by Jill Hoyer, CPCP.

Section 4 - Safe Practices for Permanent Cosmetic Technicians

Banning Artificial Nails from Healthcare Settings, The American Journal for Infection Control. Retrieved from http://www.ajicjournal.org/article/S0196-6553(02)59151-3/abstract

Nicas, M, Best D, J Occup Environ Hyg. 2008 Jun;5(6): A study quantifying the hand-to-face contact rate and its potential application to predicting respiratory tract infection. Retrieved from http://www.tandfonline.com/doi/abs/10.1080/15459620802003896

Tattoo-Associated Nontuberculous Mycobacterial Skin Infections — Multiple States, 2011–2012, Weekly, August 24, 2012 / 61(33);653-656

This chapter was contributed by Laurna Marika, OSHA Authorized Outreach Instructor, 10-30 hr. General Industry.

World Health Organization (WHO) (2009, July). Guidelines on Hand Hygiene in Health Care: a Summary Retrieved from http://www.who.int/gpsc/5may/tools/who_guidelines-handhygiene_summary.pdf

---

Section 5 - Hepatitis & Methicillin-Resistant Staphylococcus Aureus

American Association for the Study of Liver Diseases and the Infectious Diseases Society of America (2018). Initial Treatment of HCV Infection | HCV Guidance. Retrieved from https://www.hcvguidelines.org/treatment-naive

CDC Foundation (2018). Viral Hepatitis Action Coalition | CDC Foundation. Retrieved from https://www.cdcfoundation.org/vhac#

Health Union, LLC (2018). Hepatitis C Statistics - HepatitisC.net. Retrieved from https://hepatitisc.net/what-is-statistics/

US Department of Human Services Centers For Disease Control and Prevention (2018). Hepatitis C Information | Division of Viral Hepatitis | CDC. Retrieved from https://www.cdc.gov/hepatitis/hcv/index.htm

Section 6 - Skin Anatomy

This section was contributed by Liza Sims.

Section 7 - Eye Anatomy

Central Valley Eye Association, 01/14/08, http://www.centralvalleyeyeassociation.org/centralvalleyeyeassocia- tion_002.htm. Used with permission.

http://www.cc.gatech.edu/classes/cs6751_97_winter/Topics/human-cap/senses.html 03/26/2017 http://www.zain- books.com/books/computer-sciences/human-computer-interaction_7_human-input-output-channels-1.html

http://www.rivervalleyvision.ca/your-eye-health/eye-conditions/eye-allergies/3/26/2017

Ted M. Montgomery, O.D., Anatomy, Physiology and Pathology of the Human Eye, 03/26/2017, http://www.tedmont- gomery.com/the_eye/cornea.html#keratoconus.

Ted M. Montgomery, O.D., Anatomy, Physiology and Pathology of the Human Eye, 03/26/2017, http://www.tedmont- gomery.com/the_eye/. Used with permission.

Section 8 - Important Muscles of the Face

Joseph C. Hager, PhD, DataFace, Psychology, Appearance, and Behavior of the Human Face, 01/15/08, http://face- and-emotion.com/dataface/expression/buccinator.html.

Joseph C. Hager, PhD, DataFace, Psychology, Appearance, and Behavior of the Human Face, 01/15/08, http://face- and-emotion.com/dataface/expression/caninus.html.

Joseph C. Hager, PhD, DataFace, Psychology, Appearance, and Behavior of the Human Face, 01/15/08, http:// face-and-emotion.com/dataface/expression/corrugator.html.

Joseph C. Hager, PhD, DataFace, Psychology, Appearance, and Behavior of the Human Face, 01/15/08, http://face- and-emotion.com/dataface/expression/depressor_labii.html.

Joseph C. Hager, PhD, DataFace, Psychology, Appearance, and Behavior of the Human Face, 01/15/08, http://face- and-emotion.com/dataface/expression/masseter.html.

Joseph C. Hager, PhD, DataFace, Psychology, Appearance, and Behavior of the Human Face, 01/15/08, http:// face-and-emotion.com/dataface/expression/mentalis.html.

Joseph C. Hager, PhD, DataFace, Psychology, Appearance, and Behavior of the Human Face, 01/15/08, http://face- and-emotion.com/dataface/expression/o_oculi.html.

Joseph C. Hager, PhD, DataFace, Psychology, Appearance, and Behavior of the Human Face, 01/15/08, http:// face-and-emotion.com/dataface/expression/orbicularis_oris.html.

Joseph C. Hager, PhD, DataFace, Psychology, Appearance, and Behavior of the Human Face, 01/15/08, http://face- and-emotion.com/dataface/expression/other.html.

Joseph C. Hager, PhD, DataFace, Psychology, Appearance, and Behavior of the Human Face, 01/15/08, http://face- and-emotion.com/dataface/expression/procerus.html.

Joseph C. Hager, PhD, DataFace, Psychology, Appearance, and Behavior of the Human Face, 01/15/08, http:// www.face-and-emotion.com/dataface/expression/frontalis.html.

Joseph C. Hager, PhD, DataFace, Psychology, Appearance, and Behavior of the Human Face, 01/15/08, http:// www.face-and-emotion.com/dataface/expression/triangularis.html.

Section 9 - Choosing the Right Client

Portions of *Negotiating the Dissolution of Your Relationship with a Client* were contributed by Mary Jane Haake CPCP.

Section 10 - Pigment (Skin) Testing and Permanent Cosmetics

Section 11 - Client History Files

Kate Ciampi RN, CPCP assisted with the compilation of information contained in this portion of the textbook.

Section 12 - Documenting Permanent Cosmetic Work with Photography

Section 13 - Identifying Skin Undertones

Section 14 - Working With Fitzpatrick IV–VI Skin Types

Heathman, C. (2003). *Acne and Skin of Color*. Dermascope, May 2003.

Section 15 - Traditional and Permanent Cosmetic Color Theories

Elizabeth Finch-Howell, CPCP assisted with the compilation of information contained in this portion of the textbook

Mytia Story, BS, Biologist and Chemist, assisted with the compilation of information contained in this portion of the textbook

Wikipedia The Free Encyclopedia, 1/23/08, http://64.233.169.104/search?q=cache:rOj4p82oGx4J:en.wikipe- dia.org/wiki/Color_theory+A+traditon+of+color+theory+begins+in+the+18th+century&hl=en&ct=clnk&cd=1&gl=us&ie=UTF-8.

Wikipedia the Free Encyclopedia, 01/24/08, http://en.wikipedia.org/wiki/Color_theory.

Permanent Cosmetics: The Foundations of Fundamental Applications — Second Edition

Section 16 - Selecting Permanent Cosmetic Procedure Colorants—General Information

Section 17 - Basic Facial Morphology and Placement of Procedures

Section 18 - All About Procedures

Section 19 - Pain and Anesthesia

Kate Ciampi Shergold RN, CPCP assisted with the compilation of information contained in this portion of the textbook

Section 20 - The Healing Process

This section was provided by Liza Sims.

Section 21 - Solar Care and Prevention of Premature Permanent Cosmetic Color Fading

U.S. Food and Drug Administration [FDA] (2017b). Sunscreen: How to Help Protect Your Skin from the Sun. Retrieved from https://www.fda.gov/drugs/resourcesforyou/consumers/buyingusingmedicinesafely/understandingover-the-countermedicines/ucm239463.htm

U.S. Food and Drug Administration [FDA] (2017). Sun Protection Factor (SPF). Retrieved from https://www.fda.gov/aboutfda/centersoffices/officeofmedicalproductsandtobacco/cder/ucm106351.htm

Section 22 - Herpes Simplex and Permanent Cosmetics

Kate Ciampi Shergod RN, CPCP assisted with the compilation of information contained in this portion of the textbook.

Section 23 - Medical Conditions and Permanent Cosmetics

American Academy of Family Physicians - familydoctor.org (2016). *Latex Allergy - familydoctor.org*. Retrieved from https://familydoctor.org/condition/latex-allergy/

American Heart Association (2018). *The Facts About High Blood Pressure.* Retrieved from http://www.heart.org/HEARTORG/Conditions/HighBloodPressure/GettheFactsAboutHighBloodPressure/The-Facts-About-High-Blood-Pressure_UCM_002050_Article.jsp

Kate Ciampi Shergold RN, CPCP assisted with the compilation of information contained in this portion of the textbook.

Photo example of moles is an excerpt from *Segmentation of Skin Cancer Images* by L. Xu, M. Jackowski, A. Goshtasby, C. Yu, D. Roseman, S. Bines, A. Dhawan, A. Huntley. Photo used with permission.

U.S. Department of Health and Human Services - National Eye Institute (NEI) (2015). *Facts About Glaucoma | National Eye Institute.* Retrieved from https://www.nei.nih.gov/health/glaucoma/glaucoma_facts

U.S. Department of Health and Human Services - National Institute of Arthritis and Musculoskeletal and Skin Diseases (2016). *Alopecia Areata | NIAMS.* Retrieved from https://www.niams.nih.gov/health-topics/alopecia-areata

U.S. Department of Health and Human Services - National Institute of Arthritis and Musculoskeletal and Skin Diseases (2016). *Vitiligo | NIAMS.* Retrieved from https://www.niams.nih.gov/health-topics/vitiligo

U.S. Department of Health and Human Services - National Institute of Diabetes and Digestive and Kidney Diseases (2016). *What is Diabetes? | NIDDK.* Retrieved from https://www.niddk.nih.gov/health-information/diabetes/overview/what-is-diabetes

U.S. Department of Labor - Occupational Safety and Heath Administration [OSHA] (2008). *Safety and Health Topics | Latex Allergy | Occupational Safety and Health Administration.* Retrived from http://www.osha.gov/SLTC/latexallergy/index.html

U.S. National Institutes of Health - National Cancer Institute (2008). *What You Need To Know About Skin Cancer - National Cancer Institute* Retrieved from http://www.cancer.gov/cancertopics/wyntk/skin/page6 [old link].

U.S. National Library of Medicine - Medline Plus (2015). *High blood pressure: MedlinePlus Medical Encyclopedia* Retrieved from https://medlineplus.gov/ency/article/000468.htm

U.S. National Library of Medicine - Medline Plus (2016). *Mitral valve prolapse: MedlinePlus Medical Encyclopedia.* Retrieved from http://www.nlm.nih.gov/medlineplus/ency/article/000180.htm.

U.S. National Library of Medicine - Medline Plus (2016). *Trichotillomania: MedlinePlus Medical Encyclopedia.* Retrieved from https://medlineplus.gov/ency/article/001517.htm

SECTION 24 - MRI AND PERMANENT COSMETICS

https://www.fda.gov/cosmetics/productsingredients/products/ucm108530.htm 11/26/2016

Reprinted with permission from Yale-New Haven Hospital, 1/23/08, 6/18/2017 Site is no longer active. http://www. ynhh.org/patients/diagnostic radiology/mri.html

SECTION 25 - PSYCHOLOGY AND PERMANENT COSMETICS

Adler, R., Rosenfeld, L., Proctor II, R. (2007). *Interplay: The process of interpersonal communication.* Oxford University Press:NY.

Contributions to this section were also made by Amanda Le, Permanent Cosmetic Technician and professional model.

Contributions to this section were also made by Greg Shergold, MA, LPC.

Navarro, J., Karlins, M. (2008). *What Every Body's Saying: An ex-FBI agent's guide to speed reading people.* HarperCollins Publishers:NY

Peter Noel Murray, PH.D - Doctor of Psychology - Consumer psychology practice in New York City; providing consulting and market research to corporations.

Section 26 - The Principles of Tattoo Lightening and Removal

This section contained contributions from Mytia Story, BS, Biologist and Chemist.

This section contained contributions from Shanan Zickefoose, BSN, RN, CPCP.

Appendix A - Works Referenced/Works Cited

Appendix B - List of Figures

Appendix C - Errors and Omissions

APPENDIX B

List of Figures

SECTION 1 - FACTS ABOUT PERMANENT COSMETICS

SECTION 2 - PERMANENT COSMETIC DEVICES

FIGURE 2-1: MANUAL DEVICE 17
    PROVIDED BY SOFTAP

FIGURE 2-2: MICROBLADING MANUAL DEVICE 17
    PROVIDED BY HARMONY

FIGURE 2-3: MICROBLADING MANUAL DEVICE 17
    PROVIDED BY MEICHA

FIGURE 2-4: PERMANENT COSMETIC PEN 18
    PHOTO PROVIDE BY DARIA CHUPRYS, CPCP

FIGURE 2-5: DIGITAL ROTARY MACHINE 18
    PHOTO PROVIDE BY MEICHA

FIGURE 2-6: DIGITAL ROTARY MACHINE 18
    PHOTO PROVIDED BY NOUVEAU CONTOUR

FIGURE 2-7: ROTARY (LINEAR) MACHINE 19

FIGURE 2-8: ROTARY (LINEAR) PEN MACHINE 19

FIGURE 2-9: COIL MACHINE 19

SECTION 3 - TATTOO NEEDLE INFORMATION

FIGURE 3-1: SHORT TAPER 24

FIGURE 3-2: MEDIUM TAPER 24

FIGURE 3-3: LONG TAPER 24

FIGURE 3-4: EXTRA LONG TAPER 24

FIGURE 3-5: 7-ROUND CONFIGURATION 25

FIGURE 3-6: 3-ROUND CONFIGURATION 25

FIGURE 3-7: SINGLE NEEDLE CONFIGURATION 25

FIGURE 3-8: 8 LINER 25

FIGURE 3-9: 8-SHADER 25

FIGURE 3-10: LINER (LEFT) & SHADER (RIGHT) NEEDLE COMPARISON 25

FIGURE 3-11: FLAT CONFIGURATION NEEDLE 26

FIGURE 3-12: 7-MAGNUM (STRAIGHT) 26

Permanent Cosmetics: The Foundations of Fundamental Applications — Second Edition

Figure 3-13: 7-Magnum (Curved/Round) 26
Figure 3-14: 7-Magnum (Stacked) 26
Figure 3-15: Cartridge-Type Needle 26
Figure 3-16: Cartridge-Type Needle 26
Figure 3-17: In-Line Formation Double-Row Non-Microblading Manual Device Needle 27
Figure 3-18: Round Configuration Non-Microblading Manual Device Needle. 27
Figure 3-19: Microblading Needle (Plastic Wrapped) 27
Figure 3-20: Microblading Needle (Metal Wrapped) 27

Section 4 - Safe Practices for Permanent Cosmetic Technicians

Figure 4-1: Handwashing 32
Figure 4-2: Sharps container 36
Figure 4-3: Needle affixed to manual device 37

Section 5 - Hepatitis & Methicillin-Resistant Staphylococcus Aureus

Figure 5-1: MRSA Infection 51
Figure 5-2: MRSA Infection 51

Section 6 - Skin Anatomy

Figure 6-1: The Skin 56
    Drawing by Liza Sims.
Figure 6-2: The Epidermis 58
    Drawing by Liza Sims.

Section 7 - Eye Anatomy

Figure 7-1: Reference diagram of major components of the eye 63
Figure 7-2: Frontal view of the eye 63

Section 8 - Important Muscles of the Face

Figure 8-1: Important Muscles of the Face 72

Section 9 - Choosing the Right Client

Section 10 - Pigment (Skin) Testing and Permanent Cosmetics

Section 11 - Client History Files

Section 12 - Documenting Permanent Cosmetic Work with Photography

Figure 12-1: Inconsistent Placement and Size 129

Figure 12-2: Before and After 129

Section 13 - Identifying Skin Undertones

Figure 13-1: Thinner eyelid canvas 136
Figure 13-2: Thinner lip canvas 136

Section 14 - Working With Fitzpatrick IV–VI Skin Types

Figure 14-1: Ashy Cool Healed Eyebrow 141
Figure 14-2: Immediately After the Eyebrow Procedure 142
Figure 14-3: Day 4 of the Healing Process 142
Figure 14-4: Day 5 of the Healing Process 142
Figure 14-5: Day 11 of the Healing Process 142
Figure 14-6: Hyperpigmentation on Knees 143
Figure 14-7: Hyperpigmentation on Hands 143
Figure 14-8: Hyperpigmentation around the eyes 143
Figure 14-9: Lighter warm brown formulation on Fitzpatrick 5 Skin Type 144
Figure 14-10: Black eyeliner tattooed on a Fitzpatrick V skin type 144
Figure 14-11: Black lower eyeliner tattooed on Fitzpatrick VI skin type – immediately after 145
Figure 14-12: Black lower eyeliner healed on Fitzpatrick VI skin type 145
Figure 14-13: Variegated lips with cool undertones 145
Figure 14-14: Variegated lips with cool undertones 145
Figure 14-15: Loss of pigment (hypopigmentation) 148
Figure 14-16: Healed Eyebrow Procedure 150

Section 15 - Traditional and Permanent Cosmetic Color Theories

Figure 15-1: Visible color spectrum of the human eye 157
Figure 15-2: Primary Color Wheel 159
Figure 15-3: Primary and Secondary Color Wheel 161
Figure 15-4: The Traditional Artist's Color Wheel – Primary, Secondary, and Intermediate Colors 162

Section 16 - Selecting Permanent Cosmetic Procedure Colorants—General Information

Figure 16-1: Red-orange 175
Figure 16-2: Orange 175
Figure 16-3: Yellow-Green 175
Figure 16-4: Yellow-Orange 175
Figure 16-5: More Neutral Yellow 175

Figure 16-6: Eyebrow procedure 176
Figure 16-7: Yellow-green 177
Figure 16-8: Yellow-orange 177
Figure 16-9: More Neutral Yellow 177
Figure 16-10: Green 177
Figure 16-11: Yellow-green 177
Figure 16-12: Orange 178
Figure 16-13: Red-orange 178
Figure 16-14: Dark brown 178
Figure 16-15: Black-brown 178
Figure 16-16: Brown-black 178
Figure 16-17: Black 178
Figure 16-18: Client with darker brown skin with blue undertones. 180
Figure 16-19: Gray 180
Figure 16-20: Taupe 180
Figure 16-21: Brown 180
Figure 16-22: Black-brown 180
Figure 16-23: Light Cool Blonde 181
Figure 16-24: Light Cool Blonde 181
Figure 16-25: Light Warm Blonde 181
Figure 16-26: Light Taupe 181
Figure 16-27: Light Taupe 182
Figure 16-28: Eyelash enhancement and lower liner 183
Figure 16-29: Fashion Color Eyeliner 184
   Advanced procedure technique
Figure 16-30: Thinning skin and violet undertones 184
Figure 16-31: Shaded Lip Liner 184
Figure 16-32: Lip Liner 185
Figure 16-33: Darker Lip Color 185
Figure 16-34: Brow that requires design and color correction 188

Section 17 - Basic Facial Morphology and Placement of Procedures

Figure 17-1: As the woman appears (left); two right sides of the face (center); two left sides of the face (right) 196
Figure 17-2: As the woman appears (left); two right sides of the face (center); two left sides of the face (right) 196
Figure 17-3: Natural Eyebrow 198
Figure 17-4: Natural Eyebrow 198
Figure 17-5: Natural Eyebrow 198
Figure 17-6: Client drawn eyebrow design on the client's right side 199

Appendix B - List of Figures

Figure 17-7: Classic Eyebrow Construction 199
Figure 17-8: Brow Placement Closer Together 200
Figure 17-9: Brow Placement Far Apart 200
Figure 17-10: Normal Placement 200
Figure 17-11: Inset Bulbs 200
Figure 17-12: Wide-set Bulbs 200
Figure 17-13: Oval 201
Figure 17-14: Square 201
Figure 17-15: Round 201
Figure 17-16: Pear 201
Figure 17-17: Oblong/Rectangle 201
Figure 17-18: Diamond 201
Figure 17-19: Heart 201
Figure 17-20: Woman with right eye larger than left 202
Figure 17-21: Hooded eyes and inconsistent lid space 202
Figure 17-22: Hooded eyes and inconsistent lid space 202
Figure 17-23: Top Eyelash Enhancement 203
Figure 17-24: Eyelash 203
        Eyelash enhancement dotting technique
Figure 17-25: Lower Lash Liner 203
Figure 17-26: Symmetric Lips 203
Figure 17-27: Oval Mouth 204
Figure 17-28: Thin Lips 204
Figure 17-29: Droopy Corners 204
Figure 17-30: Thin Upper Lip 204
Figure 17-31: Thin Lower Lip 204
Figure 17-32: Inappropriately placed pigment 205
Figure 17-33: Inappropriately placed pigment 205
Figure 17-34: Variegated (two-toned) natural lip coloring 205
Figure 17-35: Variegated (two-toned) natural lip coloring 205

Section 18 - All About Procedures

Figure 18-1: Irregularity on Tarsal Plate (Wetline) 218
Figure 18-2: Growth on Upper Eyelid 218
Figure 18-3: Broken Blood Vessels 218
Figure 18-4: Upper Eyelash Enhancement 220
Figure 18-5: Thin Upper Eyeliner with Taper 220
Figure 18-6: Healed eyelash enhancement 224
Figure 18-7: Healed medium upper eyeliner 225
Figure 18-8: Lower Eyeliner Closure Design 225

FIGURE 18-9: HEALED UPPER AND LOWER EYELINER 225
FIGURE 18-10: UPPER AND LOWER EYELINER 227
    IMMEDIATELY AFTER
FIGURE 18-11: UPPER AND LOWER EYELINER 227
    HEALED
FIGURE 18-12: EYELINER STRETCHING TECHNIQUES 229
FIGURE 18-13: STRETCHING TECHNIQUE FOR THE EYELINER ENHANCEMENT INNER CANTHUS 231
FIGURE 18-14: EYELINER STRETCHING TECHNIQUES PERFORMED WHILE TATTOOING WITH BOTH MACHINE AND MANUAL DEVICES 233
FIGURE 18-15: LOWER EYELINER STRETCH 233
FIGURE 18-16: MICROBLADED EYEBROW 236
    BEFORE, IMMEDIATELY AFTER, AND HEALED
FIGURE 18-17: MICROBLADED EYEBROW 237
    BEFORE, IMMEDIATELY AFTER, AND HEALED
FIGURE 18-18: MICROBLADED EYEBROW 237
    BEFORE, IMMEDIATELY AFTER, AND HEALED
FIGURE 18-19: MACHINE HAIR STROKE EYEBROW 237
    BEFORE, IMMEDIATELY AFTER, AND HEALED
FIGURE 18-20: MACHINE HAIR STROKE EYEBROW 238
    BEFORE, IMMEDIATELY AFTER, AND HEALED
FIGURE 18-21: MACHINE HAIR STROKE EYEBROW 238
    BEFORE, IMMEDIATELY AFTER, AND HEALED
FIGURE 18-22: EYEBROW POINTILLISM TECHNIQUE 238
    IMMEDIATELY AFTER
FIGURE 18-23: SHADED BROW 239
    BEFORE, IMMEDIATELY AFTER, AND HEALED
FIGURE 18-24: SHADED BROW 239
    BEFORE, IMMEDIATELY AFTER, AND HEALED
FIGURE 18-25: SHADED BROW 239
    BEFORE, IMMEDIATELY AFTER, AND HEALED
FIGURE 18-26: SHADED BROW 240
    BEFORE, IMMEDIATELY AFTER, AND HEALED
FIGURE 18-27: OMBRE EFFECT EYEBROW 240
    BEFORE, IMMEDIATELY AFTER, AND HEALED
FIGURE 18-28: OMBRE EFFECT EYEBROW 240
    BEFORE, IMMEDIATELY AFTER, AND HEALED
FIGURE 18-29: RASH IN THE EYEBROW PROCEDURE AREA 241
FIGURE 18-30: PRE-PROCEDURE EYEBROW ANESTHETICS 241
FIGURE 18-31: CONNECT THE DOTS 244
    (OR MARKS MADE) WITH A LIGHT-HANDED STROKE METHOD CREATING THE DESIRED WIDTH AND UNIQUE DESIGN ELEMENTS.
FIGURE 18-32: MARKING FOR EYEBROW DESIGN PLACEMENT 246
FIGURE 18-33: EYEBROW GUIDE 247
FIGURE 18-34: DOTTING AROUND THE EYEBROW DESIGN WITH A SINGLE-USE DOTTING PEN 247
FIGURE 18-35: MARKING LINES AROUND THE EYEBROW DESIGN WITH A SINGLE-USE MARKER 247
FIGURE 18-36: COMMONLY USED EYEBROW STRETCHING TECHNIQUES. 250
FIGURE 18-37: DARKER VARIEGATED LIPS 252

Appendix B - List of Figures

Figure 18-38: Cooler (Violet) Variated Lips 252
Figure 18-39: Lip Vermilion & Inner Lip Mucosal 253
Figure 18-40: Before Lip Liner 253
Figure 18-41: Bruising During Procedure 253
Figure 18-42: Tattooing outside the Vermilion border 254
Figure 18-43: Melting lip pre-procedure topical anesthetic 255
Figure 18-44: Before Shaded Lip Liner 256
Figure 18-45: Immediately After Shaded Lip Liner 256
Figure 18-46: Healed 256
Figure 18-47: Applying the Lip Template 257
Figure 18-48: Lip Tattoo Process 257
Figure 18-49: Lip Stretching Techniques 261
Figure 18-50: Stretching Technique 262
Figure 18-51: Stretching Technique 262
Figure 18-52: Lip Stretching Techniques 262
Figure 18-53: Working in four sections 263
Figure 18-54: Eyebrows -Fitzpatrick Skin Type I 265
  Before and immediately after
Figure 18-55: Eyebrows -Fitzpatrick Skin Type V 265
  Before and immediately after
Figure 18-56: Eyeliner -Fitzpatrick Skin Type I 266
  Before and immediately after
Figure 18-57: Eyeliner -Fitzpatrick Skin Type III 266
  Before and immediately after
Figure 18-58: Eyelash enhancement 267
Figure 18-59: Narrow width eyeliner 267
Figure 18-60: Medium width eyeliner 267
Figure 18-61: Wider width eyeliner 267
Figure 18-62: Lower EyelinerImmediately after 268
Figure 18-63: Lower EyelinerImmediately after 268
Figure 18-64: Lip Liner 268
  Before and immediately after. The lighter inner lip is due to the effects of anesthetic with epinephrine, a vasoconstrictor.
Figure 18-65: Shaded Lip Liner 268
  Before and immediately after.
Figure 18-66: Full Lip Procedure 269
  Before and immediately after.

Section 19 - Pain and Anesthesia

Figure 19-1: Client's Anxiety 281
Figure 19-2: Upper liner Anesthetic 286
Figure 19-3: Remove anesthetics away from the eye 286

FIGURE 19-4: EYEBROW ANESTHETICS 287
FIGURE 19-5: ANESTHETIC IS APPLIED TO LIGHTLY PRICKED SKIN 287
FIGURE 19-6: AFTER TAKING EFFECT, THE ANESTHETIC IS BLOTTED OFF 287
FIGURE 19-7: THE BLOTTED DESIGN AREA IS CHECKED TO ENSURE DESIGN MARKERS REMAIN IN PLACE .. 287
FIGURE 19-8: ANESTHETIZING LIPS 288
FIGURE 19-9: BE FRIENDLY AND GREET CLIENTS 289
FIGURE 19-10: CLEAN AND ORDERLY WORKPLACE SETTING 289
FIGURE 19-11: STAY OFF THE PHONE 289
FIGURE 19-12: MANAGE STRESS 290
FIGURE 19-13: DRAMA 293

SECTION 20 - THE HEALING PROCESS

FIGURE 20-1: INITIAL TATTOO PENETRATION SITE 297
    DRAWING BY LIZA SIMS.
FIGURE 20-2: TATTOO NEEDLE PENETRATION SITE AT ABOUT 28 TO 35 DAYS 300
    DRAWING BY LIZA SIMS.
FIGURE 20-3: TATTOO NEEDLE PENETRATION SITE AT ABOUT 90 DAYS 301
    DRAWING BY LIZA SIMS.

SECTION 21 - SOLAR CARE AND PREVENTION OF PREMATURE PERMANENT COSMETIC COLOR FADING

SECTION 22 - HERPES SIMPLEX AND PERMANENT COSMETICS

FIGURE 22-1: HERPES SIMPLEX VIRUS TYPE 1 313

SECTION 23 - MEDICAL CONDITIONS AND PERMANENT COSMETICS

FIGURE 23-1: LATEX ALLERGY REACTION 323
FIGURE 23-2: VITILIGO 323
FIGURE 23-3: ALOPECIA 325
FIGURE 23-4: BLOOD PRESSURE RANGE AS RECOMMENDED BY THE AMERICAN HEART ASSOCIATION[9] ... 328
    NOTE: THIS CHART IS FOR INFORMATION PURPOSES ONLY. DECISIONS REGARDING MEDICAL TREATMENT SHOULD COORDINATED WITH YOUR PHYSICIAN.
FIGURE 23-5: SMALL, SMOOTH, SHINY, PALE, OR WAXY LUMP 332
FIGURE 23-6: FIRM, RED LUMP 332
FIGURE 23-7: SORE OR LUMP THAT BLEEDS OR DEVELOPS A CRUST OR A SCAB 332
FIGURE 23-8: FLAT RED SPOT THAT IS ROUGH. DRY, OR SCALY AND MAY BECOME ITCHY OR TENDER. 332
FIGURE 23-9: RED OR BROWN PATCH THAT IS ROUGH AND SCALY 332
FIGURE 23-10: A RASH DIAGNOSED BY A PHYSICIAN AS DERMATITIS 333
FIGURE 23-11: A FEW EXAMPLES OF DIFFERENT TYPES OF SKIN ABNORMALITIES.[13] 333
FIGURE 23-12: TOP EYELINER WAS NOT CONDUCTED DUE TO THE ABNORMAL CONDITION OF THE EYELID SKIN. THE CLIENT WAS ADVISED TO SEE HER PHYSICIAN. 333

Section 24 - MRI and Permanent Cosmetics

Figure 24-1: MRI Machine 337

Section 25 - Psychology and Permanent Cosmetics

Figure 25-1: Forehead skin trauma from an animal attack 344
Figure 25-2: An example of natural as defined by nature 345
Figure 25-3: Client drawn eyebrows 346
Figure 25-4: Tattooed eyebrows 346
Figure 25-5: As the client drew on her brows 346
Figure 25-6: Tattooed eyebrows 346
Figure 25-7: The Brain Records Repetitive Image 347
Figure 25-8: The Anxiety of Change 348
Figure 25-9: The Lip Procedure Healing Process 349
Figure 25-10: Media Influence on Appearance Expectations 351
Figure 25-11: Disproportionate Eyeliner 352
Figure 25-12: Torso Shield position 353
Figure 25-13: Crossed Legs 353
Figure 25-14: Compressed Lips 354
Figure 25-15: Pursed Lips 354
Figure 25-16: Two Handed Handshake 354
Figure 25-17: The Friendly Handshake 354

Section 26 - The Principles of Tattoo Lightening and Removal

Figure 26-1: Pointillism 365
Figure 26-2: Circles 365
Figure 26-3: Back and forth motion 366
Figure 26-4: Following the direction of a hair stroke 366
   Etching Pattern stroke pattern
   Hair Stroke Pattern
Figure 26-5: Discoloration appearance of product and body fluids 367
Figure 26-6: No discoloration of salt-based product and body fluids 367
Figure 26-7: Application of a product with different ingredients and pH 367
Figure 26-8: Before 368
Figure 26-9: Nine months later 368
Figure 26-10: Before 368
Figure 26-11: Eight-week progress check 368
Figure 26-12: Twelve weeks after original procedure 368
Figure 26-13: Before 369
Figure 26-14: Immediately after 369

FIGURE 26-15: THREE-WEEK PROGRESS CHECK 369
FIGURE 26-16: EIGHT WEEKS AFTER THE ORIGINAL PROCEDURE 369
FIGURE 26-17: BEFORE 370
FIGURE 26-18: IMMEDIATELY AFTER THE FIRST LIGHTENING PROCEDURE 370
FIGURE 26-19: SIX MONTHS AFTER SECOND LIGHTENING PROCEDURE 370
FIGURE 26-20: SIX MONTHS AFTER THIRD LIGHTENING PROCEDURE HEALED, AND AFTER LIGHT TOUCHUP ON THE BROW ARCH AND TAILS. 370
FIGURE 26-21: BEFORE 371
FIGURE 26-22: TWO-MONTH PROGRESS PHOTO SENT 371
FIGURE 26-23: FOUR-MONTH PROGRESS PHOTO SENT 371
FIGURE 26-24: SIX-MONTH PHOTO SENT 371
FIGURE 26-25: BOTH BROWS 372
FIGURE 26-26: RIGHT BROW 372
FIGURE 26-27: RIGHT BROW STRETCHED 372
FIGURE 26-28: LEFT BROW 372
FIGURE 26-29: LEFT BROW STRETCHED 372
FIGURE 26-30: BEFORE 374
FIGURE 26-31: HEALED AFTER FOUR SECTIONAL LIGHTENING PROCEDURES 374
FIGURE 26-32: NEW COVER-UP TATTOO 374
FIGURE 26-33: BEFORE 374
FIGURE 26-34: IMMEDIATELY AFTER 374
FIGURE 26-35: HEALED TWO MONTHS LATER 374
FIGURE 26-36: BEFORE 375
FIGURE 26-37: TEST AREAS SIX MONTHS LATER 375
FIGURE 26-38: TEST AREA 375
FIGURE 26-39: TEST AREA TWO MONTHS LATER 375
FIGURE 26-40: BEFORE 376
FIGURE 26-41: IMMEDIATELY AFTER. 376
    NOTICE THE CHUNKY APPEARANCE OF THE TITANIUM DIOXIDE AT THE TAIL
FIGURE 26-42: EIGHT-MONTH PROGRESS CHECK 376
FIGURE 26-43: THIRTEEN MONTHS AFTER THE PROCEDURE 376
FIGURE 26-44: COMPARISON OF BEFORE AND THIRTEEN MONTHS LATER 377
FIGURE 26-45: BEFORE 378
FIGURE 26-46: IMMEDIATELY AFTER 378
FIGURE 26-47: AFTER FOUR LIGHTENING PROCEDURES AND TWO COLOR CORRECTIONS 378
FIGURE 26-48: BEFORE, IMMEDIATELY AFTER & HEALED TWO MONTHS LATER
FIGURE 26-49: MIGRATION OF EYELINER 379
FIGURE 26-50: BEFORE 379
FIGURE 26-51: HEALED AFTER FOUR TATTOO LIGHTENING PROCEDURES SIX MONTHS APART 379

Appendix A - Works Referenced/Works Cited

Appendix B - List of Figures

Appendix C - Errors and Omissions

APPENDIX C

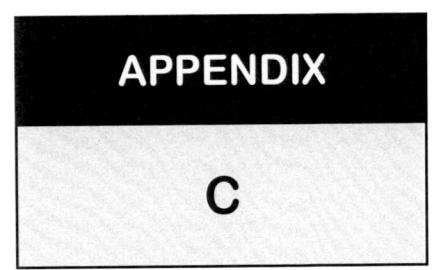

Errors and Omissions

The SPCP is proud to present an accurate and factual permanent cosmetics textbook. In the event the reader feels there are errors or omissions, it would be helpful to obtain this information for future publications.

Please identify the page number, the specific problem, and suggested ways to improve the section. While feedback is always important, specific references will be required for instances of *errors* beyond typographical errors or layout issues.

Contact the SPCP at admin@spcp.org with any comments or suggestions.